PROGRESSIVE WOMEN'S MOVEMENTS IN AUSTRIA AND HUNGARY

STUDIES IN HUNGARIAN HISTORY
László Borhi, editor

PROGRESSIVE WOMEN'S MOVEMENTS IN AUSTRIA AND HUNGARY

CONFLICT, COOPERATION, CIRCULATION

DÓRA FEDELES-CZEFERNER
TRANSLATED BY DAVID ROBERT EVANS

Indiana University Press

This book is a publication of

Indiana University Press
Office of Scholarly Publishing
Herman B Wells Library 350
1320 East 10th Street
Bloomington, Indiana 47405 USA

iupress.org

© 2025 by Dóra Fedeles-Czeferner

Translation funded by the László Tetmajer Fund of the Hungarian Studies Program, Department of Central Eurasian Studies, Indiana University Bloomington.

All rights reserved
No part of this book may be reproduced or utilized in any form or by any means, electronic or mechanical, including photocopying and recording, or by any information storage and retrieval system, without permission in writing from the publisher.

First Printing 2025

Cataloging information is available from the Library of Congress.

ISBN 978-0-253-07277-1 (hdbk.)
ISBN 978-0-253-07278-8 (pbk.)
ISBN 978-0-253-07279-5 (web PDF)
ISBN 978-0-253-07280-1 (ebook)

Originally published as *Dóra Fedeles-Czeferner* © Department of Central Eurasian Studies, Indiana University, 2023.

Contents

Acknowledgments vii
List of Abbreviations ix
Chronology xi

Introduction 1
1. Scholarship on the Bourgeois-Liberal, Feminist Movement in Hungary and Austria 17
2. Austria-Hungary in the Fin de Siècle 27
3. The Austro-Hungarian Women's Movement until the Fin de Siècle and the Different Branches of the Women's Movement 40
4. The Austrian Association: The Allgemeiner österreichischer Frauenverein 61
5. The Hungarian Associations: Nőtisztviselők Országos Egyesülete and Feministák Egyesülete 111
6. Similarities and Differences among the Three Associations 189
Conclusion 198

Notes 205
Bibliography 245
Index 267

Acknowledgments

This volume is the result of more than a decade of research, at the conclusion of which I would like to express my gratitude to all those whose assistance I was able to rely on throughout this project or during some part of it. Most of all, I am indebted to the supervisor of my doctoral dissertation, Judith Szapor, who from the moment of our first acquaintance has given me consistent encouragement and who has striven to contain and refine my sometimes rhapsodic ideas. She was the first to adorn the various versions of my draft with valuable comments and critical observations. Our conversations, whether virtual or in person, allowed me to move on from moments of scholarly difficulty.

I am always thankful for the helpful advice I received from Katalin Kéri, who has followed my attempts to spread my wings as a researcher from the outset. Perhaps even more important than her academic advice has been the example she has set as a researcher, teacher, and woman, one who has inspired me greatly over the years. I also thank my colleagues Gábor Gyáni, Attila Pók, and László Szarka. I owe a great debt of gratitude to Sándor Horváth, who was always able to provide indispensable suggestions and advice when I was in the final phase of writing this book. I also received valuable suggestions from Péter Apor, Zsuzsa Török, Mária Palasik, and Róbert Kerepeszki. I would also express my gratitude to Johanna Gehmacher for her valuable suggestions related to my manuscript. My workplace, the HUN REN Hungarian Research Network Centre for the Humanities, Institute of History, provided me with a secure and supportive background and a peaceful working environment throughout the preparation of the book. Without this, its completion would certainly have been impossible.

I must also give my sincerest thanks to my close friend Beáta Márkus. Beáta's reassurance was a great support during the phase of the work when almost nobody believed in the feasibility of the research. In addition, I also received a great deal of help from her in transcribing and translating the handwritten German sources.

A major challenge in collecting the material was that the sources were fragmented and available in different collections in Europe and the United States. I consider myself blessed to have been able to spend much time in archives and libraries in New York and Vienna thanks to different scholarships and research grants. During the often seemingly endless months of scholarships, in addition to archival and library research, I tried to contact internationally renowned scholars of the history of women's movements, to whom I also owe a great deal of help. I received valuable professional advice from Hanna Hacker, Corinna Oesch, and Susan Zimmermann, among others. In addition to them, I am grateful to Iván Bertényi Jr., from whom I received the most support at a time when I myself least believed that this volume would be completed. During my stays in Vienna, I also had exciting and valuable professional conversations with Eleonóra Géra and Dávid László Törő. I would also like to express my gratitude to László Borhi, who encouraged me to prepare this manuscript from our first meeting in 2018.

Last but not least, I would like to thank my parents and my brother for their loving and caring support and for helping me to believe that, unlike that of the other women in my family, my path in life would lead toward not teaching but research. Neither would these expressions of gratitude be complete without mentioning my husband, Tamás Fedeles, without whom I would not be writing these lines. As the first reader of my works, he has given me helpful comments and guidance for more than a decade. His patience and supportive affection have helped me past every moment of despair; my appreciation cannot be expressed in words.

Vienna, 24 February 2025
Dóra Fedeles-Czeferner

Abbreviations

AdF	Allgemeiner deutscher Frauenverein
AöF	Allgemeiner österreichischer Frauenverein
BdF	Bund deutscher Frauenvereine
BöF	Bund österreichischer Frauenvereine
EWdF	Erster Wiener demokratischer Frauenverein
FE	Feministák Egyesülete (Hungarian Feminists' Association)
HaN	Sammlung von Handschriften und alten Drucken
ICW	International Council of Women
IWSA	International Woman Suffrage Alliance
MANSz	Magyar Asszonyok Nemzeti Szövetsége (National Alliance of Hungarian Women)
MME	Magyarországi Munkásnő Egyesület (Working Women's Association of Hungary)
MNL OL	Magyar Nemzeti Levéltár Országos Levéltára (National Archives of Hungary)
MNSz	Magyarországi Nőegyesületek Szövetsége (Alliance of Hungarian Women's Associations)
MS	Musiksammlung
N	*A Nő. Feminista Folyóirat* (The Woman. Feminist Journal)
NF	Nachlass Fickert
NFL	*Neues Frauenleben*
NOE	Nőtisztviselők Országos Egyesülete (National Association of Female Clerks)
NT	*A Nő és a Társadalom* (Women and Society)
NYPL	New York Public Library
ÖNB	Österreichische Nationalbibliothek
RSP	Rosika Schwimmer Papers
VfF	Verband fortschrittlicher Frauenvereine
VLE	Verein der Lehrerinnen und Erzieherinnen
WFE	Wiener Frauenerwerbverein
WILPF	Women's International League for Peace and Freedom
WR	Wienbibliothek im Rathaus

Chronology

- **1848–1849**: Revolution, then unsuccessful liberation struggle against Austria, seeking to attain complete independence for Hungary
- **1855**: Birth of Auguste Fickert
- **1867**: The Austro-Hungarian Compromise is signed; creation of the Austro-Hungarian monarchy
- **1872**: Birth of Vilma Glücklich
- **1877**: Birth of Rosika Schwimmer
- **1893**: AöF is founded
- **1896**: Austrian and Hungarian universities open their faculties of medicine, pharmacy, and humanities to women
- **1897–1910**: Karl Lueger is mayor of Vienna
- **1898**: NOE is founded
- **1899–1902**: Publication of *Dokumente der Frauen*
- **1902–1918**: Publication of *Neues Frauenleben*
- **1903**: MME is founded
- **1903**: BöF is founded
- **1904**: MNSz is founded
- **1904**: Meeting of ICW in Berlin; IWSA is founded
- **1904**: FE is brought into being
- **1906**: Publication of *Feminista Értesítő* (Feminist Bulletin)
- **1906**: AöF separates from BöF
- **1906**: Austria and Hungary become full members of IWSA
- **1906–1919**: István Bárczy is mayor of Budapest
- **1907**: All Austrian male citizens over twenty-four years of age are given the right to vote
- **1907–1913**: Publication of *A Nő és a Társadalom* (Women and Society)
- **1910**: Death of Auguste Fickert
- **10–12 June 1913**: Preliminary IWSA conference in Vienna
- **15–22 June 1913**: Seventh Congress of IWSA held in Budapest

- **1914**: Schwimmer is press secretary of IWSA in London
- **28 July 1914**: The Austro-Hungarian monarchy declares war on Serbia
- **1914–1928**: Publication of *A Nő. Feminista Folyóirat* (The Woman. Feminist Journal)
- **1915**: Women's International Peace Congress in The Hague, and the convention of WILPF with the participation of delegates from FE and AöF
- **December 1917**: Vilmos Vázsonyi's electoral reform proposal is submitted
- **June 1918**: The Hungarian parliament rejects Vilmos Vázsonyi's legislative proposal
- **October 1918**: Schwimmer is elected a member of the Hungarian National Council led by Count Michael Károlyi
- **30 October 1918**: The Austrian law on associations (*Vereinsgesetz*) is repealed; women are able to participate in political activism
- **3 November 1918**: A delegation from the Austro-Hungarian monarchy signs an armistice near Padua, ending its involvement in World War I
- **November 1918–January (March) 1919**: Rosika Schwimmer is Hungary's nominated envoy to Switzerland
- **12 November 1918**: Universal suffrage for Austrian women is written into law; the Austrian Republic is announced
- **23 November 1918**: The government led by Count Michael Károlyi in Hungary decides on universal suffrage for men over twenty-one and women over twenty-four
- **April 1919**: NOE is disbanded
- **January 1920**: Schwimmer leaves Hungary for Vienna
- **1922**: AöF is disbanded
- **1927**: Death of Vilma Glücklich in Vienna
- **1937**: Rosika Schwimmer is awarded the World Peace Prize
- **1948**: Schwimmer is nominated for the Nobel Peace Prize
- **3 August 1948**: Schwimmer dies
- **1949**: FE is disbanded

PROGRESSIVE WOMEN'S MOVEMENTS IN AUSTRIA AND HUNGARY

Introduction

FOR A WEEK IN 1913, Budapest became the center of the international women's movement. Contrary to expectations, the seventh and last congress of the International Woman Suffrage Alliance (IWSA, 1904–, Berlin) before World War I was held in the Hungarian capital, not in Vienna. The right to host the event was granted to the Hungarian Feminists' Association (FE, 1904–1942, 1946–1949) in the summer of 1911. The association had existed for barely over half a decade, but it had successfully caught up with international organizations and the bourgeois-liberal and feminist associations of western Europe, and it had grown to roughly a thousand members.

The Budapest conference of 15–22 June 1913 and the accompanying programs in several locations outside the capital put the FE and its leadership in a spotlight previously unimaginable. Vilma Glücklich (born 1872 in Vágújhely [today Nové Mesto nad Váhom, Slovakia] and died 1927 in Vienna), who was president of FE at the time and was becoming an increasingly prominent and familiar figure in the international women's movements, and Rosika Schwimmer (born 1877 in Budapest and died 1948 in New York), head of the association's Political Committee, had begun organizing the event as early as September 1911. In the course of their work, they enjoyed the financial support of several ministers of the Hungarian government, as well as of István Bárczy (born 1866 in Pest and died 1943 in Budapest), the mayor of Budapest from 1906 to 1919, who was sympathetic to feminist ideas.

The event in Budapest, which received mostly positive press in Hungary and other countries, attracted some twenty-five hundred to three thousand Hungarian and foreign delegates from twenty-six countries. These delegates included the IWSA leaders, as well as representatives from the US, Canada, the UK, Germany, the Netherlands, Sweden, Finland, and Italy. The women's movements of Serbia and Russia were also represented. Leaders of women's associations from parts of the Austro-Hungarian monarchy, such as Austria, the Czech Republic, Moravia, Croatia, Slavonia, Galicia, and Bukovina, were also invited. Austrian women were represented by the leaders of the Bund österreichischer Frauenvereine (BöF, 1902–, Vienna, an umbrella organization for Austrian civic-bourgeois associations), including Marianne Hainisch (born 1839 in Baden bei Wien and died 1936 in Vienna), the president of the organization. The Allgemeiner österreichischer Frauenverein, which had maintained close links with the FE since its foundation, also sent delegates to Budapest, including Leopoldine Kulka (born 1872 in Vienna and died 1920 in Vienna), their vice president. The event was regarded as a demonstration of power for the Hungarian feminist movement, and Glücklich and Schwimmer were particularly proud of the fact that it drew such an impressive crowd of participants from so many parts of the empire, given the series of conflicts between women's organizations in the different regions of the monarchy.

The Viennese organizations, which for years had assumed that the Imperial City would host the 1913 IWSA Congress, did not let their humiliation go unanswered. In a brilliant move, the BöF's Women's Voting Rights Committee (Frauenstimmrechtskomitee) decided to organize a preconference (*Vorkonferenz*), and on 11–12 June, Vienna hosted IWSA delegates from western European countries on their way to Budapest.

On the one hand, this illustrates the close links between the civic as well as the bourgeois-liberal and feminist movements in Austria and Hungary before 1914. On the other hand, it shows that these relations were sometimes problematic and full of conflict. Who were these women with progressive and sometimes radical ideas? How were they involved in the women's movement? To what extent did they contribute to the political socialization of Austrian and Hungarian women who did not yet have the right to vote? These are the main questions addressed in this book.

Women's historiography, apart from its short boom after the 1989 change of regime, continues to be hugely ignored in Hungary, although in much of the rest of the world it has been a leading subject of discourse for decades. This marginalized position holds true for scholarship on the women's movement during the dualist era in the Habsburg monarchy and, within this, for the feminist activism that was an integral part of the rich, diverse political tradition of the nineteenth and twentieth centuries yet which never earned its rightful place in Hungarian historical research. Today, we can at least note one achievement: Hungarian historians and social scientists are beginning to recognize the significance of the women's associations that were burgeoning at the turn of the twentieth century. These cannot by any means be dismissed as "gatherings for bluestockings"; rather, they have to be seen as groups of women (and in some instances the men who joined them) whose thinking was progressive and whose range of activities went far beyond offering charity and helping disadvantaged female teachers or perhaps women in public office with retraining or financial assistance. Yet beyond their names, their leaders, and their primary objectives, to this day we have hardly any specific information about most of the women's associations of the period.

In this book, I discuss, analyze, and compare the development of the most significant bourgeois-liberal and feminist associations in the Austro-Hungarian monarchy, as well as their integration into the international organizations, from the 1890s to the interim period following the end of World War I. There are many points of overlap between these associations, and a great many threads connected them. I focus on the Viennese Allgemeiner österreichischer Frauenverein (AöF, General Austrian Women's Association) in Austria and the Budapest-based Nőtisztviselők Országos Egyesülete (NOE, National Association of Female Clerks) and the Feministák Egyesülete (FE, Hungarian Feminists' Association) in Hungary. NOE came into being in late 1896 but did not survive 1919. By contrast, FE, created in December 1904, reinvented itself in 1918–1919. Banned in 1942 and then reformed in 1946, it played a role in defending women's rights until the end of 1949. All three associations were formed and thrived in a middle-class milieu of educated professional women who represented the radical wing of feminism in their societies and who also had strong international relations.

In addition to their shared objectives, their working methods, the significant overlaps in their membership, and the manner in which they approached and used the press, many other strands directly linked the Austrian and the Hungarian organizations. The three associations grew out of the middle-class and partly upper-class milieu of educated women (teachers, doctors, female office workers, and university students of Jewish origin, as well as the wives of aristocrats and the members of the grande bourgeoisie),[1] and they had strong relationships with each other. Furthermore, AöF, NOE, and FE were linked to several transnational women's organizations, such as the International Council of Women (ICW, Washington, DC, 1888–) and the IWSA.

I argue in support of the importance of a transnational perspective in the study of the history of these organizations before 1918, and I challenge approaches that restrict their analysis to the national frameworks. In contrast to the existing Hungarian scholarship, I argue that, if we seek better to understand pre–World War I Hungarian women's activism, it is more relevant to compare it with the activism of Austrian and German women than to that of women in countries such as the United Kingdom or the United States, which are considered among the birthplaces of modern radical feminism. Thus, I suggest a more inclusive approach to the social history of Austria-Hungary, which, after the collapse of the monarchy, tended to be studied within the frameworks of national histories by the majority of the historians. I call attention to the close connections among the members of the women's organizations, and I focus on parallels and differences between the characteristic features of the Austrian and Hungarian movements. Of course, the Austrian, Hungarian, and, indeed, Viennese and Budapest-based women's movements are too diverse to cover exhaustively in a single volume, partly because these movements did not emerge and gain traction in exclusively German-speaking and Hungarian-speaking contexts. This volume thus furthers a more nuanced understanding of the women's movements in the Habsburg monarchy as distinct yet intricately interrelated parts of social trends and tendencies that crossed class and national boundaries.

Among the three branches of the women's movement (Christian-Social, Social Democratic, and bourgeois-liberal, feminist), it was the bourgeois-liberal, feminist branch on which the largest amount of research has been carried out in the 1990s and 2000s.[2] It should be emphasized that, in Hungary, after the changes of regime in 1918–1919, the domestic policy of the interwar period and the view of women it tended toward were distinctly unfavorable to the feminist cause. In the years that followed, Marxist ideology and state socialism also left their mark on the research into this subject, strive as they did to eradicate the very memory of organizations that by the early 1950s had been banned.

The three organizations at the center of my research represented the radical, liberal, and feminist associations of the bourgeois branch of the women's movement. At the time, this was defined in Austria as *bourgeois-liberal (bürgerlich-liberal)* and in Hungary as *feminist*.[3] The Austrian academic literature rarely uses the term *feminist (feministisch)* to refer to the historical women's movement—that is, the one before 1918—as these associations did not use it for themselves. The FE, however, was one of the few women's associations—both within the monarchy and on the international stage—that, from their inception, were proud to wear the feminist badge.[4] At many stages in this book, I reflect on the changes to the meaning of feminism and on the different characteristics of the various branches of the women's movement. As a result of the different terminology used at the time, publications on this subject tend to categorize the various branches of the women's movement on an ad hoc and inconsistent basis.

For similar reasons, we cannot avoid placing the women's organizations under investigation in relation to the women's movement of the time. The fundamental political, socioeconomic, and cultural problems of the Austro-Hungarian empire at the turn of the twentieth century provide a broader context for the women's movements and help to explain the organizations' objectives. Although

I do not undertake to provide a detailed portrayal of the social movements in the Habsburg monarchy, I will attempt to position the bourgeois-liberal, feminist operations within it. Thus, I aim to provide new contributions to the understanding of the system of relationships between Vienna and Budapest.

The Hungarian organizations took the Viennese AöF as a role model, and their aspirations were strongly influenced by German concepts of feminism filtered through AöF. Thus, we can only arrive at a subtle understanding of the history of these organizations and the ways in which they related to one another if we adopt a comparative perspective. After all, the histories of Austria and Hungary were intertwined for centuries. Nevertheless, even in the 2020s, research comparing the diplomatic, economic, and social history of the two halves of the monarchy is scant. Beyond discussion of the "common affairs" of the two countries (foreign, defense, and financial affairs), the secondary literature on the diplomatic and economic history of dualist-era Hungary rarely includes any comparative study with Vienna and Austria. Such research is even rarer in the case of social history. Furthermore, since their establishment, the Hungarian associations regarded AöF as a model to be followed, as their approaches to politics and the strategies they adopted to promote women's rights reveal. Thus, AöF stimulated the activism carried out by the Hungarian organization. Finally, the Austrian-Hungarian comparison offers a much more detailed picture of the backdrop against which the Hungarian feminist movement emerged and evolved than any comparison of the Hungarian movement with the movements in western European and American countries could. These countries may well be seen as the birthplaces of radical feminism, but their economic and social development differed significantly from that of Hungary. Thus, any comparison of trends in Hungary with trends in these countries would hardly yield analytically relevant findings. In contrast, it is logical that Hungarians were influenced by Austrian and German norms, as during the dualist era Vienna provided the relevant example to be followed in many aspects of civil society.

At this point it also needs to be clarified why it is important to include two Hungarian associations in the research. Until early 1915, the activities of NOE and FE were entirely inseparable. Alongside the considerable overlap seen in the leadership, elected committees, and membership of the two organizations, we should not forget their joint publishing project, their combined programs, or their coordinated wartime employment agency work—to touch on only their most basic activities. All in all, NOE and FE together covered the objectives and activities that AöF from its inception claimed as its own.

In its two most important and also most comprehensive chapters, this volume answers the following questions: What circumstances surrounded the establishment and operation of the three women's associations? Who were their leaders, from which social echelons did their (committee) members come, and what methods did they use to attempt to mobilize women (and, for that matter, men)? Were their leadership and membership characterized more by fluctuation or by stability? What conflict-resolution strategies did they employ? How did they revisit the basics of their activities when World War I broke out, and to what extent could they accommodate to these changed circumstances? How did the interim period of 1918–1920 erode NOE and AöF? And, finally, how was FE able to redefine itself and its objectives within the women's movement of the interwar period, which had to be established on an entirely new foundation, and in what way did the organization break up over the course of 1949?

Additionally, I demonstrate that the impulses coming from the international women's movement allowed FE to make up for much of its lost ground relative to the equivalent branch of the Austrian women's movement. I also analyze the role of NOE in this advance. I reflect on the favorable conditions that caused the 1913 biennial international congress of IWSA, formed in Berlin in the summer of 1904, to be hosted not, as expected, in Vienna but in Budapest. Furthermore, I confirm my hypothesis that NOE and FE were more practical and determined in their initial wartime work in the first days of August 1914 than AöF was and that this was an essential part of their working strategy. At the same time, I show that, toward the end of the war, an exceptionally intensive and innovative pacifist movement came into being within the framework of the Austrian organization, and I present the key aspects of this movement.

At a number of stages in the text, I highlight the parallels that are to be found not just in the objectives of the three women's organizations and the composition of their memberships, as well as nature of the challenges they faced, but also in the way they presented themselves and their activities to the general public. Both AöF and the Hungarian associations, almost from the moment of their inception, viewed the existence of independent press publications as the most basic form of self-representation, something for which they fought over many decades and at huge financial cost. This is precisely why another focus of this study is on the press history of the three associations. The words of Ulla Wischermann and Ute Gerhard, pioneers in research into the press output of the German women's movement, reassured me of the necessity for this line of inquiry: "The periodicals associated with the women's associations . . . are of inestimable value, and in the past presented almost entirely unprocessed sources to learn about the movements and women's career paths."[5]

AöF presented its first periodical, *Dokumente der Frauen* (Women's Documents), between 1899 and 1902. Its successor from 1902 to 1918 was *Neues Frauenleben*, which did not survive to see the last days of World War I.[6] The first official publication of the associations in Hungary, *A Nő és a Társadalom*, the result of cooperation between NOE and FE, would only appear in 1907. Until 1913, like the periodicals in Austria, it usually appeared on a monthly basis. The joint publication enterprise of NOE and FE run—not without some serious moments of disagreement—continued in 1914 with the printing of *A Nő. Feminista Folyóirat*. In January 1915, NOE withdrew from the project and embarked on the publication of its own independent periodical, *Nőtisztviselők Lapja* (Journal of Women Office Workers). *A Nő* was published on a fortnightly basis before World War I, but otherwise both journals were printed monthly. Apart from various interruptions, *A Nő* was in print from the early 1920s until 1928, while *Nőtisztviselők Lapja* survived only until 1919, when NOE was disbanded. Last but not least, we should mention the paper *Nők Lapja* (Women's News), published by FE from 1916 to 1919 and targeted at lower social groups. Despite the relative simplicity of its writing style, the content of *Nők Lapja* displayed a strong overlap with the articles in *A Nő*.

To illustrate the image of the Habsburg monarchy as portrayed, sometimes in a negative light, in the foreign press, I have included some leading German women's movement periodicals in this study. I collected articles written by Austrian or Hungarian activists and reports on the constitutive parts of the monarchy. A study of the German press was needed because the Hungarian women's organizations observably took the lead from the German example. According to the correspondence among the associations, there was an exchange of knowledge among AöF, FE, and NOE and the progressive branch of the German women's movement. It was exclusively its Austrian antecedents that motivated me to include *Frauen-Rundschau* (Women's Review), published in Leipzig between 1903 and 1913 and then in Berlin between 1921 and 1922. This fortnightly publication, which, despite its subtitle (*Offizielles Organ deutscher Frauenverbände und Vereine*, or The Official Organ of German Women's Associations and Women's Organizations), stood in between women's and feminist press publications, was the successor title to *Dokumente der Frauen*. Of the associations' publications, I analyzed the issues from 1902 to 1918 of *Neue Bahnen* (New Paths, 1865/1866–1933), the journal, established in 1866, of the Allgemeiner deutscher Frauenverein (General German Women's Association, AdF, 1865–, Leipzig).[7]

To understand the arc of the progress of the women's associations, we need to place them in their local political and ideological context. Although, in the intellectual ferment of the fin de siècle, the Viennese group began its work in a more progressive milieu, the Hungarian feminist movement was more virulent by the eve of World War I, while certain aspects of its activities had successfully caught up with those of comparable women's organizations in western Europe. They even eclipsed the imperial capital's AöF, by then largely kept alive by private initiatives. As a possible explanation for this, we might mention that throughout her career, Auguste Fickert (born 1855 in Vienna and died 1910 in Maria Enzersdorf)—who was generously endowed with authoritarian character traits, at least according to her life partner, Ida Baumann (born 1845 in Schwarzburg-Sondershausen and died

1913 in Greifenstein bei Wien)—endeavored to keep any fellow members of Jewish extraction at arm's length both from the group's leadership and from the editorial board of *Neues Frauenleben*.[8] She did so despite the fact that many such members wanted to become highly involved in the association's work. In the case of NOE and even more so of FE, by contrast, a great many women of Jewish heritage—if not themselves observant Jews—occupied positions in the top leadership as well as the elected committee and the broader membership. Among them we find Vilma Glücklich, president of FE, and Rosika Schwimmer, who, alongside her role at the Political Committee of FE, for years also held a leading position at NOE before being elected press secretary of IWSA in January 1914. The social capital of the two women—at the outset, Schwimmer in particular—greatly contributed to the Hungarian feminist movement's sharp rise and close connection to the international arena of women's organizations. Overall, the groups in Budapest proved to be much more effective in terms of their political agency than AöF.

Contrary to popular belief, neither the Austrian nor the Hungarian organizations followed the example of the British militant suffragette movement, which was far from the only branch of the women's movement in England that fought for women's political emancipation. Large campaigns for women's suffrage had already begun in the 1890s, after all.[9] To clarify, militant suffragettes were members of the British Women's Social and Political Union (WSPU), which was established by Emmeline Pankhurst (born 1858 in Manchester and died 1928 in London) in 1903 in Manchester. Only women could be members of this group, which under the banner "Votes for Women" fought for the political emancipation of women in the United Kingdom. WSPU engaged in direct (militant) acts of civil disobedience. They interrupted political rallies, chaining themselves to iron bars and fences in an attempt to achieve their aims. After refusing to pay the fines they were given by the police, they were sent to prison, where they went on hunger strikes and were force-fed.[10] By calling attention to this important difference between the methods and specific aims of different tendencies within the women's movement, I seek to emphasize that the women's organizations studied in this volume were campaigning not only for women's suffrage but for the emancipation of women in every aspect of life. Furthermore, as pacifists, they rejected the violent and disruptive methods used by the British militant suffragettes, from whom they repeatedly distanced themselves in various forums and in articles published in their official publications. They supported the nonmilitant British suffragists, who like them campaigned for suffrage through the press and did not use violent or disruptive demonstrations to get the right to vote.[11]

The associations studied in this volume placed at the focus of their activities the general defense of women's rights, and both as organizations and in their publications, they repeatedly emphasized the significance of this. Overstating the issue of the franchise by the researchers relative to the other goals of the women's movement—such as employment, education, the "social question" (*soziale Frage*), and the protection of children—would not have been fortunate, just as it had not been in earlier works on this period in the Hungarian literature. In the 1840s, then again from the 1860s, the primary goal of the modern women's movement, as elsewhere, was the extension of women's educational and economic rights, as will become clear from chapter 3 presenting the general characteristics of the women's organizations of the period. It was only in the decade before World War I that this came to include the struggle for political rights, one that was intense in some periods but restrained in others. The extension of the franchise to women was only one of the aims of these organizations, which categorically rejected all forms of disruptive behavior. The ability to elect their own representatives was seen rather as a means by which women could shape the legislative agenda and political life more in their own image.

Besides, FE and NOE were able to address and mobilize far broader social groups than AöF was. An association, at least in principle, was open to both ends of the social spectrum. I will reflect in detail on, among others, the Balmazújvárosi Szabad Nőszervezet (Free Women's Association of Balmazújváros), a group of female agricultural laborers in eastern Hungary who joined FE in 1908 in an official capacity. Yet we must not overestimate the role of the Balmazújváros women within the feminist movement, as for the most part they were a showcase Schwimmer and her colleagues used to reach their objectives. FE used them to demonstrate to the broader public that women employed in agriculture were involved in the "women's vanguard."

By contrast, AöF could not, throughout the time it was active, extend its sphere of influence beyond Vienna. Even directly before her death in 1910, Fickert had hoped that this situation might improve, but her successors were never able to implement her plans to establish subsidiary associations in the provinces. Smaller settlements were not involved, even after the emphasis was placed on work for the peace movement, as, after war broke out, AöF attempted to open up to international organizations rather than to those in provincial capitals in Austria. From 1914 to 1918, AöF played next to no active role in any practical steps taken to prevent economic and social collapse on the home front, yet within its ranks an exceptionally intensive and innovative pacifist movement was to form. FE and NOE, on the other hand, attempted to reconcile their antimilitarist stance and participation in the international peace movement with their aid work done on the home front. From the first days of August 1914, Schwimmer and her coworkers, aside from constantly emphasizing the principles of the peace movement, applied all their energies to work on the home front—like labor exchange, childcare, vocational training for women, and communal kitchens.

Unlike AöF, the Hungarian associations were active on all three levels: the local, the national, and the transnational or international. Archive sources provide a complex picture of the network of contacts, within the monarchy and beyond, of NOE, and particularly of FE. It is within this system of coordinates that I portray the relationship that the Hungarians established with the Austrian organizations and with AöF. It is vital to reconstruct these networks of relationships. There can be no further delay in searching out concrete examples to underscore Judith Szapor's claim that FE, from its creation through 1914, attained significant influence within the arena of the international movement and "developed along the lines of the bourgeois women's movements of Western Europe."[12] I was motivated to conduct deeper research by the claim generally accepted in theoretical literature in Hungarian on women's history—a claim that needs to be set straight—that in women's emancipation before 1918, Great Britain, the United States, and France provided the model for the Hungarian associations. In my opinion, as I have already mentioned in connection with the publications of the women's groups, the examples given by Germany, as related by Austria, were just as important, if not, in some senses, more so.

To draw the whole trajectory of the associations' development, we have also to relate (a portion of) the road to their demise. After the end of World War I, NOE was simply unable to adapt its objectives to the pressing challenges of the new, interim period in Hungary. When the association disbanded in the summer of 1919, part of its membership joined the Hungarian Communist Party, while others joined FE. The latter, although it proved incapable of recovering its former position in the women's movement as it tried to find a new footing in the interwar period, continued to operate until 1949, despite the ban placed on it in 1942. In chapter 6 of this volume, I look at the most crucial moments of the almost three decades of FE's operation after 1919. In the case of AöF—although the existing literature claims otherwise—the association was not suddenly disbanded in early 1919. It is much more probable that this was a drawn-out process of decline, to which the death of the president in 1920 contributed, as did a number of other factors. Of these, we should mention the continuous retirement of older members from roles in public life, their deaths, and the turn toward other specialist associations among younger members.

The book foregrounds the biographies and influence of the leading figures of the associations—Auguste Fickert (AöF), Rosika Schwimmer (NOE and FE), and Vilma Glücklich (FE)—and analyzes the different forms of relationships among them and the other leading activists as well as their different styles of communication. At this point, it has to be emphasized that while the biographies of the leading activists of the Western women's movement were hot topics in international academic and popular literature, they were unreasonably forgotten about by both Hungarian and Austrian historiography, apart from a few writings and encyclopedia entries. This is absurd, if only because during 1918 and 1919 Schwimmer entered the world of big-time politics, when the government of Count Mihály Károlyi (born 1875 in Fót, Hungary, and died 1955 in Vence, France), leader of the Democratic Republic (acting between 16 November 1918 and 11 January 1919), delegated her to the position of envoy to Switzerland. I pay attention not only to the leading figures in the associations but also to other leading activists. I outline whether they worked in intellectual, artistic, or other fields and whether they hailed from families with Jewish roots, whether they were observant, or whether (either because of their role in the women's movement or for other reasons) they left their Jewish communities behind. I also indicate how they came into contact with the women's movement and what role they played in the struggle for women's emancipation in the states of the Habsburg monarchy or indeed in umbrella organizations operating at the international level.[13]

Sources and Methodology

The most important sources are the Rosika Schwimmer Papers in the New York Public Library and those of Auguste Fickert at the Wienbibliothek im Rathaus as well as in the manuscript archive and musical history collection of the Österreichische Nationalbibliothek. Besides archival sources, I rely on the official organs of the three associations. I reconstruct the history of their publication and emphasize the importance of the associations' publishing activity as a key aspect of their multifaceted political agency.

A major challenge has to be highlighted regarding the papers of Fickert: the archive was established after her death and relied on public donations from family members, friends, and correspondents.[14] In this material—in contrast to the Schwimmer Collection—the outgoing letters have survived only in negligible numbers. Harriet Anderson, Renate Flich, and Hanna Hacker pursued more intensive research in this collection in the 1990s. In the Viennese archives, I surveyed the documentation of a number of members of AöF, though these did not provide more than a few folders' worth of material.

Regarding the Hungarian associations, key reference points were provided in the Hungarian National Archive and by the papers of one of the leading members of FE, Mrs. Oszkár Szirmay (1886–1959). These sources offer an insight into the activities of FE, everyday life within the association, and the sometimes distinctly heated debates at sessions of the board and at editorial meetings. They also give us a picture of the domestic and foreign press publications (and the books bought for the associations' library) the association used to acquire fresh, or sometimes less fresh information about the women's movement—information that it then regularly shared in its own periodicals.

Study of the material of the Rosika Schwimmer Collection in the manuscript archive of the New York Public Library proved invaluable in learning about the publication of *A Nő és a Társadalom* and in understanding provincial and international relationships before 1918. Although a number of other historians working on the unique aspects of the development of Hungarian and western European feminist movements have undertaken selective research in this archive, they were limited to individual issues or particular periods.[15]

Previously, exploration of the rich sources in Budapest and New York, of interest not just to scholars of women's and social history but also to those working on political and diplomatic history, was limited. The archive in Budapest has preserved not only the minutes of almost every general assembly the association held between 1906 and 1949 but also the documentation of the monthly meetings of the committee. In addition to this, a multitude of other types of source material can be found in the almost six hundred boxes preserved in the New York Public Library, which, thanks to Schwimmer's extended network of contacts, also provide interesting information on the development of the Christian-Social and Social Democratic women's movements.

In the discussion below, I briefly reflect on the methodological framework of the study, the framing of the comparison, and some of the challenges related to this perspective. Since I first began my research on NOE and FE, I have sought as one of my main goals to destabilize the national narrative.[16] This is one of the reasons I have tended to emphasize the roles played by women who became internationally well known. One such figure is Rosika Schwimmer, who was the best-known Hungarian activist worldwide because of her international network. She was also a link between the women's movements in Hungary and Austria. A previous content and discourse analysis of mine on the periodical press of the Austrian, Hungarian, and German progressive women's movements confirmed unambiguously that the activities of NOE, FE, and AöF were comparable, that there was an intense relationship among them, and that NOE and FE as associations had only limited contact with the ethnic women's organizations of the monarchy.[17] Thus, I am far from claiming that it is necessary to compare these three organizations simply because they represented the radical wing of women's movements both in Vienna and in Budapest.

Before discussing the methodology, I consider it essential to highlight the limitations of this discussion. Of course, an analysis of progressive women's movements of the entire Austro-Hungarian monarchy would have been impossible, as the women's movements in Vienna and Budapest alone were too diverse to be discussed in a single monograph. Furthermore, women's organizations existed not only in German-speaking and Hungarian-speaking contexts, as both halves of the monarchy were multiethnic. Due to my language skills, I was not able to review the archival materials of women's organizations established in the territories inhabited by national minorities but could get only impressions of them from my sources. These sources showed very clearly that the Hungarian associations had the closest contacts with the Austrian bourgeois and progressive women's movements. In other words, a comparison of the history, activism, networks of contacts, and knowledge transfers of NOE and FE with organizations other than AöF would not have yielded much in the way of meaningful insights. Regarding the associations I selected, I had to consider the availability of archival sources. In the cases of AöF, NOE, and FE, we can rely on the documentation and press organs of the associations, as well as the collections of their presidents. These kinds of sources were not available in the case of every organization, as the documents concerning certain associations (e.g., BöF) are unfortunately inaccessible to the researchers.

Another limitation of this study (and this is true of most of the secondary literature on the subject) is that it primarily focuses on upper-middle-class women's movements in the capital cities of the monarchy except for a short chapter on the local auxiliaries of NOE and FE. In the case of Hungary, apart from a few exceptions,[18] it is impossible to study the workings of these auxiliary associations systematically, as most of the archival sources documenting their operations were destroyed during World War II.

As I have stated, my primary aim was to place my research in an inter- and transnational context. Until the new millennium, historical scholarship focused primarily on women and women's movements within national frameworks. As Francisca de Haan argued in 2017, "Many feminist historians today continue to work within the national paradigm. It was and remains important to write these histories in order to understand the central place of gender and gender struggles in national economic, social, political, and cultural contexts."[19] However, as Haan and her colleagues observe in another paper, historians have started to explore inter- and transnational dimensions of the history of feminism and women's movements because of the rise of postcolonial perspectives and transnational perspectives in historiography since the 1980s and 1990s.[20] I agree with them entirely on the necessity of the inter- and transnational perspective, as feminism and women's movements did not operate in isolation within national borders. From the beginning of the nineteenth century, more and more transnational links were formed between individual women and women's associations.[21] This is also true of the period I examine in this volume, as from the beginning of the twentieth century, much of the struggle for women's emancipation was already taking place on international platforms.[22]

ICW, IWSA, and the Women's International League for Peace and Freedom (WILPF) became the most important platforms of this inter- and transnational arena, but *inter-* and *transnational* can refer to activism that crossed national borders. As Francisca de Haan observes, inter- and transnational dimensions were of key importance, as congresses and other formal and informal meetings framed by them provided not only information but also inspiration and support for the associations.[23] In a paper that examines the construction of the above-mentioned international organizations and seeks the prospects and limits of internationalism, Leila J. Rupp asks the following questions: "What drew women together across the borders of nationality? Who fell within the circle of we? What did it mean to profess ties across national, ethnic, and other identities?"[24] As Haan again notes, membership in this kind of international community gave activists self-assurance in their attempts to face challenges in their own countries, and it also created conditions within which they could take their cases to international forums, as will be illustrated several times in this volume. This way of thinking is also mirrored in the structure of the international organizations, as each had national organizations with additional local auxiliaries. Haan also points out that these "national building blocks . . . may even have strengthened the nationalization of women's movements by encouraging women to form national organizations," as happened in FE's case.[25] And as I demonstrate in the volume, collective identity was the most important factor that kept these groups together.[26] However, as I note in my discussion several times, ICW and IWSA aimed to organize internationally by drawing on Western experience, on "a nation-by-nation basis," which proved an impossible task in the multiethnic Austro-Hungarian monarchy.[27]

Thus, the workings of these three associations can (and should) be interpreted as an entangled history. Julie Carlier refers to "the forgotten transnational influences that shaped the pre-war movements for women's rights" in the case of the history of Belgian women's movements, and her observation is almost entirely applicable to Austrian and Hungarian conditions.[28] One could adopt and slightly adapt her scheme and interpret Hungarian feminism as follows: Political, economic, and social transfers in the Austro-Hungarian monarchy triggered the birth of organized feminism in Hungary in the mid-1890s (NOE). This was followed by the growing influence on organized Hungarian feminism of the Austrian (such as AöF), German, and Dutch progressive women's associations and then by the interventions of IWSA, which aimed to establish their Hungarian auxiliary associations—in other words, FE. This is a perfect example of an entangled history.[29] As Carlier argues, these external influences "were often one of the engines that fuelled the birth and the development of national women's organizations."[30] It would thus be quite an oversight not to adopt transnational perspectives in the study of the history of the Hungarian and Austrian women's movements. If we insist on national frameworks, we will inevitably overlook certain aspects of these movements without which we cannot possibly hope to arrive at a subtle understanding of their histories.

The concept of entangled history (*histoire croisée* or *Verflechtungsgeschichte*) was outlined by Michael Werner and Bénédicte Zimmermann in 2006 as a multifaceted research approach that offers new critical perspectives in the study of inter- and transnational history. According to the underlying premise of *histoire croisée*, "entities and objects of research are not merely considered in relation to one another but also through one another, in terms of their relationships, interactions, and circulation." *Verflechtungsgeschichte* in turn puts emphasis on the importance of self-reflexivity,[31] a critical concern that, according to Haan, "strongly resonates with feminist studies, including women's history, which have always criticized the professed objectivity of mainstream scholarship."[32]

Again, Carlier makes it clear that national and inter- or transnational approaches do not contradict or compete but rather supplement and reinforce each other. Thus, the methodology of entangled history blurs the boundaries of trans- and international. Carlier also argues that while comparative and transfer studies give a static character to the research, entangled history provides relational and reflective approaches. It can be considered relational, as it considers interactions among cross-national actors objects of the analysis. If more than two actors are included in the research (as is the case in this volume), issues of reciprocity and asymmetry can also be discussed, and this in turn calls into question any simplistic notion of "unilateral transfer from one nation to the other."[33] The critical perspectives and the methodologies involved in the study of entangled history provide much more than a static picture of the women's associations. They enable us to outline the workings of these associations over comparatively long spans of time, as well as the way in which the associations influenced and were influenced by trends and events on the international scene.

While comparative history tends to concern itself with similarities and differences between the ways in which similar or analogous events or shifts took place on (usually two) different national stages,[34] cross-national history follows topics across national boundaries. This is closely connected to transnational history and entangled history (or in other words connected or shared history), which examine transfers and cultural and social connections between nations.[35]

Another methodological aspect of my inquiry is that I investigate the everyday workings of the associations, describing their aims, inner structures, publishing policies, most prominent members, and changing (growing and shrinking) memberships. The archival sources and press products documenting the activities of the three associations essentially capture the moment in the social history of the region when a more educated and thus more self-aware (though not yet enfranchised) group of (upper-) middle-class women began to make their mark by leaving their homes. The (leading) members of the associations thus effectively stepped out of the shadows and began to create documents related to their activism. We are speaking, admittedly, of a relatively small and homogeneous group of women. Their activism and their role in the public sphere distinguish them from a large group of "ordinary" or "everyday" women who did not leave the walls of their homes and who thus remained in their traditional roles as wives and mothers. The women in the first group became active as organizers and raised their voices for the emancipation of women. Thus, they produced new types of sources (e.g., press products, petitions, and speeches). While these women made efforts to change the existing social relations, the masses of women in the second group, who remained in their traditional roles, followed the existing rules and thus remained essentially silent.[36]

I suggest with this volume, as Francisca de Haan has done with her research, the importance of "decentralizing" the scholarship on the history of women's movements and women's activism.[37] Thus, I suggest the more vigorous and intensive inclusion of Central European regions in this scholarship, instead of continuing to focus on the countries in the West. I thus echo the urgings of Deborah Simonton, who explains that, although postcolonial and transnational approaches took root in the 1990s, experts on the subject of women's activism continue to wrestle with fact that the European and global perspective does not mean simply the study of shifts and events in the United Kingdom, France, and Germany. In 2006, Simonton warned that more intense inclusion of research into northern Europe and East-Central Europe should be delayed no further.[38] Progress has unquestionably been made in this area since the 2000s, but historians still have a lot of work to do to make women's history of this region visible. This requires not only sedulous research and a strong knowledge of several languages but also the support of foreign publishers and a significant amount of funding.

I examine AöF, NOE, and FE within the framework of entangled history, thus making it possible to shed light on "shared dimensions of our European and transnational histories."[39] In doing so, I challenge a belief widespread in Hungary according to which there are not enough archival sources on these associations or on their network systems to allow any serious study of their day-to-day operations or their place against the backdrop of international trends. I hope that the discussion in this volume will serve as an inspiration for feminists in Central Europe today. I also hope that it will help debunk the conviction still prevalent in the region that the idea of feminism is "foreign."

1

Scholarship on the Bourgeois-Liberal, Feminist Movement in Hungary and Austria

"THE HISTORY OF WOMEN'S MOVEMENTS has been sadly sidelined by Hungarian academe.... The documents relating to them were not republished, ... at least not since World War I."[1] The changes of regime in 1918–1919, the domestic policy of the interwar period, and its preferred images of women were not at all beneficial for the bourgeois women's movement, which, from the 1920s, proved unable to win back its earlier significance. As is made clear by the 2004 writings of Judith Szapor, there have been few publications on the pre-1918 history of the Hungarian women's movement, and there are key works of research that have yet to be written.[2] A later study coauthored by Szapor and Andrea Pető speaks of an "infrastructural vacuum" and "institutional resistance" to studying women's activism, the causes of which they trace back to the "patriarchal power relationships of the academy."[3] Following on the optimism of the early 1990s, this analysis suggests a significant step backward, strengthening the impression that research subjects sidelined in the socialist period are never able to regain their rightful place. To this day there are no studies relating to the everyday life of the women's associations; indeed, we can confidently state that research into women's associations themselves has primarily taken place through political historical approaches.

In the 2010s and 2020s, we have been witnesses to a few positive changes. This is a development of note if we consider that Marxist historiography buried the memory of the bourgeois women's movement even more deeply than the domestic politics of the interwar period had done.[4] Following Susan Zimmermann's 1999 monograph titled *Die bessere Hälfte? Frauenbewegungen und Frauenbestrebungen im Ungarn der Habsburgermonarchie 1848 bis 1918* and discussing the particularities of all three branches of the Hungarian women's movement between 1848 and 1918, however, a number of Hungarian-language studies and popular scholarly articles have emerged on the feminist movement and its press.[5] Among these, we have to mention papers in Hungarian by Judit Acsády and Judith Szapor.[6] Alongside the social historical (women's historical), sociological, and literary historical aspects of feminist activism, research projects in this field have been focusing on the strategies and rhetorical practice of discourses on gender and touch on the discursive spaces of feminist journals. Yet these works cannot by any means be termed comprehensive. Most of this research is centered on Budapest and does not generalize to Hungary as a whole.

Study of the feminist movement in Hungary has required and will in the future continue to require a number of academic infrastructural innovations. Until 2020, the most important such innovation was the Gender Studies Department established at the Central European University (CEU) in 1995. However, in the fall of 2020, CEU transferred its entire teaching and research staff, as well as its library, to Vienna. This left Hungary with the Research Center for Women's History at the Faculty of Humanities at Eötvös Loránd University (ELTE) and gender studies team at the Institute of Modern Philology at the University of Miskolc. The gap left by the removal of CEU cannot be filled by these two groups alone.

No discussion of the development—or rather deterioration—of the institutional framework for women's studies in Hungary can fail to mention the abolition of the Gender Studies master's course at ELTE. The establishment of the Women's History Working Committee of the Hungarian Academy of Sciences could have been an important step forward, but without any budget and financial basis, its role is only formal. Since the early 1990s, at the Faculty of Humanities at Szeged University, there has also been a workshop in which students of English language and literature can complete courses on the subject of women's history. In the fall of 2010, the gender research group at the university's English-American Institute founded the journal *TNTeF* (*Társadalmi Nemek Tudománya Interdiszciplináris eFolyóirata* [Interdisciplinary eJournal for Gender Studies]).

In the summer of 2018, two important representatives of Hungarian women's history and gender studies, Katalin Kéri and Andrea Pető, were still optimistic about the future of the discipline.[7] Kéri was convinced that the creation of research workshops in Budapest and in the provinces could be cause for hope, if only because of their dynamically expanding network of professional contacts. But Kéri also considered that more intensive collaboration among research groups was critical for work to flourish; this dialogue still has not visibly emerged. In promoting discussions among researchers in women's studies, Kéri hopes that younger researchers might soon feel the effects of this development. As of 2018, Andrea Pető considered the most important aspect of progress to be the expansion of the institutional framework. Her premonitions that this would not come to pass, which so accurately sensed the predicament we are now in, have never been more relevant. For her opinion was that at a certain point, the process of institutionalization would run aground, which in the medium and longer term would have the consequence that young researchers would no longer be motivated to work on women's history.

According to Pető, "women's historians in Hungary are good at integrating into the international community."[8] This is underscored by the studies and monographs of Hungarian authors publishing both in Hungarian and in English and either fully or partially centering their focus on the women's movements of the nineteenth and twentieth centuries. From this body of work, we have to first mention the volumes and studies by Judith Szapor, as well as book chapters by Judit Acsády, Tibor Glant, Mária M. Kovács, and Claudia Papp. The works of Agatha Schwartz, who focuses on the literary tradition, and the shorter writings of Anna Loutfi, Margaret H. McFadden, and Susan Zimmermann all also make useful contributions to the field.[9]

A much more positive picture emerges in the 2009 volume by Johanna Gehmacher and Natascha Vittorelli on certain regions of the Austro-Hungarian monarchy.[10] For in Austria, the Czech lands (Prague), the Slavonian areas, and the region around Zagreb, the publication of works surveying writings on the subject of women's emancipation continued even after 1918.[11] Indeed in these regions, efforts were made to arrange exhibitions, to erect memorials to women's movement activists, and to celebrate anniversaries after World War I.

We need to only think of sculptor Franz Seifert's memorial statue of the founder and leader of AöF Auguste Fickert, who is one of the central protagonists of this volume, in the Türkenschanzpark of Vienna, erected in 1929, or the celebration of the sixtieth anniversary of the Bund österreichischer Frauenvereine (BöF), an umbrella organization for Austrian civic/bourgeois associations.[12] The Auguste Fickert statue found a home in the Währing district of Vienna and is still in place, close to where she once lived and indeed where the Allgemeiner österreichischer Frauenverein (AöF) office once was. Seifert's statue of Fickert is unique in that it is the first public statue in the erstwhile imperial capital to depict a woman who was not a member of the Habsburg family.[13]

Soon after 1918, the early pioneers of research into women's history appeared in Vienna. Of note is Käthe Leichter (born 1895 in Vienna and died 1942 in Ravensbrück), who studied the situations of working women in Austria in the 1920s. In contrast to Hungary, Austria's development of women's studies followed the tendencies prevalent in western Europe and across the Atlantic,[14] though in the years before World War II, Austro-fascism would bring a halt to this work.[15]

Johanna Gehmacher and Maria Mesner marked the 1970s as the next important renaissance in women's studies: by this time, thanks to the success of the international women's movement, even in Austria, there was demand for the

Figure 1.1. Memorial for Auguste Fickert. The following text is on the plinth: "Der Vorkämpferin für Frauenfrage / Auguste Fickert 1855–1910 / Voll Mut und Tatkraft hat sie ihr Leben hohem Idealen dargebracht." *Photograph by the author.*

uncovering of "the utterly ignored stories of women,"[16] in the interests of "making the female gender visible" (*Sichtbarmachung der Frauen*).[17] This trend may have been inspired by such subdisciplines as sociology, family studies, and political historical research. Germany and the United States led in the formation of methodological tools in these fields, providing models others would often follow.[18]

Yet it would be a mistake to claim that women's history was a discovery of the 1970s in Austria. For from the 1970s onward, however, a great many national and international conferences, workshops, and summer schools were organized in Vienna and a number of regional centers that would for many years determine the direction of research.[19] At Austrian universities, the repertoire of courses on women's history and gender became increasingly broad, and research teams were soon established. As a result of the positions obtained by the new or second women's movement (*neue oder zweite Frauenbewegung*), centers were established in several Austrian cities—Graz, Linz, Salzburg, and Klagenfurt—that began to research and then to teach the history of the old or first women's movement (*alte oder erste Frauenbewegung*).[20] The most prestigious of these are the Forschungsschwerpunkt Frauen- und Geschlechtergeschichte research group, operating under the direction of Johanna Gehmacher and Dietlind Hüchtker at the Institut für Zeitgeschichte (Department of Contemporary History) at the University of Vienna, and the Sammlung Frauennachlässe am Institut für Geschichte an der Universität Wien, led by Li Gerhalter, which collects the documented experiences of all women, from celebrities and activists to ordinary citizens. In addition to processing the collections of key figures in the Austrian-German women's movement (e.g., Yella Hertzka [born 1873 in Vienna and died 1948 in Vienna] or the German-born Käthe Schirmacher [born 1865 in Danzig and died 1930 in Merano]), researchers with connections to these organizations have worked on the history of gender in periods from the sixteenth to the twentieth century.

Since the 1980s, thematic exhibitions at the Wienmuseum and at other galleries outside Vienna, which have attracted broader public attention to the subject, have been foundational. Here I list only those exhibitions that produced catalogs for researchers. The series begins with a 1984–1985 exhibition held at the Hermesvilla, presenting the everyday lives of the female population of fin de siècle Vienna.[21] This was followed by an event in 1989–1990 that evoked the feminism of the turn of the century[22] and then a 1998 exhibit in Laa an der Thaya in Lower Austria that dealt with various aspects of the lives of Austrian women.[23] This list, which could be continued at length, ends with the very successful display at the Vienna Volkskundemuseum organized in 2018–2019 to commemorate the hundredth anniversary of female suffrage.[24]

We must make special mention of the grandiose project of the Austrian National Library and the Department for Contemporary History of the University of Vienna, titled Ariadne, Frauen in Bewegung 1848–1938.[25] This resource, begun in 1992, was significantly extended in 2009. It has since moved online and has, by digitizing the Austrian periodical press (including the majority of women's journals), come to provide key information for a study of any branch of the women's movement. In addition to short biographies of women's rights activists, we find key details about almost every women's group, whether in Vienna or the rest of Austria: years of foundation, years of disbandment, addresses of headquarters, names of founders and committee or board members, institutional connections in Austria and abroad (if applicable), and a list of the journals and volumes they published, together with sources and academic citations. This publicly available database remains unique to this day and would be an example to follow in Hungary,[26] where, for the time being at least, any such initiative is unthinkable.[27]

Johanna Gehmacher and Natascha Vittorelli's monograph *Wie Frauenbewegung geschrieben wird* (2009) is relevant because its authors, along with other Austrian scholars, present an overview of the history of research into the women's movements in Hungary, Transylvania, the Czech and Moravian lands, the Banat, Galicia, and the South Slav territories.[28] This volume represents an important attempt to move the discussion of women's studies in Europe forward. This field of research and its dissemination continues with the academic and financial support of the Institute of History of the Austrian Academy of Sciences and of the Austrian Science Fund (Fonds zur Förderung der wissenschaftlichen Forschung), as well as that of other higher education institutions.

Over the decades, of course, Austrian researchers have also faced a number of methodological challenges. These have been described in the columns of *L'Homme—Europäische Zeitschrift für feministische Geschichtswissenschaft*,[29] a journal associated with the University of Vienna and published since 1990, and in the chapter "Opinions" (*Stellungnahmen*), authored by Gehmacher and Vittorelli in their 2009 edited volume, *Wie Frauenbewegung geschrieben wird* (How the women's movement is written). In the "Opinions" chapter, Gehmacher and Vittorelli asked researchers such as Krista Cowman, Francisca de Haan, Karen Offen, and Gabriella Hauch to share their practical experiences and any questions or doubts they might have relating to their current or previous projects. Irene Bandhauer-Schöffmann, who studies the two World Wars and the women's movements after 1945, related her personal experiences from the 1980s: "We were convinced that women are different from, indeed better than, men, and that we, like all other women, were 'victims' of men and male society. This was tangible in our [research] findings."[30] In a similar vein, in 1990, Herta Nagl-Docekal warned with foreboding that some women researchers considered the investigations of the period into women's history and feminism to be outdated and that she recommended a large-scale, comprehensive project be launched to resolve these conceptual problems.[31] By contrast, in 1995, Brigitte Mazohl-Wallnig emphasized that "for some years now historiography has finally taken the history of women seriously."[32] Yet she also warned of the subjects of such research being "blunted," meaning that "the trivialization of women's themes" implies that such studies have done "more harm than good."[33] By this time, the greatest challenge was presented by the fact that "much of the basic research . . . has not yet taken place in systematic form."[34] Her observations remain every bit as relevant today.

In her authoritative 1997 book *Die Frau mit Eigenschaften* (The Woman with Qualities) on the subject of women's publications, Eva Klingenstein stresses that in the first half of the 1990s, interest focused on fin de siècle Vienna on account of the excellent availability of source material. Historians, literary scholars, philosophers, psychologists, and art historians all attempted to immerse themselves in the pre-1914 history of the imperial capital and in the everyday life of its female population. Yet Klingenstein considered there to be only a few works that focused on women's activism and their press publications in this period.[35] Since then, steps have been taken to address that historical gap, but researchers still have a tremendous hill to climb.

Natascha Vittorelli did not think the writings published on the Austrian women's movements to be too few; she turned her attention instead to the problem of research methodology. Most scholars had—in her opinion, misguidedly—studied the issue within a national framework.[36] Although Susan Zimmermann repeatedly pointed to the interpretational problems resulting from focusing only on the national contexts, it was only in the second half of the 1990s that the attention of researchers was attracted to the transnational/international nature of women's movements.[37] Yet we should be aware that, thus far, the broader context has been entirely missing from almost all the works discussing the operation of the AöF. The only exception to this is Birgitta Bader-Zaar's work dealing with the AöF's legal aid section (*Rechtschutz-Sektion*) and its German connections.[38] Austrian researchers focusing on the operation of the AöF such as Eva Geber, Renate Flich, Hanna Hacker, Edith Prost, and Petra Unger all conducted their studies within the national framework.[39]

Birgitta Bader-Zaar saw the root problem as the small number of English-language works on women's history that had been translated into German, even by the late 2000s; there has not been much progress since. The situation is nevertheless worlds apart from that in Hungary. At the National Library of Austria or the libraries of the University of Vienna, the most recent works written in English, French, or smaller European languages are available, which is a great help to researchers. In Budapest—not to mention provincial cities in Hungary—historians have nowhere near this access to international materials. For some years the National Széchényi Library has not been in a position to acquire the foreign-language works of even Hungarian authors. The CEU library being moved to Vienna only serves to make research even more difficult.

Of the works translated into German, one of the most important is Harriet Anderson's 1992 book *Utopian Feminism: Women's Movements in Fin-de-Siècle*

Vienna. Like the English original, its German edition (1994) remains standard reading to this day. It has inspired countless studies and analyses.[40] The first book to highlight the extension of rights for women is the 2006 volume, which deals with civil society in the monarchy, in the series *Die Habsburgermonarchie 1848–1918*.[41] I should add that a good part of the literature on this subject—including the manuscripts of graduate theses and doctoral dissertations from the 1940s onward—can only be accessed in reading rooms of libraries and research institutes. These student works—as Klingenstein herself emphasizes—are often based on mistaken basic concepts that determine their quality. In my view, however, the questions they raise are sometimes distinctly thought provoking, and they often rely on documents, manuscripts, or even oral history sources,[42] which today are hard or impossible to access.[43] Worthy of special mention is the work by Karola Auernig, who weighs up the relations between bourgeois and Social Democratic women's movements.[44]

According to Bader-Zaar, researchers into women's movements mostly make use of various associations' minutes and press publications. Accepting that these provide extremely useful information, an opinion that I share, she argues it would also be vital to study the unpublished sources, like the archives and correspondence of associations.[45] This is meticulous and tiring work, but it does bear fruit. And even if the circumstances in Austria are incomparably better than those in Hungary, researchers here, too, have to face burgeoning infrastructural and financial challenges.

Central to Austrian research in the 1970s and 1980s were issues relating to women's employment, including the rights of domestic servants, social welfare for women workers, the role of women in the workers' movement, and other related topics.[46] But by the 1990s, following the German model, the study of the history of women of a bourgeois background became more popular.[47] This was when most of the studies on the AöF were published. From the early 2000s, attention was increasingly focused on "Jewish Vienna"; to this was added the subject of female homosexuality.[48] Michaela Raggam-Blesch and Elisabeth Malleier examined the place, importance, and (in)visibility of Jewish women in the context of various women's organizations in Vienna.[49] Raggam-Blesch makes efforts to answer the question of "why Jewish women were hardly mentioned in connection with the feminist movement." As she explains, with regard to religion, the movement was neutral with regard to religious affiliation, an attitude captured in the AöF's vehemently anticlerical attitude. Raggam-Blesch also argues that within the women's movement, it was tacitly assumed that Jewish women would give up their religious identity in favor of assimilation.[50] Margarete Grandner and Edith Saurer have also published edited volumes on the topic of gender and religion and on the participation of Jewish women in women's movements.[51] By the early 1990s, it nevertheless became clear that it was among literary historians that the bourgeois-liberal women's movement became a really popular subject—we need to only think of

Harriet Anderson or Eva Klingenstein. It is also worth mentioning the project researching the international networks of women's movements in the nineteenth and twentieth centuries by Elisabeth Frysak, Margareth Lanzinger, and Edith Saurer,[52] although new questions on this subject have not been raised in the 2010s and 2020s. The only exception to this is research conducted by women on the effects of gender on the history of their own professions, for example, on the feminization of librarianship or the partial feminization of the archival profession.[53]

Austria is also further ahead in work on women's activism on the home front in World War I than Hungary, where only a few studies and no monograph have been published on the subject. We should note that while interest in Austrian historiography has become more intensive in the last decade, a large part of that work is associated with Christa Hämmerle.[54] Outside the academy, as seen in the number of published catalogs of exhibitions organized on the centenary period between 2014 and 2018, women's work and progress have attracted intense attention from the general public, if not quite on a par with that paid to the hundred years of work to gain female suffrage.[55] These exhibition catalogs hardly mention the radical wing of the bourgeois-liberal women's movement, however; there is much more active interest in the role played by the BöF,[56] which in 1914 was made up of ninety subsidiary associations and which could hardly have been more different in its profile from the AöF.[57]

Finally, research into the careers of activists in women's movements has to be discussed. Given the somewhat sporadic nature of relatively rare publications on the subject, the chasm between the specialists and experts, on the one hand, and the curious reading public, on the other, seems virtually unbridgeable.[58] Although biographies have been published on a number of the key figures in the German-Austrian Social Democratic women's movement, in the case of the bourgeois women's movement, the only monograph to appear in the early twenty-first century is an eponymous book about Rosa Mayreder (born 1858 in Vienna and died 1938 in Vienna), who was a painter, musician, author, and women's rights activist. Alongside establishing a career as a literary author, Mayreder worked with Auguste Fickert as vice presidents of the AöF and editors of *Dokumente der Frauen*.[59] Austria's literary and cultural tradition has preserved and continues to celebrate Mayreder's memory: in addition to exhibitions bringing her work into focus, her name is immortalized in the name of one of Vienna's parks, Rosa Mayreder Park, and in that of an educational institution dedicated to the feminist outlook (Rosa Mayreder College). She became well known in the Austrian households when her portrait appeared on the last 500-shilling note, printed in 1997.[60]

Following a dearth of work on bourgeois women's movements in the early years of the twenty-first century, Corinna Oesch's 2014 biography of Yella Hertzka, the women's rights and peace activist who in 1912 founded the first two-year secondary horticultural school for girls in Vienna-Grinzing and directed it until 1938, represents a great step forward, as does Johanna Gehmacher et al.'s

2018 monograph about German writer and women's rights activist Käthe Schirmacher.[61] In the 1890s, Schirmacher was one of the leading figures of the radical wing of the bourgeois women's movement, from which she later turned away. Of Fickert's immediate associates and the leading members of the AöF, shorter studies have been written on literary historian and editor Christine Touaillon (born 1878 in Jihlava and died 1928 in Graz), gynecologist and urologist Dora Teleky (born 1879 in Hinterbrühl and died 1963 in Stäfa), philologist and university professor Elise Richter (born 1865 in Vienna and died 1944 in Theresienstadt), and Therese Schlesinger-Eckstein (born 1863 in Vienna and died 1940 in Blois), who joined the Social Democrats after a brief stint with the bourgeois-liberal movement.[62] As a result of the power battles (*Machtkämpfe*) following Fickert's death, Touaillon became one of the editors of *Neues Frauenleben*, though she performed her duties not from Vienna but rather from Stainz, a small village in the direct vicinity of Graz. Fickert and her coworkers showered their attention on the linguist Elise Richter, the first woman to serve with accreditation by the University of Vienna as a private instructor at a university, whose professional progress was regularly covered by *Neues Frauenleben*. Only a few book chapters and encyclopedia entries have dealt with Fickert, one of the greatest role models for the new women's movement in Austria, most notably works by Karola Auernig, Käthe Braun-Prager, Renate Flich, Hanna Hacker, and Dora Leon.[63]

The situation in Hungary is less favorable. Hitherto, there was next to no information about Rosika Schwimmer and Vilma Glücklich, two prominent figures in not only the Hungarian women's and peace movements but also international women's movements. In addition to her work as a women's rights activist, Glücklich was the first woman to earn a degree at the Faculty of Arts of the University of Budapest. In recent years, a few articles have been published on Schwimmer, both academic and popular,[64] but Glücklich's name is hardly mentioned in the literature.[65] To this day, the project at the CEU Gender Studies Department is unique: as a result of it, in 2006, a lexicon was published that included biographies of 150 women's activists from twenty-two countries, including Hungary and Austria.[66] Its articles all included sources and bibliographies. At the time of its publication, its editors were motivated by books appearing in the early 2000s whose titles had promised an overview of the history of European women but which in point of fact passed over the East-Central European region entirely. There are also few or no articles to be found on less significant activists from this region on the world stage. The next groundbreaking volume in this field has just been published at the end of 2024. It was edited by Zsófia Lóránd, Adela Hîncu, Jovana Mihajlović Trbovc, and Katarzyna Stańczak-Wiślicz and contains one hundred sources, which are preceded by short author's biographies and an introduction, and offers a selection of the most representative texts on feminism and women's rights in East-Central Europe during the interwar period, between the end of World War II and the early 1990s.[67]

2

Austria-Hungary in the Fin de Siècle

THE TURN OF THE TWENTIETH CENTURY was one of the most turbulent periods in the development of Central Europe in general and of Austria and Hungary in particular, from both an economic and a social and cultural point of view. Vienna was at the vanguard in bringing modern culture to the Austro-Hungarian monarchy, but Budapest also contributed eminent composers, writers, and artists to the cultural life of the empire and of the world. Yet this is the same era that Hermann Broch, Austrian modernist writer (born 1886 in Vienna and died 1951 in New Haven), interprets as the "fröhliche Apokalypse" (jolly apocalypse), referring to the economic, social, and cultural problems that threatened to tear this multiethnic state structure apart.

The innovations of the Industrial Revolution and the development of modern transportation and communication expanded the world of traditionally closed communities; distances previously considered unbridgeable became manageable, and the flow not just of goods but of ideas and news quickened.[1] The political spectrum gradually broadened, and alongside liberal, conservative, and nationalist schools of thought, various antiliberal and antisemitic ideologies flourished. Society in both halves of the empire was strongly influenced by the "Jewish question," with it "enkindling and distorting . . . the movements and political battles of the public life of the period." The upswing in right-wing radicalism and conservatism was in large part thanks to this influence.[2] In the sociocultural community that gave birth to the ideas of Friedrich Nietzsche (born 1844 in Röcken and died 1900 in Weimar) and Sigmund Freud (born 1856 in Příbor and died 1939 in London), among others, it was no surprise that many were critical of the existing system.³

In the discussion below, I reflect on the main aspects of the history of the Austro-Hungarian monarchy. I do not seek to give a detailed account or analysis of individual historical or socioeconomic processes, which would go well beyond the framework of my inquiry. Rather, I provide a general overview of the political system, circumstances of the national minorities, economic life, and culture. My intention is merely to provide an adequate backdrop since this newly established state provided the framework for the birth and evolution of the women's organizations examined in this volume.

Political Establishment

The Compromise (*Ausgleich*) of 1867 created a new country, the Austro-Hungarian monarchy (Austria-Hungary), and became its basic law. After the annexation of Bosnia and Herzegovina in 1908, Austria-Hungary was the second-largest country in Europe in terms of area (after the Russian Empire) and the third largest in terms of population (after the Russian and German Empires), with 52.8 million people in 1914. The Habsburg Empire was divided into two legally equal countries, and in principle, relations between the two were based on parity:[4] the kingdoms and lands represented on the Imperial Council, unofficially Cisleithania (it was called Austria unofficially until 1915), and the lands of the Holy Hungarian Crown, unofficially Transleithania (or Hungary).[5] The territory of Bosnia and Herzegovina was occupied by Austria in 1878 and incorporated into the monarchy as a condominium in 1908. The joint head of state was the emperor of Austria and apostolic king of Hungary from the house of Habsburg-Lorraine. Franz Joseph I (born 1830 in Vienna and died 1916 in Vienna) reigned from 1867 to 1916, followed by his grandnephew Charles IV/I (born 1887 in Persenbeug and died 1922 in Madeira), who ruled until 1918. There was no common constitution for the dual state. The legal basis of the Austro-Hungarian monarchy was formed by different constitutions and laws, among which the first one was introduced in 1713 (Pragmatic Sanction) and the last one in 1878 (Customs and Trade Alliance).[6]

Regarding their internal affairs, Austria and Hungary became sovereign states, with their own legislatures, as well as legal and law enforcement organs. Common affairs between the two states, such as foreign policy, defense, and the associated finances, were managed through common ministers, who were appointed by the emperor. Among the ten ministers of foreign affairs during the five decades of the dualist era, three were either Hungarian or Hungarian subjects.[7] Among the eleven ministers of finance, four were Hungarian, but none of the common ministers of defense was Hungarian.[8] Diplomatic posts were filled according to lineage and wealth. Tibor Frank argues that higher offices were slowly opened to people of different national origins, and differences were clearly visible by the end of the dualist era. According to Frank, "The number of Hungarians serving in the diplomatic corps reached 30 percent by the turn of the century, but only 5–6 percent in the leadership of the common armed forces."[9]

A common currency and customs barriers also strengthened the unity of the Austro-Hungarian monarchy. In addition to the joint decision on the amount of finances the two halves of the monarchy would provide, customs, trade agreements, the entire monetary system, the national bank, excise taxes, and the operation of common railroads were common affairs. The constitutional compensation agreements ensured the equal rights of the two (partial) states. As Frank observes, "In political, economic, and military affairs, Austria-Hungary remained a centralized state retaining some absolutist features."[10]

Right after the Compromise, the government that came to power under the leadership of the older Count Gyula Andrássy (born 1823 in Oláhpatak and died 1890 in Volosko) began to build the modern bourgeois-liberal state. The government, which represented the party of Ferenc Deák (born 1803 in Söjtör and died 1876 in Budapest), who had been an instrumental contributor to the Compromise, renewed some of the laws of 1848 (in less radical forms) and dramatically altered the social-political system, though many feudal features remained. The most important measures taken by the government addressed the issues of freedom of the press, freedom of assembly, and freedom of association. The government lowered the amount of money to be deposited by those launching a new periodical but increased its own ability to intervene in libel suits by making press-related issues subject to jury trials. The government, while representing itself as liberal, restricted basic freedoms when those freedoms were seen as a potential threat to Hungarian supremacy. The rights of assembly and association were freely given to those groups who did not threaten the state power.[11] In 1867, an important law gave the Jews equal citizenship and political rights. This period can be characterized by political consolidation, as after Andrássy had served as prime minister of Hungary from 1867 to 1871, the king appointed him common minister of foreign affairs, a position he held between 1871 and 1879. This made it clear to all parties that Hungary enjoyed parity with Austria in the dual monarchy.[12]

In the 1890s, the first mass Social Democratic parties were established both in Austria and in Hungary. Besides this, various radical antisemitic groups grew stronger. The papacy also began to exert more political influence, and relations between the state and the church had to be settled. In 1893, soon after the organization of the Social Democratic parties, Karl Lueger managed to bring together the various Christian democratic groups into a unified party.[13] At the time of the funeral of Lajos Kossuth (born 1802 in Monok and died 1894 in Torino) in Budapest, the Viennese administration was afraid of the rebirth of the Hungarian national spirit of 1848, but on the whole, society and the political elites accepted the dualist system.[14]

Universal male suffrage was introduced in Austria in 1907.[15] More than a decade would pass before this would take place in Hungary. In 1913, the property census in Hungary was extended to include an education census, which meant that only a narrow elite of the male population could exercise the right to vote. Meanwhile, the nationalities question became ever more pressing. The political elites among the national minorities remained, in general, opposed to dualism until the end of the dualist era, and they used antidualist sentiment (which included both anti-Habsburg and anti-Hungarian sentiment) as a tool "in gathering and organizing widespread dissatisfaction."[16]

Until 1918, Hungary acted in the international arena of politics as part of Austria-Hungary. The appointment of Count Gyula Andrássy as minister of foreign affairs proved important, as his nationalist and liberal orientation greatly differed from the dynastic and usually conservative Austrian policies. It was Andrássy who concluded the Emperor's League in 1873, tying Austria-Hungary to Russia and Germany and framing the directions of foreign policy for the next few decades framing the monarchy's foreign policy around its relations with Russia and the Eastern question. Both Austria-Hungary and Russia were interested in solving the problems in the Balkans, where Ottoman rule had started to crumble. Andrássy demanded the organization of the Congress of Berlin, after which the monarchy occupied Bosnia-Herzegovina.[17]

The relative stability after the Compromise began to fray toward the end of the century. Free trade gave way to protectionism, and state intervention became more and more common. Germany, the United States, and Japan were also growing stronger and changing the power constellation on the international scene. European states attempted to reestablish the old balance with various alliances, such as the Triple Entente of Britain, France, and Russia, which faced the Triple Alliance of the monarchy, Germany, and Italy. Nationalism was also on the rise, and it posed a major threat to the multinational monarchy. The monarchy's international position had weakened by the turn of the century, and it adopted an increasingly defensive posture in its foreign policy.[18]

The murder of Crown Prince Franz Ferdinand (born 1863 in Graz and died 1914 in Sarajevo) and his wife, Sophie Cothek (born 1868 in Stuttgart and died 1914 in Sarajevo), led to the outbreak of World War I.[19] In the monarchy, as in every other European country, there was widespread enthusiasm and support for the war, and people believed that the conflict would be short. Public opinion in Austria-Hungary soon changed, however, after the poorly equipped army suffered several defeats.[20] Austria-Hungary was even less prepared than Germany for a long war, especially in the economic sphere. Some historians see the monarchy as the least prepared state of the major European powers.[21] Its weak political and economic structure made it particularly vulnerable to modern total war. It had fewer resources for war than any other great power.[22] But its political leaders had expected only a brief conflict that would resolve political problems without threatening the monarchy's political and economic structure.[23] After Franz Joseph died in November 1916 at the age of eighty-six, signs that the empire had reached a state of exhaustion became ever more visible around the coronation of Charles IV/I. In the hinterland, there were major supply crises and strikes in the winter of 1917–1918 (*Hungerwinter*).[24] Total economic and military exhaustion compelled the monarchy to seek an armistice on 2 October 1918. The dissolution of the multiethnic dualist monarchy after the signing of the peace treaties (in the case of Austria in Saint-Germain-en-Laye on 10 September 1919 and in the case of Hungary in the Grand Trianon château in Versailles on 4 June 1920) transformed Austria-Hungary from an imperial power to two small, defeated, economically vulnerable, and ethnically and religiously more or less homogenous countries.[25]

The National Minorities

The Compromise of 1867, which gave Hungary extensive powers as a virtually autonomous state, was met with protests among the national minorities, especially the Slavic minorities. The Austrians criticized certain elements of the Compromise, while the Czechs were totally opposed to the dualist transformation. The Poles in Galicia were also critical and demanded broad autonomy for themselves. Relations between the Hungarian and Croatian states were reestablished one year after the Compromise had been signed. Croatia received important autonomous rights, and the Croatian political elites agreed that "Croatia and Hungary were part of the same state complex," as well as part of the reorganized monarchy. Transylvania became an integral part of Hungary again, a change that met with strong opposition among the Romanian inhabitants of the region.[26]

The potential threat national minorities posed to a multinational state had been an issue across the Habsburg lands since 1848 at the latest. Nationalist sentiments had taken hold of people's imaginations, and the national minorities in the Habsburg Empire were increasingly falling under the sway of political elites who entertained visions of breaking away from the monarchy and becoming independent. Indeed, in a Europe of emerging nation-states, where nationalism was seen as the strongest political force, the national minorities of Austria-Hungary (and political elites across Europe) increasingly saw the supranational multiethnic state as an anachronism. Opponents of the monarchy infamously characterized it as a "prison of peoples" (this precise phrase was first used by Lenin in 1914 to describe Russia).[27]

In Hungary, there were five national minorities numbering over one million: Romanians, Germans, Slovaks, Croats, and Serbs. There were half a million Rusyns and six other ethnic groups (Roma, Bunyevaks and Socacians, Slovenes,

Poles, Czechs and Moravians, and Bulgarians) whose number did not exceed ten thousand.[28] Before 1867, Hungarian political leaders had guaranteed the rights of the other national minorities. The Compromise, however, killed any hope of a federative state system. The 1868 nationality law did not recognize the existence of separate nationalities and did not grant them collective national rights or political institutions. It was only liberal in terms of the language used. Although the state could perhaps have been saved had the political elites been willing to accept a transformation into a kind of federation in which the national minorities enjoyed some level of autonomy and rule, the Compromise's failure to offer genuine recognition of and power to the national minorities may have sown the seeds of the collapse of the monarchy in the wake of World War I.[29]

In the 1910 census, 54.5 percent of the population of Hungary (the Kingdom of Hungary within the dual monarchy) declared Hungarian as their mother tongue, compared to 42 percent in the 1851 census (which, unlike the 1910 census, had not included Transylvania). Thus, over a period of sixty years, the population of the country had increased by 57 percent, while the non-Hungarian population grew by 29 percent. The number of Slovaks increased by 13 percent, and the number of Rusyns, by 5 percent. In the other half of the monarchy, the dominant nation (German speakers) did not increase its share of the total population during this period. These trends can be explained by higher birth rates among the Hungarian-speaking population, as well as emigration and assimilation, which affected the national minority communities more than the Hungarian communities.[30]

Assimilation was particularly strong in the cities and in areas in which national minorities lived scattered among the majority (Hungarian) population. People who belonged to the educated and geographically and socially mobile sections of society were more likely to assimilate (i.e., to use Hungarian and to come to consider themselves Hungarian). The Hungarian political elite made concerted efforts to encourage and accelerate the adoption of Hungarian with various regulations. Their main instrument was schooling. Until the 1880s, their efforts did not involve any kind of forced linguistic or ethnic Magyarization.[31] Beginning in the 1880s, however, emphasis was placed on offering classes in which Hungarian was used and taught in all the schools, including those in communities that contained few or almost no Hungarian speakers. However, the state's efforts to encourage Magyarization (and the potential economic incentives of adopting the majority language) ultimately had little effect on members of the national minorities who lived in coherent ethnic blocks, and in many parts of Hungary, the linguistic composition of many communities hardly changed over the course of the dualist era. In 1910, only 1.8 million people who belonged to one of the national minorities in Hungary (which numbered 8.3 million people) spoke Hungarian.[32]

In the reigning mentality of the period, the place of the individual was determined not only by social background but also by nationality. In Hungary, the majority society regarded Germans and the Saxons of Upper Hungary and Transylvania as ethically and culturally healthy minorities. The same was true, if slightly less so, of attitudes toward the Croats, followed by Serb merchants and intellectuals and Slovaks. Romanians were not regarded favorably, and the Roma were at the bottom of the ranking.[33] The non-German nationalities enjoyed better treatment and circumstances in Austria, where all nationalities had at least de jure equal rights. In Hungary, the non-Magyar nationalities were denied voting rights, in contrast with Austria, where the franchise had been extended to all adult males after the 1907 Imperial Council elections. By the time universal and equal male suffrage was introduced in Hungary, the dual monarchy had collapsed.[34]

Between 1876 and 1910, about 3.5 million (some figures give up to 4 million) inhabitants of the monarchy emigrated. They were poor and unemployed and hoped to find better living conditions in another country. About 1.8 million of them came from the Cisleithanian half of the empire, and about 1.7 million came from the Transleithanian half. Almost three million of them had the United States as their final destination, while others chose Argentina, Canada, Brazil, and Australia. In 1907 alone, about half a million people left their homeland. The governments of Austria and Hungary were concerned because many young men who would have made a valuable contribution to the workforce were among the emigrants.

Economy, Society

Compared to Germany and western European states, the Austrian half of the monarchy was economically backward but still significantly more developed than Hungary, which was dominated by agriculture. This economic backwardness was caused in no small part by the fact that the feudal system had only been brought to a formal, legal end in Hungary in 1848 with the liberation of the serfs. Furthermore, the guild system, which greatly inhibited the freedom of trade, had only been dismantled in 1859, more than fifty years later than in Prussia. Finally, the protective tariff system, which formed a massive hindrance to economic development and shielded (or rather isolated) the country from the world economy, was supplemented by its own internal customs border. Nevertheless, the Austro-Hungarian economy changed significantly during the dualist era. Technical changes accelerated both industrialization and urbanization. While the old institutions of the feudal system gradually disappeared, capitalism spread across the territory of the Danube monarchy.[35]

Railroad transportation expanded rapidly in Austria-Hungary. From 1854 to 1879, the length of the lines increased in Cisleithania by 7,952 kilometers and in Hungary by 5,839 kilometers, making new areas accessible by railroad.[36] It became possible to reach distant areas and integrate them into the processes of economic growth, which had not been possible when transportation depended on rivers.[37] In 1879, the governments of Austria and Hungary began to nationalize the railroad network again because of sluggish development during the world economic crisis of the 1870s. Between 1879 and 1900, more than 25,000 kilometers of new railroad lines were built in Cisleithania and Hungary.[38] During this period, the monarchy used railroads to reduce domestic transport costs and gain access to new markets outside the country. Austria also had several seaports, among which the most important was Trieste.[39]

The Compromise created the political and legal preconditions for economic development. Large-scale industrialization began. The government placed emphasis on the capitalistic transformation of agriculture, where the majority of the working population was employed. Cereal production remained the most important sector of the Hungarian economy after the Compromise. Hungary became one of the period's leading grain exporters, and milling became the most important sector of its industry. One important aim was the creation of a modern credit and transportation system. Foreign capital was welcomed from France, Germany, Austria, and even the UK, Belgium, the Netherlands, and Switzerland.[40] Foreign investments disappeared for a while after the economic crisis in 1873, but they again began to play an important part in the 1880s, contributing to the construction of the railroad network, the increasingly rapid processes of urbanization, and the establishment of a modern bank system in Budapest. During the first decades of the dualist era, skilled workers arrived in high numbers from outside Hungary—from the other half of the monarchy and from Germany.[41]

The crisis of 1873 brought the economic development that had begun after the Compromise to an end. The Vienna stock exchange panic of 9 May 1873 (so-called Black Friday), followed by a similar crash at the stock exchange in Pest (which had been founded in 1864), led to the collapse of several businesses and the withdrawal of foreign capital from the country.[42] The economic crisis was to become the most serious depression in Europe before 1914, and according to Tibor Frank, "while it affected the entire continent, it probably hit Austria-Hungary the hardest."[43] Its impact was made particularly strong by the fact that the first truly major capitalist cyclical crisis and the last traditional type of demographic and food crisis coincided and reinforced each other. And on top of that, 1873 saw the last great cholera epidemic sweep through Hungary.[44]

The optimism that had contributed to the economic boom after the Compromise did not return after the crisis of 1873.[45] Deficits had to be covered, and national debt had to be diminished, so the Hungarian government took on new debts. It also began new negotiations with the Austrian government in the summer of 1875, with the intention of modifying the commercial and customs unions. After three years of negotiation, only smaller compromises had been reached. The new customs agreement included light protective tariffs that allowed the Austrian industry to continue to enjoy a dominant position in Hungary, and this created tension among the political parties. The tension was exacerbated by the creation of the independent Hungarian National Bank to end the Austrian National Bank's monopoly on issuing the official currency. Thus, the Austrian National Bank was reorganized into the Austrian-Hungarian National Bank, with either Austrian or Hungarian governors and vice-governors at the helm.[46] In 1898, Hungary managed to achieve a position of equal influence in this bank. In 1892, the entire monarchy underwent a fiscal reform, and a new currency, the crown, backed by gold, was introduced.[47]

The social changes brought by industrialization, and the increasing surplus of women compared to men, added to the growing number of widows long before the arrival of World War I, a process only intensified by the economic crisis of 1873 and the ensuing recessions.[48] Even if the economy had recovered to some degree from the crisis of 1873, which permanently disrupted the livelihoods of so many families that marriage and child-rearing now offered financial security only to a narrower set of social groups. The rise of poverty in the 1890s affected more and more parts of society. While the 1900 census indicates that 41 percent of Austrian woman were working, this proportion in Hungary was only 27.6 percent. It should be noted that the Austrian data include women working part-time, while the Hungarian statistics do not. In Vienna, by the 1860s, only 50 percent of the population over twenty were married. In tandem with this, the number of children born out of wedlock grew in both halves of the monarchy, especially in the capital cities. The attempt to reduce discrimination against women in the workplace was made first by the short-lived organizations of 1848–1849 and then from the 1860s by the new associations brought into being across the monarchy to defend women's interests.[49]

As a direct result of industrialization, the period also bore witness to the emergence and growth of the labor movement in Austria and Hungary. While skilled workers were relatively well paid, unskilled workers had very low wages. Skilled workers had higher standards of living and higher social status. In both countries, workers in the capital cities became increasingly active in calls for protections and reform, especially after the Paris Commune, which made a strong impression on them.[50] The formation of the first mass-based parties occurred toward the end of the 1890s: in Austria, the journalist and politician Victor Adler (born 1852 in Prague and died 1918 in Vienna) founded the Social Democratic Party of Austria (Sozialdemokratische Arbeiterpartei) in 1888–1889, and the United Workers' Party of Hungary was established in 1880. Radicalization resulted in the organization of the first congress of the Social Democratic Workers' Party of Hungry in 1890.[51] The last decade of the century also saw, alongside various incarnations of liberalism, nationalism, and conservatism, the appearance of the ideology of socialism. While the labor parties were given permission to celebrate May Day, Sunday became an obligatory public holiday, and obligatory health insurance was introduced.[52]

In 1890, the population of Vienna was close to 1.5 million (in fact 1,342,000); at this time, by incorporating surrounding settlements, the so-called Greater Vienna (Groß-Wien) was created. The city's growth had political ramifications: a great number of laborers and tradesmen became Viennese citizens in this period. Partly as a result of this, the liberals' once-prominent role in city administration started to decline, leading to an election win for the Christian-Social Karl Lueger (born 1844 in Vienna and died 1910 in Vienna), mayor of Vienna, who enjoyed the support of craftsmen and the petit bourgeois. Lueger first acted as deputy mayor of the imperial capital and then from 1897 until his death in 1910 held the position of mayor.[53] Grand urban development projects bore his name, and his politics, blending openly antisemitic and anticapitalist elements, came to bear a strong influence on the flourishing civil sphere. He made every effort to support Christian-Social associations and hinder the operation of progressive women's organizations.[54]

The Hungarian capital, too, underwent enormous change: from the Compromise to 1910, its population grew from 270,000 to 865,000—it tripled.[55] In 1873, Pest, Buda, and Óbuda were administratively united, legally creating a new municipality, Budapest, the capital of Hungary. It is worth noting that the government could not remove the mayor of Budapest from his office. This new "metropolis," whose population was diverse from the outset, continued to attract residents of different nationalities, economic circumstances, and cultural backgrounds.[56] This fast progress and population growth had a dark side: alongside the glittering palaces in the city center, shelters were filling with the homeless, and, as in other European metropolises, including Vienna, the number of prostitutes was also on the rise.[57] As a result, Budapest had a population—and particularly a bourgeois population—that was much more heterogeneous than that of the imperial capital.[58] The Budapest bourgeoisie was much newer, with many of its members suddenly or at least very quickly acquiring considerable wealth, and so they were much less socially embedded than Vienna's historic cultural bourgeoisie (*Bildungsbürgertum*) or its propertied bourgeoisie (*Besitzbürgertum*).[59] The bourgeoisie of the Hungarian capital only began to emerge in the years after the Compromise, and it was primarily made up of assimilated middle-class Germans and Jews.[60]

Toward the end of the era, Hungary's most serious challenge came from the social issues that arose from the increasingly pressing need to better the fates of the lower classes. The tensions between the national minorities and the majority societies in the two halves of the empire were also worsening, as were those between the German speakers of the empire and the Hungarians.[61] The ascent of the groups that had mostly migrated to Budapest from abroad, or from other regions of the monarchy, led to a number of conflicts because their social standing was much weaker than their economic and political influence, and in political terms, they came to be a marginalized faction. The transformation of the officer and intellectual class into an independent social group was not an incidental development, nor was that of the appearance of women in various careers in state and private office. With a rise in the number of female teaching staff, women were also present in intellectual careers in ever-greater proportions.[62]

Alongside the capital cities, major provincial centers also began to establish and popularize the bourgeois way of life. The urbanization of this era left an unmistakable mark across the monarchy that is still there today: its stylistic touches can be seen not just on railroad stations and public buildings but also on schools, hotels, and coffeehouses. The decades of the dualist system even saw the uniformization of leisure pursuits: theaters and cafés became arenas of public entertainment in the same way as did casinos, cabarets, and bathhouses.[63]

The period from the second half of the nineteenth century to the outbreak of World War I was seen in Austria and Hungary—in line with trends in western Europe—as a golden age for the organization of civil society.[64] It is wrong, however, to think that the state supported every initiative to establish a new association. At numerous points in the volume, I refer, for example, to the *Vereinsgesetz*, the law on associations in place in Austria from 1867 until 1918, which presented obstacles for women's groups wishing to muster support for a political objective.[65] Over six points, the second section of the legislation, beginning with § 29 of the introduction, limited the rights of associations founded with political objectives. In addition to § 30, on the prohibition of women and children in the establishment of organizations with political objectives, it covered the following: The board of an association had to have at least five and at most ten members (§ 31), and the names of new members had to be registered with the local authorities within three days of their enrollment (§ 32). They were not allowed to establish branch offices (§ 33), could not have subordinate organizations (§ 34), and could not display badges (§ 34). For the women's associations forced to leave any political aims out of their constitutions, however, the last paragraph, § 35, prohibiting them from being accepted as full members, was the most significant.[66] However, the operations of certain women's groups, such as the Verein der Lehrerinnen und Erzieherinnen (Association of Women Teachers and Educators, 1870–1938, Vienna) and AöF, demonstrate that women did in fact participate in various political activities. This, in light of the law on associations, can be considered as a paradox today because of the following factor. While the AöF's fight for women's emancipation is considered political today, contemporaries judged it in a moral framework. Besides fighting for women's emancipation, AöF continued to pursue a rich variety of politics related to women's economic and social interests.[67]

Yet, regarding individualization and the self-organization of civic communities from below, Gábor Gyáni deems it characteristic that in Hungary "there were no legislative steps taken on the freedom of organization and on citizens' rights of association and assembly," either directly before the Compromise or after it. While the authorities quickly obstructed the activities of social groups seen as "dangerous," like the initiatives of agrarian socialists in the 1890s or of the ethnic groups that questioned the legality of the dualist state system, "unrestricted opportunity arose for activity in culture, entertainment and social thought to blossom." Yet an edict of 1875 barred associations from explicit political opinions here too.[68]

Cultural Life

In cultural life, compulsory education led to a steady decline in illiteracy, which was still widespread, especially in the eastern and southern parts of the empire. However, illiteracy remained a major educational problem and hindered the participation of large sections of the population in social and political life. On 14 May 1869, Emperor Franz Joseph I sanctioned the law on elementary education (Reichsvolksschulgesetz), which came into effect in the following school year. The provinces had the option of enacting appropriate regulations to implement the new legislation and thus adapt the law to regional conditions. The elementary school system now consisted of the "general elementary schools" and the "citizen schools." In the general elementary schools, the subjects taught included religion, language, mathematics and geometry, natural history, geography, history, writing, singing, and physical education. Girls were still taught handicrafts associated with homemaking and childcare. At the citizen schools, which were based on this curriculum, the children received instruction in the aforementioned subjects along with essay writing, bookkeeping, and drawing. Non-German citizen schools added instruction in German. The regional school authorities were free to establish additional instruction in another language.[69]

Educational reform was also introduced, as the organization of a modern state would have been impossible with a population in which only 41 percent of the male and 24 percent of the female population over six was literate.[70] The elementary school law was introduced in 1868 by Baron József Eötvös (born 1813 in Buda and died 1872 in Pest), minister of religion and education. The law left the confessional schools in the hands of the churches, but it also allowed for the municipal takeover of these schools. Elementary schools were designed to teach basic skills, as well as religion and morals, singing, physical education, history, geography, and practical skills in the mother tongue of the children. Around half of the schools were Hungarian, a third ethnic Hungarian, and the rest mixed-language. This law ensured dramatic improvement in the country's general educational level.[71]

The decades before World War I were characterized by the vigorous development of Vienna, Budapest, and, in third place, Prague.[72] Since 1862, Vienna had enjoyed relatively comprehensive autonomy in local administration, although

Franz Joseph I established executive rights on a number of settlement-planning questions. After he ordered the demolition of Vienna's medieval city fortifications in 1857, space was made for a boulevard encompassing the entire inner city. Vienna's Ringstrasse, was completed in 1865. On either side of the new boulevard at the city center, one found the palaces of wealthy bankers and big industrialists, as well as an extension of the imperial Hofburg, large museums housing the imperial art and nature collections, a parliament building for the Imperial Council, the new buildings of the university, the New City Hall, the Hofburg Theater, and the Votive Church, donated in memory of the emperor's rescue from an assassin in 1853.[73]

Economic and social progress brought with it advances in the sciences and technology. Vienna, Budapest, and Prague were appealing destinations for many scientists. Theoretical physicist Albert Einstein (born 1879 in Ulm and died 1955 in Princeton, New Jersey) worked briefly as a university professor at Karl Ferdinand's University in Prague. Modernist philosophers such as Ludwig Wittgenstein (born 1889 in Vienna and died 1951 in Cambridge), son of the Austrian industrialist Karl Wittgenstein (born 1847 in Leipzig and died 1913 in Vienna), and philosopher Ernst Mach (born 1838 in Brno and died 1916 in Munich) significantly influenced the later Vienna Circle. Sigmund Freud's most important work on the Medical Faculty of the University of Vienna fell in the period around 1900. In Hungary, physicist Baron Loránd Eötvös (born 1848 in Buda and died 1919 in Budapest) was one of the last prominent representatives of classical physics, and Tivadar Puskás (born 1844 in Pest and died in 1893 in Budapest), inventor, telephone pioneer, and inventor of the telephone exchange, was a pioneer in the field of communication technology. In medicine, Ignác Semmelweis (born 1818 in Buda and died 1865 in Oberdöbling), early pioneer of antiseptic procedures, who has been described as the "saviour of mothers," became world famous.[74] Even more than the visual arts, music had a great heyday during the dualist era. Vienna, already known as the "capital of music" since the days of Mozart and Beethoven, still had a leading position both in classical music and in light music. The most famous representatives of musical life were members of the Strauss family (Johann Strauss [born 1825 in Vienna and died 1899 in Vienna] and Richard Strauss [born 1864 in Munich and died 1949 in Garmisch-Partenkirchen]) and Franz Lehár (born 1870 in Komárom and died 1948 in Bad Ischl). In Hungary, the Academy of Music was established in 1875 under the leadership of Franz Liszt (born 1811 in Raiding and died 1886 in Bayreuth). In both empires, one could observe the stratification of culture and the emergence of mass culture.[75]

This framework defined the relationship between Austria and Hungary until 1918 and also provided the backdrop against which the women's associations discussed in this volume emerged.

3

The Austro-Hungarian Women's Movement until the Fin de Siècle and the Different Branches of the Women's Movement

IN THIS CHAPTER, I present the characteristic features of the civil sphere of the period that were relevant to the Austrian and Hungarian women's organizations, and I offer an overview of the process that led to the establishment of the associations. I also answer questions relating to the broader social context of the women's movements.

Among the associations that were established in line with political, economic, social, occupational, or religious subjects of interest, "the organizations created by women form a distinct group."[1] By the 1880s, these organizations were operating in ever-greater numbers not just in the two capitals of the monarchy, Vienna and Budapest, but also in provincial cities.[2] Harriet Anderson dates the beginning of the "era of women's organization" in Austria to the 1860s, while emphasizing that three decades would pass before the creation of Allgemeiner österreichischer Frauenverein (AöF), the most important organization for bourgeois-liberal women.[3] Susan Zimmermann places the first Hungarian golden age for women's associations a little bit later, in the 1870s—the period after the Compromise. The resulting "organization-founding rush" can in general be traced back to the dynamic economic and social restructuring, to urbanization, and to the cultural development of the period, and within this to the gradual extension of the framework for institutional women's education.[4]

When discussing the similarities between the two halves of the monarchy on the question of women, we should mention the strong and well-organized women's movement of the fin de siècle period, as well as its long list of women writers. We need to only think of writer and journalist Irma von Troll-Borostyani (born

1847 in Salzburg and died 1912 in Salzburg) or of Júlia Kende (born 1864 in Pest and died 1937 in Budapest), wife of Count Sándor Teleki. Júlia Kende was also known as Szikra ("Spark"), who as a writer, journalist, and editor played a leading role in Feministák Egyesülete (FE) and in the operation of its official organs. Both of these women, and their literary work, played a part in the fight for women's rights.[5] A number of women writers (e.g., Grete Meisel-Heß [born 1879 in Prague and died 1922 in Berlin], Margit Kaffka [born 1880 in Nagykároly/Carei and died 1918 in Budapest], and Emma Ritoók [born 1868 in Nagyvárad/Oradea and died 1945 in Budapest], who was also member of FE) enjoyed the support not only of their fellow writers but also of critics, whether men or women. All this would have been utterly inconceivable just a few decades previously. The writers publishing on the rights of women at the time of the Compromise were a generation before those who joined the new types of women's associations in the 1890s. The former were mostly born in the 1840s and 1850s, while the latter, the generation of Rosika Schwimmer and Vilma Glücklich, were born in the 1870s and 1880s. In Austria, these generation gaps were rather blurred, as the women authors born between 1830 and 1850—including Rosa Mayreder and Marianne Hainisch (born 1839 in Baden bei Wien and died 1936 in Vienna)—were the prominent figures in the women's movement two and a half decades before the war. While most of the women writers and women's movement activists in Austria were born in the imperial capital, those in Hungary mostly arrived in the capital from the provinces.[6] This era also brought with it broadening of opportunities for women—albeit not in enormous numbers—to succeed in the fine arts. Mayreder, who also tried her hand at painting, even had a work on display at the 1893 world exposition in Chicago.[7]

Before the 1890s, in both halves of the monarchy, the dominant organizations focused on charity work, in line with the traditional role of women and the traditional system of values.[8] An increasing number of groups, whether newly founded or well established, raised their voices in objection to the exploitation of women in various areas of life. By the last decade of the century, the various branches of the women's movement had become clearly defined: alongside charitable groups, which had often brought together female members of a particular religious affiliation, there also appeared Social Democratic (working women's/proletarian) and Christian-Social associations, as well as bourgeois organizations offering a home to women without or with only partial religious affiliation.[9] Among the latter, we equally find more conservative and more radical (progressive) groups, including AöF, Nőtisztviselők Országos Egyesülete (NOE), and FE.

In the course of the decades before World War I, the center of women's emancipation in both Austria and Hungary was clearly the capital. Yet, while just about every leading figure in the Austrian women's movement was born in Vienna,[10] in Hungary it was much more common for the pillars of the women's community to have arrived in Budapest as children or young adults.[11] In both countries, most women joined an association that was not charitable in its work because of unfair treatment experienced in education or at the workplace.

In the following sections, I present the major turning points in the development of the bourgeois, Social Democratic, and Christian-Social tendencies of the Austrian and Hungarian women's movements from the revolutionary years of 1948 to the turn of the century. I do not discuss each of these movements in detail but mention only their main characteristics and the most important women's associations belonging to them. I briefly refer to other provinces of the monarchy as well, but my discussion focuses on Austria and Hungary. It is not my intention or aim to focus on the women's associations created by members of the national minorities, nor do I examine the networks among them. I must note, however, that the monarchy was significant in part because of its multinational and multifaceted women's movements, the members of which came from different classes and spoke different languages. Several associations maintained contact across crown land borders, formed common umbrella organizations, and joined together to form transnational associations.[12]

It should be pointed out that the national minorities had loose relations with the Hungarians associations. In other words, NOE and especially FE as associations built up closer networks with the Austrian women's organizations throughout the period. This is why I do not touch on the women's movements in the territories inhabited by national minorities. An exception to this was the period of preparation for the International Woman Suffrage Alliance (IWSA) congress in 1913, to which the women's associations in the national minority communities were invited, and these associations did indeed send large numbers of representatives.

Civic/Bourgeois Women's Associations

"They say that homemade apple strudel no longer satisfies women's ambitions, so they long for the apple strudel of public life."[13] This is just a single sentence taken from the memoirs of an unknown author,[14] which were penned on the occasion of a so-called first Austrian Women's Day convened in May 1892.[15] This brief excerpt tells us how a small part of the female population of Vienna (principally female teachers at elementary and civic schools)[16] had moved up to the next level of organization. In contextualizing this line of progress, I cite the works of Susan Zimmerman, who believed that the French Revolution and the wave of revolutions in 1848, together with the creation of a bourgeois public sphere, played a key role not just in industrialization and social transformation but also in the development of the women's movements of the time.[17]

In Austria, the origins of the bourgeois women's movement organized on a modern basis can be traced back to 1848, before those of the movement in

Hungary. For unlike most of the Austrian and Hungarian women's associations of the period, the short-lived Erster Wiener demokratischer Frauenverein (EWdF),[18] founded in the last days of August 1848 by Karoline von Perin (born 1808 in Vienna and died 1888 in Neu Isenburg),[19] did not only have charitable goals on its agenda. In addition to providing social welfare assistance for "orphans of the revolution," it sought to stand up for women's educational and democratic rights, including women's suffrage.[20] Yet in the group's statutes, its objectives are rather vague, and there is no mention of how it hoped to accomplish them.[21] However, women's assemblies were held in 1848 in several cities in the Habsburg monarchy, such as Prague, and also in Galicia. Before and after the revolutionary months of that year, most of the women's associations had philanthropic aims, and their members came from the (upper) middle class and the aristocracy.[22]

Although the members of EWdF never had the chance to achieve their objectives, as the association was banned in October 1848, the direction they set would not be forgotten over the decades to come. This indicates that in its initial phase, the Austrian women's movement gained an advantage of many decades over its Hungarian equivalent. I agree with Hilde Schmölzer, however, in considering Daniela Weiland's claim that "the bourgeois women's movement in Austria developed in parallel with the German one" to be an exaggeration.[23] For it was in the fall of 1865, in Leipzig, that the bourgeois women's association Allgemeiner deutscher Frauenverein (AdF) was founded. Led by Louise Otto-Peters (born 1819 in Meißen and died 1895 in Leipzig) and Auguste Schmidt (born 1833 in Breslau and died 1902 in Leipzig), AdF belonged to the moderate school and was considered a key voice right up to the 1930s. The basic rules of the association display a considerable overlap with those of AöF from thirty-two years later and those of FE from thirty-nine years later. The foundation of the German women's endeavors was their struggle for educational and economic rights for women.[24] From the time of the establishment of AdF, which had few members at the beginning, Otto-Peters bore in mind that "women have to stand up for themselves, else they will be a lost cause from the outset."[25]

Both direct and indirect factors led to the foundation of AöF.[26] Wiener Frauenerwerbverein (WFE, Vienna, 1866–1938), which also belonged to the bourgeois branch—and whose foundation, according to Harriet Anderson, marked the beginning of the modern women's movement in Austria—considered it imperative that the framework for women's higher education and vocational training be improved. The highly popular German Lette-Verein (Berlin, 1866–) served as the model for the association,[27] and a German-language association of similar profile had been established in Prague in 1871 (Prager Frauen-Erwerb-Verein) as well.[28] The primary objective of WFE's members was to improve middle-class women's position on the labor market, and they wished to achieve this goal through educational activities such as lectures or published articles.[29] As new professions were opened to women, several new associations were established for their support—for female teachers (1870), post officers (1876), music teachers, midwives, actresses, writers, and artists (1885)—not only in Vienna but also in the provinces, such as in Innsbruck and Czernowitz.[30]

Marianne Hainisch, a member of WFE and later president of Bund österreichischer Frauenvereine (BöF), the umbrella organization for Austrian bourgeois women's groups, a position she retained over three and a half decades, played her part in the activism. In 1870, she made her famous speech on the necessity of secondary education for girls, intertwining, for the first time, the women's movement with the struggle for the extension of women's right to institutional education.[31] Throughout the 1870s, Hainisch fought for the establishment of *Realschule* for girls, and in 1888, working with the Verein für erweiterte Frauenbildung (Vienna, 1888–1939), she began striving to give female pupils the chance to study at *Gymnasien* (in the German and Austro-Hungarian school systems, the *Realschule* was a type of secondary school between the *Hauptschule*, or elementary school, and the Gymnasium was roughly equivalent to the grammar school in the English school system).[32] In Vienna, this women's association was urging comprehensive educational reform. This civic movement, associated perhaps first and foremost with Hainisch, considered the broadening of women's educational rights important because of the economic implications of this issue—the impoverishment of the middle class and women's rights in the labor market. Finally, Vienna's first girls' Gymnasium opened its doors in 1892, four years before its first equivalent in Budapest. In Germany, girls could graduate from four-year high schools from 1895 onward, while in Prussia, for example, universities only opened their doors to women in 1908. Linda L. Clark also points out that many sought to compensate for institutional education's unfair treatment of women with private schooling. The Országos Nőképző Egylet (ONE, Hungarian National Society for Women's Education, Budapest, 1867–?), for example, established a course from 1893 to give further teaching to girls who had completed their fourth year of high school. The board of the society ultimately decided in January 1896—after the opening of the medical, pharmacological, and humanities faculties of universities to women by the regulation of Gyula Wlassics (born 1852 in Zalaegerszeg and died 1937 in Budapest), minister of education—to establish the new form of school.[33]

The struggle for institutional educational rights for women was progressing well in Austria by comparison not just to Hungary but also to Germany.[34] It is worth noting, however, that the first women's association campaigning for the admission of women to universities' faculties of arts and medicine was founded in Prague in 1890 under the name Minerva. According to Irene Bandhauer-Schöffmann, this was no accident. The Bohemian women's movement was pioneering in the monarchy when it came to educational matters.[35] This initiative facilitated the first petition for women's education rights in Austria, signed by 3,644 members of six Viennese women's organizations. They called for the opening of both regular student admission and university faculties of pharmacy for women. In 1892, women demanded the opening of all university faculties to female students. The initiative was spearheaded by Auguste Fickert, who worked alongside Marie Schwartz (born 1852 in Vienna and died 1920 in Vienna). Schwartz was a schoolteacher who later became president of the Verein der Lehrerinnen und Erzieherinnen, but this association did not enjoy the support of the Viennese women's associations. This lack of support foreshadowed the objectives of AöF.[36]

On 19 March 1896, a decree of the Ministry of Culture and Education allowed the nostrification of medical doctorates obtained by women abroad. This decree was the first step. In a second step, the Faculty of Philosophy was opened to women. Then came the decree of the minister of education of 23 March 1897, according to which women who were Austrian citizens, over eighteen years old, and had passed their matura exams were admitted to the Faculty of Philosophy as regular students. After this second decree, three full-time female students, one of whom was Elise Richter, enrolled at the University of Vienna in the winter semester of 1897–1898. When women were admitted to the Faculty of Medicine and Pharmacy in 1900, the decree in question was drafted with the greatest respect for the obstinate opponents of the issue. After the admission to the Faculty of Philosophy, however, it took another two decades before women were allowed to study at the Faculty of Law. The VeF (Verein für erweiternde Frauenbildung [1888–1939, Vienna]), BöF, and the Akademische Frauenverein (Academic Women's Association), founded in 1908, petitioned for a long time for the opening of this faculty to female students.[37]

We should at this stage also highlight a fundamental difference between the Austrian and Hungarian movements: in contrast to its Hungarian equivalent, the radical wing of the Austrian bourgeois-liberal women's movement, which Harriet Anderson and Birgitta Bader-Zaar claim can in many respects be compared to the Social Democratic elements of this activism,[38] took shape in the early 1890s in response to one particular event. An 1888 legislative proposal of the provincial assembly for Lower Austria[39] held that tax-paying women should lose their community voting rights (*Gemeindewahlrecht*) at sessions that they had enjoyed since the patent of February 1861. This patent was introduced in the name of liberalism, and the fact that women were granted community voting rights was unique at that time.[40] After the 1888 legislative proposal was made public, it was not only those associated with the bourgeois women's movement who raised their objections but also the Social Democrats. The female elementary school teachers of Vienna began to mobilize first. In the December 1889 issue of the journal *Lehrerinnen-Wart* (Vienna, 1889–1901), the more actively self-aware in the profession called on "every female elementary school teacher in Lower

Austria" to oppose the attempts to relegate them to "political nothings" (*politischen Nullen*) compared to their male colleagues.[41]

The petition, submitted to the provincial assembly by the Verein der Lehrerinnen und Erzieherinnen (Association of Female Teachers and Governesses, Vienna, 1870–1938), as represented by Auguste Fickert and Marie Schwartz, makes it clear that the escalating conflict was caused not only by suffrage but also by the inequitable treatment of male and female teachers and the resulting difference in wages.[42] The phenomenon was universally familiar in the period: women teaching staff were paid less in wages and benefits than men doing the same work, while their hopes of professional advance were almost nil. Indeed, at one point a law prohibited married women from working in the profession. Because of this dispute, the overriding objective of AöF, which was formalized by 1893 and considered itself "progressive," became not universal suffrage for women but rather the extension of rights to women in every walk of life.[43]

The Industrial Revolution, the extension of social legislation, and the development of institutional education all brought important changes to women's everyday lives, even in the Hungary of the late nineteenth century. Modernization had a positive effect on their organizations, although here, too, we find a lag in comparison to developed western European states. Yet, in 1901, Malvi Fuchs, Hungarian journalist and author, who was trying her luck in the Hungarian- and German-language press, would, in rather provocative fashion, show off her skill with words by stating that in Hungary there did not exist such a thing as the women's question.[44] Since the rule of Emperor Joseph II (1780–1790), Hungarian women (like Austrian women) had enjoyed certain legal rights not available to the female population of other (western) European countries. In principle, Hungarian women could make decisions about their own property, inherit, and take jobs. That they could not really make use of these rights in practice—and that not even middle-class and upper-class women were necessarily aware of them—was a different matter. According to Mrs. Sándor Teleki, the cause of women's unawareness of their rights can be traced to the low level of education for women.[45]

While in Vienna the women's movement received an institutional framework in the revolutionary year of 1848, Budapest was only really home to charitable women's associations from the time of the Napoleonic Wars at the beginning of the nineteenth century to the Compromise of 1867.[46] Blanka Teleki (born 1806 in Kővárhosszúfalu and died 1862 in Paris), one of the pioneers of Hungarian women's education, had already demanded equal rights back in 1848, but it would be four decades before Hungarian women turned to political activism. Yet for all this—as the following examples will show—it cannot be said that the question of women was not present in Hungarian public life.

I only list a few associations, which were often based on religious affiliations or on the patronage of the ruler or the female members of some aristocratic family: Budai Jótékony Nőegylet (Charitable Women's Society of Buda) and Pesti Jótékony Nőegylet (Charitable Women's Society of Pest, 1817), Magyar Gazdasszonyok Országos Egyesülete (National Association of Hungarian Housewives, 1861), Pesti Izraelita Nőegylet (Israelite Women's Society of Pest, 1866), and Országos Nőiparegylet (ONE, National Women's Industrial Society, 1868). As more women entered the workforce toward the end of the nineteenth century, even more women's rights organizations were founded, a prominent example of which was Zsuzsanna Lorántffy Association (1892). Protestant in its outlook, it took on many tasks assisting women's education. Judith Szapor's claim holds for these groups: "Apart from the year of their foundation, we know little of the activities of and the extent of the influence of the women's associations, which made up a third of the organizations that played a key role in the social foundation of bourgeois society."[47]

These groups primarily championed the development of vocational education for women.[48] In addition, they functioned as antechambers for the political socialization of women, and their role in the history of the monarchy should not be underestimated, even if the majority of them operated with relatively modest income and few members. The state of women's education displays numerous similarities between Hungary and Austria throughout the period. For a long time, girls could only join elementary and civic schools, with the institutions of secondary and higher education closed to them. The same was true of specialist educational institutions. WFE, which recognized the need for women's training, similarly to ONE, attempted to overcome the fact that the doors of institutional education remained closed in front of women by organizing courses in tailoring, commerce, and industry; as we will see, NOE and FE followed their example in this. The associations' long-term goal was to open up every level of institutional education to women. Yet by 1918 this had not been fully realized in either half of the monarchy.

In addition, the associations strove to ease those social tensions that state social policy could not deal with.[49] If we survey the profiles and founding dates of the key Hungarian women's organizations in the period, we can draw certain conclusions: In the mid-1890s, the bourgeois wing of the Hungarian women's movement was behind that in Austria; ONE, which fought to improve women's position in education, was only founded in 1867, the year of the Compromise, under the leadership of Mrs. Pál Veres née Hermin Beniczky (born 1815 in Lázi and died 1895 in Budapest), a pioneer of Hungarian women's education and the founder of the first girls' secondary school.[50] In this period, Emília Kánya (born 1828 in Pest and died 1905 in Fiume), a publicist and writer and the country's first woman journal editor, expressed her support for the expansion of the institutional framework for women's education, and yet it would be almost two decades before the foundation of the Mária Dorothea Association (Budapest, 1885–?), which fought for women's rights and undertook labor exchange and advanced training for women. Yet the Mária Dorothea Association—created in part at the instigation of Janka Zirzen (born 1824 in Jászberény and died 1904 in Budapest), a Hungarian educator, one of the outstanding figures of Hungarian women's education, and the director of the first women's teacher training school, which was established in 1869—improved opportunities for unemployed female teachers and found positions for them while also taking on a considerable amount of charitable work.[51] In this period, however, several leading campaigners in the Hungarian women's movement did not speak Hungarian, as they came from upper-middle-class families of German origins. Hermin Beniczky can be considered "the German-speaking mother of the Hungarian movement for national girls' education."[52]

The associations I investigate represented the radical left wing within the bourgeois branch of the women's movement, which at the time was described in Austria as bourgeois-liberal and in Hungary as feminist or liberal feminist.[53] FE was one of the few women's organizations in this period that proudly bore the feminist label.[54] Rosika Schwimmer and her coworkers did not wish to lose this label, even when it garnered negative connotations in certain press publications and in public life.[55] Agatha Schwartz argues that in Austria the women's movement would normally refer to itself as "progressive," and she also claims that for a long time the German term *Feminist* referred to the male supporters of the women's movement, while the term *Feministin*, used to refer to women, would only start to be used more generally around 1914.[56] Johanna Gehmacher has studied the meaning of the term *feminist* in a transnational context while examining translation practices in the international women's movements at the turn of the century. She argues that the term *feminism* "itself, as well as parallel expressions, moving from time, fields of agency, language and disciplines since the beginning of the twentieth century, can be analysed as a 'travelling concept' that has had a sinuous career of changing meanings."[57] She highlights that several uses, ideas, and ideologies are interconnected with this term and the concept itself. She also notes that "historians of feminism are confronted with the fact that feminism is both a term used in historical sources in a variety of ways and an analytical concept of feminist theory."[58] She claims that the term *feminism* was coined in France at the end of the nineteenth century, though at the same time, "parallel concepts" appeared in other languages and soon became connected with the original term. The word *Feminismus* was first employed in German at the centenary as well, but as Gehmacher states, "it was obviously not yet identified with the women's movement at that time."[59] Gisela Bock contends that the new term served as a title for women's congresses and also for some works written by male historians in the 1890s. In 1896, at the international women's congress in Berlin, the word *Feminismus* was reported before a large audience to have been spread by the press. It should be noted that *feminism* was occasionally used to refer to the "radical left wing" of the women's movement.[60] Karen Offen insists on using *feminisms* in the plural, as the concept acquired different meanings in different countries and periods. She puts the birth of European feminisms at 1622.[61]

The 1932 novel *Radetzky March* (*Radetzkymarsch*) by Austrian writer Joseph Roth (born 1894 in Brody and died 1939 in Paris) paints a lucid picture of the stereotypes concerning women living through the twilight years of the Habsburg monarchy. According to the novel, the majority of men did not object to women only having limited political, economic, and social rights, and they even considered it natural for men to have control over women's affairs or for women to be able to access only superficial education compared to men. In Austria it was only the bourgeois women's movement, and indeed its more radical branch, that reflected on "the whole problem of the women's question."[62] We need to only think of the works of Rosa Mayreder, later vice president of AöF. These works from the 1890s onward regularly attracted widespread public outrage.

The political turning points of the decade also brought change to the nature of the Austrian-Hungarian women's movement. After so much charitable giving and the decade-long struggle for educational rights, a small group of women was demanding political rights. The means the women's associations had at their disposal were various and depended on their political affiliations (or lack of them). While AöF, for example, campaigned from its establishment for the rights of children born out of wedlock, BöF sought to improve the situation of women within the family. For instance, BöF opened maternity clinics and information centers for pregnant single women, and it also fought for the introduction of maternity leave or the installation of breast-feeding rooms in factories, usually without success. As the result of a fight lasting almost four decades, in 1910 they did at least see to it that vocational schools opened their doors to girls.[63]

FE refused to ally itself with any political party, just as AöF had avoided doing so. Indeed, AöF had been created by women's groups that did not want to oblige themselves either to the Social Democratic or to the Christian-Social Party.[64] Harriet Anderson argues that the Austrian bourgeois women's movement came into being thanks to the work of a handful of dedicated individuals. Their objective in expanding women's rights was similar, but they had very different ideas as to how to get there. Marianne Hainisch as future leader of BöF wished to take the more moderate path, while Rosa Mayreder and Auguste Fickert as leading members of AöF wanted to follow the more radical one.[65] BöF, brought into being in 1902 by Hainisch's organizational genius, integrated not only Viennese women's associations but also those of the various Austrian provinces. Most of them were German-speaking groups. Among its member organizations, we find the Frauenbund in Brünn (Brno) and the Frauenerwerbverein in Prague. BöF proved unsuccessful only in its appeal to Christian-Social women's organizations: these bodies remained at a distance from the Bund from the outset and mobilized themselves independently for religious reasons.[66]

In the light of the above, AöF's and FE's aspiration to include all Austrian and Hungarian women in their work, regardless of their social differences, is incomprehensible. I am convinced that this goal was nothing more than a publicity stunt, or perhaps some utopian dream destined for a time far in the future: neither Fickert nor Schwimmer can seriously have thought that these associations, which mostly consisted of (upper-) middle-class members, with a few aristocratic ones as well, would appeal to the masses of female industrial and agricultural workers.

The relationship between the governments and the associations was in continuous flux. If we think in terms of longer processes, we can state that AöF, throughout its existence, put pressure on the governments and on the city of Vienna. Yet at the same time, it found answers and substantive solutions—for example, to the problems of women's housing or legal rights—that the state was unable to provide. The connections between FE, NOE, and the political authorities proved to be turbulent as well. In 1913, Budapest's leadership recognized that the feminist organizations had significant resources with which to address social issues, something it could turn to its own benefit. The role of these organizations became particularly significant during the IWSA congress of 1913, at which, finally, it was possible to present Budapest's primacy over Vienna. Contrary to expectations, the leadership of IWSA accepted the invitation not of the imperial capital but rather of its Hungarian counterpart, which suffered from a certain inferiority complex compared to its neighbor. This weeklong meeting must have been important for Mayor István Bárczy, as he appeared at the official events and receptions on a number of occasions. This relationship was to be recalibrated by the war years, however: for their wartime work on the home front, NOE and FE received (financial) recompense both in Budapest and in the provinces, while the government attempted to suppress their antiwar propaganda and their active participation in the peace movement.

Social Democratic Women's Organizations

Social Democratic women in Austria also started to make their voices heard after the revolutionary years of 1848–1849, but they then remained silent for two decades. From the second half of the 1860s, an increasing number of prominent people in the movements pushing for social change recognized that working-class women also needed vocational and further education, so they founded various *Arbeiterinnen-Bildungsverein* organizations in the districts of Vienna inhabited by industrial workers. The first *Arbeiterinnen-Bildungsverein* was established in 1890.[67] These also laid the groundwork for women's political socialization. Initially, the bourgeois women's groups were involved in their operation: we need to only think of Auguste Fickert, who worked as a teacher in the first *Arbeiterinnen-Bildungsverein*. Their influence on the Social Democratic movement was short-lived, however, as working-class women started to fight for their rights on an individual basis.[68] From the outset, both in Austria and in Hungary, they mostly rejected any form of cooperation with the bourgeois-liberal feminist groups. These working women believed that the bourgeois women's movement had almost exclusively been fighting to wear modern women's clothing and arrange afternoon women's clubs. And they did not keep their feelings quiet: when not lampooning Fickert, Schwimmer, and their coworkers in the pages of the *Arbeiterinnen-Zeitung*[69] and the *Nőmunkás* [Woman Worker], they ridiculed them at their events and rallies, accusing them of only representing the interests of women in the middle and upper classes.[70]

The greatest difference between the organizational arrangements of the bourgeois women and those of the Social Democrats was that the latter, following a very different dynamic, "did not only happen on paper."[71] For AöF, FE, and NOE, the most important methods of activism were publishing independent journals and launching petitions, while the women workers used strikes and street demonstrations to demand an extension of women's rights, and in both countries, they did so within the frameworks of Social Democratic parties dominated by men.[72] They, too, used petitions to assert their interests, as it was in the form of submissions that they demanded the introduction of universal and equal suffrage with a secret ballot, and the immediate suspension of the law governing associations.[73]

In Austria, the Social Democrats' commitment to unrestricted political rights had begun in 1893 with the draft electoral law, which was handed in to the government of Eduard Taaffe (born 1833 in Vienna and died 1895 in Nalžovské Hory). This draft law sought to accommodate the demands of the working class as it proposed the universal male suffrage to the curia, alongside those conditions, which were based on large-scale land ownership and the tax census. In 1892, the Social Democrats had added "without distinction of gender" to the suffrage clause, and they incorporated this principle in their party platform. In particular, Adelheid Dwořak (born 1869 in Inzersdorf and died 1939 in Vienna), feminist and socialist politician, who later went by her married name, Adelheid Popp, after marrying Julius Popp and who served as editor of the *Arbeiterinnen-Zeitung*, emphasized the importance of female suffrage in this campaign. The first Social Democratic women's meeting campaigning for women's suffrage was held on 1 October 1893, with the participation of approximately one thousand women and many men. However, male members of the party showed a reserved attitude toward the issue of female suffrage. For example, the cofounder of the Sozialdemokratische Partei Österreichs (Social Democratic Worker's Party), Victor Adler, said that the first step would be the introduction of male suffrage. Once women had supported men in the campaign for their rights, the introduction of female suffrage would follow.

Taking Adler's promise seriously, the Social Democratic women joined the party's campaign for male suffrage. However, after the formation of the Sozialdemokratische Partei Österreichs's Frauenstimmrechtskomitee in 1898, they increasingly insisted that the party take a stronger stand in support of female suffrage. They also urged the introduction of female suffrage within the framework of demonstrations on 1 May. Subsequently, debates within the party on female suffrage intensified, culminating at the Frauenreichskonferenz on 8 November 1903. Therese Schlesinger, one of the few activists who had converted from the political leanings of AöF to social democracy, strongly criticized the ongoing debates on suffrage and argued that suffrage would put women in a much better position to participate actively in the Social Democratic movement. Charlotte Glas-Pohl (born 1873 and died 1944), a founding member of the Sozialdemokratische Partei Österreichs and a leading figure in the public sphere during the late imperial period, took a contrasting view. Her priority was first to achieve universal male suffrage; in other words, she toed the party line. Finally, in the struggles for the introduction of universal and equal suffrage in 1905–1906, the party gave priority to the achievement of male suffrage and thus postponed the campaign for the equal political participation of women.[74] Social Democratic women's organizations were also established in the provinces, in Graz, Linz, and Salzburg. Most of their members worked in the textile and tobacco industries, which employed many women. In 1902, the Gewerkschaft der Näherinnen (Union of Seamstresses) was formed within the Reichsverband der Heimarbeiterinnen und aller im Hause beschäftigter Frauen und Mädchen (Reich Association of Home Workers and All Women and Girls Employed in the Home).[75]

In both countries, the key figures in this movement had working-class backgrounds; we need to only mention Adelheid Popp or Mariska Gárdos (born 1885 in Nagyberény and died 1973 in Budapest). In the first half of the 1890s, they held the first organized strikes in Vienna and Budapest, at which hundreds and soon thousands and tens of thousands of women demanded better working conditions, a maximum working day first of ten hours and then of eight hours, restrictions on child labor, and the recognition of 1 May as a public holiday. Their radical methods meant they often found themselves in conflict with the authorities. As a result of the actions of the police, their official journals were repeatedly banned.[76]

A turning point in these efforts was the foundation in 1902 of the Verein sozialdemokratischer Frauen und Mädchen (Association of Social Democratic Women and Girls): its leaders, ignoring the law on associations, started to involve themselvés in political activism,[77] and from 1905 onward, their efforts to win female suffrage became ever more determined throughout the monarchy. The first women's days in Vienna and Budapest were held in 1911,[78] and both were subject to disparaging leading articles in *Neues Frauenleben* and *A Nő és a Társadalom*. At the Vienna event on 19 March 1911, it was not only Adelheid Popp who spoke but also Victor Adler, whose support the leaders of AöF could count on at any time during their activity.[79] If there was one thing that the progressive and Social Democratic women's organizations could heartily agree on before 1914, it was that the law on associations had to be repealed. The differences between the two schools ultimately softened to some degree during the years of World War I, when they acted together on a number of aid efforts, and in 1917–1918 they organized joint (mass) demonstrations.[80]

The protection of the interests of female workers in fin de siècle Hungary was without strong foundation, partly on account of the utter lack of workplace safeguards for women and partly because of the apathy of workers' groups dominated by men.[81] Alongside the bourgeois women's organizations, the majority of the Christian-Social groups also condemned industrial work being done by women, and the General Workers' Society did not accept female members. Nor did the trade unions throw their weight behind the protection of the rights of women workers; indeed, they often sought to undermine them. The mobilization of women workers began at the turn of the century in Budapest among female laborers of German extraction who worked in light industry. In terms of the nature of the Social Democratic organization, the Austrian and German examples were followed by the Hungarians.

The foundation and subsequent growth of the Social Democratic Party of Hungary (1890), which finally paid heed to the interests of female workers, gave considerable impetus to the movement. Almost two decades later, the Women's Organization Committee was established within the party (1908), and even before this, the Magyarországi Munkásnő Egyesület Working Women's Association of Hungary was founded (1903).[82] Schwimmer and other elements associated with the bourgeois women's movement appear in its creation and in the early operation of the Working Women's Association of Hungary. The president of the association was Mariska Gárdos, who was also editor of *Nőmunkás*, its official publication. Alongside the questions of female labor, education, and child protection, the bourgeois-liberal feminist organizations also allocated space in their publications to discussions of alcoholism, prostitution, sex education, and the trafficking of girls, but these topics were all still considered taboo in the press of the Social Democratic (not to mention the Christian-Social) movement.[83]

Christian-Social Women's Organizations

Unlike the liberal and Social Democratic women's associations, Christian-Social women's associations followed paternalistic models, and the boards of the associations were established with the participation of women but mainly by men from the church hierarchy. The 1848 revolution mobilized Christian women in Austria, who began social and charity work without having committed themselves to any kind of political role. Separate women's branches of the Katholikenverein für

Glauben, Freiheit und Gesittung (Catholic Association for Faith, Freedom, and Morals) and the Frauen-Wohltätigkeits-Verein für Wien und dessen Umgebung (Women's Charity Association for Vienna and the Surrounding Area) were also founded in Vienna in August 1848. In both halves of the monarchy, a duality is observable in this line of organization, as women joining the associations, despite having left their domestic lives behind, joined supportive and charitable activities in accordance with their traditional "natural roles." In Austria, the Verein katholischer Erzieherinnen (Association of Catholic Governesses) was founded in 1868, while Erster Verein Katholischer Lehrerinnen und Erzieherinnen (First Association of Catholic Female Teachers and Governesses) came into being three years later. One of the most important aims of the latter association, similarly to the aims of the bourgeois women's organizations, was to improve the poor financial circumstances of female teachers; this aim was unique within the whole Christian-Social movement. Meanwhile, the overall opinion of the Christian-Social women's movement was that a woman's place was in the home, alongside her husband, and that her primary task was not success at the workplace. The Verein katholischer Arbeiterinnen (Association of Catholic Women Workers) was founded by the pastor of the Votive Church, Adam Latschka, in 1893, and its statutes were officially approved within one week. In contrast, this process took roughly a year in the case of the liberal and Social Democratic associations. The main aim of the association was to provide representation and protection for its members through unemployment benefits, an employment agency, a health support fund, legal advice services, and a savings bank. It also strove to cultivate religious life and provide home economics training for women workers. They organized auxiliary organizations in Vienna, of course, and also in Laibach, Tirol, Steiermark, and Troppau.[84]

Under the leadership of Karl Lueger, in 1887 the Christian-Social associations founded a mutual umbrella organization (Vereinigte Christen, United Catholics) in which the influence of men was traditionally strong. The first public meetings of Catholic women took place in 1892, when the Christliche Famile (Christian Family) association arranged meetings on economic issues, from which the first political women's gatherings emerged on the occasion of the 1895 municipal elections. Subsequently, Frauencomitees (women's committees) were established in several districts of Vienna to promote agitation and further the establishment of new associations.[85] Christlichen Wiener Frauenbund (Catholic Women's Association of Vienna) was formed in 1897, and one decade later (1907), the Katholischen Reichsfrauenorganisation (Catholic Women's Association of the Empire) was established. Women who joined these associations were unlikely to have joined others.[86] Christlichen Wiener Frauenbund, which was similar to the Christian-Social Party in terms of its structure, became a powerful association within a few years, with twenty thousand members who joined not only from Vienna but from the other crown lands. They were called the "amazons of Lueger."[87] The function of the Catholic Women's Association of the Empire was similar to that of BöF within the bourgeois women's movement: to show the cooperation between Catholic women's organizations in the Austrian half of the monarchy. Finally, in 1910, the Erster allgemeiner österreichischer katolischer Frauentag (First General Austrian Catholic Women's Day) was held. AöF pilloried the event for months. The improvement of conditions for working women was included in the program of those women's associations, who participated in this Women's Day, even if they still did not campaign for the extension of the vote to women.[88]

Although the church continued to function as a kind of "women's guesthouse," or the most essential institutionalized female public space in Catholic Austria, it faced potential competition because of the emerging women's associations with other profiles. Like the Christian-Social women's clubs, Social Democrats also combined education with social activities. Dances were frequently organized in workers' educational societies, for instance, and they were met with disparaging criticism and mistrust. On the bourgeois-liberal side, various women's clubs were founded, from the swimming club to the Wiener Frauenclub (Vienna Women's Club), which opened in 1900 in its own rooms, with a library, billiards, and a bathroom. Men, of course, were not allowed to come.[89]

In Hungary, too, the 1890s brought change to the activities of women's groups organized on the basis of religious values. In addition to the nascent mass parties, Christian-Social ideas were spreading at great speed, which was further hastened by the encyclical of Pope Leo XIII (Rerum Novarum, 1891). The National Catholic Society for the Defense of Women was formed in 1896 and grew both in Budapest and in the provinces at a breakneck pace.[90] Within the remit of this society, the National Alliance of Catholic Women Office Workers and Commercial Employees was formed during the 1890s, and the Alliance of Catholic Housewives was established in 1907; a year later, it would operate according to its own constitution. An announced objective was "the establishment of an assertive type of housewife who uses her religious outlook to protect the ethical purity of the family," not to mention one who can run a household. Unlike the feminists, Christian-Social women's dealings with the rights of domestic servants and related issues (relations between housewives and domestic servants, the shortage of such servants, and their moral behavior) were not limited to newspaper articles and discussion evenings. In Budapest, they opened training centers and labor exchanges for domestic servants and also organized various community groups for them.[91]

As Anna Loutfi argues, women's philanthropic associations also existed within the framework of Christian-Social groups. These associations (for instance, the Hungarian Christian Women Workers' Section, which was established in 1904) launched initiatives in the field of welfare in an effort "to win women workers away from the 'immoral' or 'anti-family' ideologies of socialism, and [their] ideologists explicitly criticized feminism in Hungary as an expression of Western 'anti-family' and anti-Christian trends."[92] On the other hand, like their Austrian counterparts, the Hungarian bourgeois and working women's organizations believed that religious groups and charity work could not solve women's problems. They considered the operation of Catholic women's societies to be no more than "treatment for the symptoms" rather than a "cure for the real disease."[93] It speaks volumes of the relationship between the Christian-Social and feminist organizations that there was no forum at which FE designed to comment on the former's achievements in easing the "misery of the maids." Instead, it strove to interpret the problems as ones that no one else was doing anything to assuage. This despite the fact that the difficulties faced by this social class could hardly be resolved with a few editorials in A Nő és a Társadalom or with a lecture evening. During the war years, there were attempts to effect some rapprochement between the two sides, when FE did its best to cooperate with representatives of all branches of the movement, irrespective of their position or attitude.

After 1910, all three branches of the movement shared a common feature: they wished to defend the interests of working women. But while behind the Social Democratic and Christian-Social women's movement stood parties dominated by men, the bourgeois-liberal feminist groups fought their cause alone, independently of political parties. This, together with the events that preceded it, as discussed above, gives an adequate sense of how, in the ideologically so differentiated Austrian and Hungarian societies, the women's movement from the outset developed along such separate and distant paths—a phenomenon that can also be observed in several European countries.

Women's Movements in the Territories Inhabited by National Minorities

At the end of this chapter, I briefly allude to the theoretical literature discussing the women's movements in the territories inhabited by national minorities. This is necessary because, as I highlight at various points in the book, the Austro-Hungarian Empire was a multiethnic state in which women's organizations with widely differing profiles were sometimes loosely and sometimes comparatively closely linked to one another. In spite of these connections, however, the Hungarian women's organizations had only minimal contact with women's associations in the areas inhabited by ethnic minorities, at least as far as the archival research so far has revealed. Closer contacts were only established with the Austrian associations, which were active throughout the period under study. Furthermore, it is important to highlight, as Anna Loutfi does, that "'Hungarian feminism' or women's movements would assume that Hungary was a linguistically national context unmarked by religious, ethnic, and linguistical and class and locational differences."[94]

The language of communication between the associations was primarily German. There are still a few indications of contact between them, but these contacts were only occasional. Nevertheless, as the women's associations under examination here emerged and pursued their aims in a multiethnic, multilingual empire, we cannot ignore the women's organizations in the areas inhabited for the most part by Slovaks, South Slavs, Czechs, Moravians, and Ruthenians. In my discussion of the women's associations in these regions, I mention their sporadic interactions with the Hungarian progressive women's movement. In almost all of these territories, the women's movement was intertwined with movements for national cultural awareness, political presence, and even political independence.[95] In my study of the theoretical literature on women's movements in these areas, I rely exclusively on works in German and English, as I do not speak any of the abovementioned languages.

The Slovak secondary literature has only partially dealt with the history of the women's movement until the 2010s. As Gabriela Dudeková observes, contemporary feminist journalism among the ethnic minorities in the Habsburg monarchy until 1918 addressed a double form of discrimination against women: national or ethnic and gender. The center of women's emancipation was obviously Pressburg (Bratislava). It is also worth noting that no real research has been done on possible ties between the Slovak and Hungarian women's movements after 1918. One does find considerable secondary literature on Živena, however, which was the most important women's association before 1918 in the region inhabited primarily by Slovak speakers. Particular emphasis was placed on the important contribution of Živena to the national emancipatory movement. The activities of other women's associations (i.e., charitable, Christian, and bourgeois organizations) have been largely ignored in the secondary literature, as the focus has been placed on the roles of women in Slovak national-patriotic education and agitation. Gabriela Dudeková also argues that women were important figures in the national minority movement because they raised children. Among the Slovak political elites, conservative attitudes toward women's emancipation prevailed, although feminist ways of thinking did begin to be discussed and partly accepted by the early years of the twentieth century. Despite the democratic developments in the interwar period, which included equal suffrage for women and a number of emancipatory initiatives, the public discourse in these two decades saw the woman's role as housewife, educator, and sometimes agitator, as was true in Hungary. From the perspective of my discussion, it is important that one often comes across the claim in the Slovak secondary literature (which tended to distance itself from the Hungarian scholarship) that women's organizations closely cooperated with the Czechs. This can be explained by the fact that the Czech women's movement, which was more advanced organizationally and ideologically, was seen as a role model for the Slovak movement in the interwar period. However, researchers seem to forget, for example, that auxiliary associations of FE in the Slovak territory of the new Czechoslovak state were in relatively loose contact with local women's organizations. Dudeková highlights this: "New research has shown that despite the distancing of the national Slovak, Czech (and later Czechoslovak) women's movement from the associations and association headquarters in Budapest, which were assumed to be Hungarian, FE developed its activities also in [the] territory of today's Slovakia."[96]

In the Czech Republic and Moravia, the centers of women's emancipation were found mainly in the larger cities, primarily Prague, but recently a few researchers have pointed to women's organizations active in Brno that also merit study.[97] Representatives of the women's movement in the nineteenth century sought to legitimize women's rights by calling attention to the examples set by famous Czech women from the Middle Ages and early modern times, and they even named the first women's association after the first female Czech saint, Ludmilla. As Jitka Malečková argues, it has been mainly foreign (non-Czech) historians who have emphasized the strong connection between the women's movement and nationalism at the turn of the century.[98]

In the first half of the nineteenth century, women were only expected to be good wives and mothers. Their second most important task was to teach their children Czech and make them proud of Czech history and culture. Women's associations at that time had primarily educational and charitable aims. By the 1890s, the women's movement was already focused on ensuring that middle-class women had the same opportunities as men in education and that women could work in the trades and professions for which they had acquired the necessary qualifications. As the writings published in the women's press at the turn of the century clearly reveal, the women's movements became increasingly diverse in their profiles and also increasingly radical. Society was also beginning to pay more and more attention to women's activism, despite the many problems and contradictions that plagued Czech political life. As women were prohibited from forming political organizations (as was also true in Austria), the Committee for Víbor pro volební právó zeny (Women's Voting Rights) was set up in 1905.[99] Natascha Vittorelli argues that some activists in the region had networks with Polish and Slovenian women's organizations.[100] Women's associations in Prague maintained much closer relationships with similar organizations in Germany (and in particular in Saxony).[101] The Czech lands joined the IWSA in 1909, together with France and Belgium.[102] As Malečková argues, however, the Czech women's associations' relations to the international arena were controversial. Their relationships with Austrian women's associations, furthermore, were marked by national controversies. Czech women refused to join the work of all-Austrian umbrella organizations because of the cultural and linguistic differences between them and the members of these organizations.[103]

Research on women's organizations in Galicia has been published in a Polish and a Ukrainian volume of studies. Scholarship on women's movements in Jewish and even German-speaking communities in Galicia is still in its initial stages.[104] However, Natali Stegmann has clearly demonstrated that between 1863 and 1905 in the Kingdom of Poland and Galicia an extremely powerful women's movement was organized that fought for the extension of women's institutional educational rights. These women's associations started to demand political rights after 1905.[105] With this statement, Stegmann challenges the secondary literature and some primary sources on the issue, which insist that there was never any such thing as a Polish women's movement.[106]

In Transylvania, in the Banat, Crişana, and Maramureş, the women's movement was characterized as "a widespread epidemic" in the local press. These territories were incorporated into Hungary after the Austro-Hungarian Compromise in 1867. The situations differed in each of these regions, as the national minorities that inhabited them—Hungarians, Romanians, Saxons, Serbs, Armenians, Jews, and Roma—lived alongside one another in varying proportions. The relations (and tensions) among the various national groups, together with the prevailing political conditions, influenced the main features of the women's movements in the region. The most important activist women were Romanians and Saxons (the German-speaking communities in Transylvania were descendants of Saxon settlers and spoke Saxon as well as Hoch Deutsch), as well as some Hungarians who were tied to the Unitarian movements. Only a few women's associations were established at the beginning of the nineteenth century. Most were formed toward the end of that century or at the beginning of the twentieth. However, as is also true of the women's associations that were formed in Hungary, it is often difficult to determine precisely when the associations were founded. By 1914, 103 organizations of Romanian women were operating in about ninety towns and larger villages. Saxon women had 245 organizations in Transylvania and 9 in the Banat, with a total of thirty-four thousand members. According to a 1929 statistic, Hungarian women had formed 106 associations operating in seventy municipalities in Transylvania and in the Banat before 1918. These organizations, however, have not yet been studied in detail. Most of the rather conservative associations that were founded at the time were concerned with social welfare. Furthermore, the Romansh and Saxon communities played a major role in the fight against Magyarization through a strong commitment to their language and distinctive traditions. Publications that focused specifically on women's issues were rare. Only a few appeared at the beginning of the twentieth century. Activists who belonged to one of the national minorities expressed their views in newspapers and local papers, which were printed in their languages.[107] Romania joined IWSA at the 1913 congress in Budapest.[108]

Progressive Women's Movements

As Vittorelli has shown, the claim found all too frequently in the earlier secondary literature that there were no women's movements or activists for women's rights in Zagreb or elsewhere in Croatia is not true. Several women's organizations in Croatia were actively demanding equal rights for women in education and on the labor market and urging the introduction of female suffrage. Around 1900, Zofka Kveder (born 1878 in Ljubljana and died 1926 in Zagreb), one of the first Slovenian feminists and also a writer, playwright, translator, and journalist who wrote in Slovenian and later in Croatian, was already working on the establishment of a feminist organization.[109] Vittorelli emphasizes that the Slovenian, Croatian, and Serbian women's movements were clearly linked by Zofka Kveder, who lived and was active in Ljubljana, Trieste, Zagreb, and even Prague, where she was in contact with women's movements of all nationalities.[110]

4

The Austrian Association

The Allgemeiner österreichischer Frauenverein

IN THIS CHAPTER, I reconstruct the history of the Viennese organization Allgemeiner österreichischer Frauenverein (AöF), which operated from 1893 to 1922. I argue that the golden age of AöF was in the first decade of the twentieth century, under the leadership of Auguste Fickert. Fickert was AöF's vice president from 1893 to 1897 and its president from 1897 to her death in 1910. I demonstrate that the association and its journal, *Neues Frauenleben*, which existed for more than a decade and a half, were symbiotic. AöF, which operated with a modest membership throughout its span, was connected in myriad ways to Vienna and to its (upper) middle class, which limited the extent of its influence. Fickert and the other leading members of AöF never managed to establish bridgeheads in the provinces, even though the founding of branch organizations was on their agenda until 1910. Yet AöF's influence was not entirely limited to a few districts in Vienna, and around the turn of the century and during World War I, it became embedded in both national and transnational women's movements.

Foundation

AöF, created amid the intellectual ferment of fin de siècle Vienna, began its work in a progressive milieu. The organization of female teachers played an essential role in its establishment.[1] In this chapter, I examine the turning points in the first three years of AöF's existence. I draw on legal documents concerning the regulation of the mobilization of women, coverage of women's activism in the contemporary Viennese press, and AöF records, including the minutes of the founding session of AöF and its annual reports up to 1895–1896. To understand the process of the formation of the AöF, we need to take into account the undying optimism of Auguste Fickert, who started her activism as a schoolteacher. As early as 1888, she was convinced that § 30 of the law on associations regarding women's activism would be removed from the regulations within a year. Not in her wildest dreams did she imagine that granting women the fundamental right to organize politically might take a full three decades.[2] During these thirty years, AöF members and *Neues Frauenleben* authors, like several other Austrian women's organizations, demanded that the law be retracted. Their outrage grew after 1908, when the repeal of similar legislation allowed German women to participate in associations that had political objectives.[3]

The intense activism of the female teachers in Vienna and Lower Austria can be linked to a single event—a legislative proposal from the Lower Austrian provincial assembly, which was one major antecedent to AöF's establishment.[4] In *Utopian Feminism: Women's Movements in Fin-de-Siècle Vienna*, Harriet Anderson stresses that the difficulties of organizing AöF foreshadowed the main directions of its activity.[5] A look at contemporary newspaper articles raises a question: How do we explain why, unlike Britain, Austria—or rather Vienna—had no organization "motivated by a single objective" but only groups that, following the direction set by the German women's movement, wished to reflect on "the women's question in its entirety"? In "Bürgerrechte und Geschlecht," Birgitta Bader-Zaar indicates that the skeptical attitude of participants in the Austrian women's movement ruled out women's participation in organizations from the start.[6] Fickert offers a more subtle explanation: she claims that the already existing associations simply proved inadequate to improve the situation of women. In her speech evaluating the first (partial) year of AöF, filled with highfalutin rhetorical elements, she set out no smaller goal than the following: "We are to our goal, the goal of women preparing the human race adequately for the times to come."[7] This contradicts the law on associations, at that time more than thirty years old, which forbids women's associations to publish articles or journals with political content. The formal establishment of AöF was also delayed for half a year by this law, according to which statutes of women's associations must not include any references to members' political commitments. As Fickert, already dismissive of advice from others, would not abide by these restrictions, the authorities at least once (and, according to some sources, three times) returned the statutes submitted by the association—which even at the end of 1892 were riddled with references to political ambitions.[8]

The internal contradictions in the law on associations, however, left a loophole that was similar to the anomaly in Germany: in Germany, § 21 stated that during elections women could actively join in political activity. In Austria, it was declared in 1867 that every citizen was equal before the law.[9] Fickert interpreted this declaration to mean that even if women's organizations could not announce meetings or demonstrations, women, as private individuals, could do both.[10] In this spirit and as members of the Verein der Lehrerinnen und Erzieherinnen (VLE), Fickert and Marie Schwartz, who had worked as a principal of civic schools since 1891, immediately convened two protest meetings, held on 3 October 1890 and 14 May 1891. The largest group of attendees was composed of female elementary school teachers employed in the outskirts of Vienna,[11] and their goals were not by any means limited to the formulation of a few petitions that made only a modest impact. Far more important than these were their plans for the foundation of AöF.[12]

Although Fickert left no diary from her adult life, her correspondence from these few months reveals a number of things. First, at this time, the horizons of VLE proved too narrow for her wide-ranging objectives: her interest in activism constantly expanded. Alongside the mobilization of women teachers, she now rose to the defense "to be realized on all platforms" of women's social and political rights. Second, the two protest meetings provided a perfect training ground for dealing with the challenges faced by the leadership of AöF. As the excerpts from her speeches published in the journal *Volksstimme* indicate, it was at this time that Fickert learned the skills that would allow her to move with freedom and abandon in the public arena dominated by men. From the early 1890s, it became typical of her rhetoric to build on a question-and-answer structure.[13]

The next protest meeting, organized for Pentecost 1892, was announced as the first Austrian Women's Day. It provided a good example of activism's progression and outlined the more radical directions the nascent AöF sought to follow.[14] To this meeting, Fickert invited Bertha von Suttner (born 1843 in Prague and died 1914 in Vienna), the internationally renowned peace activist, but she rejected the invitation.

> It is with a heavy heart that I cannot agree to put my name to every word in the text. But were I to accept the request, even though I am in agreement, then I would, so to speak, appear as a member of the convened operative committee, as an organizer of the Austrian women's day, and in this way I would be taking on obligations I would not be in a position to satisfy. For me, if nothing else, this would mean an extension to my correspondence, but I would not be in a position to attend to this. . . . For this reason, I have rejected requests from a number of other associations (e.g., Frauenwohl in Berlin) in which I was similarly invited to speak—and you know that if one does not want to cause offense with a rejection, then one must consistently act in the same way with everyone—by those outside my chosen areas of activity.[15]

It was months before the association was actually established, as four of the speakers (including Marie Schwartz) closer to the conservative wing of the bourgeois women's movement or to Social Democratic circles canceled their appearances at the event.[16] Although the relationships between the Viennese bourgeois-liberal and Social Democratic women's associations were always burdened by conflict, Fickert did not object to involving these groups to a certain degree.[17] Although Fickert rejected any institutional form of cooperation between AöF and the Social Democratic (women's) movement, she did feel an affinity for their values.[18]

In my evaluation of the first Austrian Women's Day, I challenge the existing literature in some respects. The existing scholarship's claim that participants canceled their involvement at the last minute is contradicted by a February 1892 letter from the most important Austrian realistic woman writer Emilie Mataja (born 1855 and died 1938 in Vienna) telling Fickert of her decision made "for reasons of principle." According to Mataja, the event would not necessarily have been of use to the "cause of [their] gender," and she warned Fickert against making a fool of herself:

> "It is unfortunately for reasons of principle that I am not able to play an active role in the women's day, so I have to ask you not to count on my support. And from an entirely objective standpoint, I cannot avoid expressing my fear that with the program provided for 'Frauentag' you will do little to advance the cause of our sex. You demand too much at once, and the likely consequence of this will be that your demands are laughed at . . . [and] rejected out of hand."[19]

Fickert was strongly influenced by the ideas of the Marxist politician and founder of the German Social Democratic movement August Bebel (born 1840 in Cologne and died 1913 in Passugg), with whom she had already exchanged a few letters before 1893. From these, it is clear that Bebel tried to talk Fickert out of founding an association with political objectives.[20] In an undated letter, Bebel indicates that the "Führerin"—as her fellow women activists often referred to Fickert—originally thought in terms of founding an alliance (*Bund*) broader than the framework of an association. However, she did not have up-to-date information on the formalities of acquiring official permissions from the authorities for establishing a women's organization. In his letter, Bebel advises Fickert to found an association with educational objectives.

> The endeavor you are planning is a highly worthy one, if its implementation will require great challenges to be confronted. Primarily the prejudices of your own gender, a prejudice that will be even greater there than in Germany, because the social conditions are less developed. I would not recommend that you use the appeal to prepare the foundation of an alliance. I think this would not make a favorable impression and would likely end in failure. I suggest that first you generate publicity in smaller groups for the foundation of a women's training organization, and once a smaller but permanent body of people has come together, then you can come forward with a public meeting. I cannot help you with the statutes, alas. The women's society here in Dresden was condemned to its demise by the regulations imposed by the authorities.[21]

At Bebel's suggestion, Fickert turned to Victor Adler, who, in addition to fighting successfully for the introduction of adult male suffrage, had played a key role in the foundation of the Sozialdemokratische Partei Österreichs (Social Democratic Party of Austria). For the Social Democrats, Fickert's ideas—especially those relating to women's education—were overly "bourgeois," despite the fact that the AöF leadership would later enjoy a close working relationship with Adler.[22] Harriet Anderson in her work titled *Utopian Feminism: Women's Movements in Fin-de-Siècle Vienna* and Gabriella Hauch in her book *Frauen bewegen Politik: Österreich 1848–1938* emphasized that women belonging to the more conservative wing of the bourgeois women's movement considered the preliminary agenda of AöF to be too radical. They include Marie Schwartz among those women, despite the fact that Schwartz's name is present on the list of AöF members in 1897; indeed, Fickert also remained a member of VLE for the rest of her life.[23] Furthermore, in highly innovative fashion for the time, the association included in its program not just general issues of education and training but also the rights of domestic servants and prostitutes and women's rights to participate in the legislature.[24]

Among the achievements of the Women's Day were the nomination of the temporary AöF committee and the beginning of a dialogue on the composition of the organization's statutes. It is evidently due to Fickert's pigheadedness—and, as she would later admit, her naivete—that the inaugural assembly would only take place in the following year. For a long time, she continued to believe that the authorities would approve the AöF's original statutes. She was to be disappointed in this, and the rejection of the statutes—a successful display of force on the part of the authorities—shows that the bourgeois-liberal women's movement did not represent a strong enough force to openly and successfully stand up for women's rights.[25]

The celebratory first meeting of the AöF was finally convened on 28 January 1893 in the grand meeting hall of Vienna's old town hall.[26] Auguste Fickert was elected vice president—a few years later, she would become president. It is important to highlight that in the minutes of the inaugural meeting, there are no rules as to the nomination of committee members or presidents.[27] The annual reports, published separately, do not include the election of the leadership for the following year among the items on the agenda; the names of the committee are to be found only within the list of members. Reports on the pages of *Neues Frauenleben* merely name each group's officers without telling readers what positions they were nominated for.

The lengthy process involved in the establishment of AöF shows the group's uniqueness among the contemporary Viennese women's organizations and indicates that it was ahead of its time in its aims, but it also foreshadows the difficulties presented by Fickert's resolute attitude, as she was only rarely open to taking advice from others.

Auguste Fickert as Leader of the Organization

As the key figure of AöF, Auguste Fickert merits a more detailed introduction. In this section, I reflect on her family background and on the possible relevance of the fact that she lived with a woman. I also analyze her complicated character, which made it difficult for her to share tasks in the leadership of AöF with others. She was seemingly surrounded by adoring coworkers, but her conflicts with them left their mark on the national and international standing and reputation of the association. I also touch on her apparent inability to share influence with others when it came to her role as the leader of the association.

Christine Touaillon, who played a key role both in the editing of the literary section of *Neues Frauenleben* and in the leadership of AöF after 1910, said of Auguste Fickert in 1911, "It seems this woman had no private life."[28] While this was something of an exaggeration, it suggests that Fickert's private and professional connections operated within a constrained system of coordinates throughout her life. Auguste—known to those close to her as Gusti—was born in Vienna on 25 May 1855 to a family with Silesian roots. Her father, who was the child of a Protestant family in northern Germany, worked at the imperial printing press. Her mother, who was born to a Catholic family in Vienna, was a housewife, as was expected of women in the era, and she raised Auguste and her one elder and three younger siblings.[29]

Auguste attended elementary school, and because of her talent, her parents wanted her to continue her studies.[30] Her correspondence with her cousin Karoline Fellner, known within the family simply as Lina, indicates that in 1869–1870, Auguste studied at one of the Bavarian teacher training institutes operated by Englishwomen in Burghausen.[31] Her grades for most subjects (including theology) were "very good"; in literary writing, mental arithmetic, history, and handiwork, her grade was "good."[32] On her return to Vienna, she enrolled at the Saint Anna Teacher Training Institute, from which she graduated in 1876.[33] Her 124-page diary kept from 1871 to 1910 reveals that at the school in Vienna, she already had given up on her dreams of becoming an actress or author and that she was aware of the disadvantages her gender brought with it. Even at this stage, she repeatedly asked herself, "Why did I have to be born a woman?"[34] It is worth noting that then and later, her diary often took the form of poems. At the teacher training school, Fickert met the woman who would later become her life partner, Ida Baumann. Baumann was from a Jewish family of teachers from Thuringia, Germany. Her fraught relationship with Fickert would last until the end of Fickert's life. For Fickert's part, she makes no mention of the foundation of AöF in her diary, even though it was important to her; the pages from 1893 onward contain details only of a conflict with Baumann. Of the last twenty years of her life, she left only five pages in total.[35]

From 1876 until her death, Fickert worked as a teacher at both elementary and civic schools. It was after her father's death in 1881 that she began publicly to declare her radical views concerning the exploitation of women teachers. From this time onward, her obligations grew, as she had to support her mother and her younger siblings financially. To increase her earnings, she took on teaching work outside school, while Ida Baumann—to support her partner—came to live with the family for a time. Together, Fickert and Baumann joined the VLE in 1882, already objecting to the fact that the female teaching staff earned 20 percent less than their male colleagues.[36] Soon afterward, Fickert and Baumann moved into their first home together at 15 Neubaugasse, though in 1890, Baumann's name did not appear on the list of residents.[37] Their everyday life, beyond difficulties

Figure 4.1. Portrait of Auguste Fickert. Österreichische Nationalbibliothek, Bildarchiv und Grafiksammlung Signatur: NB 528268-B (CC BY-NC-ND 4.0).

in making ends meet, was burdened by troubles caused by Baumann's Jewish heritage. Baumann was also earning her living as a teacher, although her previous goal had been to open her own kindergarten in Vienna, something she did achieve, only to have to close it again little more than two years later.[38]

Toward the end of the 1880s, clouds were forming in the skies of Fickert and Baumann's relationship—clouds that became darker and thicker with the increase in Fickert's speaking commitments. To explain this situation fully, I highlight a few aspects of the partnership of two women in Vienna at that time and the response of the broader public. Hilde Schmölzer, who gives a thorough analysis of the question, states that such relationships were not considered lesbianism in the literal sense but were rather defined as a sort of "romantic friendship." As these women predominantly represented themselves as asexual, they only partially attracted the attention of society, which in general was tolerant of partnerships between unmarried, financially independent women. Yet one might well wonder why they had to move roughly every two years. The sources do not offer any answer to this question.

Baumann's letters—which give us the most rounded picture of Fickert—reveal that their relationship was saddled with constant conflicts caused by their different personalities. In the end, they could not avoid tragedy, and three years after her partner's death, Baumann killed herself by jumping into the Danube. Fickert had remained an idealist even after the growth of her public appearances, her departure from the Catholic Church in 1893, and the two disciplinary proceedings (1897, 1900) instituted against her by the local education authority.[39] Baumann, for her part, continued to be introverted and shy, with no other desire than to live together with "her dearest Fickert."[40] Baumann was more private, while Fickert was drawn to the public fight for women's rights, with which, perhaps, she was able to satisfy something of her theatrical ambitions.[41] For many long years, Baumann wrote enthusiastically of her partner, whose intellectual superiority is at many points evident in the letters. At one point, the rhapsodic Fickert—who was constantly recommending reading matter to Baumann—even attempted to convince her partner to join her in immigrating to the United States.[42] In these years, despite having lived together for a protracted period, Fickert and Baumann continued to use the formal form of address in their correspondence, a habit with which they would only break at the end of the 1880s.

Fickert's temperament made their private life difficult; their conflicts only became worse after Baumann became involved in the efforts to bring AöF into being. Around that time, a man named Ernst also appeared in Fickert's diary, only to disappear from her entries without trace.[43] This section of Fickert's life is relevant for two reasons. It was then that helping others became an integrated part of her everyday life, and as a result of this, her character as known later and seen on the 1929 memorial statue came into being. Leopoldine Kulka, her immediate coworker in AöF, referred to her character in *Neues Frauenleben*, noting that the door to Fickert's apartment was always open to those in need of support.[44] Thus, the 1890s were of crucial significance in the building of Fickert's character. It was then that, because of the foundation of AöF, she came in close contact with Julius Ofner (born 1845 in Hořenec and died 1924 in Vienna), a member of the Austrian parliament and later keen supporter of AöF; Rosa Mayreder; and the Norwegian writer and poet Bjørnstjerne Bjørnson (born 1832 in Kvikne and died 1910 in Paris). These new contacts were detrimental to Fickert's private life, though, and this was when Baumann first left their joint home, after they had been living together for twelve years.[45]

After the temporary collapse of a partnership that was rich in arguments and intrigue, Fickert invested the energies thus freed into AöF—something it badly needed. This raises a number of questions, and the answers are to be found in Fickert's character. First of all, why did the newly established association fail to nominate a president for years? While the personality at the helm of an organization is important at any stage of its activity, it is of particular importance at its outset, when the objectives and working methods are laid out. So why can we find no president of AöF before 1897 or after 1910?[46] The minutes of the first meeting held after Fickert's death (11 November 1910) indicate that the board wanted to leave the president's position unfilled for at least a year to mourn Fickert's death.[47] But the later lists of the association's leaders show that the post remained unfilled until 1918, and indeed probably until the body was disbanded.[48] This cannot be unrelated to the way that Fickert's immediate colleagues deified her in their recollections, referring to her variously as their "Fürstin" (princess), "Meisterin" (mistress), or even "Führerin" (leader).[49] After 1910, they saw the president's position as some kind of mystical, posthumous role that even in death only Fickert could fill. This raises a question as to the progressive nature of the Austrian bourgeois-liberal women's movement, that it was able—albeit only indirectly—to maintain empty positions for deceased members of its committee.

The answer to the question of why the committee did not elect a president between 1893 and 1897 is also to be found in Fickert's personality. After her extraordinary organizational efforts from 1889 to 1893, it would surely have been the obvious decision for the inaugural meeting to nominate her as AöF president. Yet her conservative religious upbringing—even if she turned her back on the Roman Catholic Church in the year the association was founded—and her martyr complex, which had only become stronger over the years, may have hindered her ambitions to lead the organization. The letters she exchanged with her family give a picture of a mother none too pleased by her daughter's radical views.[50] This raises the question of just how much strategy could have been in the mind of this unmarried woman, already thirty-six years of age, who had an unrelenting desire to prove herself.[51] She can only have had a single clear plan—namely, to nominate herself for president of the association once she, as vice president, had accumulated unquestionable achievements in the blossoming of AöF. One indication of Fickert's determination might be that after her nomination as president in 1897, Baumann's name disappeared from the list.[52] This was when they started living together again after their separation, although unreserved trust had not yet been established between them. The name missing from the list might be a coincidence, but given Fickert's discipline and Baumann's refusal to leave the women's movement behind in later years, this seems unlikely.[53]

Apart from ensuring press publicity for AöF, Fickert was constantly fighting against the "Christian-Social danger." She even published a satirical poem criticizing the policies of Mayor Karl Lueger, titled *Würde der Frauen (Women's Honor)*. As a result of the second school board disciplinary proceedings begun against her because of the poem, she was moved from the elementary school close to the Volksoper in Vienna (18 Schulgasse) to another school just a few streets away (9 Grüne Torgasse).[54] The information about her from this time onward is from the documentation of the association and from AöF's official journals. She considered the publication of these journals to be one of the organization's most important tasks. This is why it is worth looking at the complicated relationships between these journals and the bargains they struck, as a result of which *Neues Frauenleben* came into being in 1902. The earlier literature concludes that the collapse of *Dokumente der Frauen* in September 1902 was in large part thanks to AöF's new mouthpiece, yet its authors do not mention why the editorial board marked the pilot edition of *Neues Frauenleben* as being in its fourteenth year.[55] Neither do they mention that the journal had no fewer than three legal predecessors, two of which are not mentioned in AöF reports,[56] and that none of these periodicals was connected to AöF in any institutional or contractual way.

The key turning points in the process that led to the publication of *Neues Frauenleben* were as follows: The first step was the establishment of *Lehrerinnen-Wart. Zeitschrift für die Interessen der Lehrerinnen und Erzieherinnen* (Magazine for the Interests of Female Teachers and Educators) in 1889, in which Fickert regularly published articles on the circumstances of women teachers and the work of organizing AöF. The journal was taken over by Helene Littmann (born 1866 in Paris), later a member of the committee of BöF, who published it between 1889 and 1892 under the title *Neuzeit. Blätter für weibliche Bildung in Schule und Haus, zur Förderung der Frauenbestrebungen und Vertretung der Fraueninteressen* (Modern Times. Journal for Female Education in School and at Home, for the Promotion of Women's Aspirations and Representation of Women's Interests).[57] From 1894 to 1901, the journal appeared with another new title (*Frauenleben*, Women's Lives) but was still edited by Littmann. Littmann ultimately "left this [journal] to Fickert" "as a gift," although the motivation behind this gesture is unknown.[58] She cannot have died in 1901, as hardly a year later she was among the founding members of BöF. In "Die Frauen müssen ganz andere Worte hören" (Women Must Hear Completely Different Words), Eva Klingenstein says that the periodical "fought for its survival" as the official journal of two Viennese and one Praguian women's groups.[59] We know that it came into the hands of AöF—that is, of Fickert—at no charge.[60] This was an important moment, as under the law on associations, AöF could not appear as a publisher (*Herausgeberin*), but Fickert could do so as a private individual.[61]

In the January 1902 pilot edition of *Neues Frauenleben*, Fickert welcomed its readers, whom the editors later referred to as the friends (*Freunde*) of AöF.[62] The editor in chief from the beginning of the project to 1918 was board member Adele Gerber (born 1863 in Vienna and died 1937 in Vienna), and after the power battles that followed the death of Fickert, the members of the editorial board and the leaders of the publishing company became Leopoldine Kulka, Christine Touaillon, and Emil Fickert (born 1870 in Vienna and died 1957 in Vienna), Fickert's younger brother. The first premonition of these battles must already have been felt by the time of Fickert's death in the sanatorium in Wällischhof, where Fickert was dying. As the sanatorium bills settled by Emil Fickert reveal, every one of Fickert's close colleagues lined up next to her bed: after Emil Fickert, Leopoldine Kulka, and Christina Touaillon, Adele Gerber and Ida Baumann also arrived. Kulka and Emil Fickert spent the longest time, five days, there.[63] After Fickert's death, Baumann attempted to blend herself into the editorial threesome, but her efforts were in vain. She favored the teacher and writer Antonie Hug von Hugenstein (?–1915), secretary of VLE, and wanted to see her on the editorial board, and "the non-Jewisch compromise figures" were Christine Touaillon and Emil Fickert. Although Baumann's relations with Fickert's younger sister, Marianne Fickert, were cordial, she and Emil Fickert could not see eye to eye at all, so she stood little chance of attaining a more significant role in and around the journal's offices.[64]

In the schedule Auguste Fickert forced on herself with military precision, she undertook her tasks relating to *Neues Frauenleben* during school lunch breaks and free slots between lessons. It was then that she dealt with editorial correspondence.[65] She regularly received postal communications relating to AöF at her home address or her office, thereby engendering Baumann's resentment. Despite the joint issues published every summer, she did not give up on her work in July and August: she would often be found at some stop along an Alpine hiking route copyediting the articles that Adele Gerber had sent her.[66]

Although the editing of *Neues Frauenleben* followed a more clearly defined concept than that of *Dokumente der Frauen*,[67] Fickert only delegated tasks to a close-knit group. None of the sources mentions any of her direct colleagues being disappointed in her work, so I assume that she maintained her perfectionism in this too. In truth, as an author and editor, she could only rely on Kulka, whose work ethic did not flag even after Fickert's death: from 1907 to 1918, alongside her tasks as editor, Kulka published an average of over 10 articles a year (128 in total). This number is particularly impressive in comparison to the output of her colleagues: Adele Gerber, who had overseen the publication of the journal from the outset, wrote only 16 articles, while Christine Touaillon had 35 to her name.

Emil Fickert, who only joined the editorial board in 1910 and mostly worked to stabilize the financial backing of the journal, published just 1 article.

Fickert's correspondence relating to the journal and the association was almost exclusively conducted with Germany's intelligentsia, artists, leading women's movement activists, and a few lawyers and economists. We encounter one or two isolated letters from members of women's associations in Galicia, Switzerland, or France or from women teachers in the Austrian provinces. Oddly, AöF was not able to profit from Fickert's friendly connections with northern Europe.

The atmosphere among the members of AöF was often tense because of Fickert's autocratic behavior, and this tension remained even after her death. Within the association, Fickert behaved the same as she did as a teacher at school: she would not accept dissenting opinions, and her fellow members, who otherwise had the fullest respect for her, described some of her actions as tyrannical. Fickert outrightly refused to treat her fellow members as equal partners.

For as long as she lived, Fickert remained strictly formal, reserved, and even downright cold with her closest colleagues, Kulka, Gerber, and Touaillon. Her fellow women never called her by her forename, and—with the exception of Marie Lang (born 1858 in Vienna and died 1934 in Altmünster), a founding member of AöF with whom Fickert and Rosa Mayreder published *Dokumente der Frauen* for a short time in 1899—they all addressed her formally. Kulka generally called her "Geehrte Frau" or "Sehr geehrtes Fräulein," while Touaillon usually called her "Hochverehrte Frau." Their interactions were almost entirely limited to the operation of AöF or to formal greetings sent on festive occasions. Within these constraints, Gerber perhaps managed to establish the closest bond with her; she once addressed a letter to "Dearest Miss Fickert."[68] Fickert's relationships with people usually remained static. Only her interactions with Marie Lang showed signs of change: in 1893, they held each other at a polite distance, but Lang then came to be very close to Fickert.[69] An 1899 conflict over the editing of *Dokumente der Frauen* made them more distant, but they became (a little) closer again toward the end of Fickert's life. In a 1907 letter, Lang again calls Fickert "Dear, dear Madame" before rounding off "with kisses" and signing it "Your Marie."[70] All of this grew out of Lang's idolization in the 1890s, which Ida Baumann, presumably out of jealousy, considered overdone.

By the end of her life, Fickert had perfectly honed her leadership strategy. She convinced single women much younger than she to join her on the AöF board. Of the "Fickert epigons" treated as her "disciples" (*Schülerinnen*),[71] it was Leopoldine Kulka, a nonobservant member of a Jewish family, who shone through. In 1911, she was not only elected vice president of the association but also selected for the committee publishing *Neues Frauenleben*.[72] Elisabeth

Malleier highlights that Kulkat came from a family in which writing and revising were common practices, as her father also worked as an editor. Her father had taken part in the revolution in 1848 and had been one of the first to publish poems untouched by the censors. As Malleier has demonstrated, the word *freedom* appears often in Kulka's articles.[73] According to Baumann, this was what Fickert had feared the most: her association and her journal "fell into Jewish hands."[74]

The editing of the journal, alongside the direction of AöF, increasingly tested Fickert's stamina and tolerance, and by the mid-1900s, conflicts in her private life had also escalated. On one occasion Rosa Mayreder encouraged her to make decisions concerning the association on her own, without discussing them with Ida Baumann.[75] Fickert's excessive workload is evident from her correspondence as well. Her words to Maikki Friberg (born 1861 in Kankaanpää and died 1927 in Helsinki), a leader of the Finnish women's movement and Fickert's confidante, indicate that her excessively dictatorial reflexes resulted from her disappointment in her work. As she saw it, intrigue had poisoned every aspect of her life—the association included.[76] As the years progressed, Baumann also became increasingly selfish and demanding, even conspiring against AöF because, as she saw it, her beloved Fickert had become estranged as a result of her endless work for the association.[77]

Fickert's health never fully recovered from her infection with an influenza virus (*türkische Influenza*) in 1905. Baumann pleaded with her to rest, but Fickert refused. She continued to wear herself out at the association, at the editorial board of the journal, and in her work on her "favorite project," the "Heimhof," the single-kitchen building (*Einküchenhaus*) of AöF. It was a reform model of urban housing in which a centrally managed large kitchen within an apartment building replaced individual kitchens. The concept was based on the ideas of the German women's rights activist and Social Democrat Lily Braun (born 1865 in Halberstadt, Germany, and died 1916 in Zehlendorf, Germany), and Fickert adapted it in Austria. To establish the Heimhof, in addition to collecting donations, AöF made a generous contribution from its own capital. The first call to help acquire the necessary funds was published in May 1909 in *Neues Frauenleben*, and construction took two years. Fickert did not survive to see its completion; the Heimhof was opened in October 1911.[78] Succumbing to pressure from Friberg, in 1909 Fickert finally traveled to Finland, where she was regarded as an exemplar in the fight for women's education and political emancipation, but this voyage only weakened her further. After another academic year in which she had worked herself to the bone at school, Fickert passed away on 9 June 1910 at the Maria Enzersdorf sanatorium.[79]

With Fickert's death, AöF entered a new phase. However, as the "Führerin" had not ensured who would succeed her as president of the association and publisher of *Neues Frauenleben*, the power struggles after 1910 and her influence even after her death left a controversial mark on the work of AöF in the years to come.

Objectives and Press Policies

In this section, I discuss the objectives of AöF, which touched on almost every aspect of women's lives. I clarify which of their aims were successful (e.g., their publishing activity and the expansion, at least to some extent, of the scope of women's institutional education) and which were not (e.g., the regulation of the law on prostitution). I pay particular attention to the way in which Auguste Fickert and Leopoldine Kulka communicated the association's successes and failures to members and in its press. I examine the press policies of AöF, which underwent hardly any changes and which constituted an exceptional success in the era, as the association managed to keep their official organ alive for almost two decades, which was quite unprecedented at the time.

We do not have the collection of statutes related to AöF. The Fickert estate, however, did retain detailed minutes of the inaugural meeting in January 1893, with which we can reconstruct a relatively precise picture of the organization's key goals.[80] At the beginning of the minutes, the editors announced with pleasure that this was the association's first publication, which anyone could acquire for ten crowns. The pre-1902 minutes are available in similar form; these provide important information on the slowly increasing membership.[81] A similar publication was produced for the association years 1909–1910, when Auguste Fickert died. There are no surviving minutes from the remaining periods. It is possible that these were left out of the Fickert estate or were destroyed, or it may be that after 1910, such minutes were never produced. It is also possible that after the inception of *Neues Frauenleben* in 1902, the association did not consider it necessary to distribute these reports in a separate volume. If this is true, then the 1909–1910 publication might have been a tribute to the association's departed "leader."[82] Apart from the years 1916–1917, the *Neues Frauenleben* gives precise information about the work of AöF.

The January issues of the journal repeatedly and verbatim published the following goals, laid down in 1893, which did not change at all as the decades passed: "The goal of the Allgemeiner österreichischer Frauenverein is to support the intellectual improvement and economic interests of women, and to improve women's social standing by organizing them and providing them with written and verbal education."[83]

The reports of the annual meetings were usually published in May or June but were often much delayed: they appeared in the August issue of *Neues Frauenleben* in 1908 and in the September issue in 1909.[84] This was probably because during the summer months they tried to keep editing work to a minimum. The reports can hardly be described as detailed: mostly they give a glimpse into the events organized by the association and the election of committee members. Unfortunately, they do not touch on a question of great importance: how the membership numbers developed. Even the exhaustive statistical details published on the operations of the human rights section (*Rechtschutz-Sektion*) do not make up for this lack of information. It is worth noting that the reports of the Rechtschutz-Sektion were from the outset much longer than those of the entire AöF. They kept a careful record of the number of legal cases and the social classes the clients had come from.[85] Most likely, they provided this information to prove that women from any social background could turn to them for advice or legal assistance.

The reports repeat a few elements until they almost become clichés. Until the annual meeting held in late April in almost every year of the association's operation, Fickert welcomed the members on every occasion. In speeches imbued with pathos, the "Meisterin" radiated never-ending optimism, but by the late 1890s, her enthusiasm was replaced by pessimism; from this time onward, her words instead reflected a general mood of gentle melancholy while remaining full of fight and encouragement. The first signs of her gloomier outlook can be seen in 1895: "We can look back over a long year at our association. This gives a certain motivation to the association members and much work to its leadership. The results do not match the effort involved."[86]

This changing attitude did not for a second mean that Fickert's fervor had abated; indeed, her disappointment relating to the journal and its provincial distribution only further girded her resolve. Her speeches regularly touched on political actualities and the situation of the women's movement in Austria and, within this, AöF's successes or challenges. She did not forget about the anniversaries of the bourgeois women's movement; in 1898, for example, she paid lengthy tribute to the role played by Karoline von Perin and her fellow women in the series of revolutionary events in Vienna and in the short-lived but exemplary Erster Wiener demokratischer Frauenverein.[87]

After the welcome given by the (vice) president, the reports cover, in chronological order from September of the previous year to the current assembly, on the lectures, debate evenings, courses, and museum visits the association had initiated. This was followed by the report of the *Rechtschutz-Sektion*. After detailing the financial receipts and outgoings of this section and then of the journal, the documents list the names of the members of the committee. The largest items of income always included membership fees and, before 1902, the enrollment fees (*Einschreibegebühr*). Over the years—until 1917, which is the last year we have information for—these changed only twice. Until 1897, the annual membership fee cost one gulden, and the enrollment fee was twenty-five kreuzers.[88] The membership fees were adjusted for the first time in 1902, when the *Neues Frauenleben* started to appear. Association membership alone cost three crowns, and a journal subscription with membership cost six crowns.[89]

Donations represented a significant item on the list of revenues, as did stock market investments and interest payments. Like the capital needed to establish *Neues Frauenleben*, these came from a bequest from Baron Otto von Springer, one of the founding members of AöF living in Vienna, who left 60,000 crowns to the association before his death in 1900.[90] The largest item of expenditure up to 1902 was the organization of events: in addition to room rental, they paid for receptions following lectures and even for certain speakers. They regularly held meetings at the town hall of the ninth district, where the rental was initially free, as well as at the city center rooms (first district, 11 Tuchlauben) of the Neuer Frauenclub (Vienna, 1903–1938) and the building of the Commercial and Industrial Chamber, also in Vienna's first district (1 Wipplingerstrasse).[91] Given a lack of resources, however, few foreign speakers came to Vienna, and AöF was accordingly modest in its entertainment allowance. Meanwhile, the budget only rarely contains items related to Fickert's lecture tours or participation in conferences abroad.[92] And although the publication of *Neues Frauenleben* was in principle covered by a separate account, it nevertheless was a great financial burden for AöF.

The reports included membership lists in alphabetical order. These detailed the members' addresses and subscriptions paid. The lack of these details is very much felt in those periods in which *Neues Frauenleben* published the reports, as these do not even indicate changes in the numbers or composition of the membership.

Now that we have looked at the general characteristics of these reports, let us return to the minutes of the first celebratory meeting in January 1893, which reveal much about the circumstances of AöF's foundation. First of all, telegrams of congratulation had arrived from the Czech Lands, Moravia, Germany, Switzerland, Belgium, Holland, France, and Great Britain. The following institutions and activists celebrated the creation of AöF: the Allgemeiner Studentinnen Verein (General Association for Women University Students) from Zurich, the Union nationale des femmes (National Union of Women) and the Internationale Gesellschaft der Wissenschaften und Künste (International Alliance of Researchers and Artists) from Paris, the Women's Progressive Society from Great Britain, the Freie Frauengesellschaft (Free Society of Women) from Amsterdam, and the Ligue belge du droit des Femmes (Belgian League of Women's Rights) from Brussels. The leaders of Allgemeiner deutscher Frauenverein (AdF), Louise Otto-Peters and Auguste Schmidt, sent separate letters from Leipzig welcoming the new organization. Schmidt said she was sorry she could not participate in the illustrious event. A number of members of the Austrian parliament, including Ferdinand Kronawetter (born 1838 in Vienna and died 1913 in Pottschach), a supporter of Fickert and AöF, also sent their best wishes. So, too, did the author Irma von Troll-Borostyani, who married a Hungarian and for a while earned a living as a music teacher in Budapest and whose writings were regularly published by *Neues Frauenleben*. I quote just one of these messages, as the others all follow the same pattern: "The best of luck to this nascent association that it turn into a force for good capable of uniting the real values of women's emancipation in the fight for freedom of the downtrodden classes."[93]

The inaugural session nominated the members of the board, with whom Fickert had been in negotiations since the fall of the previous year. Alongside the vice presidents, two keepers of the minutes (*Schriftführerin*), a treasurer (*Kassierin*), a secretary (*Sekretärin*), and a librarian (*Bibliothekarin*) were chosen.[94] Yet—at least in this document—the board failed to lay down the principles according to which members of the leadership, including the president, vice presidents, and secretaries, would be selected in the future. We might trace this back to Fickert's lack of experience, as already discussed, though we could also see it as an expression of her autocratic tendencies. The former hypothesis is not borne out by her letters addressed to the educational committee, which reveal that she must already have been a member of VLE by 1875.[95] We should not forget, though, that mere membership in an association did not necessarily imply familiarity with its management. The latter hypothesis, meanwhile, is corroborated first by the predominance of Fickert's speeches and comments throughout the inaugural meeting and second by the fact that only a single subject was brought up and debated. This related to the enrollment fee, which was ultimately set not at the original suggestion of twenty kreuzers but instead at twenty-five kreuzers.[96]

The electorate of eighty-five (appears to have) agreed spontaneously on everything, though it is possible that comments were deleted from the published minutes. It is unlikely that attendees would have been inexperienced at leadership, as a good number of them were Viennese teachers socialized within VLE circles. According to the published material, the meeting's participants were of like mind regarding the level of membership fees: they were convinced that keeping these low would attract new members.

The meeting was probably conducted according to a preestablished order of events, as was the general session of 31 March 1906, which decided on the departure from BöF and at which the comments and reflections had been agreed on in advance.[97] A total of five speeches were made at the inaugural meeting, and three of these were formal congratulations.[98] This cannot fully be explained by the fact that the material of the session was posted to the members in advance. Fickert even saw to it that the statutes were voted on not paragraph by paragraph but en bloc.[99]

With the fourth item on the agenda, beyond acknowledging her own naivete, Fickert sought answers to the question of how AöF could get around § 30 of the law on associations. This is unique; the archival material contains no other example of her accepting that her judgment of a situation was mistaken: "At that time [after Women's Day in May 1892], I was so naive, I thought that the second demand, namely, that § 30 of the law on associations, which prohibits women from joining political associations, be repealed, could be achieved in a year or even earlier.... How wrong I was!"[100]

Fickert explained that the authorities and the Interior Ministry would only allow the foundation of a group with a general (*allgemein*) profile and removed the part of the statutes that would have fought for women's rights as citizens: "The goal of the association is to mobilize Austrian women with the objective of protecting and broadening their civil rights, of supporting their economic interests and their intellectual development, and the improvement of their social status."[101]

In the end, Fickert, in conjunction with two lawyers (who are not named), decided that they would not renounce even this part of the AöF program. Quite the opposite, in fact: they would seek to realize women's political rights "outside the association"—that is, as private individuals.[102]

There was no obstacle preventing AöF from standing up for women's educational and economic rights or organizing lectures on these subjects. In any case, they believed the comprehensive solution to the women's question to be attaining "the economic independence of women," for which the acquisition of adequate (vocational) education would prove vital.[103] Precisely for this reason, Fickert, who considered an expansion of institutional women's education to be the most important step toward their legal equality, had already urged action in 1893. She stated that AöF not only campaigned for the establishment and operation of certain types of schools but also demanded a comprehensive revision that would put the imperial educational law on a modern footing.

> Let there be no misunderstanding ... we are not just making a stand for any given specialist or middle or higher education—on which, thankfully, other women's associations in Austria are already working, with varying degrees of success—but rather we are making a stand for the reform of the whole system of adult and child education, for the creation of girls' schools, which might be mentioned in the Imperial Primary Education Act, but of which none have come into being.[104]

The radicalism of AöF was most obvious on the issues of domestic servants and prostitution. Its members did not believe that the legislation in place would restrict commercial sex; meanwhile, they sought in every possible arena to stress the importance of sexual education for children, which might also have represented a partial solution to the "misery of the maids." They stood for the introduction of maternity support and the reform of marital legislation. From their inception onward, they urged the reform of the civil law code in effect since 1811; they would, however, "celebrate" the centenary of the civil law code in *Neues Frauenleben*.[105] Unlike other associations, they wanted to interpret the questions generated by the extension of rights for women by "getting to their root" and intended to use their proposed solutions to broaden the outlook of women in the longer term.[106] At the jubilee assembly celebrating twenty-five years of the association, Kulka and Gerber looked back on this.

> The Allgemeiner österreichischer Frauenverein could never have come into being if the need for such an organization had not been urgently felt. The existing women's associations are unable to satisfy our needs: to grasp the women's question in its entirely, the explore its roots, which extend to every part of human coexistence, and to the realization that the movement as a whole requires intellectual foundations. This is why the association had to be founded. . . . Back then the Austrian women's movement was dominated by questions relating to education and work.[107]

All we find in the report about the composition of the membership is that women over the age of sixteen could become full members.[108] Men could join as supporting members; they were most valued in their role in the human rights section and as writers for *Neues Frauenleben*.[109] Men paid the same subscription fee as women, although men contributed with larger donations not just to the establishment of the journal but also, for example, to the association's library. Baron Schwarz-Seeborn gave fifteen volumes to help found the library in 1893, after which the collection grew to 202 volumes by 1895 and 330 by 1910.[110] As the years passed, the association's extensive network of lawyers and business specialists close to parliamentary circles grew, providing an opportunity for its leaders, at least indirectly, to influence political life.[111]

One other aspect of the 1893 report must be emphasized: the clarification of the question of the association's headquarters and meeting hall. AöF's general meetings and speaker and debate evenings were usually held at the community hall (*Gemeindehaus*) of the ninth district (Alsergrund) of Vienna, at 43 Währingerstrasse. Franz Lölich put the hall at the disposal of the association for free (*unentgeltlich*) at its inception, although, according to the financial statements, AöF would later be obliged to pay room rental fees and lighting and heating expenses.[112]

Let us move on from the association's objectives to the application of its principles. To what extent could AöF's (self-)representation be successful in the press and other areas of public life, and what methods could Auguste Fickert or Leopoldine Kulka use to achieve their goals? Did they succeed in attracting the attention of Viennese women to their work? How did they motivate those women to join them? And which social groups did they intend or manage to appeal to? We can use a variety of sources to answer these questions. In the Wienbibliothek, a collection of women's movement journals contains articles written by Fickert and sent mostly to Austrian and German women's movement journals. These provide insight into the work of AöF, but, as they are essentially long-form journalism articles, we have to treat them with suitable caution. From the early 1890s, Fickert mostly sent articles to the following journals: *Die Frauenbewegung* (Women's Movement), *Die Frau* (The Woman), *Frauenleben: Blätter zur Verbesserung der Frauen-Interessen* (Women's Life: Journal for the Improvement of Women's Interests), and *Österreichische Rundschau* (Austrian Review).[113] The daily press also reveals the influence of the association, both local and national.

Finally, annual reports are a valuable source too, mainly because Fickert and Kulka were not in the habit of papering over the association's failures. At the general meetings, they spoke openly of problems, including the conflicts that developed within the Austrian women's movement and within AöF.[114] They made no secret of the fact that almost every fiscal year of the association—which began in the fall and ended in May—came to a close with a deficit.[115] Moreover, we can consider the announcements and times of lectures, courses, and debate evenings as entirely authentic sources of information, as these disclosures served as invitations for members and those expressing an interest.

According to Hanna Hacker, the most successful period for AöF was that between 1900 and 1910, the year of Fickert's death.[116] Fickert and Rosa Mayreder made it public in January 1900 that they had left the editorial board of *Dokumente der Frauen* in October 1899 and that they were distancing themselves from any collaboration with Marie Lang.[117] I myself date the beginning of the upswing to 1902, as the establishment of *Neues Frauenleben* was a long-term guarantee of all-important publicity for AöF. According to the sources, the other high point for the association was the planning and implementation of the Heimhof. In addition to protecting and improving the living standards of women working as officials and attending university, the Heimhof constituted another attempt to settle the domestic servants issue.

After 1910, Kulka and her colleagues were only willing to continue along the line of attack set out by their instructor; they had no intention of deviating from the standard Fickert had set. As 1914 approached, they became ever more unequivocal in their support for the peace movement, and in the journal they reflected on Austria's chances in a war and the options for avoiding armed conflict. Fickert had in fact followed the activities of the peace movement ever since the creation of Österreichische Friedensgesellschaft (Austrian Society for Peace, Vienna, 1891–, since 1965, Suttner-Gesellschaft, Suttner Society), as she had personal connection with Bertha von Suttner, the organization's creator. Suttner even invited Fickert to the inaugural meeting of the group:

> "The inaugural meeting and the general meeting can only be held after the statutes have been accepted by the authorities. The registered preliminary meeting will be held on 28 January. I would be very glad if you and your close female associates might wish to attend. I will inform you of the choice of venue in good time. I would ask you to send me a list of their names and addresses of those ... whom I can add to the list of members."[118]

It is not sure, however, whether Fickert and her coworkers genuinely represented VLE at the event, as their association met on the very same day, as indicated by Fickert's words to Ottilie Turnau, later board member of AöF: "Above [can be read] Suttner's response to our letter of approval. I asked her to send the location of the preliminary meeting to your address as soon as possible, because we will have a general meeting (of the teacher's society) on 28 January."[119]

As the years passed, AöF increasingly focused its day-to-day activity on its human rights section. Alongside dealing with legal cases, from 1895 onward members provided an advisory service that was free for anyone to use; at the time, this was unique not only in Austria but also in Germany.[120] They held consultancy hours on a weekly basis in a number of different locations in Vienna, dealing with around fifteen hundred or two thousand legal cases a year.[121] And although the agitation for educational rights for women remained emphatic throughout, it lost much of its significance after Fickert's death. According to articles published in *Neues Frauenleben* and the petitions submitted by AöF, the attempt to thoroughly reform education did not succeed. They campaigned for the opening of schools to girls, the adjustment of the wages of female teachers, or their right to be married instead of trying to figure out the "root of the problems" or revise the imperial education law. In 1908, they raised their voices on two occasions in support of the opening of the university of law to women; three years later, they fought for the revocation of the ban on women teachers marrying—known at the time as "celibacy."[122]

They also gradually lost ground in their movement to extend the franchise and get around legal regulations. The most visible sign of this was the Frauenstimmrechtskomitee (Vienna, 1905–1918) established within BöF in 1905. On account of the law on associations, the organization was formed as a "committee." As its leader, they selected Ernestine Fürth (born 1847 in Prague and died 1946 in Washington, DC), who regularly published in *Neues Frauenleben*. In addition to playing a leading role in several Viennese women's associations, Fürth, who was of Jewish origin, helped found the Neuer Wiener Frauenclub (New Women Club of Vienna, Vienna, 1903–1938); she was also the editor of *Zeitschrift für Frauenstimmrecht* (Journal for Women's Suffrage, Vienna, 1911–1918).[123]

As the Frauenstimmrechtskomitee was connected to the International Woman Suffrage Alliance (IWSA) via BöF, and as AöF left BöF in 1906, its international contacts from 1906 to around the time of World War I stagnated. The antecedents to the conflicts between AöF and BöF could be traced back years, in fact, to when AöF joined BöF in 1902. At the founding of BöF on 5 May 1902, the first disagreements with AöF became visible. Fickert declared at this meeting that her organization would join BöF only if a representative of AöF were included on the board of BöF. She also published several lengthy articles in *Neues Frauenleben* criticizing BöF and Marianne Hainisch. According to Fickert, BöF remained too conservative and even apolitical. The tension between the two groups increased after the establishment of Beamtinnen-Sektion within the framework of AöF. In January 1906, with the announcement of the founding of the Reichsverein der Post- und Telegraphenmanipulantinnen und Posthilfsbeamtinnen (Reich Association of Postal and Telegraph Operators and Postal Assistants), cooperation between AöF and BöF grew increasingly problematic and rife with conflict, as each association claimed that it represented the interests of female post officers. This conflict ultimately led to AöF leaving BöF during its extraordinary general assembly on 31 March 1906, where questions and speeches had been planned in advance. This break was later interpreted as a split between a radical and a moderate wing of the bourgeois women's movement.[124]

This tendency did not affect Fickert's friendly relationships, especially her closest, the one she had developed with Maikki Friberg, one of the leaders of the international women's movement who was also active in IWSA. It is hard to deduce exactly when their friendship became so close, as Friberg's letters are mostly undated and Fickert's writings have not survived. But Friberg was the only person, other than Lang, who used the informal with Fickert, generally calling her "My Love."[125] Their communication, however, was not very practical in nature. After reporting everyday developments (like her lecture tours), Friberg would regularly ponder the big questions of life: "In spirit, I am so often with you, and I would like to worry together with you . . . dear Auguste, as we are both tortured animals. And it is questionable whether or not people will become better as a result."[126]

We can conclude from the letters that Friberg attempted to convince Fickert to travel away from Vienna, repeatedly tempting her with the notion of a trip to Finland, which she did in the end take place in 1909. She also thought it important for Fickert to avoid hiding from the world and to seek out new acquaintances: "The best thing you can do is a pleasant journey, to find new friends and connections. So please come away. Decide the day and the location where I can collect you. . . . Why can't you take on this trip instead of going to Semmering?"[127]

The best indicator of an association's influence and socioeconomic position is the capital at its disposal. Budgets—especially in the absence of further statistical data—can provide a measure of the response that an association generated. AöF's 1893 budget does not provide a satisfactory reference point, as this was only a partial year for the association, and the 1894 budget has not survived. The 1910 budget, meanwhile, is important primarily because the costliest work on the Heimhof took place that year. The government financed around 90 percent of the construction and fitting costs of a communal living space, and the association had to raise 30,000 crowns from private donations.[128] Fortunately, the association marked the smallest items of income and expenditure in their reports, and so the rows of data can be compared meaningfully.

In the course of 1895–1896, AöF's income was 705.28 gulden, which was less than Fickert's salary as a teacher in 1892.[129] And more than a third of this amount (276.54 gulden) had been carried over from the previous year. The most significant item of income was membership subscriptions, which, together with enrollment charges, made up 305.75 gulden. Then there were fees for courses (57.18 gulden) and donations sent, which at this stage were not very significant (25 gulden). There were receipts from brochures sold (6.31 gulden) and the amount remaining from returned membership cards (12 gulden).[130] Among expenditures, the largest item was the postage cost for invitation cards (94.60 gulden). It is no surprise that AöF soon stopped sending these cards: they asked their supporters to follow their program of events in the *Volksstimme* (People's Voice) or the daily newspapers. Lectures and academic courses ran to 64.36 gulden—that is to say, they made a loss—while the printing of documents cost 60.30 gulden. AöF spent 58.35 gulden on postage, and room rentals (15 gulden) and lighting costs (16.39 gulden) appeared among the outgoings. They spent 39.55 gulden on the upkeep of the library, 10.80 on bookbinding, and 8.75 on stationery.[131]

The financial circumstances of AöF became more stable as time went on, even if the association did not exactly witness a stampede of those wishing to become members. Membership requests, cancellations, and changes of address had to be reported not just to the secretary but also to the cashier, and cancellations were only accepted in the first quarter of the year.[132] To guarantee the trouble-free publication of *Neues Frauenleben*, whose deficit was growing every year, and, in line with the principles outlined in 1893, to keep subscription fees low, there was a pressing need for cost-cutting measures. All this is also relevant related to describing the financial circumstances of the association because in 1910, Otto von Springer's younger sister followed the example of her brother and left 30,000 crowns to the association.[133] The courses organized by the association, fewer and fewer of which were publicized, fell victim to the trimming of the budget.

According to the cashier's report for 1909–1910, AöF had 8,647.56 crowns at its disposal.[134] One crown was worth 0.50 gulden; in pre-1900 currency terms, its holdings in 1910 amounted to 17,295.12 gulden. In effect, the association increased its capital twenty-four-fold. But with the launching of *Neues Frauenleben* and with the construction works of the Heimhof, its costs also increased greatly. In 1910, membership fees brought in 1,144 crowns, meaning that the number of members stagnated since the 1890s at around three hundred. Temporary increases in membership were sometimes restrained and sometimes more dynamic. The foundation, bearing Auguste Fickert's name and established with the nurturing care of Emil Fickert, had soon after the death of the "Führerin" brought in revenues of 575.25 crowns, which gave cause for optimism. But we should not forget that Leopoldina Kulka and her coworkers set aside the money collected from donations from individuals (e.g., Rosa Mayreder and her husband, architect Karl Mayreder [born 1856 in Mauer and died 1935 in Vienna], or Julius Ofner) for the completion of the Heimhof and then for the support of the underprivileged women who lived in it.[135]

The largest item of income, 2,792.51 crowns, was generated by the sale of stocks and shares. On the other side of the balance sheet, AöF faced an ever-greater burden financing its periodical: by 1910, it was subsidizing it to the tune of 5,124 crowns. To this were added the members' subscription fees (552 crowns), which were due to the publisher. Thus, in 1910, AöF covered 5,676 crowns, or a full three-quarters (76.73 percent) of the publisher's budget of 7,397.53 crowns.[136]

It is evident that the association mobilized capital beyond its means to maintain its press presence. AöF spent relatively small amounts on organizing lectures and gatherings (167.84 crowns in 1910), and the receipts made no mention at all of joint travel or outings. The only exceptions to this were the visits to the Naturhistorisches Museum in Vienna, when the museum's director, who supported the ideas of the progressive women's movement, gave members a tour of the collection.[137] AöF did not arrange any community activities, which can be explained not only by a lack of funds but also by a shortage of enthusiasm or indeed by the social differences between the group's members. Fickert's correspondence indicates that every summer, the committee members would set off on tours of the Alps that lasted many weeks; she herself usually went on vacation with her mother or Ida Baumann.[138]

In 1909–1910, AöF spent 156.50 crowns on the organization of its library, the upkeep of its books, and subscriptions to various periodicals, as well as 88.70 crowns on printing and 25.56 crowns on official documents. They gave 50 crowns of support to the Vienna meat boycott; if not very intensively, they joined the battle against rising food prices.[139] On the basis of all this, it is possible to conclude that, aside from its publication, AöF was modestly represented in Viennese public life. The committee members must have been aware of this shortcoming, as they attempted to compensate for it in a number of areas: for example, with the courses held at the Arbeiterinnen-Bildungsverein by Fickert and her coworkers;[140] Mayreder's literary output, which could from time to time be linked to the association's activities before 1903; or indeed the lectures by Adele Gerber, Leopoldine Kulka, and initially Marie Lang.[141] The inauguration of the Heimhof is a good example of how AöF—if it had to pay a high price for this—could mobilize serious capital or use its influence over the Christian-Social city administration, which at the time was still dominated by Karl Lueger, and over the political party leaders.[142]

AöF's courses began in 1894 and, in line with the association's calendar, lasted from January to April, then September to December.[143] They focused on the development of a healthy lifestyle and physical fitness, as well as on the "social question" (*soziale Frage*) and care work.[144] Working with AöF, Dora Teleky, the eminent gynecologist and urologist, who was a pillar of the community involved with a whole list of specialist medical societies, held courses on anatomy. With these courses, the association had as its evident objective not so much polishing the intellect of its members or advancing their professional work so much as instilling in them the values of social care that Auguste Fickert was so keen to emphasize.[145] For the benefit of younger members, physical education and singing classes were held; the latter primarily gave them a change to learn folk songs and popular works by Mozart and Mendelssohn, from a contemporaneously "relatively famous Viennese female opera singer."[146]

As participation in these courses was almost always free, they, too, only generated further expense for AöF. Reports on the courses tend to dwell on the moral lessons to be drawn by the students. We do not have quantitative data on the numbers of those who took an active interest; at most, we have some mention of how "well-attended" the programs were: "dicht besucht" (densely attended), "gut besucht" (well attended), "sehr gut besucht" (very well attended), "viel besucht" (much attended), or "glänzend besucht" (brilliantly attended).[147] Fickert and her colleagues were delighted if sixty-five to eighty-five people turned up to the annual general meetings.[148] And as these were AöF's most prestigious events, it is unlikely that an average lecture evening could have drawn a crowd of more than thirty or forty. Lectures were, pragmatically, held by those in the broader social circle around AöF, probably because they did not have to be paid.[149] Neither could the association allow itself to invite women's movement leaders to Vienna from northern or western European countries. The greatest departure from convention for AöF was when, in fine weather, it held its events in the Türkenschanzpark of Vienna. Even in this, it did not manage to break out of its usual neighborhood—namely, the eighteenth and nineteenth districts of Vienna, where the Heimhof had its home.[150]

Finally, we must mention key aspects of AöF's press activity in the short decade after its creation. Before *Neues Frauenleben*, AöF was involved in the publication of a party journal and two association journals. Thanks to the network of contacts that Fickert had built up in Viennese political circles, the group found itself in the fortunate position of acquiring a publication outlet immediately after its inception. Initially, from 5 March 1893 to the summer of 1897, AöF published its news in *Volksstimme*, a Social Democratic journal only superficially aligned with the bourgeois-liberal women's movement. Fickert and the journal's proprietor, Ferdinand Kronawetter, laid out the details of this cooperation in an exchange of letters in January 1893. They outlined these details to the membership at the ceremonial inaugural meeting of AöF. By this stage, Kronawetter was a well-known left-wing politician who took his seat in the Reichsrat from 1885 to 1901 as a sworn enemy of Karl Lueger.[151] According to the agreement between Fickert and Kronawetter, the association received two or three pages of space in the weekly publication *Das Recht der Frau* (The Rights of Women). This provided a perfect training ground for Fickert to hone her editing skills. AöF did not have to provide anything in return for the column inches it received, although members probably did not receive the journal for free. In an 1897 report, Fickert complained that few members had taken out a subscription to *Volksstimme*. Aware that changes were taking place at the journal's editorial board and that AöF's column would no longer be published from the fall of 1897, she argued that AöF needed to create a periodical of its own, calling for "a paper that keeps readers up to date on key events in the women's movement both at home and abroad, and that publishes articles illuminating the various aspects of this movement."[152]

In the absence of financial sources, there was no question of AöF having its own periodical, let alone a weekly one: at the time, its annual revenue was a mere 1,419.27 gulden, a quarter of which was spent on entertainment costs. Precisely for this reason, Fickert considered it "exceptionally fortunate" that in 1897 they could enter into an agreement with the journal *Die Frauenbewegung*, published in Berlin.[153] It was the official organ of the relatively new Verband fortschrittlicher Frauenvereine (Organization of Progressive Women's Associations, VfF, Berlin, 1899–), which had been founded two years earlier by Minna Cauer (born 1841 in Freyenstein and died 1922 in Berlin), a member of the association's committee, who continued to publish it until 1919.[154]

This cooperation, too, was based on personal connections: Cauer had been corresponding with Fickert since 1894, and the two had a good working relationship. Even after Fickert's death, Cauer continued to send reports on the events of VfF, an alliance of Germany's more progressive women's organizations, to the editorial board of *Neues Frauenleben*.[155] The letters make no mention of the details of this joint publication enterprise, so we can only put the pieces together from the annual reports in 1897 and 1898. According to these, members did not have to pay to receive the journal; however, AöF committed to purchase three hundred copies every two weeks.[156] Because of this, they raised the annual membership fee from one gulden to three gulden.[157] The reports do not tell us anything about the practical questions, such as whether the association would be given a full column or how often members would submit articles on news of AöF and the Austrian women's movement.[158]

It soon became clear, however, that this cooperation was not crowned with success. At the general meeting in 1898, Fickert reported on the establishment of their own, stand-alone journal, pointing out the conditions for making it viable and the tasks it would involve: "The agreement made over the last association year with the publication Die Frauenbewegung from Berlin has been rescinded, and preparations have begun on establishing an organ of our own. This will appear in the first quarter of the forthcoming association year. . . . We need relentless propaganda to recruit followers and subscribers of the new journal, for it to have a sound financial foundation, and for it to be a useful accessory in the great battle with prejudice and the reaction of the ruling class."[159]

Cauer was happy to congratulate them on the new periodical, expressing her hope that the journals in Vienna and Berlin would complement one another in serving the women's cause. She did allude, though, to the difficulties inherent in such acts of cooperation stretching over country borders: "I am glad to hear that you have decided to set up a newspaper for those with an interest there. I always knew that it is impossible fully to represent the interests of another country, and I hope that the journals of our two organizations will complement each other in informing readers of how women's affairs are developing in our two countries."[160]

The first journal of the Austrian bourgeois women's movement was *Dokumente der Frauen*, which was published fortnightly. When it was founded, Marie Lang, as one of its editors and as the founder of the publishing company, emphasized that the periodical would represent the interests not only of AöF but also of all Viennese and Austrian progressive bourgeois women's groups.[161] The members of the editorial board, Fickert, Mayreder, and Lang, had begun collecting donations and publishing invitations to subscribers a year before the first issue came out.[162] Yet by March 1899, a mere 684.60 gulden had been collected for this purpose.[163] We do not know the total cost of publication per year, but AöF contributed 1,742.20 gulden toward that cost in 1899.[164]

In the introduction to the pilot issue (15 March 1899), the editors clearly explain the reason for the journal's title: "Irrespective of the directions and attitudes of the parties, it has to assist *women* by providing them independent, matter-of-fact, strictly fact-based proof—*documents*—on real-life circumstances."[165]

Fickert and her colleagues announced *Dokumente der Frauen* as the "mouthpiece for the interests of all working women (and men)," foreshadowing that "in its articles it [would] limit itself to questions of fact." But there are contradictions between these two statements. The press articles of the women's movement—with the exception of some brief stories published in newspapers—were not exactly famous for their objectivity at the time.[166] There is no chance that leading articles, journalistic columns, and internal articles had objectivity as their goal. This question can also be seen through the lens of the three editors, who all had extremely strong personalities and never refrained from publicly expressing their opinions.

I do not discuss the conflict that emerged between the three editors, as several researchers have done so before me;[167] they do not fail to mention Lang's fascination with Fickert, which was not without erotic elements and which turned into hatred. Because of irreconcilable differences, Fickert and Mayreder left the editorial team half a year after *Dokumente* was launched, as Fickert reported at the AöF annual general meeting. They continued to be credited as editors on the title page, and they even submitted their own articles for publication for a few

88 | Progressive Women's Movements

months, but Lang opened the year 1900 with the following announcement: "To the reader: at the end of last year, Miss Auguste Fickert and Mrs. Rosa Mayreder resigned from the publication of 'Dokumente.' Both remain employees at the journal, which I will continue to direct, in a similar direction and manner."[168]

At the same time, Lang left her post as AöF vice president.[169]

The publication of *Dokumente der Frauen* was not a great success, although it had 1,281 subscribers in 1899, according to Irmgard Sparholz's calculations.[170] Lang's limited experience as an editor may have played a role in this failure, as may a lack of readers, not to mention the fact that in 1900 the annual subscription fee was increased from four gulden (two crowns) to twelve crowns. This seems an unjustifiably high amount for a newspaper of sixteen to twenty-four pages, with no illustrations, especially if we compare it to the same twelve-crown subscription fee for the magazine *Wiener Mode* (Vienna Fashion, Vienna, 1888–1948; 1949–1955), which for decades was the most prestigious and attracted the most readers. Indeed, *Wiener Mode* reached its readers once a week, over about thirty-five to fifty pages, with more than fifteen hundred illustrations a year.[171] But not even this lack of success could deter Fickert and her colleagues: in 1900, they were already inviting donations for a new periodical (*Neues Frauenleben*). By the time this was launched in 1902, they had ten years' experience in publishing and editing work.[172]

AöF's objectives were far ahead of their time, but the association lacked the necessary means to achieve them. Without these means, its activism remained limited in certain areas. Its achievements, such as the creation of the Heimhof (the first centralized residential building in which a single kitchen replaced the kitchens in individual apartments) and their progress in the struggle for women's right to institutional education, were remarkable for the period and received the continued support of several politicians, including Julius Ofner and Ferdinand Kronawetter.

Membership

When it was founded, AöF had just over 200 members, and membership never went above 1000. Nevertheless, the influence of the organization was considerable, not only because of Auguste Fickert's determination and constant work but also because important representatives of the Viennese intellectual and artistic world were among its members. I offer below a short description of the most important members, followed by a discussion of conflicts within the association and the *Neues Frauenleben* editorial board that led to setbacks in its efforts to achieve its aims.

While many scholars have attempted to evaluate the size of the AöF membership, these estimates, with the exception of the data provided by Hilde Schmölzer, are not accurate. In her Rosa Mayreder monograph, Schmölzer mentions 5 founding members, 208 full (female) members, and 12 supporting (male)

The Austrian Association | 89

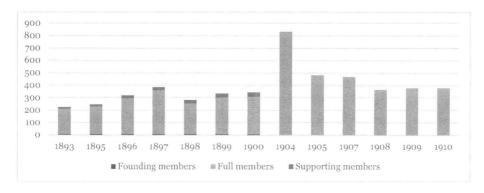

Figure 4.2. AöF's membership from 1893 to 1900 and from 1904 to 1910. Sources: *Tätigkeitsbericht 1893–1900, 1910; NFL 1904, 6, 16; 1905, 5, 18; 1907, 6, 23; 1908, 8; 1909, 9, 208.*

members, a total of 225 for 1893. Harriet Anderson writes of 207 full members, and Gabriella Hauch, citing a 1974 dissertation by Elisabeth Guschlbauer, assumes 208 founding members, which rose to 288 in 1897.[173] Elisabeth Malleier's figures are exaggerated: she claims the association was established by 250 women and 50 men.[174] These last numbers—the sources of which are not given—are improbably large even if Malleier has blurred the minutes of the inaugural meeting with the report of the first, partial association year. 85 women were present at the celebratory event, and by October, membership had grown to 250.[175] Other authors also provide approximate numbers: Hacker mentions a few hundred, and Lydia Jammernegg speaks of 200–300 members, but Jammernegg's writings do not tell us which period of the association's activity this refers to.[176] It is essential to reconstruct the operation of the associations in the course of longer processes, so I have outlined the development of membership numbers in figure 4.2.

The data for 1893–1900 come from the lists of names attached to the annual reports. They suggest that in the first stage of its operation, AöF did not appeal to more than 200 people, and it was only in 1896 that it gained more than 300 members. And there was a marked decline in 1898: 101 of the full members left the organization, dropping the total membership from 385 to 284.[177] These sizable fluctuations remained typical throughout, even though the number of supporting members continued to grow: it tripled from 1893 to 1900. Taken together with the 6 founding members, in 1900 they represented 13.8 percent of the membership. Anderson reckons with 300 members for 1900,[178] while the ledgers of names suggest a figure of 346. 46 members one way or the other made an enormous difference for a small association, if only because of the membership fees.

The growth in membership numbers was disappointing for Fickert too. At the general meeting in 1895, she attempted to compensate for the failed attempts at recruiting members by elaborating the credo for the next 23 years. She held that high membership levels could not be the right measure of success: "Our task is not to win members for ourselves at any price—quite the reverse. People have to reflect on their own nature and on the direction followed by the association, and only choose to join it if they are convinced that they are able to represent and support that direction."[179]

She also stated that the membership fee was far from the most important contribution made by new members: "The membership fee is the least that someone can do for the objectives of the association, while rights are the least that one can gain through membership of the association. Moral values are much more important . . . and the motivation developed through discussion with those of like or different mind is much more valuable than 'rights' can be."[180]

She emphasized the moral value of membership and the importance of taking part in activism and actively contributing to events, as this was how AöF could demonstrate its strength to the public. All of this is very principled, of course, but it did little to contribute to the financial foundations required for guaranteed operation.

No document from between 1900 and 1904 mentions membership numbers. The sources are also limited for the years that followed, but the items in the treasurer's reports up to 1910 allow for a quick calculation. From 1911 onward, we have no sources at all, and so we are left with many unanswered questions as to how membership numbers developed during World War I, or indeed the period after 1918. Neither does *Neues Frauenleben* offer us any pointers, but the fact that as late as 1918 Leopoldine Kulka still cited Fickert's 1893 speech on the membership suggests that there were never great crowds joining AöF.[181]

Let us now glance at how many joined AöF in 1910 and how many left. This is the result of a simple calculation: the annual cash records listed the membership subscriptions paid and the amount that AöF paid the publishing company to cover members' journal subscriptions. We can use these figures to deduce the number of members, even if we cannot divide the total between founding, full, and supporting members.

Why did AöF membership rise to more than 800 by 1904? Was this turn for the better the result of a consistent increase? Never had such a high sum (2,504.72 crowns) come in from membership fees before.[182] One possible explanation could be the Viennese membership of the Beamtinnen-Sektion, which operated for years as a subsidiary branch of AöF. The organization, with around 1,000 members, became independent in 1908 under the name Zentralverein der Postbeamtinnen.[183] We cannot yet include the youth section (Sektion-Jugend) of AöF to this calculation, as this was only established in 1906. It is also possible that part of the membership conducted its activism efforts within the framework of the BöF's Frauenstimmrechtskomitee as well. This hypothesis is supported by

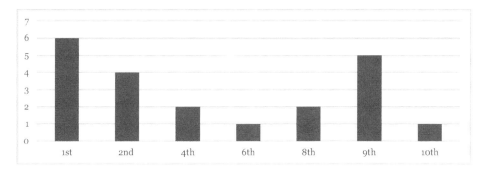

Figure 4.3. The distribution of supporting members of AöF living in Vienna in 1897, by district. Source: *Tätigkeitsbericht 1897*.

the presence of Olga Misař (born 1876 in Vienna and died 1950 in London)[184] and Marie Schwartz—who both had previously been on the AöF committee for many years—among the founding members and board members of Frauenstimmrechtskomitee.[185] The 1906 report of *Der Bund* (Union), the official organ of BöF, indicates that the separation between AöF and BöF also reduced the number of AöF members. At least 24 full members left the association, including Marianne Hainisch; Henriette Herzfelder (born 1865 in Brünn and died 1927 in Vienna), who became a leading member of BöF and the Frauenstimmrechtskomitee; Ernestine Fürth; Marie Lang; and Daisy Minor (1860–1927), who was later involved in editing *Der Bund*. They argued that AöF board did not understand the goals of BöF.[186] After the 1908 low point of 368 members, the membership appeared to stabilize at 380–381 members in 1909–1910.

To answer questions about AöF's social base, it is worth examining which parts of the city its Viennese membership hailed from. It is possible to compile such a list of figures from 1897 onward; before then, the ledger of names did not include the exact addresses of new members. After that time, for about 70 percent of the 283 members in Vienna, the ledgers show which district they were from. Figures 4.3 and 4.4 display the 21 supporting (male) members and the 262 full (female) members. In figures 4.3, 4.4, 4.5, and 4.6, districts one through nine represent the central area of Vienna.

In line with my hypotheses, all the male members, with one exception, lived in the center of Vienna. Six of them were from the most prosperous first district, four from the also central second district (Leopoldstadt), five from the ninth district, and two from the eighth district. One man gave a sixth-district address, and only one, an address in the more outlying tenth district. None of this is a surprise, as AöF evidently attempted to appeal to wealthier men, who might supply significant donations over and above the membership fee. The association had

92 | *Progressive Women's Movements*

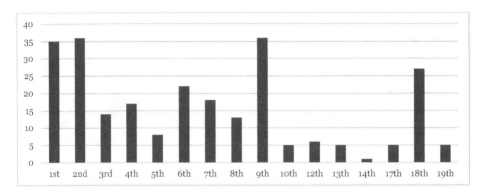

Figure 4.4. The distribution of full members of AöF living in Vienna (262 persons) in 1897, by district. Source: *Tätigkeitsbericht 1897*.

used this same strategy to try to win over the founding members, like Baron Otto von Springer, who from the outset financially helped to bring AöF to fruition.[187]

The distribution of the 262 female members is more complex. My preconceptions that women from ninth district (Alsergrund) and eighteenth district (Währing) would be overrepresented, as these were home to the association and most of its events, did not hold up: only 63 people came from these parts. A significant proportion of their fellow members (107 people, or 40.8 percent of the Viennese female membership) were not only from the center of the city but, as in the case of the men, from the first, second, and ninth districts. Only after this in the rankings do we find Währing, from which 27 women joined. A further 27 members, or little more than 10 percent of those from Vienna overall, came from one of the city's outskirts. Of these, 5 were from the tenth district (Favoriten), which at the turn of the century was considered Vienna's largest working-class district and in which in 1879 no more than 1.9 percent of girls went on to civic school. In the first district, this ratio was 63.3 percent.[188] 22 of the members lived in the sixth district, known as the general headquarters of Arbeiterinnen-Bildungsverein.[189]

For the sake of comparison, it is worth taking a look at the situation three years later. Figure 4.5 juxtaposes the data from 1897 and 1900, and the numbers of supporting members in Vienna doubled to thirty-six in this period.

Their distribution by district hardly changed over the three years, with 35 of the 36 in Vienna, mostly in the heart of the city. By this time, supporters came from a few even more outlying districts, of which the eleventh (Simmering), an industrial part of town, was the farthest from the center.

While supporting members came from twelve different districts, full members were based in sixteen. In 1900, 277 of the 304 female members provided a

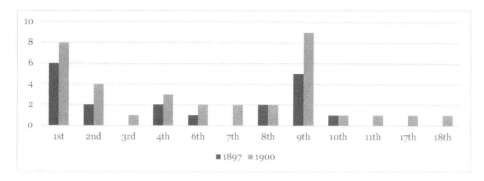

Figure 4.5. The distribution of supporting members of AöF living in Vienna in 1897 and 1900, by district. Sources: *Tätigkeitsbericht 1897, 1900*.

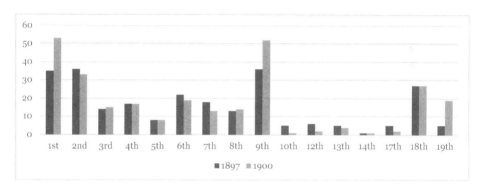

Figure 4.6. The distribution of full members of AöF living in Vienna in 1897 and 1900, by district. Sources: *Tätigkeitsbericht 1897, 1900*.

Viennese address; less than 9 percent lived in the provinces, in other regions of the monarchy, or farther afield. As before, most came from the first, second, and ninth districts, but there was also a significant proportion from the eighteenth.

In the years in question, almost 75 percent of members lived in the heart of Vienna. Alongside Währing, Döbling was home to the most members, as it was relatively close to the association's rooms and to the offices of the human rights organization, and it was here that Fickert lived and taught for a while (9 Schulgasse and then 45 Schulgasse). Indeed, in 1903–1904, the editorial staff of *Neues Frauenleben* operated at 43 Schulgasse, close to Fickert's home.[190] By that time, the proportion of members from Favoriten had declined. Not a single woman joined from the traditionally working-class, industrial areas of Simmering and Ottakring, so we can conclude that, by this stage, not even the human rights section of AöF could appeal to those working women who were in the most vulnerable circumstances.

This raises three questions. First, why did so few people join the association? Second, can the effectiveness of AöF have been affected—and, if so, to what degree—by members coming from different districts of Vienna and from different social classes and backgrounds? Third, what might explain the overrepresentation of women living in the center of the city? What may have motivated women traditionally seen as more conservative to join this radical group?

The answer to the first question is relatively simple, and I have already touched on it: the membership of AöF—which, relative to other progressive organizations, was not so small—did not rise any higher because its objectives were too radical. Thus it is pointless to compare its effectiveness with Social Democratic or Christian-Social women's organizations with thousands or even tens of thousands of members. Neither is comparison with more moderate bourgeois women's groups relevant. While the conservative organizations joining BöF imagined the improvement of women's circumstances as taking place within the family, adapting to existing party power relationships,[191] AöF espoused reformist views that overrode party politics, on the domestic servants and prostitution issues,[192] and not even the open-minded Vienna of the fin de siècle was really able to make these views its own. Yet alongside the misery of the maids, commercial sex really was an enormous social problem at the time: in the summer of 1896, a total of 2,400 prostitutes were registered in the city of 1.5 million, and some estimates suggest that the total of those unregistered may have been ten times higher. Meanwhile, Austria had no radical and progressive umbrella organization like VfF in Germany, which AöF could have joined. Although some of AöF's views were not far from those of the Social Democrats, because the association did not count as revolutionary, so by the second half of the 1890s, it had become distant from this movement too. Before 1895, Therese Schlesinger-Eckstein had made a number of attempts to integrate bourgeois-liberal and Social Democratic branches,[193] but Auguste Fickert rejected this out of hand, and Rosa Mayreder was deeply averse to the Social Democratic principles on account of how dogmatic they were.[194] Last but not least, with her divisive personality, anticlericalism, and possible antisemitism, Fickert was probably not well placed to attract a great number of Social Democratic devotees.

Harriet Anderson suggests an excellent starting point for answering the second and third questions. She indicates that the conflicts arising within AöF can be traced back to two factors: to the differences in the social backgrounds of the leaders and the members and to their varying interpretations of feminism.[195] All this certainly had an effect on the atmosphere surrounding the group and on the effectiveness of its activism. While a large part of the membership was unified by having grown up in the cultural ferment that was Vienna as it took its place on the world stage, their life experience, level of education, living circumstances, profession (if they had one), preferred leisure activities, and worldview were entirely heterogeneous.

How could we expect Therese Schlesinger-Eckstein, brought up by a liberal and highly educated father, and Rosa Mayreder, raised in a conservative family but taught Latin, Greek, and French alongside her brothers, to think about the issues of the subordination of women in the same way as Fickert, who first at a Bavarian convent school and then at a teacher training college had maintained her dream of becoming an actress?[196] Fickert never dreamed of not going to work; the same was true of her partner, Ida Baumann. Not to mention Marie Lang, who, although she never actually needed to earn a living, did live in constant financial insecurity after leaving her first husband, as the love of her life was still a student of law when they got married. The bankruptcy of *Dokumente der Frauen* further worsened her situation, which put her seriously in debt; she also had to deal with her son's suicide in 1904.[197] Lang's personal success was also cramped by her dictatorial nature, similar to Auguste Fickert's, because of which she attempted from the outset to dominate the editing of *Dokumente*. Mayreder's life, meanwhile, was made more difficult by her husband's worsening depression. Therese Schlesinger-Eckstein, for her part, was already a widow when she became a member of AöF. Furthermore, an infection caught during childbirth permanently damaged her health.[198]

The factors outlined above probably affected the effectiveness of AöF's success in the recruitment of new members and contributed to the failure within AöF's limited membership to establish collegiate and even friendly relationships. The vast majority of the AöF membership withdrew from any real contribution to its work; it was only the "most committed" leaders, and their family and friends, who made any particular effort. This personal network of connections was extended to include certain Viennese intellectuals, lawyers, politicians, artists, and sociologists. Rosa Mayreder joined, together with her husband and her sister, while sociologist-philosophers Rudolf Goldscheid (born 1870 in Vienna and died 1931 in Vienna) and Otto Neurath (born 1882 in Vienna and died 1945 in Oxford) also played an active role in AöF's work, as did their wives, Marie Goldscheid and Anna Schapire Neurath (born 1877 in Brody and died 1911 in Vienna). Fickert also tried to arouse her family's activist longings: her younger brother Emil, her younger sister Marianne, and her mother are all to be found on the membership lists. Of the members I have listed here, Rosa Mayreder, Otto Neurath, and his wife, Anna Schapire, as well as Rudolf Goldscheid, were all regular contributors to *Neues Frauenleben*.[199] Emil Fickert, who worked as a banker, undertook a more significant role in AöF after Fickert's death, and it was essentially limited to protecting the association's finances.

Figure 4.7. The membership of AöF, without Fickert. Leopoldine Kulka is seated in the front row, third from right. *Photograph by Josef Bopiel, 1904.*

At its inception, AöF selected four vice presidents: Ottilie Turnau and Marie Musill (born 1854 in Zagreb)—of whom, beyond their publications and association activities, nothing is known—as well as Fickert and Mayreder.[200] The position was held longest by Mayreder, whose family background gave her no firsthand experience of the grievances women had, in the workplace, for example. In an 1894 lecture on the subject of prostitution, however, she outdid and indeed stunned the majority of the AöF membership with her radicalism.[201] Her family, which did not approve of the extent of her devotion to the cause, as well as her conflicts with Lang and Fickert, made Mayreder retire from her leadership of the association in 1903 and devote all of her time to building her career as a writer.[202] Musill and Turnau filled the vice presidential positions since 1893. Fickert—whom Mayreder referred to as "a champion of morality"[203]—promoted from vice president to president in 1897. Soon, Mayreder left her position as vice president because she wanted to focus on her literary career. Due to these factors, there was a need to elect two new vice presidents. On this occasion, however, the only name put forward was Marie Lang, who would perform these duties for two years. She was then replaced by Marie von Dulemba, of whose career we know nothing. Given Fickert's type of leadership, though, it is logical that for altogether seven years, the group remained without a vice president around the turn of the century. In this period, the autocratic hand of the "Führerin" can also be felt in the newly launched journal, a state of affairs that would be nuanced after Leopoldine Kulka joined in 1904.[204]

The confusion that reigned over the AöF committee after Fickert's death can surely be linked to her exaggerated power. The 1910 election of vice president Sophie Regen (?–1918), who had led the legal aid section for sixteen years, also took place amid the power struggle that was underway due to the death of Fickert, and she lasted only for one year in that position. She did not take on another role, either before or after this one.[205] In 1911, Leopoldine Kulka became vice president, a position she would maintain until her death in 1920. Her management methods were a little different from those of her beloved Fickert: until 1914, she shared the role with Mathilde Hanzel-Hübner (born 1884 in Oberhollabrunn and died 1970 in Vienna), who also worked as a teacher and became a school principal in 1920. Afterward, Kulka shared it with the painter Marie Rosenthal (born 1869 in Lemberg and died 1942 in KZ Banjica,).[206]

Finally, let us glance at the generational differences between the women involved in running AöF, as around the time of Fickert's death a generational transition took place: with the exception of Adele Gerber, editor in chief of *Neues Frauenleben*, the women who joined the committee and the publishing house were born in the 1870s and 1880s. Christine Touaillon and Olga Misař, who would determine the content of the journal from 1910 onward, together with Emil Fickert, who would become invaluable with his financial advice and financial support, were members of the cohort of Schwimmer and her colleagues.[207] And they had five to ten fewer years' experience of organizing themselves than had Fickert and her associates.

The strength of AöF and the nature of its activism were thus significantly influenced by the size of its membership, its social composition, and the generational conflicts that increasingly created fault lines within the association. It is important, however, that throughout the existence of the association, the board was able to unite and act as one to achieve certain goals. The most striking evidence of this, alongside the uninterrupted publication of *Neues Frauenleben*, is the centralized household Heimhof and the fact that the association once again fought its way back into the international arena of the women's movement after 1914 and also took on important roles.

Changing International Embeddedness

It is difficult to study the social influence of women's associations, which holds true for AöF as well.[208] Such investigations are complicated: the measure of effectiveness cannot be based exclusively on the membership numbers or the copies of its publications printed or sold. It would be a mistake to base conclusions purely on the numbers of those participating in their events or visiting their libraries. To receive a more complex picture, it is vital to reconstruct the network of connections between (leading) members. Thus, in the discussion below, I examine the national and international network of connections of AöF, and more specifically those of Auguste Fickert. AöF's international network began to wither after it left BöF as a result of the two associations' conflict in 1906, and these tendencies became even more visible after Fickert's death. This process lasted until World War I, when the organizations started to take an active role in the national and international peace movement and thus reintegrated themselves into the international arena of women's movements.

A shortage of sources makes it difficult to ascertain the level of AöF's international connections. Daily newspapers can provide the first reference point: the *Aerbeiter-Zeitung* (Worker's Newspaper), the *Neue Freie Presse* (New Free Press, Vienna, 1864–1938), and the *Neuer Wiener Tagblatt* (New Gazette of Vienna, Vienna, 1867–1945) all regularly published the association's invitations, event programs, and general meeting dates. We can also read reports on these, but nowhere can we find information about the numbers present.

It surely seems to have been an overly ambitious and highly unrealistic objective in 1983 for Fickert and her committee to mark out the whole territory of Austria as covered by their association. The majority of the membership was from Vienna; the ledger of names lists few members from Germany, South Tyrol, the Czech Lands, or Hungary. In 1896, for example, of the 320 members, 293 (91.6 percent) were from the imperial capital, with a total of just 2 Hungarian women, 1 from Budapest and the other from the eastern Hungarian city Szolnok. The group could take pride in having 3 women from Munich, 1 from Dresden, 3 from Salzburg, 2 from Graz, and 1 each from Bad Ischl, Prague, and Corfu.[209] In the medium and longer term, this tendency meant that AöF failed to set up a single provincial branch; there is no sign that Fickert or any of the committee members visited any provincial centers with a view to promote activism or held any speeches beyond the boundaries of Vienna. For all this, the association's leaders placed importance on the propaganda circulated in the provinces every summer, with leaflets handed to those members heading off on vacation elsewhere in Austria.[210] As late as 1910, Fickert hoped the situation could improve, but not even her successors were able to put her plans into place.[211] In her last speech—having already warned her listeners against the "Christian-Social peril"—Fickert opined: "It is my opinion that a broad group of Austrian women who have hitherto not been affected by the notion of the women's movement, namely, women of Catholic convictions, should be able to join the movement."[212]

The appeal to smaller cities did not take place even after the peace movement made its presence felt, as after 1914 AöF still turned its attentions not to the provinces but rather to the international arena. As Gerber interprets it, the association publications served as a tool for propaganda in the provinces, even though I would argue that the members looked to it more as a source of revenue. They sought to use the royalty payments for the articles that ran in provincial papers to settle the deficit run up by the publishing company. This seems a rather brave plan, and there is no sign that any of the long, five-to-ten-page articles in *Neues Frauenleben* ever found their way into any publications outside the capital.[213] With the increase in printing and editing costs, from 1909 they fought even harder to find new subscribers, and, from time to time, they would harass the "friends of the journal" with requests along these lines: "We urgently request all our readers and friends to support our work by publicizing *Neues Frauenleben*. We have to break through both in Vienna and in the provinces, in town and in villages, at home and abroad. It is the responsibility of all those who love light and hate the darkness to do their utmost to acquire new readers."[214]

Before concluding that the effect of AöF's activities could be felt only in few districts of Vienna, we should look at how the organization joined in the activity of the international women's movement and how its foreign relationships progressed. Three periods can be distinguished in the dynamics of these relationships: the first stretches from AöF's foundation to its separation from BöF. Until 1910, it was almost exclusively connected to the international women's movement via Fickert herself. The primary focus of these advances—as we have seen with regard to her publications—was Germany.

Fickert enjoyed friendly relations with Auguste Schmidt and Louise Otto-Peters, considered the pioneers of the German women's movement, as well as with Marie Raschke (born 1850 in Gaffert and died 1935 in Berlin), who played a huge role in the establishment of legal rights for German women.[215] Fickert corresponded with the leadership of Deutscher Verband für Frauenstimmrecht (German Union for Women's Suffrage, VfF 1902–, Hamburg), Anita Augspurg (born 1857 in Verden and died 1943 in Zurich) and Minna Cauer.[216] Augspurg was from a family of lawyers in northern Germany and became known as one of her country's first female advocates. In 1902, she was involved in founding the VfF, together with Minna Cauer, who worked as a teacher, journalist, and editor; they also cooperated in organizing the IWSA congress in Berlin. On account of her Jewish heritage, Augspurg was forced to leave Germany with her life partner, Lida Gustava Heymann (born 1868 in Hamburg and died 1943 in Zurich), who also made vital contributions to the women's and peace movements. In 1933, they settled in Zurich after a journey disguised as just a visit.

After a series of family tragedies, Minna Cauer — who lost her two-year-old son and her first husband at almost the same time, and only a few years later, her second husband also died—devoted her life to the women's movement. She campaigned not only for women's right to vote but also for the protection of single mothers and freedom for women to choose a career, and so she soon became the face of the radical women's movement in Germany. Fickert acquired a good part of her journalistic and editorial experience with and from Cauer. Fickert also enjoyed good relations with the more moderate branch of the German bourgeois women's organizations: it was also vis-à-vis the association's press publications that she came into contact with Gertrud Bäumer (born 1873 in Hohenlimburg, today part of The Hague, and died 1954 in Gadderbaum), one of the key figures in the umbrella organization Bund deutscher Frauenvereine (BdF, Alliance of German Women's Associations, Berlin, 1894). Bäumer edited one of the movement's most important publications, *Die Frau* (The Woman, Berlin, 1893–1944). She also corresponded with Henriette Fürth; Marie Stritt (born 1855 in Segesvár and died 1928 in Dresden), president of BdF from 1899 to 1910; and leading Social Democratic politician Clara Zetkin (born 1857 in Königshain-Wiederau and died 1933 in Arkhangelsk oblast, Russia). She asked many of them to contribute articles to *Neues Frauenleben* and invited them to hold lectures.[217]

The other main direction for international connections was the countries of northern Europe, through Maikki Friberg. The importance of the Finnish model was felt in the content offered in *Neues Frauenleben*. Like other contemporary women's activists, Fickert was a devotee of Bjørnstjerne Bjørnson, with whom she came into contact through the association's publications. In letters exchanged in 1899, they discussed the German translation of one of Bjørnson's poems, and in 1902, they corresponded about an edited version of one of Bjørnson's speeches, destined for *Neues Frauenleben*.[218] Fickert also exchanged numerous letters with the Finnish women's rights activist Alexandra Gripenberg (born 1857 in Kurkijoki and died 1913 in Helsinki), with feminist writer Ellen Key (born 1849 in Västervik and died 1926 in Ödeshög), with the Swedish literary Nobel Prize winner Selma Lagerlöf (born 1858 in Mårbacka and died 1940 in Mårbacka), and with Aletta Jacobs, who spent some time in Vienna within the frames of a 1906 lecture tour.

If I am right in my hypothesis that Fickert failed to involve a single one of her coworkers in her international correspondence, then the almost complete lack of connections in the English-speaking world immediately becomes conspicuous. This cannot be put down to Fickert's language skills or lack thereof: among her letters, we find some written in English.[219] Rather, she had neither the fondness nor the opportunity to participate in foreign conferences and lengthy lecture tours—that is, to network.[220] When in June 1898 AöF was invited to take part in the abolitionist congress in London, Fickert sent Marie Lang in her place. Lang described her impressions of the London event to Fickert in writing.[221] Furthermore, Kulka participated in the IWSA congress in 1904, from which she sent reports to Vienna on a daily basis.[222]

By breaking off from BöF, AöF isolated itself from valuable foreign connections: after 1906 it had no formal link with either the International Council of Women (ICW) or the IWSA. This meant it would only learn of any news of the international movement from German coworkers or from press reports. *Neues Frauenleben* did publish reflections on these developments, so there was at least some indirect communication between AöF and international groups. In 1910, for example, AöF sent an open letter to ICW suggesting they make their joint voice heard in opposition to the Russian Empire's Finland policy, and in 1913 they addressed Emmeline Pankhurst, who had just been released from jail.[223]

Meanwhile, the correspondence of Martina G. Kramers (1863–1934), the editor of the IWSA's official journal *Ius Suffragii* (1906–1924), fails to put BöF's international connections in a positive light. Kramers repeatedly asked her Hungarian coworkers to relay news of the Austrian women's movement, as neither Marianne Hainisch nor Auguste Fickert had managed to do this. She wrote the following lines to Rosika Schwimmer during the breakup of AöF and BöF: "Please send me a newspaper again so I can know what the situation in Austria is. . . . You really are one of our best colleagues, as you have . . . sent me so many things about Austria and in such good time."[224]

She was not afraid to disparage Fickert's qualities as an editor,[225] and she said the following of *Neues Frauenleben*:

> "It is true that newspapers run by men do everything in their power to make us see that we have a need for our own women's press. But Neues Frauenleben does not much improve on this situation. Did the editor not read pages 34/35 of the [IWSA] Copenhagen [congress] report? I have not yet received anything from Fickert, but Aletta [Jacobs] has acquired enough [information] on Austria from [Henriette] Herzfelder."[226] Not even by 1914 did AöF manage to return itself to the international level of the movement. A considerable change in this occurred after the outbreak of war.

Before 1914, the personal contacts of the association's leaders and Fickert in particular determined the direction of AöF's efforts against the larger international backdrop, but after the outbreak of World War I, AöF emerged as an effective group in the international arena. The association built, of course, on the networks of contacts established by their late president, but the members of the board were more eager to expand their foreign contacts each year. The IWSA congress in Budapest in 1913, which was attended by the AöF leaders, including Leopoldine Kulka, played a prominent role in this process.

Passivity and Pacifism during World War I

One could easily form the impression that AöF was completely passive at the outbreak of World War I, as it did not take part in almost any relief activities coordinated by women's associations, especially between 1914 and 1916. Its pacifist aspirations, however, were actually more intense than before. Inside AöF, an intense and innovative pacifist movement emerged and obviated all activities intended to prevent economic and social collapse on the home front. The association also found its way back to international organizations and even played a leading role in the establishment of the Women's International League for Peace and Freedom (WILPF) in 1915.

The year 1914 redrew the map of the goals of the Austrian women's movement.[227] Harriet Anderson interprets it as "ironic" that in a moment the war bonded together the organizations in BöF's broader circle with the Social Democratic and Christian-Social groups.[228] Associations that had previously been "at war," taking every smallest opportunity to berate one another, now combined forces to prevent the "economic, social, and moral collapse" of their heartlands.[229] As early as the day on which war was declared on Serbia (27 July), Marianne Hainisch published an announcement in which she encouraged the women of Austria to join the assistance plans (*Frauenhilfsaktionen*): "Women of Austria, come together and work for those dearest to you; if we are not able to prevent war, then we can contribute to lessening some of the pain and horror. Let us stand by our men in Austria's honor!"[230]

The first wartime issue of *Neues Frauenleben* provides detailed information about these initiatives: the associations established a Zentralkomitee (central committee) with seventeen members "without regard to party affiliations."[231] Across the twenty-one districts of Vienna, this committee coordinated the welcome, provision of aid, and search for paid work for the dispossessed.[232] In the twenty-first district, a working committee was established to deal with labor exchange and advice; sewing workshops were set up here. Members of the committee attended to children left without a guardian, and "they provided financial support only in exceptional circumstances" for the needy.[233]

Its pacifism prevented AöF from actively taking part in almost any wartime work on the home front; mostly it passively observed events. In the face of wartime censorship, issues of *Neues Frauenleben* were increasingly predictable. Its articles downplayed the practical implications of the war for domestic life (labor exchange, childcare, training for unemployed women) in its treatment of problems on the home front or its coverage of the operation of the Nationaler Frauendienst, established by the initiative of the German bourgeois women's movement.[234] In addition, they published lengthy leading articles on the efforts of the international peace movement.

How could an association that, before 1914, emphasized the protection of the rights of working women and an increased awareness of social care adopt a position of almost complete passivity during the war years? How could *Neues Frauenleben* record the horrors of war with a distance almost typical of an outside observer? And, in general, why did Leopoldine Kulka and her coworkers appear to let slip any last shreds of pragmatism? In 1914, Auguste Fickert had been dead for four years, and Kulka's health continued to decline. Besides these circumstances, I have not managed to find any material in Vienna that would have provided a more detailed glimpse into the association's role during the war. In the mirror of this, we can only rely on articles published in newspapers and association journals and the references to Austria in the Hungarian press and archive material.

The explanation for AöF's attitude can be found in Auguste Fickert's intellectual legacy. She was an ardent pacifist, so her association declared similar views. From August 1914, Kulka and her associates were consistent in their communication to members and to readers of *Neues Frauenleben* that the war, which men had started, was meaningless and that the slaughter had to be stopped as soon as possible.[235] Within this scheme of things, even the assassination in Sarajevo only deserved a brief story in the July 1914 issue, in which the leading article was an excerpt from *Die Waffen nieder* by Bertha von Suttner, winner of the Nobel Peace Prize.[236]

When the war was declared, the relationship between AöF and BöF was even frostier than it had been, as the pages of *Neues Frauenleben* indicate. In point of fact, Kulka's said, "The majority of the membership are not well informed and have no clue about the objectives of the association; little is left apart from a corpse that with its dead weight makes every action so difficult that it ends up not feeling the life in its veins."[237]

While BöF's subsidiary groups made every effort to ease the wartime pain of those left at home, disillusionment took over among the ranks of AöF. Rosa Mayreder saw the war, and a few years later the collapse of the monarchy, as the bankruptcy of male dominance and patriarchal values.[238] Meanwhile, Christine Touaillon lost all her faith in normal ethical standards, noting, among other things, in the first days of the war, "In the world there is no such thing as culture."[239] Mayreder, also an earnest pacifist, considered not just the war but also her own homeland to be sick; not even in the euphoria of August 1914 did she believe Austria would prevail.[240]

AöF's last proper annual report was published in *Neues Frauenleben* in July 1914.[241] We only learn from this that the members of the board, alongside Touaillon, were Elsa Beer-Angerer, the teacher and Zionist activist Nadja Brodsky (born 1891 in Kostelec nad Černými lesy and died 1961 in Haifa),[242] Adele Gerber, who I mentioned several times in this chapter as editor in chief of *Neues Frauenleben*,[243] Toni Mark, the writer and journalist Mathilde Prager-Holm (born 1844 in Prague and died 1921 in Vienna),[244] Anitta Müller-Cohen (born 1890 in Vienna and died 1962 in Tel Aviv),[245] and the teacher Marianne Zycha (born 1874 in Vienna and died 1946 in Vienna).[246] Apart from their names and years of births and deaths, we have almost no biographical information about them. The 1916–1917 volume of the journal reports nothing about AöF's activity; it does not even mention the election of committee members. I think it unlikely that censors, who revised every issue of the periodical press during the war years, would have removed these details. They primarily deleted the provocative passages of articles relating to (mass) demonstrations, as well as those letters that members of the international women's and peace movements had sent to AöF. This is borne out by the fact that reports from BöF, Wiener Frauenerwerbverein (WFE), AdF, and the Schweizer Verband für Frauenstimmrecht (Swiss Association for Women's Suffrage), none of which had any closer working ties with Leopoldine Kulka and AöF, could be read in the journal in their entirety.

From 1916, the work of the legal rights section of the association was no longer presented to readers, who were, however, given details of the donations sent by Sektion Mutterschaftsversicherung, which had been operating under the auspices of AöF since 1914.[247] From time to time, the financial reports of the Auguste Fickert Stiftung also appeared in the publication. The foundation had only modest funds at its disposal: its balance sheet for 1915 notes income of a mere 332.17 crowns.[248] By 1917, the statements of Sektion Friedenspartei (Peace Party Section), the Austrian branch of WILPF established in The Hague, had become a regular feature.[249] This association was closely connected to AöF, as founding members and leaders were Elsa Beer-Angerer and Leopoldine Kulka. In 1920, this organization grew into WILPF's full Austrian subsidiary, called the Internationale Frauenliga für Frieden und Freiheit, österreichischer Zweig (International Women's League for Peace and Freedom, Austrian branch), led at that time by Yella Hertzka; it operated until 1938 and then again from 1948 to 1980.[250]

A sign of the passivity of AöF can be found in the writings published in Viennese and national newspapers, which mention only a few association lectures. The Arbeiter-Zeitung reported on a lecture given in Vienna by Lida Gustava Heymann, Neues Wiener Tagblatt covered the twenty-third annual congress of AöF, and Neue Freie Presse had an article on the foundation of the Friedenspartei.[251] Yet, in late 1915, articles in the Neue Freie Presse, the Reichspost (Imperial Post), and the Neues Wiener Tagblatt all made it clear that AöF had in principle put itself on the same platform as BöF, and indeed as many proletarian and Christian-Social women's societies. On 11 December 1915, they protested in a joint declaration against the military leadership's initiative to include a greater proportion of women in war work.[252] According to the signatories, this could only come to pass if the state were to offer services in return for the tasks the women undertook, in the form of crèches, maternal assistance, and health insurance. The article in Neues Frauenleben covering this proposal again voiced AöF's skepticism. AöF still did not believe that the war would bring equality for women in all areas of life: "There really is a tragic irony in the list of demands that decades of the women's movement had fought for now being satisfied by the war."[253]

We know of only two wartime aid programs that AöF contributed to: one was in January 1916, when Adele Gerber represented the association at the newly established Zentralstelle für weibliche Berufsberatung (Central Office for Female Career Counseling, Vienna, 1916–1936). In addition to newspapers, Gisela Urban (born 1871 in Teschen and died 1943 in Theresienstadt), vice president of BöF and editor of its official organ, *Der Bund*, reported the creation of this organization. Neither here nor with regard to the political demonstrations in the fall of 1918 does she mention AöF. She merely emphasizes its role relating to the peace movement.[254] Alongside members of AöF, VLE, and BöF, a number of Social Democratic and Christian-Social women's associations also joined the initiative. Among these groups, we find WFE, Katholische Frauenorganisationen für Niederösterreich (Catholic Women's Organizations for Lower Austria, Krems an der Donau and Vienna, 1907–1938), Österreichisches Frauenstimmrechtskomitee, Reichsorganisation der Hausfrauen (Austrian Women's Suffrage Committee, National Organization of Housewives, Vienna, 1910–1938), Sozialdemokratische Frauenorganisation (Social Democratic Women's Association, Vienna, 1898–1934, 1945–), Vereinigung der arbeitenden Frauen (Association of Working Women, Vienna, 1901–1938), Reichsverein der Postoffizienten (Imperial Association of Woman Post Office Workers, Vienna, 1905–?), Katholische Lehrerinnenorganisation (Catholic Women Teachers' Organization, Vienna, 1885–).[255] Alongside the groups based in Vienna, only a single organization can be found among the signatories that operated in the provinces for any of its existence. As, however, we cannot find a single article either in daily newspapers or in *Neues Frauenleben* that reports on the role of AöF in this operational committee, I am convinced that the association's involvement was nothing more than a formality.

In August 1914, the majority of the women's associations in Vienna put aside their differences in the interest of assisting those left behind at home (*Hinterbliebende*).[256] They also suspended their battle for women's right to vote—a struggle that would only return to the fore after the Russian Revolution in 1917.[257] Not even in this did AöF subscribe to the same position: from 1914 to 1917, *Neues Frauenleben* and lectures given by members continued to champion female suffrage.

In contrast to the German AdF, in January 1915 AöF welcomed a proposal from Anita Augspurg and Gustava Heymann for the women's groups of various countries to convene in Bern to (among other things) keep the international women's movement alive: "We heartily welcome these proposals, not merely as a sign that the suffragist organizations continue to observe their international obligations . . . but also for the reasons we lay out on the leader page of our journal. Despite limited expectations, it seems to us highly opportune for the international women's movement to join [an international organization] urging peace."[258]

In the light of this, can AöF be accused of ignoring its national obligations? I argue that within the association national feelings had lost nothing of their strength; the leadership simply did not wish—or did not dare—to deviate from the points of reference laid down by Fickert. Their willingness to confront the issue of women's frontline work is evidence of this. In 1916–1917, the association paid close attention to lectures given in Vienna by activists visiting from abroad, such as Glücklich Vilma and Lida Gustava Heymann.[259] It wished to use different measures to promote a speedy end to hostilities, however: at Kulka's suggestion, AöF became intensely involved in the international peace movement. While in this regard BöF increasingly turned its back on supranational initiatives and became ever more introspective, AöF more and more "became open to internationalism."[260] Although, apart from newspaper reports, we have only Rosika Schwimmer and Leopoldine Kulka's correspondence and Schwimmer's diary notes to prove this, it seems to me that AöF never opened up so intensively to the international women's and peace movements as in the years 1915 to 1918.[261]

From 18 April to 1 May 1915, six Austrian delegates, including Kulka, Marie Lang, Olga Misař, and Rosa Mayreder from AöF circles, participated in the WILPF congress in The Hague. Kulka only published the invitation to the congress in the pages of *Neues Frauenleben* in April 1915—immediately before it took place. Given this, it is a trifle strange that they encouraged private individuals, not just the association's delegates, to attend.[262]

Together with Elsa Beer-Angerer, Kulka founded the Sektion Friedenspartei within AöF in 1917, as it has been mentioned before. By this time, *Neues Frauenleben* regularly published letters addressed to AöF from foreign activists. From October 1914 onward, the publication also reported on Rosika Schwimmer's US lecture tour and the peace talks she held for the Central Allies.[263] In the same vein as these events, from early 1917 AöF organized a number of assemblies with the Social Democratic women's groups in the interest of a peace treaty being signed as soon as possible. It did so despite wartime regulations that restricted freedom of speech and banned public demonstrations. The number of demonstrations in Vienna grew rapidly, which can be put down not only to the famine, the domestic political crisis, and the untenable economy of shortage all seen in the winter of 1916–1917 but also to the increase in corruption. One of the largest demonstrations was held on 19 January 1918, at which every branch of the women's movement was represented.[264]

Overall, we can conclude that while BöF hurried to prove that women had "come of age" through its loyalty to the state and its participation in aid programs,

AöF meanwhile saw its opportunity to ensure the broadening of women's rights in its involvement with the international peace movement.

Questions and Problems: Fast Disbandment or Lengthy Agonizing?

In this sub-chapter, I challenge the contention found in the secondary literature according to which AöF rapidly collapsed and dissolved in 1919. I discuss the lengthy death throes of the association, which lasted until 1922 and which were certainly accelerated by the death of Leopoldine Kulka and by the fact that several leading members left AöF and either continued to pursue their work as activists in other associations or gave up activism entirely.

"The association is disbanded in 1919."[265] This is the only piece of information the Ariadne database provides those curious about the history of AöF after World War I. Lydia Jammernegg's survey shows only that after 1918 members continued their activities within the institutional framework of WILPF.[266] Gabriella Hauch is similarly succinct, but she does reveal that the women belonging to the potential base for AöF mostly favored the Social Democratic Workers' Party or the Communist Party.[267] Thus the literature tells us next to nothing about the disbandment of AöF, although it provides considerable detail about the political changes that took place in the fall of 1918, and indeed about the legislative amendments regulating the participation of women in politics.[268]

While in Hungary issues of *A Nő*, and until 1919 *Nők Lapja* and *Nőtisztviselők Lapja*, offer an insight into the everyday life of the movement after the war, in this regard *Neues Frauenleben* provides little in the way of clues. The April–May 1918 double issue of the journal, celebrating the twenty-fifth anniversary of the association's foundation, was to be its swan song.[269] Of the original 1893 leadership, by that time only Anna Frisch was still alive.[270] At this point in the research, I could not rely either on archive sources or on publications associated with AöF. As I did not find documents pertinent to the dissolution of the organization, even in the sources relating to Hungary, I brought further source material into my investigation. I also attempted logically to deduce the possible date of AöF's disbandment. Hanna Hacker's papers seemed to make 1919 a less likely answer, as she ambiguously suggested that the association drew further and further into the background, but made no reference to it suddenly disappearing after the war.[271]

At the end of World War I, the collapse of the monarchy in October 1918 and the accompanying radical political upheavals provided the occasion first for the revocation of the law on associations (on 30 October 1918) and then for the introduction of equal, direct, and secret voting rights for all citizens without any distinction based on gender for the electoral regulations of representative bodies at the parliamentary, state, and municipal levels (on 12 November 1918). How might these two newly introduced laws[272] and the temporary inclusion of female deputies in the Austrian national assembly[273] have contributed to the gradual disappearance of AöF from public life? It has been repeatedly argued that women's performance in the war caused such a revolutionary change in public opinion that the introduction of their suffrage could not be postponed.[274] While Marianne Hainisch saw the right to vote as the "well-deserved reward" for the bourgeois women's movement ("unsere große Errungenschaft"), Rosa Mayreder was not at all convinced it was a "reward" at all.[275] On the other hand, Social Democratic activists like Adelheid Popp rejoiced that, "now suddenly without struggle, without effort, without serious resistance being offered," women had been "freed from the ignominy of political lawlessness."[276]

Many of the former territories of the monarchy also introduced female suffrage at the time; for instance, Galicia, which became part of Poland, did so in 1918 and Czechoslovakia in 1920, after women there had already received equal municipal suffrage in 1919. In the Slovenian territories, which were united with Serbia and Croatia in the new Kingdom of Serbs, Croats, and Slovenes, this breakthrough was not achieved, although Slovenian Catholic politicians supported women's suffrage.[277]

Birgitta Bader-Zaar thought that the first participation by women in an Austrian election on 16 February 1919 was the prelude to a new stage of their legal emancipation.[278] If with considerable difficulty, a number of associations managed to redefine themselves in the flux of the years 1918–1919, so why was AöF incapable of doing so?[279] We know for certain, for example, that on 30 October 1918, the Frauenstimmrechtskomitee stated that it was an association operating with a political objective, changing its name to the Verein für Frauenstimmrecht (Association for Women's Suffrage). When women were given the franchise a mere two weeks later, it again altered its profile, and from then on, it came to be known as the Verband österreichischer Staatsbürgerinnen (Association of Austrian Woman Citizens) and espoused the educational rights of middle-class women.

Finally, some pointers in press reports make it possible (at least approximately) to reconstruct the process of the association's disbandment. According to the obituary of Leopoldine Kulka in the Arbeiter-Zeitung on 4 January 1920, "She was close friends with the unforgettable Auguste Fickert, and a founding member [of AöF] of which she remained the life and soul after the death of her dear friend."[280] As the author of the article did not mention the association's collapse, there were two ways to put the pieces of the puzzle together: one was Harriet Anderson's already much-quoted work. She undertook such thorough research in the Vienna archives in the early 1990s that she should also have found existing information about AöF's end.[281] And yet, despite her detailed discussion as to why the association was not fully able to make women aware of their situation,[282] she says nothing of any developments after 1918. In the end I turned to the association journals and newspapers distributed in Vienna. On the basis of articles in the Arbeiter-Zeitung, the *Der Bund*, the *Neue Freie Presse*, the *Neues Wiener Tagblatt*, and the *Zeitschrift für Frauenstimmrecht* (Journal for Women's Suffrage), we can exclude the possibility that AöF was disbanded in 1919. As late as September 1922, the *Allgemeiner Tiroler Anzeiger* (General Tyrolean Gazette) of Innsbruck (1907–1937) lists the association among the active, left-wing liberal groups. As there is no information about the group's activity for the two preceding years, however, I am more or less certain that the information the author, surely living in the provinces, received from the capital was out of date.[283]

I am still unable to provide a precise date for the disbandment of AöF. With the help of press sources, however, I can reconstruct the continued existence of the organization until about the end of the postwar interim period—until the acceptance of the law establishing the Austrian federal constitution (1 October 1920).[284] In the May 1918 issue of *Der Bund*, Gisela Urban, who earned her living exclusively as a journalist, reported on the general meeting celebrating twenty-five years of AöF, which eight years after Fickert's death was still "devoted" to the memory and intellectual heritage of the "Führerin."[285] This, among other things, indicates that until the fall of 1918, the membership was constantly pushing for the law on associations to be repealed, and in February 1919, it, together with many other groups, including the Ethische Gesellschaft (Ethical Society, Vienna, 1894–1938), again raised its voice against its sworn enemy for decades, the Christian-Socials.[286] In late September 1920, the Arbeiter-Zeitung published an announcement from the human rights section of AöF indicating that it still welcomed women for free legal advice on Fridays between 5:00 p.m. and 7:00 p.m. at 5 Keplerplatz (Favoriten), the address of the rooms the association had furnished soon after its foundation.[287] Even if in the course of 1918–1919 the limits of the association's activities had become more restricted, AöF simply must have continued to operate for some time after Leopoldine Kulka's death in January 1920.

Finally, given the spirit of AöF, I would like to mention an article also published by *Der Bund* in late 1918. In this, too, Urban reports on AöF's first public political meeting, held on 13 November 1918. Can it be a coincidence that this event occurred the day after universal, equal, and direct suffrage and the secret ballot were all extended to women? All we learn from the text here is that a large number of attendees crowded into the meeting hall. Those unable to fit inside eventually demanded that a second smaller meeting also be held. It hardly needs saying that the event was opened by Kulka, who was seriously ill by this time, and that in her words of greeting she cited Auguste Fickert.[288]

If the BöF journal is to be believed, AöF was not idle in the last days of 1918, and there was no reason for it to be dissolved. And we have no reason not to believe this information, given that BöF, after so many decades, was hardly interested in portraying AöF in an overly positive light. This is further borne out by a source that has recently emerged relating to the international women's movement: according to this, AöF was still in existence in the summer of 1920.[289] At the IWSA congress in Geneva held on 6–12 June, Lisa M. Goldmann was an official delegate of AöF.[290] Her name is not mentioned in the Austrian literature, but I managed to reconstruct some aspects of her life from the Rosika Schwimmer Papers. She corresponded with Schwimmer from the 1910s until the end of the 1920s. Schwimmer for her part assisted Goldmann's planned but finally never realized emigration to the US not just with advice but also with finances; in doing so, she may indirectly have played a role in AöF falling apart. Further research is needed, however, to resolve the problems arising from this information.

All in all, bearing in mind the temporal distribution of newspaper articles after 1918, there is no justification for speaking of the sudden disbandment of AöF; it is much more likely that the decline was a prolonged process. Kulka's death must have acted as a catalyst, as must the fact that the more active but also older (committee) members slowly retired from public roles or themselves came to the ends of their lives.[291] From the 1920s, the younger members of the organization dedicated their time and energies to other specialist associations. We find Dora Teleky, for example, among the founding members of the Organisation der Ärztinnen (Association of Women Doctors, Vienna, 1919–1938, 1945–), while Elise Richter, dealt with as a prominent member by the AöF leadership on account of her academic career as a university lecturer, joined the Verband der akademischer Frauen Österreichs (Association of Austrian Academic Women, Vienna, 1922–1938, 1947–).[292] The Social Democratic, feminist activists dedicated to the international women's movement, who previously would probably have become part of AöF, were from the early 1920s much more likely to join other specialist groups or the Social Democratic or Communist Parties.[293]

After 1914, inside AöF a highly intense and innovative pacifist movement emerged, one that obviated all activities intended to prevent economic and social collapse on the home front. However, the association was unable to redefine itself and its goals after the transitional period after World War I, and it lost its iconic leaders and slowly frayed and disbanded in the early 1920s.

5

The Hungarian Associations
Nőtisztviselők Országos Egyesülete and Feministák Egyesülete

IN THE DISCUSSION BELOW, I examine the work of the two most important Hungarian feminist associations, which were organized according to the ideas of the women's movement. Nőtisztviselők Országos Egyesülete (NOE) and Feministák Egyesülete (FE) were inseparable from 1904 to early 1915 and in some respects until the dissolution of NOE in 1919. This can be explained partly by the strong overlap between their leaders and memberships and their similar objectives. The most important person linking the two organizations was Rosika Schwimmer, who took on the leadership of first NOE and then FE.

The progressive women's movement in Hungary and in Budapest started to develop later than in Vienna. The work done by Allgemeiner österreichischer Frauenverein (AöF) in Vienna had a decisive influence on developments in Budapest through the indirect and direct contacts of the (leading) members of AöF, NOE, and FE. Thus, I argue that NOE and FE largely followed the path set by AöF in Vienna, but after a time, they began to adopt different strategies to achieve their goals. While studying the workings of NOE and FE and their place in the international context, I analyze the factors that allowed FE in some ways to catch up with AöF by 1914. I also examine the circumstances under which the 1913 International Woman Suffrage Alliance (IWSA) congress came to be held, contrary to expectations, in Budapest and not in Vienna. Furthermore, I discuss the characteristic features of wartime work of NOE and FE.

The Establishment of the Associations

In this chapter, I show that while a group of women office workers organized NOE as a spontaneous response to problems in their workplaces, FE was established largely as an international initiative. As I demonstrate, several women (and men) were actively involved in the founding and operation of both associations, and some were also involved in the activities of other women's organizations, sometimes linked to a completely different branch of the women's movement. However, this was quite normal at the time.

NOE begins its activity in 1896 in Budapest.[1] Mrs. Gizella Bíró, née Kaiser (born 1850 in Budapest and died 1930 in Budapest), the first qualified female teacher of stenography in Hungary, led the group.[2] We have already learned of the element of spontaneity in its formation: a smaller group of women attempted to elaborate meaningful responses to problems that had been around for decades—namely, the lack of vocational training for female office workers and their exploitation at the workplace—and that the state had failed to solve.[3] At the outset, Miksa Iritz, the executive secretary of the National Alliance of Private Office Workers (Magántisztviselők Országos Szövetsége, Budapest, 1893–?), also played a role, as revealed in the exasperated letters exchanged between him and Rosika Schwimmer, who at that time was also a key figure of the association. In one letter from 1900, Iritz wrote:

> I would like to fly forward on eagle's wings with the association's affairs, which at present are not carried along with wings of lead. I began organizing the office in March, and patiently waited more than two months, going to the association every day. Progress is great relative to previous results, but disproportionately limited relative to my efforts. I cannot watch for much longer as the carriage totters, endlessly needing to be pushed, now from the left, now from the right.... So from now on I will only go up to the association office on Thursday and Saturday evenings ... and if there is something to attend to.... But for the time being, until the situation changes, I ask you to be so kind as to call every day, so the office not be entirely without leadership.[4]

It should be mentioned that before 1900, the sources refer to the association by a number of different names but usually use Tisztviselőnők Országos Egyesülete (National Association of Office Worker Women) or Női Tisztviselők Országos Egyesülete (National Association of Female Office Workers). Later, the leaders of the association would insist on the consistent use of the NOE name.[5]

In the absence of a separate archival source, we have little information on the early stage of the association's operation. As to group's membership and activities, we find merely a few details among the association papers of FE and in the estate of Mrs. Oszkár Szirmay.[6] The Rosika Schwimmer Papers in New York does not reveal much more, despite the fact that Schwimmer was a member from

1897—from the age of twenty—then vice president from April 1899 and president from May 1901 to 1908. She submitted her resignation from the vice presidency in May 1900, but the society's committee did not accept it.[7] Her letters dated around this time offer a glimpse into NOE's activities that helped women find work: we see a "one-woman labor exchange" whose initial successes were entirely down to Schwimmer. In the short term, however, the growing workload was more than her energies could bear, and so, at a relatively young age, she learned to divide tasks among her colleagues.[8]

The amount of source material increases from the time that *A Nő és a Társadalom* was first published, and from 1915, *Nőtisztviselők Lapja* (The Journal of Women Office Workers) gives us a detailed picture of everyday life in NOE. Between 1901 and 1914, the association had only two presidents. Until May 1908, Schwimmer formally held this position, but in fact, from the year 1906–1907, it was primarily "Janka Grossmann directing the association's affairs, after [the] president was abroad for a prolonged period. . . . She visited a number of sister societies, like those in Vienna, Cologne, and Berlin, all of which [they] were already in constant friendly contact with."[9] Schwimmer must have been nudged to give up her position in NOE both by her growing number of foreign trips and by her work for FE and *A Nő és a Társadalom*. Henceforth, she was only a board member.[10] After she resigned, no new president was nominated in 1908; that year, the organization was run by vice presidents Janka Grossmann (1881–1954), who around 1910 Magyarized her surname to Gergely, which I will insist on in this chapter, and Paula Pogány. By May 1909, Gergely had filled the position of president, a role she retained until 1914.[11] Naturally, both women made their living as office workers; they boosted their wages with the honoraria they received for their articles published in the joint journals of FE and NOE.

Those participating at the April 1908 general assembly witnessed the following small-scale public shenanigans:

> As Rosika Schwimmer did not nominate herself for the position of president, the board has proposed to the assembly that out of respect for the departing president the position of president not be filled in this year. Despite this, the assembly did elect Miss Schwimmer as president, but she did not accept the decision. She also objected to the proposal from Gizella Szenczy and Nelly Schnurr [sic] [a member of the board of NOE] that she be elected as honorary president. Miss Schwimmer explained at length that our association must not follow the path of handing out vacuous titles, until the assembly ultimately took on her view as its own.[12]

While the literature generally says little regarding NOE,[13] it is rather more forthcoming as to the origins of FE. According to Eszter Kaba, FE came into being in late November or early December 1904 as the fourteenth women's association in the Hungarian capital and as the direct Hungarian subsidiary of IWSA.[14]

There is no universal agreement regarding dates here either: citing various Budapest press sources, Judit Acsády dates the foundation to 14 December 1904, while Susan Zimmermann says it took place in December 1904 or January 1905.[15] Meanwhile, on 4 December 1904, Auguszta Rosenberg (1859–1946), vice president of the Hungarian bourgeois women's associations' umbrella organization Magyarországi Nőegyesületek Szövetsége (MNSz, Alliance of Hungarian Women's Associations), had already congratulated Schwimmer on the founding of FE.

She also foreshadowed the challenges the association would face: "I am only now able to thank you for your kind announcement of the association of feminists. I think that with time it will really fill a niche. . . . I say 'with time,' as at the moment no one really understands that niche: as such [society] is uninterested in the necessity of the movement, just as it is little interested in all forms of social issue."[16]

On the circumstances of the foundation of FE, I highlight one element typical of Schwimmer. From the outset, she wanted to see Vilma Glücklich as executive president but knew that she would probably not accept the nomination. To avert this refusal, she organized the first committee meeting in December so that Glücklich's school obligations would prevent her attending. In this way, the experienced teacher was chosen as their leader behind her back. Of course, she did not take this lying down: instead of sending Christmas greetings, she wrote an outraged letter informing them that she was unsuitable for the role. Not even Glücklich's mother approved by this stage of her association work, as in the first days of 1905 she surprised Schwimmer with the following New Year's greetings: "Mrs. Ignác Glücklich, widow, greatly regrets that her daughter finds no better betrothal than that to lunatics like you, and wishes more sensible thinking for the new year."[17]

In the end, Glücklich only left her presidential position when her otherwise secret terminal condition became worse in the spring of 1927, though, even before 1918, she had announced her intention to retire at just about every board election.[18] In 1908, "she consider[ed] the inclusion of fresh blood, and a separation of ideas from personalities in the eyes of the public, as in the interests of the cause." In 1911, a conflict of opinions led her to request that "the board make use of this symptom of difference of opinion to nominate a new director."[19] In 1910, she would have been happy to see either Schwimmer or Countess György Haller, a new recruit to FE with the social prestige of her aristocratic background, in the role of president.[20] Both women refused the nomination, however; the latter even emphasized that she "[did] not accept any kind of official role as a matter of principle."[21] Finally, in 1918, Glücklich wished to retire because of an escalating conflict with Mrs. Szirmay.

> If further proof was ever needed that I am not cut out for leadership, it is provided by this insistently disapproving attitude that you displayed to the steps I took in your absence; it did not cross your mind that there might be rational

reasons or extenuating circumstances that you could wait to be provided; neither did you stop to think that I exclusively and ruthlessly defended the interests of the cause, even at my own expense; you simply brought judgment upon me without hearing me out. One only does such a thing to a leader whose motivations and good intentions one does not fully trust.[22]

As for IWSA, at first Aletta Jacobs and the organization's president, Carrie Chapman Catt (born 1859 in Ripon and died 1947 in New Rochelle), were surprised that Schwimmer was not elected president of FE. Catt sent the following lines to Schwimmer after receiving official information about FE's creation from Glücklich:

> I am delighted to learn that the Hungarian Association has consented to become auxiliary to the International Alliance. We are glad to welcome it. I shall write a letter at once in reply to the official one which I have received from the secretary of the President. One thing puzzles me greatly. At the head of the letter is the name 'Glücklich Vilma' but then the name is signed Vilma Glücklich as President. I do wonder why this is so.[23]

The much friendlier response from Jacobs at least revealed that Glücklich had made a positive impression on the IWSA leadership.

> Of course I remember Vilma Glücklich—she is not the sort . . . one might ever forget. She made a very good impression. She sent me the printed matter, but I cannot read them, as they are all in Hungarian.[24]

After these initial difficulties, the mild-mannered, hardworking Glücklich, who apart from Hungarian also spoke fluent German, English, French, and Italian and who, as an unmarried woman, dedicated her entire life to her calling as a teacher and to social activism, soon became a valued figure in the international women's movement. Her personal and work relationship with Schwimmer, who was president of FE's Political Committee, was an excellent one that developed into a lifelong friendship. The first written evidence of their cooperation is from 1901, when Glücklich, citing ill health, returned a ticket for a ball.[25]

The torrent of messages that survive indicates that a collegial and even friendly relationship developed between the members of NOE and FE.[26] Schwimmer, Janka Gergely, and Glücklich—all from Jewish families—joined their associations at a young age. Of the three, Glücklich was the most disciplined. Gergely and the other pillar of the FE board, Szidónia Willhelm, who also worked as an official, both had rhapsodic temperaments. Schwimmer's younger years, meanwhile, were embittered by the conflicts caused by her eccentric character, her melancholy, the morphine addiction she developed after moving to Budapest, and the alcohol problems that emerged in some of her darker periods. As early as 1897, when briefly moving back to Temesvár, she wrote her will and also designed her own gravestone, with meticulous detail and impressive draftsmanship.[27]

Descriptions from her childhood friends hint at Schwimmer's emotionally volatile personality, and throughout her life, she was thirsty for recognition.[28]

The four childless and unmarried women spent a great amount of time together even outside the NOE and FE events, and they continued their correspondence when they were far apart. Aside from the "cause," constant themes included their state of health, that of their parents, and the subjects of Schwimmer's lecture tours. Alongside these obligations, they were also quite partial to a bit of discreet gossip. Initially, Auguszta Rosenberg and MNSz, which she led, were the focus of this gossip, which then turned to the leaders of the foreign women's movement and, of course, politicians. As an example, an entirely typical letter written by Glücklich and Gergely tells Schwimmer of the already well-established German activist Käthe Schirmacher's 1906 Budapest lecture, surely bringing a smile to her face.

> Dear Schwimmer! [Szidónia] Willhelm says that you will be most forlorn if I write with a pencil, but to get my pen I would have to take at least 20 steps, and God save me from that. . . . Just for a change, Willhelm is ill. Sore throat and all that. Yesterday evening we had a meeting. Really stupid and boring. Grossi [Janka Gergely].

Vilma Glücklich's lines follow on the same letter paper:

> I hope you got my letter sent to you . . . in Bremen; I cannot write it again, struggling as I am with this miserable cold. [Käthe] Schirmacher made a grand fool of herself . . . Captain [Adele] Schreiber [one of the leaders of Bund deutscher Frauenvereine, a founder of the also German Bund für Mutterschutz [Federation for Maternity Protection], and the editor of the journal Die Staatsbürgerin], then at [Auguszta] Rosenberg's there was tea, in a small, boring company; Mrs. Perczel [Flóra Kozma, born 1864 in Baracska and died 1925 in Budapest, a member of the FE board and a prominent activist of the Christian-Social women's organization] is a blockhead, but is making good progress, and right now is reading literature on abolition instead of me. . . . Mrs. Meller [Eugénia Miskolczy, born 1872 in Budapest and died 1944 in Auschwitz, also a member of FE board and then president] is very eager, and [Paula] Pogány will hopefully bring a little order, as I am utterly lazy and always tired. Vilma.[29]

Not even the challenges the organization of the IWSA congress in 1913 posed for the FE board could sour the relationship between Glücklich and Schwimmer. Meanwhile, the cheery atmosphere in the association's offices and at the easygoing summer gatherings surely had a positive influence on the members' attitudes. The effect of all this could also be felt in the numbers of new members.

Until January 1914, Schwimmer and Glücklich exchanged messages on the various administrative affairs of the association on an almost daily basis, whether they happened to be in Budapest or not. It is clear from their letters and postcards that Schwimmer's volatile personality—which would soon become the "face of the movement"[30]—was perfectly offset by Glücklich's calm, considered manner. Their correspondence became less regular after the outbreak of World War I but did not die out. The lines they wrote, however formal, were distinctly affectionate, and their tone was full of concern for the other. They lacked that faux gloss that gleamed from the communication between Auguste Fickert and her Austrian colleagues. After 1914, most of Glücklich's letters outline FE's wartime work, often asking for Schwimmer's opinion on contentious issues.[31]

Main Protagonists of the Organization: Rosika Schwimmer and Vilma Glücklich

The central protagonist of the narrative I am presenting, alongside Auguste Fickert, is Rosika Schwimmer. Unlike Fickert, Schwimmer became a key figure in the international women's and peace movements as the press secretary of the IWSA and a contributor to the founding of the Women's International League for Peace and Freedom (WILPF). In November 1918, she even stepped onto the international political stage when the government of Count Mihály Károlyi made her Hungarian envoy to Switzerland. As an immigrant to the US, she was awarded the World Peace Prize in 1937 in recognition of her work, and she was nominated for the Nobel Peace Prize in 1949. Thus, to put FE's efforts and accomplishments in a larger context, we must examine the most important turning points in her life and her work as an activist, not only in the pre-1918 period but also during the years she spent as an émigré in Vienna and the US.

Rosika Schwimmer, a now mostly forgotten leader of the Hungarian and the international women's movements before 1918, was born on 11 September 1877 to a nonobservant Jewish family in Budapest.[32] After the failure of her father's business, her parents moved to Temesvár with her and her younger sister, Franciska (1880–1963), and younger brother, Béla. We get a picture of young Schwimmer's personality from the letters she exchanged with her childhood friend from Temesvár, mentioned above, and with Aletta Jacobs (born 1854 in Sappemeer and died 1929 in Baarn), a leader of the Dutch women's movement and later mentor and friend to Schwimmer. Jacobs once reflected on Schwimmer's morphine addiction,[33] and on another occasion, her sexual orientation was the subject of discussion: "I would be glad if one fine day you would report that you had found a good boyfriend, and only after that would you have to tell me whether, in a sexual sense, you are normal or abnormal. You don't have to consider marriage for a long time, but you could, and indeed should, take a lover."[34]

The young Schwimmer, who struggled to find her place in the world and who often had suicidal thoughts, made a home for herself in Budapest in the mid-1890s. She initially earned her living as a governess, which seemed to her a favorable state of affairs, as her employers provided her board and lodging in the capital, which even at this time appeared prohibitively expensive compared to the provinces. After what must have been a romantic disappointment (with a man), Schwimmer gravitated toward a career as a woman office worker, one that, with Budapest's economic boom, a growing number of women were opting for. At that time, she and her coworkers in the associations, first within the framework of NOE and then within that of FE, placed the Hungarian women's movement on a new foundation. Indeed, she even participated in the founding of the Social Democratic Hungarian Working Women's Association (Magyarországi Munkásnő Egyesület), corresponding for a few years with its president, Mariska Gárdos, before their relationship deteriorated to the point where they made fun of each other in their associations' newspapers.[35]

Schwimmer and her coworkers at NOE and FE were associated with no less an achievement than the creation of the modern women's movement and the spreading of its innovative ideas first in Budapest and then in provincial cities in Hungary. Her closest associates, in addition to coordinating the everyday affairs of NOE and FE, also supported Schwimmer in building her international career over a number of decades. Vilma Glücklich noted, half joking, in late 1906, "What an international star of a lady you will become."[36] With this, Glücklich was referring to the guile with which her colleague, still in her twenties or thirties, was establishing connections within the international network of the women's movement. Thanks to her journalistic vein, her astonishing motivation, and her excellent capacity for languages, Schwimmer was already in the early 1900s publishing articles in eminent Austrian and German journals. She used her journalistic work to establish close friendly connections with, among others, the leaders of the women's organizations in Holland and the US. This form of building one's career was not at all unknown in this period, as the development of women's journalism went, in Austria and Hungary as in Western countries, hand in hand with the expansion of the women's movement.[37]

Of the editors of and contributors to Hungarian feminist journals, Schwimmer was the first to publish not just at home but also internationally,[38] and from the mid-1900s, she was able to survive entirely on her income as a journalist and from her annual lecture tours.[39] Her first attempts to test her journalistic skills appeared in the Austrian journal *Frauenleben*, which was also followed by women's organizations outside the monarchy.[40] NOE and particularly FE profited greatly from the results of her distinctly intentional building of her international career. Even the leaders of IWSA proved to be open to her innovative insights: the organization had its badge and brooch made at Schwimmer's initiative, and it was she who suggested the publication of its official record, *Ius Suffragii*, in 1906.[41]

After the founding of FE, Schwimmer spent most of her time, apart from her duties on *A Nő és a Társadalom*, on her lecture tours of western and northern Europe and on women's congresses. A contract proposal detailing her tasks as

Figure 5.1. Portrait of Rosika Schwimmer. Atria Institute, Amsterdam.

editor of *A Nő és a Társadalom* dates back to late 1906.[42] Glücklich considered it to be reasonable; Paula Pogány strongly objected to its fixed time period, the commission for two years. At the last annual board meeting, the proposal was finally modified to include an indefinite commission, and this was accepted in late December.[43]

Of course, Schwimmer was not always present when the issues of *A Nő és a Társadalom* were in preparation. In the summer of 1907, for example, she coordinated the editing work from Strasbourg, remaining in constant contact with Vilma Glücklich, Janka Gergely, and Janka Dirnfeld, the secretary of FE. In these letters, Glücklich jokingly called Schwimmer "Respected Editor." Being a schoolteacher, Glücklich performed her duties both for the association and for the journal during school breaks. From the outset, she made great efforts to prepare the journal for publication.

FE, meanwhile, was less inclined to trust Glücklich to balance the books, and so this task fell to Schwimmer. Over the years, Schwimmer was repeatedly forced to turn to IWSA, or to Aletta Jacobs in person, for loans. Her efforts were not usually rewarded with success.[44] In addition to selling *A Nő és a Társadalom*, the FE tried to support itself with various donations; this was also in line with the practice in the AöF. Even so, we find only one reference, from December 1909, to the financial situation of the journal "turning for the better": at that time, they only owed the publishing company the price of a single copy.[45]

Schwimmer's doubts as to her sexual orientation seemed to be put to rest for a while by her marriage in 1911 to journalist Béla Bédy. After two years, however, the couple decided to divorce. As her sister Franciska Schwimmer, together with her secretary, Edith Wynner, carefully removed Bédy's letters from the correspondence, we can only guess the reasons for the divorce. It may have been a product of Schwimmer's tempestuous nature or her constant foreign travel.

It is surely thanks to Schwimmer's network of contacts that in 1913 Budapest became home to IWSA's seventh congress. This event, which reinforced FE's convergence with Western organizations, put Schwimmer into the limelight for a prolonged period, as she was elected one of the leaders of IWSA (its press secretary). She filled this post from January 1914 in London, which did not prevent her from following the work of her colleagues back in Budapest from a distance.[46]

After her move to London, Schwimmer handed her editorial tasks at *A Nő* over to Mrs. Sándor Teleki and to Paula Pogány. Schwimmer herself remained editor in chief at the new journal. No draft contract similar to the one from 1906 but covering the responsibilities and rewards of the journal's direct employees has survived. We do know, however, that FE board member Adél Spády, employed by the committee to run the publishing company from 1 January 1914, received "monthly 200 K pay and 100 K for lodgings." This added up to 3,600 crowns a year, and we can infer that Mrs. Sándor Teleki may have had, and Paula Pogány probably had, pay packages in excess of this.[47] The sources indicate that Schwimmer really did step back for a while from coordinating the everyday affairs of the association and from publishing its journal. In 1915–1916, she was only listed as the author of one or two articles in the publication.

In response to the outbreak of war, Schwimmer's pacifist views were rekindled even more markedly. After the mobilization, she gave up her leading role in IWSA at once and put all her contacts, in Europe and in the US, to use in the interests of declaring a peace treaty as early as possible.[48] In addition to the Peace Ship financed by US magnate Henry Ford (born 1863 in Springwells Township, Michigan, and died 1947 in Dearborn, Michigan), Schwimmer held talks in many countries, representing IWSA and then, in 1917–1918, the left-wing Hungarian

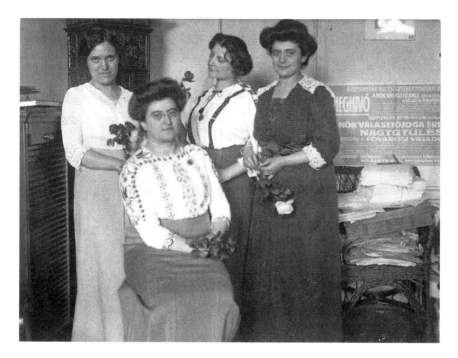

Figure 5.2. Group photograph with the invitation to the IWSA congress in the background. *Left to right:* Paula Pogány, Rosika Schwimmer, Janka Dirnfeld, and Franciska Schwimmer. Schwimmer-Lloyd Collection, The New York Public Library.

political grouping led by Mihály Károlyi. She sent warm, affectionate letters to her coworkers back in Hungary, reporting on her achievements or rather the lack of them. This is what she was doing on 4 December 1915, when the Ford Peace Ship (*Oscar II*), with her and members of the US elite on board, left New York harbor—and indeed when, a few months later, the mission proved to be a complete failure. Afterward, Schwimmer returned home to Hungary and "again [took] on the editorial tasks at *A Nő*, but [was] not willing to accept the fee due her for this. [The] association [saw] it as its obligation to honor her highly significant efforts not merely with moral recognition."[49]

In the light of all this, Dagmar Wernitznig was obviously wrong to speak of Schwimmer's increasing isolation from 1914 onward, in terms of her positions in the Hungarian and international women's movements.[50] They corresponded even after Schwimmer left Hungary in January 1920 first for Austria and when she immigrated to the United States in 1921. Until 1939, Schwimmer regularly exchanged letters, in English, with FE board member Eugénia Meller, née Miskolczy. They informed each other in detail about news of the movement, their everyday lives, and the ever-worsening atrocities inflicted on Jews. In 1939, after a comprehensive description of the state of her health, Schwimmer writes that, despite her diabetes and her coughing fits, she was regularly pleased to receive sizable packages of desserts and cigarettes from Mrs. Meller and from Janka Dirnfeld.[51] Much more important was what Schwimmer requested from Mrs. Meller in early February of that year:

> "And now I have a very important request both to you and to the Fem [FE]. Will you please get all your archives and the Fem[inist]. archives expertly packed and shipped to me to New York. If Vilma's [Glücklich] papers are available, please send those too. Don't weed out anything. Nothing is unimportant. I will take care of the expenses as soon as you let me know. And please attend to it without delay."[52]

Schwimmer was asking for this material—of which she was only to receive one box's worth—for the women's movement archive she had established in 1935 with Mary Ritter Beard.[53] After this, the most important subject in their correspondence was to arrange for Mrs. Meller, a Jew, to escape from Hungary.[54]

After the end of World War I the government of Mihály Károlyi in Hungary sent Schwimmer on a diplomatic mission to Switzerland, making her the world's first ever female envoy, albeit one with no accreditation. She performed this role in 1918–1919 in Bern, but, despite her broad network of contacts, she, as a woman, was unable to deliver on Károlyi's expectations of her. In the end, she was forced to resign her position in the last days of 1918. This short-lived Bern mission—from which Schwimmer would return to Hungary in the last days before the Hungarian Soviet Republic was announced at the end of February 1919—would cast a shadow over her entire life. In January 1920, with the help of a friend of the family, who is not named in the sources, Schwimmer escaped to Vienna under the pseudonym Ilona Kovács.[55] She continued her emigration into the first half of 1921; then, after traveling through Rotterdam, she stepped onto US soil in the first days of September by entering Ellis Island in New York, the location of the federal immigration checkpoint for immigrants from southern and eastern Europe.[56] Her journey and her residence in the United States were supported by the well-known US peace movement activist Lola Maverick Lloyd (born 1875 in Castorville and died 1944 in Winnetka), who would continue to send various sums of money as long as she lived. Rosika Schwimmer was soon followed by her sister Franciska and their mother. Rosika and Franciska Schwimmer could not be granted US citizenship on account of their pacifist beliefs, and so their documentation would henceforth always describe them as "stateless."[57] They thus had to continue their lives as citizens of nowhere, knowing they would never see Hungary again.

It was not easy for Schwimmer to settle in in her "new home country," as she was considered to be a Bolshevik spy both in Hungary and in the US. The Schwimmer sisters and their mother lived first in Chicago and then in New

York, where they tried to make ends meet with the assistance from the Lloyd family, the fees paid to Schwimmer for her articles and lectures, and the money brought in by the piano lessons Franciska gave. Even at that time, Rosika Schwimmer did not neglect her activities in the women's and peace movements: she was in close contact with Carrie Chapman Catt and those who came after her as president of IWSA, in addition to her colleagues in Hungary and the leaders of the western European women's movement. Among her correspondents, we find not only women's movement activists but also politicians, such as Herbert Hoover, Vladimir Lenin, and Winston Churchill; artists, such as Thomas Mann; and, within the Hungarian world, the liberal politician Anna Kéthly, the composer Zoltán Kodály, and the poet Endre Ady. Schwimmer exchanged letters with German revolutionary socialist and antimilitarist Karl Liebknecht, who was member of the Social Democratic Party of Germany, English comic actor, filmmaker, and composer Charlie Chaplin, and the German-born theoretical physicist Albert Einstein. She was in close contact with the US birth-control activist and eugenicist Margaret Sanger,[58] who, as well as popularizing contraception devices and forced sterilization, dealt with sex education.[59] From the end of her Swiss fiasco to her death, Schwimmer continued to correspond with Mihály Károlyi and his wife.[60] She also established a broad network of contacts with those Hungarians who had immigrated to New York and other parts of the United States.

Schwimmer, as an émigré in the US after 1921, did not turn her back on her Austrian contacts: from her correspondence with Renée Lovas, a women's movement activist who lived in Vienna for a while, we can build a picture of how FE assisted women of Jewish extraction in their university studies in Vienna or elsewhere in Austria. Meanwhile, from the letters Schwimmer exchanged with her younger brother Béla, who after World War I lived in Vienna, we see that she kept her eye on domestic politics in Austria, which she regularly touched on in her diary notes. She did not break off communication with the leadership of AöF either: she corresponded with Leopoldine Kulka until the latter's death in 1920 and also with the previously mentioned Lisa M. Goldmann, a member of AöF who had appeared at the IWSA congress in Geneva.[61]

After her US immigration in 1921, the year 1927 was another turning point in Schwimmer's life. This was the year that brought the death of Vilma Glücklich, who for decades had been her closest coworker and confidant in Hungary. In the letters they exchanged about the challenges related to the publication *A Nő*, Glücklich from January 1926 regularly complained that she did not have time even "to write a single decent article" for the journal, and on one occasion, she mentioned, "You would laugh at me if you saw how much I struggle with it [the editing of the journal, which after 1925 she did together with Mrs. Szirmay] and how poor it is!"[62] One question is how great a role Glücklich's death played in the gradual decline of the periodical in 1927–1928, or indeed why Mrs. Szirmay, who

Figure 5.3. Portrait of Vilma Glücklich (1912). Schwimmer-Lloyd Collection, The New York Public Library.

took over the running of FE, did not consider it important to keep the official publication—through which it communicated with its supporters—alive.

Even in her new life as an émigré in the US, Rosika Schwimmer continued her extensive work on publications and for the peace movement: as well as her vast number of journal articles, the texts of her lectures in the US have also survived. She wrote a long treatise on marriage and also authored children's books. Her personal tragedy was not necessarily her life in emigration but rather the way that posterity would almost entirely forget about her. This happened even though she did everything in her power to avoid it: she documented almost every moment of her life in the United States, first in Hungarian and then in English. In her estate, in addition to the texts of her articles and speeches and the documentation of her 1920s lawsuits, we find receipts, shopping lists, and notes on what she read, on her outgoing and incoming mail, and on her telephone calls. We even learn about the diet she followed because of her diabetes—usually without much success. Her notes on the state of her physical and mental health, kept from 1926 onward under the title "Medical records" and updated every few months or twice a year, reflect her capacity for self-reflection. She usually concludes these reports by saying that she is always hungry and feels old.[63] The last entry in these reports, meanwhile, speaks volumes: "It would be much more useful if I wrote my article [instead of these notes on the state of my health]. Everyone reads articles, but no one will read these."[64] After lengthy treatment in the hospital, Rosika Schwimmer passed away on 3 August 1948, of complications from diabetes, at the Mount Sinai Hospital in New York.

When Schwimmer passed away, the world lost a feminist and women's movement activist who had been a leading figure in the struggle for women's emancipation in Hungary from the outset. She had made substantial contributions to the founding of the first modern women's associations and had actively participated in these associations as a leading figure. Her commitment to her ideals and her temperament often complicated her life and sometimes led to conflicts within IWSA and WILPF, but she was nonetheless one of the key figures of the twentieth-century women's movement.

Objectives of the Associations and the Founding of Their Official Organs

In the subchapter below, I offer an overview of the associations' objectives, which changed minimally over the decades, and a discussion of the strategies they adopted to achieve their goals. I also show that the career guidance and job placement office run by FE was unique among women's associations in Hungary at the time. Finally, I argue that some of FE's aims (e.g., the fight against the trafficking of girls or campaigns for sexual education for the younger generations), though far ahead of their time, led to setbacks in the association's efforts to garner support among the general population.

The NOE statutes have not survived, but the rules of its operations can be reconstructed from a 1909 brochure made up of twenty-nine clauses.[65] A 1905 publication on FE's "objectives and work plan," which includes the first amendments to its statutes, has remained.[66] Further changes to FE's regulations, with approval from the Ministry of the Interior, were made in 1911, on three occasions between 1915 and 1917, and finally in 1946, when the association was reestablished after its suppression since 1942. We do not know of any general assemblies to amend NOE's constitution.

NOE's objectives were summarized in a single sentence: "The improvement and advancement of the interests of women office workers in private, state, and other public authorities." Thirteen years after its foundation, NOE could list at length the more important steps to achieving its objectives, along with the means at its disposal. Its leaders noted with satisfaction that a good number of these steps had already been taken: the association arranged different courses, operated a labor exchange from its early days, and organized "cultural, educational, and entertaining lectures," often in cooperation with FE. NOE provided broad-based consultation and information, maintained its own library, and, during the summer months, operated a vacation facility at Lake Balaton or in the Tatra Mountains; it also did some charity work, taking care of welfare for its members who could not work and "guarantee[ing] an assortment of benefits," including free train tickets, tickets for the baths, and discounts in a variety of shops. In 1907, to increase the intensity of communication with the membership and potential new members, it published a "specialist journal" and announced its intention to mobilize women office workers in the provinces. It is worth noting that "the full range of rights and benefits offered by the association" (which included the services of its labor exchange) was reserved exclusively for full members.[67]

The creation of NOE ushered in a new era for the Hungarian women's movement, even if, under the banner of "aid for members unable to work," the association was also involved in charitable activities. It always strove to avoid merely distributing handouts and instead used the creation of jobs, the exchange of labor, and training courses to help its members to earn a livelihood. FE expressed this intention most clearly in 1915: "Our objective has been and continues to be to provide everyone with work rather than with charitable donations. Charity kills, and donations rob us of developing our energies."[68]

The need to found FE was expressed at the international level of the women's movement in 1902 (i.e., by the IWSA), at the time that Bund österreichischer Frauenvereine (BöF) was established. At this stage, Aletta Jacobs encouraged Schwimmer to cobble together an umbrella organization similar to the Austrian BöF that could also join the International Council of Women (ICW).[69] Their plan, bandied about over the space of two years, did not come to fruition in the form of an umbrella organization, as in the spring of 1904, MNSz ultimately began its activities. It was led by Countess Ilona Andrássy (born 1858 in Petronell and died 1952 in Polgárdi), the wife of Lajos Batthyány (born 1860 in Egyed and died 1951 in Polgárdi), a member of the Hungarian parliament and the governor of Fiume between 1892 and 1896. MNSz, which, with its conservative values, represented the moderate wing of the bourgeois women's movement in Hungary, held its inaugural meeting on 14 March 1904 in Budapest. Schwimmer was also invited to this event, but we do not know if she was present.[70] FE would also join MNSz just over a year later.

According to the work plan published in 1905, FE's objectives covered every aspect of women's life.

We strive to make the daughter, the wife, and the mother of great value to the family, too. We wish for a woman to acquire economic independence, such that she does not have to be restricted by financial considerations when selecting her life partner; for her to be involved in her husband's work and assertively to share in his problems, to be an intellectual partner for him, to appreciate, from her own experience, the financial rewards of her work, so that she might spend her own income, and that of her parents or her husband, on acquiring goods of only genuine value. We want to make it possible that she should raise her child not just with love, but with the knowledge that life requires of it; that she should remain its leader and guide beyond the children's bedroom, and after the end of childhood. We finally want to make use of the labor of those women who have not yet started a family: labor that is often untapped but highly important for the household of humanity.[71]

At this point, I challenge the Hungarian literature suggesting that FE had an absolutist focus on the fight for female suffrage. I would not, of course, want for a moment to belittle the role FE played in the campaigns for votes for women; I merely wish to emphasize that its activities were not limited to this one arena.

We have no sources on the inaugural sessions of NOE and FE, but the archival sources and the association columns in *A Nő és a Társadalom* and *A Nő* give us a detailed picture of their operation. These report columns formed the cornerstone of the close cooperation between NOE and FE, as noted by NOE in 1907.

We were very glad to receive the offer from the "A Nő és a társadalom" publishing company, which vouched that it was willing to allow our fellow members to have its journal for a low price. . . . *According to our contract, the publishing company is obliged to leave space in each issue for official announcements, articles and for reports that serve our special interests.* The fact that the journal is edited by our president, Rosika Schwimmer, is in itself a guarantee that "A Nő és a társadalom" will represent our interests in every respect, and that if needed it would be a brave comrade in our struggle. The journal is also the official bulletin of Feministák Egyesülete. To present the general tendencies of the publishing company to the honorable assembly, let us quote one of the points of the company's regulations, which states: "The fair profit of the company is to be divided, with half going to *Nőtisztviselők Országos Egyesülete* and half to *Feministák Egyesülete*."[72]

The "official announcements of Nőtisztviselők Országos Egyesülete" and the "official announcements of Feministák Egyesülete" usually took up about three to six pages at the back of an issue; from January 1908, they grew to include the reports of the provincial branch organizations, and from the end of 1911, they incorporated news from the "7th congress of the International Women Suffrage Alliance." Janka Gergely edited the NOE association announcements, and Vilma Glücklich oversaw FE statements from the outset, while Paula Pogány, the secretary-general of the committee preparing the IWSA congress, was responsible for the section focusing on that congress.

As the years progressed, the two associations deliberately strove to extend their social base, both in the capital and beyond it. Of course, they were not immune to naivete, as association journals rarely generated income and were more likely to do the opposite: most were loss making from the first moment of their publication. Nevertheless, NOE and FE did use their income to establish the organizational structure (practical and career advisers, the wartime committee to protect mothers) with which they assisted those in difficulty, offering not only advice but also real support.

The rhetoric of the reports in the journals was based on an imagined community of editors and readers; they usually took the form of first- or second-person dialogues. The journals generally published the associations' annual reports and treasurer's results in the form of "budget and results invoices" and "budget guidelines" in May and June, alongside the events being held (annual general meetings, lecture and debate evenings, artistic soirees, exercise and language classes, etc.).[73] They did not send "separate invitations and announcements to their events" on account of the high mailing costs; instead, they told their members, "We should first read the association pages, and note the dates of the meetings."[74] They rarely departed from this practice if, say, a foreign speaker canceled a visit. As the years passed, both associations could count on the publicity brought by countrywide daily newspapers. But the road leading to this point was long, with many articles besmirching or simply ignoring the associations' work. By 1907, however, they looked to the future with optimism: "In Hungary, where the feminist movement is still so young, it is a great achievement that the whole of society, and particularly the press, is constantly dealing with the questions and efforts of the women's movement. Some are for it, some against, but they concern themselves with it."

Two years later, they were entirely positive about the press response: "There has hardly been a month in the history of our association richer in events worthy of mention than this last March has been; and yet—an odd contradiction—we have never had a shorter report [in the association column]. There are two factors limiting us: 1. shortage of space ... 2. the fact that the daily press across the country has already comprehensively discussed what the association has achieved in the last two months."[75]

In what follows, I will turn to the financial circumstances of the associations and the dynamics of their operation. FE's "treasurer's reports" from before 1914 can be found among the material of the board meetings held every month. After 1914, as in the case of AöF, such reports disappeared from the vicinity of NOE and FE. But the 1909–1910 treasurer's reports for all three organizations have remained, making it possible to compare their financial circumstances.

Given the profiles of the associations and the social specificities of the age, membership fees were the largest items in the income of both NOE and FE. Compared to British, German, and Austrian women, Hungarian women were the least likely to support regular and sizable donations. Yet membership fees were higher than those in Austria, while members, both in Budapest and in provincial cities, were given free or discounted services in return for their outlay.

We have no information on the membership fees collected by NOE before 1907. From that year, however, NOE took on the significant financial burden of publishing its own journal. The membership fees had to be increased in line with this: in addition to the enrollment fee of 2 crowns, full members had to pay 12 crowns a year, supporting member 6 crowns, and members from provinces 8 crowns, all in quarterly installments.[76] Despite general price increases, these fees remained unchanged until 1914,[77] unlike those of FE, where, in the period in question, the opportunity to increase membership fees was used on no less than five occasions. Between 1907 and 1911, "full members [paid] a membership fee of at least 6 crowns a year in twice-yearly installments paid in advance." In 1908, the leaders of FE pointed out to their members that this amount was less than the membership fee "customary for associations for working women in Hungary," which was 20 fillérs a week, or 10.40 crowns a year.[78] According to the 1911 amendment to the statutes, full members were expected to pay at least 10 crowns a year, while supporting members, in line with previous practice, paid 200 crowns as a lifetime subscription.[79] After the outbreak of war, FE attempted to use hikes in the membership fee to compensate for the lost *A Nő* advertising revenue: from 1915 to 1917, full members contributed an annual 12 crowns to the budget; from December 1917 to the end of 1918, this figure was 16, and afterward it was 26. The membership fee for supporting members rose proportionately, from 250 to 1,000 crowns. For those experiencing financial hardship, in 1917, as AöF had done, FE offered a more favorable payment scheme. For those in the same household, only one member had to pay the full fee, while the others had "only" to pay 10 crowns a head.[80]

The preliminary budget calculations indicate that Vilma Glücklich and her coworkers regularly overestimated their income from membership fees. At NOE, they were more precise in their calculations of future income. Figure 5.4 compares plans with reality.

Now let us have a look at the membership fees received by the three associations in 1909. In the Austrian case, the total was 1,144 crowns; for FE, it was five times this amount, at 5,330.78 crowns; for NOE, it was seven times, at 7,881 crowns. In 1913, the year of the IWSA congress, FE attained its highest-ever membership-fee income, of 6,271.20 crowns, but even this was way below the estimate of 9,000 crowns. The actual 1914 income of 5,554.33 crowns, meanwhile, was little more than 55 percent of what had been envisaged. Thus, for Glücklich

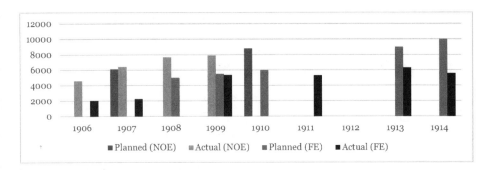

Figure 5.4. Planned and actual income from membership fees for NOE and FE, from 1906 to 1914 (in crowns, total). *Source: Annual reports and minutes of committee meetings of NOE and FE, 1906–1914.*

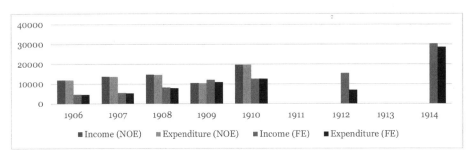

Figure 5.5. Income and expenditure for NOE and FE from 1906 to 1914 (in crowns, total). *Sources: Annual reports of NOE and the minutes of the committee meetings of FE, 1907–1914.*

and the board, as the years passed, these budgetary plans had less and less to do with reality and increasingly reflected unrealistic visions.[81]

Thanks to the size of its membership, the budget of NOE was usually double that of FE.

From the mid-1900s, the annual income of the Hungarian associations far exceeded the amounts recorded by AöF. If we use 1909 as our benchmark, we can see that while AöF's income was 8,647 crowns, FE's came to 12,220.44 crowns, and NOE's to 10,527.36 crowns. And although mayor of Budapest István Bárczy and a number of ministries contributed considerable sums to FE's and NOE's courses, the labor exchange office, and the staging of the IWSA congress in the city, the two associations never enjoyed the kind of donations that AöF received from the Springer siblings. On the other hand, Bárczy gave FE use of the grand Vigadó building in Budapest for the period of the 1913 congress without charge.

Figure 5.6. István Bárczy (*left*), mayor of Budapest, at the reception held at the Fisherman's Bastion for delegates to the IWSA congress. Schwimmer-Lloyd Collection, The New York Public Library.

The association was also allowed to open and maintain its account at the Hungarian Commerce Bank of Pest without charge. This was a generous gesture on the part of the capital.[82] FE and NOE tried to increase their revenue with the sale of publications, posters, and badges, but we have no information as to how much this came to. All we know is that by 1909 Glücklich and her coworkers had estimated that the income from these sales would come to 3,000 crowns.[83]

Exactly what free or discounted services did members enjoy? Apart from membership fees, what income and expenditure did the accounts of FE and NOE mention? Important income came from fees for training courses, entrance charges for various artistic events, and the donations given on such occasions. The jointly organized courses, which took place at 8:30 p.m. on weekdays, brought an annual revenue of more than 3,000 crowns, but the costs they incurred were not much less than this.[84] The subjects taught varied: while, like AöF, FE and NOE repeatedly started courses on social education and women's health, the most popular lessons proved to be those for beginners and advanced learners of German, English, and French. For these, attendees paid an enrollment fee of 2 crowns and a course fee of 4 crowns. The English lessons were attended by the leaders of the associations; to ensure their success, even native speakers were employed as teachers. The organizers did their best to establish an environment that was conducive to learning: despite being oversubscribed, the classes were limited to small groups and concluded with exams; students received detailed evaluations and certificates of their achievements.[85] These language courses became all the more valuable with the approach of the IWSA congress, the official languages of which were English, German, and French. To prepare for the event, the FE board advertised courses in Esperanto and proposed lessons in Italian, Swedish, and Danish.[86] After the outbreak of war, the repertoire was extended to include courses, offered without charge, at which fellow members left without employment could train or retrain.[87]

Apart from improving their members' erudition, the associations considered it an important mission to popularize a healthy lifestyle and outdoor sports. They organized expeditions and hiking trips to the hills around Budapest, to Esztergom, Dobogókő, and Visegrád, or to Lake Balaton;[88] they even rented tennis courts and held courses in Swedish gymnastics, which was very popular at the time.[89]

The statistics reveal, however, that of NOE's many thousands of members, only a few enjoyed the relaxation offered by its leisure resort: in 1907, a mere twenty members visited the Balaton facility, spending a total of 272 days there, about two weeks per person. Those vacationing there had their full board and lodging paid for and were even given cheap bathing tickets.[90] Despite this generous offer for those wishing to take a break, the association's resort never operated at full capacity, a fact Janka Gergely put down to members' carelessness.

> There are still those who apply unthinkingly, booking spaces before they know for sure if they can come, thereby robbing other members of the opportunity to have a break here. Such instances have occurred now, too, with the ultimate effect that there are still empty spaces at the resort, for which we still have to pay the accommodation, even though our fellow members have made it impossible for those spaces to be made use of. In order to avoid similar unpleasant and costly incidences, I would ask all fellow members who have applied to one of our vacation facilities to consider this registration to be o b l i g a t o r y in nature and not to cancel it unless with absolute need to do so.[91]

It was not just during the summer months that NOE provided for leisure activities: there were visits to the Museum of Applied Arts and the Museum of Fine Arts in Budapest, in similar fashion to the Austrian case.[92]

NOE's evenings and concerts, in which Franciska Schwimmer often participated as pianist, generated 2,327.70 crowns of income in 1907 and 1,847.13 in 1909. These events included performances by the greats of Budapest's artistic life, and the proceeds were generally offered to the labor exchange. The Vigadó concert hall in Pest was almost always home to these celebratory occasions.[93] Anyone could attend these events, but members could purchase tickets at a more favorable price. In 1909, members could go to the association's Wednesday evening concert for 40 fillérs, and others for 60 fillérs; this fee also covered the "tea, cloakroom, and door expenses."[94] There is a fitting anecdote about the NOE's artistic soiree of 1907, the whole income from which, around 550 crowns, was being offered to offset the costs of the vacation resort. A report on these developments praised the event's success, to which performers of similar standing to famous Hungarian actress Mari Jászai (born 1850 in Ászár and died 1926 in Budapest) contributed. It is only at the end of the article that we learn the outcome of the evening: "We were stunned to see, just a few hours after we left the soiree, that thieves had broken into the offices of the association in broad daylight, and stole the large part of the profits of the evening."[95] Although they asked members to "support the work of the organization with [their] donations, to lessen the damage caused," the enthusiasm remained limited: they managed to collect a sum of 200 crowns.[96]

As donations were vital for AöF's operation, it is worth pondering how this worked within the ranks of FE and NOE. The sum granted to Glücklich and her team in 1906 was 564 crowns, which steadily increased year by year until 1914. In 1912–1913, they received a total of 6,574.75 crowns in donations; by 1914, this almost trebled, to 16,950 crowns. While NOE's fundraising efforts did not go beyond selling postcards of its empty association rooms, FE polished its strategy to perfection in time for the 1913 congress. It operated a "Christmas shop"; indeed, thanks to the involvement of two of its members, Mrs. Izidor Megyei and her brother Alfréd Brüll, known as a patron of Hungarian sports and the president or honorary president of several sports associations, it even raised capital from football, which was becoming increasingly popular in this period. Brüll, the president of the Magyar Testgyakorlók Köre (Hungarian Athletics Circle), offered part of the income (1,500 crowns) from their fall 1912 match against Budapesti Torna Club (Budapest Sports Club) to FE.[97]

In 1909, these evening programs, the quality of which, according to the members, varied, brought in 3,472.59 crowns, which made up a quarter of FE's annual income of around 12,000 crowns. The events also incurred costs, however, which came to 3,616.12 crowns. Schwimmer's hectic organizing work, meanwhile, which went from inviting and accommodating activists from northern and western Europe and from across the Atlantic to entertaining them in Budapest for a number of days, did not bring success in any financial sense. A further expense was the honoraria of many hundreds of crowns paid to invitees, which could not be recouped from the entry tickets priced at 6, 4, and 2 crowns, seen by the leadership as suitably inexpensive. The lectures incurred losses even though they were most often also attended by NOE members. NOE often postponed its own events so its members could hear foreign activists speak.[98] FE invited at least two foreign speakers to Budapest (or provincial Hungary) a year. Besides this, leaders of the association held lectures on a monthly basis.[99] With the exception of Schwimmer, whose fee was between 50 and 100 crowns per lecture, they put themselves at the association's disposal without charge.[100] No entry fee was charged on these occasions.[101] The cooperation between FE and NOE brought the costs of events down: Schwimmer; Sarolta Steinberger (born 1875 in Tiszaújlak and died 1966 in Budapest), a gynecologist, the first woman doctor to be awarded her degree in Hungary; and Mrs. Meller were often guest speakers for NOE, while Riza Steiner, a member of the NOE board, presented the joint debate evenings.[102] NOE involved its members in the planning of its speaker meetings: its leaders often asked that if members "[had] special requests, they should urgently inform the committee of them."[103] It seems they did precisely that, and they were not afraid to offer criticism, as we can read with regard to the 1912 lecture by the German sociologist Robert Michels.

> His lecture was a painful surprise for all of us who thought we knew his decisive opinion on the question of sexuality from his very serious and valuable articles published in the most highly-esteemed foreign journals. We do not know whether to put this down to his publisher's merciless pressure on this well-known sociologist as it rushes him across half of Europe in the interests of his recently-published book, or to the information given in Budapest that "a Budapest woman has read everything, seen everything, and knows everything, and it is not possible to talk too freely in front of her," but the fact is that in lieu of any academic discussion we heard only light-hearted chat, and instead of any clear position taken, we heard rhapsodic opinions being expressed. The speaker himself became aware that this audience was expecting something else of him.[104]

After FE and NOE managed to reduce their expenditure on printing and mail costs, their largest outgoings were the upkeep of their association rooms in the city center. NOE settled at 83 Andrássy Boulevard in Budapest's sixth district until 1912, when it transferred its headquarters to the fifth district, to 3 Vigadó Square. For almost ten years, excluding the periods of small renovations, FE "enjoyed the hospitality" of the director of the Társadalmi Múzeum (Social Museum) at 12 Mária Valéria Street in the fifth district. In June 1917, it reestablished its "general headquarters" to the nearby 9 József Square. The office for the preparation work for the IWSA congress was in the seventh district, at 67 István Street. The cost of keeping these offices in 1910 was 800 crowns a year, and by 1914, this had risen to more than 1,300 crowns. In addition to this came the cost of heating and lighting, which in 1907 for both organizations reached 500 crowns. Another costly expense was the wage of the administrator of the office and of the debt collector sent to pick up overdue membership fees. As they wanted to connect the pay of these women to "market conditions," in 1909 this represented a cost of

1,240.40 crowns for FE and 2,875 crowns for NOE. Finally, both groups invested a sum of around 2,000–2,400 crowns in the publication of their official journals.[105]

The Hungarian associations made serious efforts to keep their books balanced. Their financial plans were refined at the monthly board meetings, at joint boat sightseeing tours in the summer, or at impromptu gatherings at the milk pavilion on Stefánia Street, not far from Városliget (City Park). For inspiration, or to discover what mistakes to avoid, the leaders of FE and NOE attended not only each other's general meetings but also those of the Magántisztviselők Országos Szövetsége (National Alliance of Private Office Workers) and of MNSz.[106] They did their best to hold their meetings on Sundays or in the evenings, after the end of the working day, so as many members could attend as possible. The annual general meetings were without exception held on nonworkdays—in practice, on Sundays—for "the attendance of all [their] fellow members [was] important, because [they] elect[ed] a new board and a new president."[107]

Two "annual work programs" were created: one for the summer months and one for the fall and winter period. From June to September, the associations in the capital were in their "sleepy season," when the activities of members, given the "tropical heat," were limited to one informal gathering per week and a few excursions.[108] In this regard, the summer of 1912 was the exception, as it generated "unending working time" on account of the IWSA congress.[109] This period, and the year 1913 in particular, also brought increasing friction between the two associations. Yet the pressure on FE is understandable, as what was at stake was the successful implementation of an event expected to have two thousand to three thousand guests and a total budget of around 100,000 crowns.[110] This intermezzo of about half a year notwithstanding, the cooperation between the two groups remained relatively untroubled. In addition to plans for a joint headquarters on the Pest side of the river Danube, near the Margaret Bridge, in 1912 there were also real efforts toward the opening of a centralized household (similar to the Vienna Heimhof) for working women. Their work on this front did not succeed; the outbreak of World War I stopped the plans from going further than the shelves of the archive.

To grasp fully the nature of the cooperation between the two associations, a brief outline of their joint publishing enterprise is indispensable. A suggestion from March 1906—"Rosika Schwimmer proposes that we publish a journal together with Nőtisztviselők Országos Egyesülete"—is the first piece of evidence that FE, which had 333 members at the time, was preparing to pursue its own press activity. We do not have any further details as to what Schwimmer said, only that, as always, Glücklich was commissioned to investigate the potential opportunities.[111] By this time, FE had already been publishing the *Feminista Értesítő* (Feminist Bulletin), edited by Glücklich, which was available to members without charge and to readers outside FE for an annual subscription of 2 crowns. It would be an exaggeration to call this a periodical in the proper sense of the term, as it primarily included an association calendar, invitations, courses, and reports. Both its content and its design are much more reminiscent of the annual reports published independently by AöF. Even FE members referred to this imperfect publication as a "house bulletin," one that Glücklich herself accused of having "no frills."[112]

FE had enormous hopes for *A Nő és a Társadalom* when it was launched; for NOE referred to this cooperation, using a canny contemporary metaphor, as living together in a centralized household. The preliminary negotiations—on the potential publisher, the choice of editor, the creation of the A Nő és a Társadalom Publishing Company, the authors for the first issues, and the journal's title—began in May. Members of the associations working on the publication project found subscribers for the journal by collecting lists of names and addresses on subscription lists, offering them *A Nő és a Társadalom* for 6 crowns a year.[113] Schwimmer clearly put faith in the work of her colleagues, as before the journal was launched, she set off on a lecture tour of Germany and paid a visit to Aletta Jacobs. She learned about events at home from letters sent to her; indeed, a letter informed her that she was elected editor.

NOE and FE originally planned for the journal to be published fortnightly, but in the end, this was not accepted. With the exception of one combined issue for July and August 1913, it usually came out on the first of each month, with a length of two press folios.[114] Beginning in December 1911, the journal's *impressum*, which contained the name of the authors, the publishers, the place, and the date of the publication, came to include the Budapest-based Férfiliga a Nők Választójoga Érdekében (Men's League for the Interests of Women's Suffrage), although this group did not participate in the actual editorial process. Although they were in talks with a number of printing presses, in the end they accepted the offer from Athenaeum Press also in Budapest.[115] Meanwhile, Schwimmer was at work on the list of potential authors. The first issue of *A Nő és a Társadalom*, which Marianne Hainisch, alongside the leaders of IWSA, also congratulated,[116] reached its readers in January 1907.[117] It was three years behind *Nőmunkás* (Female Worker), the mouthpiece of the Hungarian Social Democratic women's movement.

In January 1914, much greater publicity surrounded the release of *A Nő*, the successor to *A Nő és a Társadalom*. *A Nő* was established using the FE's revenues left over from the IWSA congress. Subscribers were enlisted in both Budapest and the provinces. Mrs. Szirmay made a proposal: "For those families, where two or more are members of the association, and so needlessly receive multiple copies of the journal, we will find a solution for making membership less expensive if only one copy is received, allowing us more easily to find more members within a particular family."[118] *A Nő* was by no means intended only for the members of the association, as indicated by its broader range of content and by its planned

Figure 5.7. Feminist propaganda—association members selling *A Nő*. Schwimmer-Lloyd Collection, The New York Public Library.

budget of April 1914, which estimated 5,040 crowns of revenue from street sales and 16,920 crowns from advertisements. By 24 April, however, they had only managed to raise a small fraction of these amounts, as street sales had brought in 371.93 crowns, while advertising raised 2,386.55 crowns.

Before the declaration of war in August 1914, *A Nő* was published fortnightly, on the fifth and twentieth of every month, over approximately fifteen to twenty-five pages.[119] In both its aesthetic design and its content, the periodical approached its German sister publications, which had tens or even hundreds of marks to spend every year. This makes it all the more unfortunate that *A Nő* could not blossom under the direction of its new editorial board, for the war would intervene to block its progress.

While NOE's objectives were more specific, FE, in theory, sought to advocate for the political, economic, and social rights of all women. This was impossible, of course, if only because upper-middle-class women, who made up a large part of the membership, had little information about the problems faced by working women. In their radicalism, both Hungarian organizations initially approached AöF, but they soon realized that if they were to adopt the more ambitious positions and strident style, they might well lose a significant number of supporters, so they softened their tone.

Changing Membership

In this subchapter, I survey changes in the size and social composition of the memberships of NOE and FE over the course of their existence. I challenge the studies of Susan Zimmermann, Judit Acsády, and Zsolt Mészáros, according to which the members of NOE were "simple employees" and those joining FE were "from agricultural laborers, through industrial workers, to the middle class ... the broadest classes of women."[120] I also argue that NOE and FE enjoyed a close relationship with the Jewish bourgeoisie of Budapest, and they established a harmonious cooperation. Their intellectual and social capital, as well as financial resources, surely made a significant contribution to the Hungarian feminist movement's ability to compete with those in the West.

The literature gives us only the merest inkling of the associations' membership numbers. Susan Zimmermann—and thus Claudia Papp, who relies on her data—estimates that NOE had 1000 members at the fin de siècle, 4000 in 1913, and 6000 in 1917.[121] Using the annual reports, I reconstructed the membership numbers to the end of 1914, with the exception of 1908–1909.

Ten years after its foundation, NOE had more than 1,000 members, and by 1913 it had more than 3,500. Although in 1914 the total membership for Budapest and the provinces was just short of 4,000, at 3,933, it was three times larger than that of FE in this period. While the number of those joining the main organization in Budapest was constantly growing, from 1910 to 1913, the membership of the provincial branches resolutely stagnated at 498–499. It is highly unlikely that the real membership level was fixed to this degree, but a lack of sources makes it impossible to check this figure.

The NOE statutes of 1909 made detailed provisions as to the registration and admission of members of various statuses, their rights, their obligations, and the circumstances of their departure or potential expulsion.

> §6 The general assembly can elect as honorary members those who have in any way achieved excellent results relating to the association's success or to the furthering of its goals. . . . Foreigners cannot be honorary members of the association.
> §7 Supporting members are those who have donated, once and forever, at least 100 crowns toward the goals of the association.
> §8 A full member is a woman working in the state offices listed in paragraph 2, and involved in office work of any kind. A full member is accepted by the association's board, after being nominated by two members, and on

The Hungarian Associations | 139

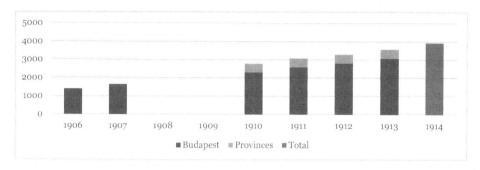

Figure 5.8. NOE membership in Budapest and in the provinces, 1906–1914. *Source: Annual reports of NOE, 1906–1914.*

the basis of a statement signed personally.... Any possible objections to their admission are to be reported to the secretary. Foreign residents cannot be full members. The board is entitled to reject admission without giving any explanation.

§9 Anyone can be an external member if they accept to pay at least six crowns a year in membership fees.

§10 Full members can enjoy all the rights and privileges offered by the association.

§11 Obligations of full members: 1) On being admitted they are obliged to pay 2 crowns in enrollment fees and three months' membership in advance.... 2) ... To support the association, to inform female colleagues of its objectives, to expand the association's membership by finding new members, and to accept and abide by the association's regulations, house rules and its interim measures. 3) To inform the secretary without delay of any job vacancies that are brought to a member's attention.... 6) A former full member who left voluntarily and applies to join again is obliged to pay a special charge of 4 crowns, which the board can forgo in certain justified circumstances.

§12 Full membership can cease in the event of: 1) Departure, which can only happen if announced to the secretariat half a year in advance. Departure is only possible after two years of membership have passed. 2) Exclusion, because of behavior damaging to the interests of the association, in which instance membership can only officially be ended if this is decided upon by 2/3 of the board in a vote by acclamation....

§15 Incorporated members are associations for female office workers and female commercial employees, with their own unique statutes, which pay as many crowns in membership fees prior to their annual general meetings as they have full members; these county organizations can, on the basis of ad hoc contracts, use the association's official journal as their own official journal. Such associations thereby become the national association's subsidiary branches: their full members can make use of all the institutions of the national association.[122]

What conclusions can we draw from these paragraphs? First of all, only female officials (either public or private) doing office work could become full members with full rights. Meanwhile, anyone could become an honorary or supporting member, irrespective of gender, nationality, citizenship, or profession. Provincial groups were integrated as "incorporated members."

From paragraphs 10–15 and the annual reports, we can conclude that the number of members fluctuated significantly. With growing unemployment in the face of repeated economic crises, an increasing number of women saw NOE as a labor exchange office that could be used without charge, and they left once they had found a position. By the summer of 1914, it had become inescapable that its president, Janka Gergely, in response to a reader's letter in A Nő, should draw attention to the importance of office workers organizing themselves. The author of the original letter asked, "But please, while I know that a membership fee of one crown a month is not going to ruin me, but what use is there for me in joining? I have a job; it is not absolutely vital for me to be a member of the association." In her answer, Gergely, as well as emphasizing the advantages for members, also tried to play to the emotions of her audience, highlighting the benefits of membership.

> As for how someone should come to like the association, I know a very simple recipe. She should work in it and work for it. Apart from the community of people with similar interests, it is primarily her work for it that ties an individual to the organization. The more effort she invests—and there is plenty of opportunity for her to do so—the more she will be attached to it, and the more the association will mean to her. . . . Doesn't this work also increase our individual worth? Isn't this a reward, too? I hope that I will soon have the honor to see you in person up at the association.[123]

Those who quit the group and wanted to rejoin it were made to pay double the enrollment fee, and the first opportunity to leave came at the end of the second year of membership.[124]

Figure 5.9 combines the full and supporting members of NOE. It is only for the years marked here that we have data for the exact composition of the membership; even here, there is no information about honorary and corporate members. We do know, however, that in 1896, thirty-one individuals were registered as founding members. The number did not change over the years; the leadership did not provide an opportunity, as at AöF, for someone later to join the association as a founding member in return for payment.[125]

The lack of sources means we cannot draw any conclusions as to the distribution of Budapest members according to gender or place of residence.

Regarding the membership of FE, Susan Zimmermann mentions 500 members in 1907 and 2,947 a decade later; Katalin Kéri calculates that there were 342 in 1906 and 507 in 1907.[126] Judith Szapor mentions around 700 members nationwide for 1910.[127] Alongside the minutes of the board meetings, the logbooks kept

The Hungarian Associations | *141*

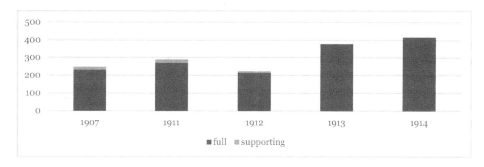

Figure 5.9. Full and supporting members of NOE from 1907 to 1914. *Source: Annual reports of NOE, 1906–1914.*

from 1912 to 1918 give a precise picture of the membership numbers, registered month by month. This source is further nuanced by the list of addresses of Budapest members. The documents make no distinction between full and supporting members. Only the 1910 collection of FE statutes pours any light on the distinctions between the status of new members.

§3 Members of the association are of three kinds:
1) Any Hungarian citizen can become a full member if they take on the fundamental principle of the association as their own and they intend to participate in the association's work. Furthermore, any Hungarian association can become a full member, with the same conditions.... A full member is accepted after [as in the case of NOE] being nominated by two members and accepted by the board with a secret vote. A full member has the right to speak, propose a motion, and to vote, can elect, and can be elected.... These membership rights can only be exercised by a member who has no membership fee arrears. Associations exercise their membership rights through their representative.
2) Anyone can become a supporting member if they pay at least 25 crowns a year or a single lifetime payment of at least 200 crowns. Supporting members have speaking rights only.
3) Junior members over the age of 16 joining the youth group of the association ... exercise their rights within this group.... Those facing school discipline cannot be members of the association at all.[128]

Foreign members are not mentioned here, but we do learn of the Ifjúsági Csoport (Youth Group), which was similar to AöF's Sektion Jugend. In this we find the children of parents actively involved in the association, including Flóra, daughter of board member Mrs. Elemér Békássy and Károly, son of Mrs. Oszkár Szirmay.[129] Flóra Békássy was president of the group. Other professional associations could become members of FE. The ceremonial act of accepting new members can be seen as a formality of the board meetings.

142 | *Progressive Women's Movements*

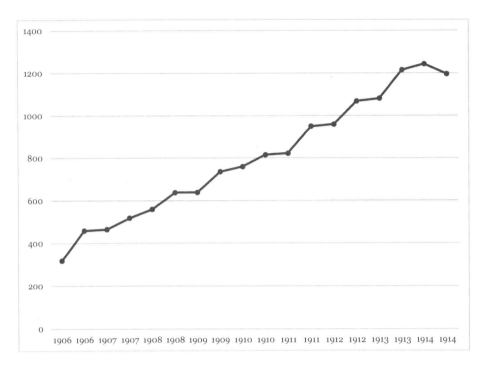

Figure 5.10. FE membership numbers from 1906 to 1914. *Source: Minutes of the FE committee meetings, 1906–1914.*

Figure 5.10 depicts changes in the membership of FE from 1906 to 1914 on the basis of the data from the first and last board meetings of each year. Three important conclusions can be drawn from this information. First of all, we gain an insight, on a monthly or sometimes even two-to-three-week basis, into the increase in the membership of FE. Compared to the 319 members in January 1906, by 1914, the number of members in Budapest and the provinces had increased almost fourfold, a fact that tells of the association's increased influence. By February 1907, membership reached the milestone of 500, and by May 1912, that of 1000. Vilma Glücklich and her colleagues had no reason to fear the strong fluctuations experienced by AöF and NOE, as only a handful of FE's member asked to leave the group. The highest number doing so was 17, in September 1910; their motivation is unknown.[130]

From January 1906 to August 1914, there were hardly any board meetings at which Glücklich failed to deal with the changes in membership numbers. Occasionally, there were significant growths and declines; the rate of growth can hardly be described as steady: in Budapest, the total membership of FE grew by 140 in 1906, 53 in 1907, 79 in 1908, 97 in 1909, 55 in 1910, 127 in 1911, 108 in 1912, and 134 in 1914. The growth continued until June 1914, followed by intermittent signs of decline, which the minutes put down to wartime mobilization and the impoverishment of members.

Table 5.1. FE membership numbers from January 1906 to August 1914, with the dates of committee meetings

Committee meeting date	Membership
19 January 1906	**319**
20 February	315
10 March	333
6 April	360
14 April	361
12 May	375
30 May	379
23 June	397
3 July	407
12 September	411
6 October	418
22 October	425
24 November	445
21 December	459
18 January 1907	**465**
12 February	504
8 March	503
24 April	506
14 May	509
17 June	510
17 September	No data
24 September	512
22 October	No data
25 November	518
20 December	No data
20 January 1908	**559**
20 February	551
16 March	556
3 April	566
4 May	566
5 June	571
14 September	591
16 October	609
11 November	626
23 December	638
25 January 1909	**639**
27 February	695
24 March	707
21 April	704

Table 5.1 (*continued*)

Committee meeting date	Membership
24 May	704
13 September	715
16 October	723
9 November	735
12 December	736
22 January 1910	**760**
24 February	781
15 March	791
2 April	801
23 April	804
20 May	808
20 September	803
11 October	812
20 December	815
21 January 1911	**822**
25 February	811
17 March	817
20 April	824
24 April	820
3 May	823
23 June	842
13 September	926
24 October	931
27 November	951
17 December	949
26 January 1912	**959**
23 February	958
15 March	970
26 March	972
9 April	979
27 May	1,002
24 June	1,017
12 September	1,043
25 September	1,050
21 November	1,060
20 December	1,067
25 January 1913	**1,080**
26 February	1,113
29 March	1,133

Table 5.1 (continued)

Committee meeting date	Membership
17 April	1,142
6 May	1,143
27 June	No data
26 September	1,160
14 October	1,169
30 October	1,176
27 November	1,195
22 December	1,214
January 1914	**1,242**
28 February	No data
12 March	1,247
23 March	No data
3 April	1,256
24 April	1,261
12 June	1,272
31 July	No data
31 August	1,195

Minutes of FE committee meetings from 1906 to 1914. MNL OL P999, box 2, item 3.

From the spring of 1915, FE attempted to counteract this tendency by offering favorable payment options (installments) and allowing membership fees to be paid late.[131]

The decline of 1914 was only to be expected, but the appearance of this same tendency in 1913 raises a number of questions: my initial hypothesis was that the euphoric atmosphere around the organization of the IWSA congress may have attracted many new members to the association. Yet the increase in members over the years was restrained, a fact that can only be explained by the effect of the economic crisis. Also, the enthusiasm of the active membership of FE did not really rub off on outside observers. These limiting factors may have been heightened by the growing conflict with NOE, which had not appeared before the organization of the IWSA congress. At first, the signs of this disagreement were kept under the surface, but by the eve of the IWSA congress, they had come out into the open. FE had by this stage long refused to share with NOE the foreign women's movement periodicals it subscribed to, a decision that left Janka Gergely, Szidónia Willhelm, and the other members of the NOE leadership dumbfounded. Meanwhile, the international congress served the interests of FE much better than those of NOE, which was only involved in the transnational dimensions of the cause in an indirect way.[132] The fact that NOE had to assist with the organizational issues of the

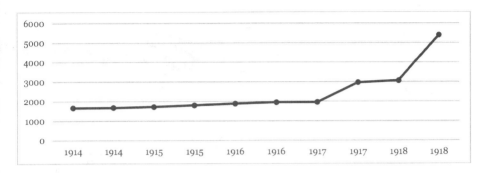

Figure 5.11. Numbers of FE members from 1914 to 1918. *Source: FE logbooks, MNL OL P999, box 23, item 32/b.*

congress but did not profit from it explained this conflict. The publication of *A Nő és a Társadalom* escalated the conflict, which was only resolved months later, with the help of Glücklich's diplomatic skills.

Table 5.1 displays FE's precise minute-keeping practices and the regularity and the dates of its board meetings.[133] In 1906, the board met on fifteen occasions; after this, the number settled at around nine to eleven each year. It held a summer gathering every June, a custom it maintained even in 1913. The mobilization of 1914 of course turned the normal dynamics of association life upside down: members began their war-related work in August with determination, as noted in the minutes of the (special) FE meetings.

It is mostly the logbooks that provide us with a picture of the growth in membership from September 1914.[134] These list the names and addresses of members both in Budapest and elsewhere in the country. The total membership in January 1912 was 1,134, with 175 members of the provincial branches. By 12 September 1914, the total had risen to 1,667, in part because of the strengthening of the provincial organizations, whose membership more than doubled, to 472. In the war years, the number of members underwent an even more dramatic rise, almost trebling in size.

As these statistics indicate, former FE member Laura Polányi's claim that the membership had risen to 30,000 by 1918 was an exaggeration.[135] Between April 1914 and the summer of 1918, the number of members shot up from 1,978 to 5,312, which was a particularly impressive increase compared to previous trends.[136] An explanation might include the electoral reform instigated by Vilmos Vázsonyi (born 1868 in Sümeg and died 1926 in Baden bei Wien), a liberal-bourgeois democratic politician who served for a time as minister of justice, as well the creation of the National Councils in Budapest and the provinces, which could have mobilized many of those committed to female suffrage. Thanks to electoral reform, a certain part of the Hungarian female population could have received the right

Table 5.2. The membership of FE from September 1914 to November 1918

Date	Membership
12 September 1914	**1,667**
19 October	1,680
27 January 1915	**1,719**
28 August	1,760
18 October	1,785
December 1915	1,802
January 1916	**1,802**
9 February	1,817
8 May	1,878
25 September	1,914
27 November	1,944
28 December	**1,949**
29 January 1917	**1,957**
26 February	1,975
12 March	1,981
30 April	1,987
30 July	2,093
September	2,177
2 October	2,214
22 October	2,310
27 October	2,406
30 October	2,469
1 November	2,542
8 November	2,730
12 December	2,960
7 January 1918	**3,062**
26 April	4,501
23 May	4,728
24 July	5,312
7 November	5,393

FE logbooks on members, MNL OL P999, box 23, item 32/b. Cf. Szapor 2018, 33.

to vote for the first time. The proposal was finally rejected by parliament in the summer of 1918. New members were, following the well-worn practice, recruited by circulating subscription lists.

The organization experienced an enormous increase in membership during these four years, even if some members decided to leave. The registrar removed only seventeen names from the logbooks.[137] Meanwhile, the list of addresses tells

148 | Progressive Women's Movements

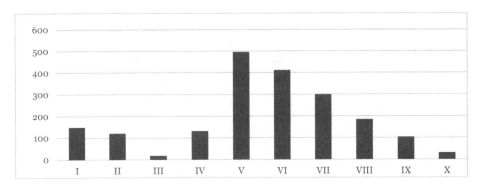

Figure 5.12. Distribution of Budapest members of FE according to district, around the turn of 1916–1917. Source: FE logbooks, MNL OL P999, box 23, item 32/b.

us that in the course of 1917–1918, it was primarily the number of provincial members that rose so strongly. Overall, this did not mean that FE swept its efforts for social and economic equality for women under the carpet, but neither does it mean that there was a great increase in the number of members active in the work of the association.

On the 250 pages of the ledger of names, written in four different hands, not once is the year noted, but it was probably kept from 1912 to 1916–1917, until the sudden growth in membership numbers.[138] As figure 5.12 indicates, most Budapest members were from the fifth, sixth, and seventh districts—from Lipótváros, Terézváros, and Erzsébetváros (497, 412, and 300 members, respectively). Compared to Vienna, the number of members in what was, strictly speaking, the center of the city (Belváros), the fourth district, was modest, at 131. Meanwhile, as in Vienna, there were few from the outlying districts in which industrial sites were prevalent: 103 from Ferencváros, the ninth district, and only 31 from Kőbánya, the tenth district. The metropolitan intelligentsia and women who had attended university were overrepresented: 280 members had doctorates; 10 members, men and women, were of baronial lineage; and 5 were from comital families.

Now let us look at the procedure the associations used to elect the members of their leadership (board) and see just who joined these organizations. A precise reconstruction of the social backgrounds of members is currently impossible, so I am limited to a few more general conclusions. In the absence of archival sources, we know, alongside the postal addresses of new members, only the family background and profession of a few more active (leading) members of FE and NOE.

The engine for the operation of both organizations was a board of some twenty-four to fifty members. The annual general meetings decided who would fill the main positions, which, in practice—with the exception of a few women who relocated or changed jobs—would be held for years or decades. In general, these officeholders enjoyed the trust of the membership and were reelected year after year. The tasks of the board members were laid down in NOE's 1909 statutes.

§19 The affairs of the association are managed by its officers, its board, and its general assembly.

§20 The officers of the association are as follows: a president, two vice presidents, a secretary, a treasurer, a controller, two clerks, two librarians, an attorney, three auditors, and a first officer. Apart from the attorney's position, only a full member can hold one of these offices. The president chairs meetings, and is deputized for by one of the vice presidents if unavailable.... The secretary arranges the affairs of the association, and its office, implements the decisions of the board, countersigns the official documents signed by the president, prepares the board's annual report, and keeps the association's books. Her wage is determined by the board. The clerks keep minutes of all the meetings. The treasurer is responsible for dealing with the membership fees and the association's funds. She keeps the books and accounts recording these amounts, and is obliged to give every board meeting a detailed report on the state of the books and the membership fees that have been paid.... The librarians maintain the association's library, keep a record of its holdings, and are obliged to report on this every month to the board. The controller countersigns the cash slips, checks that membership fees have been paid properly, that the association's financial holdings are properly managed, and that the association's books and accounts are properly kept; she is obliged to report on this activity every month to the board. The attorney can be a lawyer with headquarters in Budapest.

§21 The board is made up of 50 members chosen by the general assembly, together with one representative each from the member associations. ⅕ of the board, that is 10 of its members, can be chosen from among the external members.

Irrespective of when board members were elected, their mandate comes to an end with the full general meeting. The board is quorate if 18 board members are present. If for any reason the total number in the board decreases to 17, an extraordinary general meeting has to be convened to elect new members to it.... The board chooses all of the officeholders from its members, with the exception of the president and the auditors. The secretary can be a member who is not in the board. The board oversees the implementation of its decisions and the work of its officers; it determines the wages of or possible payments to individual employees, makes decisions on the acceptance or exclusion of members, and, in addition, is entrusted with everything that is not clearly the responsibility of the assembly. The board has the right to set up a provisional or permanent board from its own ranks and to invite full or external members for this purpose.[139]

So, alongside a president and two vice presidents, they elected a secretary, a treasurer, a controller, two clerks, two librarians, an attorney living in Budapest, three auditors, and a first officer, who were all paid for their services. We do not know the exact breakdown of the annual cost of these officeholders, but in 1907, 1,740 crowns were marked out for "payment of officers"; this sum was about the average wage for a female office worker.[140]

In the absence of membership lists, we only know the presidents and vice presidents, or at least their names. The reports do not list the fifty board members. Yet the question arises of who these female Hungarian public and private office workers were who started to mobilize at about the same time as their Austrian counterparts. Because of their close relations with the Magántisztviselők Országos Szövetsége, NOE members mostly emerged from the class of private office workers; in my opinion, not many office workers employed in state and other public authorities and in the service sector joined the group, even if principally they would have been accepted. To which social groups in particular does the notion of the private office worker refer? In the pages of *Pesti Napló* (Pest Journal) in 1893, Sándor Braun defined this class: "This name was taken on by employees at banks, savings, and loan institutions, insurance companies, mills, factories, and other large enterprises, as a way to distinguish themselves from state office workers on the one hand and from shop assistants on the other."[141] In the late 1890s, private office workers represented "only a thin echelon of society," though their number was increasing dramatically by the end of the era of the dualist monarchy.[142]

Using census statistics, Zsombor Bódy's research touched on the age and gender distribution of office workers. According to his combined data, in 1900, the proportion of women in office careers proved to be highest in industry, commerce, and "free professions in civic and church public service." The proportion of female office workers in industry declined with age (39.3 percent of those under nineteen and 14.5 percent of those aged twenty to thirty-nine), as in this sector women tended to work only until they were married. The proportion of female office workers employed in commerce was rather lower (23 percent of those under nineteen and 9.3 percent of those aged twenty to thirty-nine), while the most women, because of "the female teachers, midwives, and nuns, also present here," were employed in public service (49 percent of those under nineteen and 23 percent of those aged twenty to thirty-nine).[143] In mining, according to Bódy, in 1910 there were only 45 female office workers, alongside 1,538 men. In industry, 26,498 men were joined by 6,191 women, while in commerce and in savings and loan, the figures were 37,212 and 7,569, respectively. Roughly speaking, women earned half what men did.[144] Thus, overall, while we cannot claim that the proportion of women in office work in this period was particularly high, their growing numbers helped establish the possibility for their movement and later their own publications.

NOE found strength in the fact that its members came from similar, albeit mostly lower, social classes and so had similar professional and life experiences.

Most did not have a direct connection to the transnational level of the women's movement. As in the majority of cases we do not even know their years of birth or death, we are not able to consider the possible generational conflicts among the members. Apart from their positions in the association, usually all we know about them is whether they published in *A Nő és a Társadalom* or in *A Nő*.

We only have (more) precise details on those who had leading positions in FE or who were from Schwimmer's family or her circle of friends. These included Szidónia Willhelm, who in addition to being a member of the FE board was for many years secretary of NOE; Margit Taubner (1882–1960), clerk of NOE and auditor for FE; Nelly Schnur, treasurer of NOE and FE board member; Róza Spitzer from the southern Hungarian city of Pécs; and Erzsébet Trombitás from the western Hungarian city of Szombathely. The patterns seen in AöF are repeated here, as we encounter family members in the boards of both NOE and FE: while Margit Szenczy worked as a controller for NOE, her sister Gizella was a member of the "Audit Committee" at FE.[145] Of the NOE leadership, Béla Besenyő; Janka Blumgrund (1864–1931); Mrs. Flóra Perczel, née Kozma, who did much for the organization of Unitarian women; and Ernő Reinitz all participated in the management of FE.[146] The same holds for Schwimmer's uncle, Lipót Kácser (born 1853 in Csák and died 1939 in Lucerne), who led Magántisztviselők Országos Szövetsége, and her closest colleagues, Paula Pogány, Vilma Glücklich, and Janka Gergely. The latter were, like Schwimmer, part of the Educational Committee at NOE, where, in cooperation with FE, they organized advice on career choice and held parents' evenings.[147] From the lectures given as part of these programs, we can conclude that the majority of the (board) members undertook their tasks for the association alongside their day jobs: Glücklich, like Fickert, taught for the whole of her life, and not only Willhelm and Gergely but also the Szenczy sisters and Mrs. Perczel continued their employment as office workers.

The leadership of FE was organized on similar principles to that of NOE.

> §7 The board of officers, whose members, with the exception of the president, are chosen from among members of the board, implements the decisions of the general assembly and of the board.... The treasurer manages the association's income and its wealth, and sees that membership fees are paid.... The books and accounts ... must be put at the disposal of the audit board.... The association's attorney, who must be a lawyer operating in Budapest, deals with the association's affairs at the court or other official institutions.
>
> §9 ... The board deals with all the affairs of the association that do not fall under the jurisdiction of the association's other bodies. The board is composed of the director and 24 full board members, who are chosen by the assembly. Its mandate always comes to an end at the annual ordinary general meeting, irrespective of when it was granted. The assembly elects a further 3 substitute members, who fill any places that become empty on the

board in the course of the year and whose mandate also ends at the annual proper general meeting. Members of the board can be reelected. The board manages and oversees the operation of the board of officers. If necessary, it can establish separate boards . . . made up of its own members, which can operate independently, within the bounds of their remit. . . .

The decisions of the board are made with a simple majority; on personal questions, a vote is always in secret. In the event of voted being tied, the chair has a casting vote. 10 members are required to be present for the meeting to be quorate. Any board member who fails to be present for five board meetings in a row is considered to have forsworn their membership, and a substitute member is called in in their place.[148]

In addition to the treasurer, the attorney and the audit board members, in principle FE also elected a secretary, controller, clerk, and librarian every year, but in practice it usually extended the mandate of those already in the posts. There is no data for the fees paid to the officers here either: in 1906, among the expenditures, we find one item entitled "office costs, employees," for which the sum of 2,378.74 crowns was put aside.[149] It was customary for those (board) members who had been in their posts longer and who could cover the costs of longer foreign journeys to represent FE, together with Schwimmer, in a delegation of five to eight members, at the biennial IWSA congress.[150]

At the suggestion of Mrs. Eugénia Meller, née Miskolczy, the size of the committee was extended in 1913 from thirty to thirty-five, in 1915 to forty, and in 1918 to sixty. The measure taken in 1913 was surely because of the challenges posed by the organization of the congress, while the amendments to the statutes during the war years followed the lightning growth in FE's membership.[151] The preparation work for the congress took place in the following committees, established with distinct tasks: the Propaganda Committee, the Economic Committee, the Excursions Committee, the Provincial Committee, the Guiding Committee, the Functions Committee, the Artistic Committee, the Interpreting Committee, the Accommodation Committee, and the Press Committee. Among the presidents of these committees were the aristocratic members of the FE committee (Countess György Haller, Countess Katinka Pejacsevich, and Countess Ármin Mikes), as well as NOE president Janka Gergely. The president of the Implementation Committee was Mrs. Sándor Teleki, an aristocratic member of FE, who attempted to promote the interests of the association in Hungarian political life through her husband, who was a deputy at the parliament.[152] In early 1914, when *A Nő* was launched, FE established the Journal Publication Committee; when war broke out, they set up the Committee for the Protection of Mothers and the Committee for the Protection of Children.[153]

FE membership was much more heterogenous than that of AöF or NOE. Yet I would warn readers against concluding that the character of FE might have been determined by the women joining it who were employed in the petit bourgeois, industrial, and agricultural sectors. The social composition of its membership was not compensated for by the journal articles about women working in industry or agriculture or by the lectures on these topics. This is shown clearly by the 1911 announcement of a prize for an "in-depth" study of the issue: "The economic situation of female factory workers is made the subject of a thorough study, and the work that is most impressive in its collection and analysis of the data will be rewarded with a prize of 50 crowns."[154] It is hard to imagine that, apart from a few women, Schwimmer and her coworkers formed any kind of closer acquaintance with women of working-class or peasant backgrounds.

The majority of the (board) members who played an active role in the association's activities were surely from the Budapest middle class, with a smaller group recruited from the ranks of the aristocracy. In the former group, women and men from nonobservant Jewish families were overrepresented: let us think of Janka Gergely, the close friend of the Schwimmer family, or of Sarolta Steinberger, their family doctor; of Mrs. Meller and Melanie Vámbéry, who would become victims of the Holocaust; or of Janka Dirnfeld and her sister, who managed to survive World War II. Men also played a key role in FE. Among them we find the jurist and royal court judge Dezső Márkus and the obstetrician and gynecologist Gusztáv Dirner, director of the Midwife Training Institute in Budapest. From 1904, these men helped FE with many aspects of its activities: they gave legal and medical advice, lectured in Hungarian and in other languages, or supplied statistics to *A Nő és a Társadalom*, in which they themselves also published articles.[155]

The constant recruitment of new members was of key importance in the life of the association.[156] They attempted to appeal to female university students through every possible channel, especially when, in the second half of the 1900s, women's higher education again started to be restricted, whether formally or informally, in most institutions. Following in the Austrians' footsteps, they wished to involve Budapest's intellectuals and artists in their work: they tried to convince the actress Mari Jászai, the authoress Terka Lux (1873–1938), the painter Árpád Feszty (born 1856 in Ógyalla [today Hurbanovo, Slovakia] and died 1914 in Lovran) and his wife, and Paula Pogány's brother, Vilmos/Willy Pogány (born 1882 in Szeged and died 1955 in New York), a graphic designer who later settled in the US and who regularly fought in FE's corner. These public figures were regular guests at the association's artistic soirees and balls, and *A Nő és a Társadalom* was advertised with their recommendation in 1906, in the hope that their names would attract more readers. Among the members we find the well-known Budapest photographer Olga Máté (née Mautner before 1907; born 1878 in Szigetvár and died 1961 in Budapest), who made portraits of many FE members and international delegates on the occasion of the 1913 IWSA congress,[157] as well as Zsófia Dénes (born 1885 in Budapest and died 1987 in Budapest), dozens of whose social reports were published in *A Nő* in the World War I years. Sándor Giesswein (born 1856 in Tata and died 1923 in Budapest), a Christian-Social politician who for a decade and a half supported Schwimmer's cause in the Hungarian parliament, was an FE member, as, for a while, was the Social Democratic politician Anna Kéthly.[158]

Here, too, the board members involved members of their families in the affairs of the association. We find among them the families of Glücklich, Gusztáv Dirner, Janka Dirnfeld, Mrs. Szirmay, Károly Zipernowsky (born 1853 in Vienna and died 1942 in Budapest), and the famous writer Dezső Kosztolányi (born 1885 in Szabadka [today Subotica, Serbia] and died 1936 in Budapest).[159] The number of active members was much higher in FE than in AöF, where alongside Auguste Fickert at most four individuals (Adele Gerber, Leopoldine Kulka, Rosa Mayreder, and Christine Touaillon) were willing (or allowed) to undertake more important roles. That NOE and FE proved to be more effective than AöF can be put down to the overlap between the membership and leadership of the two Hungarian associations and also to the specialized committees they brought into being to manage particular issues. The leaders of these committees tended to make the tasks they were entrusted with entirely their own.[160] We must also mention the more democratic operation of NOE and FE, in which the leaders had no intention of placing themselves above the membership or hiding away in the mists of unapproachability. Schwimmer and Glücklich treated their direct colleagues as if they were members of the family, happily meeting them in their spare time, on (boat) excursions, hikes, tea afternoons, or dinners together, at which they could indulge their love of gastronomy.[161]

Provincial Propaganda

NOE and FE have worked from the outset to expand their institutional scope. In the following sections, I survey the more than ten provincial branches, which they founded after 1907. These groups, the characteristic features of which I also discuss, first adapted the operating model of NOE and FE to their own purposes and then began their own independent endeavors. I also challenge the existing scholarship on the role of one provincial group, Balmazújvárosi Szabad Nőszervezet, which formally became part of FE in 1908. I argue that this provided FE an excellent piece of evidence for its argument that the movement was fighting for the rights of women of every social class.

The 1910 statutes of FE read "Objective: Equal rights for women in all areas and the protection of the interests of female labor. The establishment and support of subsidiary branches in the provinces, and finally the creation of groups within the framework of the association but given independent remits for their operation."[162] Albeit adapted to the protection of the needs of female office workers, more or less the same thoughts were expressed in the goals of NOE and in *A Nő és a Társadalom*. According to an article in the latter, "The problems and needs, which today are such a burden on the lives of provincial women office workers, could easily be removed, if it proved possible to establish an association in all of those cities in which at least 25–30 women office workers are employed."[163] NOE and FE managed to overcome the odds, despite financial difficulties. At NOE, the organization in the provinces began in 1907: "Nőtisztviselők Országos Egyesülete has for years considered organization in the provinces to be an urgently needed undertaking, but hitherto, for simple reasons of a lack of resources, was not able to start work on it. It has no capital or wealth to offer for this purpose, while its sources of income are hardly enough to cover the enormous expenses of the central institutions."[164]

With what status did the provincial groups connect to the parent associations, and how did they maintain communication with one another? What changes did the national conference of FE on 25 September 1914 bring to the life of the subsidiary branches? What level of autonomy did they ask for from the capital, and how much did they get? What types of activities did they organize themselves around, what problems did they face, and were they able to influence decisions made in Budapest?

Activism outside the administrative boundaries of Budapest served to bring the members of FE and NOE even closer together: as well as encouraging the operation of "centralized kitchens," they held an increasing number of joint lecture tours of activism in the provinces.[165] Over the course of 1905, Vilma Glücklich took the first practical steps toward establishing the branch associations when, in Kaposvár and Fiume (today Rijeka, Croatia), she worked on "preparing the soil" in the form of organizing lectures to spread her message.[166] These lectures were held in German and Hungarian in Fiume, but Glücklich was able to communicate in Italian as well.[167] In the following year and a half, these initiatives occasionally tailed away, no doubt because of financial problems: in 1906, FE was only able to spend about 400 crowns of its almost 5,000-crown annual budget on various "missions."[168] Lecture tours were also a burden for NOE, which similarly had a modest budget: in 1907, it said, "Money and labor are needed for this task, as for all others. Our fellow members would have undertaken the work, if our association had been able to pay for the costs. Our association's financial circumstances did not, however, allow us to spend money on this objective."[169]

The provincial groups maintained close relationships with both FE and NOE, as, given the overlap between the membership of the two parent organizations, was logical. The question arises, however, of why the Nagyváradi Nőtisztviselők Egyesülete (Female Office Workers' Association of Nagyvárad, today Oradea), established as a branch of NOE, would appear a few years later as a subsidiary of FE, while the Nőtisztviselők és Kereskedelmi Nőalkalmazottak Egyesülete (Association of Women Office Workers and Female Employees in Commerce) of Pécs was reestablished in 1918 as the Pécsi Feministák Egyesülete (Association of

Feminists of Pécs). The former is all the more surprising because NOE reported on its achievements in Nagyvárad with enormous enthusiasm.[170] The destruction of the archive sources makes it impossible to answer these questions, but I agree with Judit Acsády and Zsolt Mészáros, who claim that "an investigation into the relationship between NOE and FE is crucial in order to see more precisely the development of the organizational framework and social group of the Hungarian feminist movement."[171]

My research shows that until 1914 there were ten branch organizations in the classical sense under the aegis of the two associations; in 1914, these were followed by a further two. From the summer of 1917—by this stage with the help of FE—the number of groups outside the capital increased; their membership was recruited from the suffrage groups that formed after 6 June 1917. Already in July 1917, Paula Pogány "ask[ed] members, if they [heard] of an inaugural meeting, to inform the office about this, so [they could] send someone." She noted, "Next Adél Spády is setting off for the more peripheric cities of the country, i.e., Arad (today in Romania), Kolozsvár (today Timişoara), Marosvásárhely (today Târgu Mureş), and Beregszász (today Берегове, Berehove)."[172] The noninstitutionalized feminist-style groups working in smaller settlements were also significant. There were usually between 50 and 200 members in these groups.[173] Apart from residents' education level, their financial circumstances, and the number of women doing paid work, this number also depended on the attitude of the city administration. While the NOE parent association had 2,093 members in 1908–1909, there were 137 in the Arad auxiliary association, 150 in Temesvár, 74 in Nagyvárad, and 169 in the western Hungarian Szombathely.

The organization of the auxiliary associations was regulated in the following way: "The creation then disbandment or disappearance of the provincial branch associations must to from time to time be reported to the minister of the interior via the relevant legal authority, in order to be acknowledged." When provincial associations were registered, the same legal protocols were required as employed for the parent organization.[174] The provincial organizations in Germany, however, had much greater autonomy from the parent association than their Hungarian counterparts did; the explanation for this is clearly to be found in the nature of their activism. The former often published entirely independent publications, which across Germany at the fin de siècle numbered more than seventy.[175] This all visibly reflects the German attitude of federalism, as opposed to Hungarian attempts to centralize. Indeed, even in 1918, Schwimmer and her coworkers, copying the principles of IWSA, rejected decentralizing initiatives when at one session Paula Pogány announced, "As for one of our provincial groups setting up its own journal, Schwimmer can, given her American experience, vouch for the ineffectiveness of this. For where a number of journals are in the service of the same cause, none of them tends to be outstanding. Also, in America having a number of journals produced such discord that Chapman Catt had to spend millions on centralizing them."[176]

The nationality question could be an interesting element of organizations in the provinces, though the first wave of the feminist movement in Hungary did not really have a nationality. NOE repeatedly emphasized that it was only willing to organize branch associations on an economic basis, regardless of the language question. With this criterion in mind, in 1911, NOE rejected the organization of the Hungarian female office workers in Brassó (today Brașov,) because there was already a group of German Saxon women office workers.[177]

In the fall of 1907, after the creation of the women office workers' associations in Pécs and Nagyvárad, Schwimmer stated, "Our movement is not worth anything as long as the other women [who were not organizing or who belonged to other branches of the women's movement] in our country are not yet in our camp."[178] NOE wanted to extend the network of auxiliary organizations in part so it could send many Budapest office workers to the "provincial jobs" that would become available. According to NOE, the practice that Budapest-based women office workers accepted jobs in the provinces had a positive effect not just on young women's independence but also on their state of mind and their health.[179]

In 1907–1909, the Pécs group came under the aegis of NOE; the same was true of the auxiliaries in eastern Hungarian Debrecen, Nagyvárad (until 1911), Temesvár, Szombathely, and Arad. In the summer of 1908, steps were taken toward the foundation of an association in Pozsony (today Bratislava), but we do not know if this enterprise proved successful. The following groups undoubtedly operated as subsidiaries of FE: Nagyvárad (from 1911), Szabadka (Суботица), the southern Hungarian Szeged (which would often challenge the Budapest association), Vágújhely (today Nové Mesto nad Váhom, the town where Vilma Glücklich was born), and finally Pécs in 1918. The spa towns of Upper Hungary (roughly equivalent to the territory of today's Slovakia)—Pöstyén (Piešťany), Tátrafüred (Starý Smokovec), Trencsénteplic (Trenčianske Teplice)—played a key role in the management of these affairs, but there was also intense activism in Brassó, Érsekújvár (today Nové Zámky), Nyitra (today Nitra), Pozsony, and the western Hungarian city of Sopron. This spa-town activism was not universally popular among FE sympathizers, however, as made clear in a letter from an unknown sympathizer of the feminist movement János Benedek.

> Who is in Pöstyén on 15 August? The part of wealthy society the world over that wants to heal its rheumatism or gout. An international crowd that is busy with its declining tendons. Why would these people be interested in female suffrage? In Budapest or Bucharest? And will we take forward the success of the feminist movement by even a hair's breadth if, among these crippled hedonists pampering their confounded bodies, we hold a meeting, the outcome

of which is always in doubt? . . . The audience at a spa wants entertainment, pleasure; they need a cabaret, not a meeting. . . . The flush of emotion at a spa, a summer love story, tends only to last until the end of the season. . . . I am not going to fight on a battleground, among the disabled and crippled of Pöstyén; I would rather they let me go to Szováta [today Sovata, Romania], where I can do something in the interests of women.[180]

The first auxiliary associations were established in 1907 in Pécs and Nagyvárad as it has already been mentioned. The Pécs group of female office workers began work with forty-two full members and thirty-six supporting members.[181] We have no information about the number of founding members of the Nagyvárad branch, but we do know the names of the leadership and the committee members.[182] Shortly afterward came the branches in Arad, Szeged, Szombathely, and Debrecen. Then activism in Temesvár and Szabadka was also organized into an association framework, and in 1909, Upper Hungary was given an association, centered in Nyitra.[183] The Nyíregyházi Feministák Egyesülete (Association of Feminists of Nyíregyháza) was formed in 1914.[184] Meanwhile, in Nagybecskerek (today Zrenjanin, Serbia), Kaposvár, and Balmazújváros, there were groups referred to by contemporaries as "feministadian."[185]

Both NOE and FE made attempts to establish a branch association in Segesvár (in Transylvania; today Sighişoara,); the correspondence relating to this takes us closer to understanding the activism in the provinces. In this regard, we should note that the associations strove always to delegate charismatic individuals to the provincial events to win over the local population.

Schwimmer's reputation was a guarantee of success in Segesvár, as shown by a February 1913 letter from a local resident influenced by feminist ideas: "Here you were, among us, while since your departure a photograph has marked your steps—it would pain me were the light to fade from one day to the next, only then to be washed away thanks to people's lack of appreciation. I would like to show our gratitude for your appearance here by seeing to it that there are very permanent reminders of your visit, inescapable memories, so to speak, which would make it clear that your words were not spoken here without leaving their mark."[186]

The resident's lines also touched on the idea of establishing an association, and Schwimmer, in a letter a mere nine days later, responded helpfully to her questions. These letters allow us to conclude that, even in the year of the IWSA congress, FE attributed a key role to activism in the provinces. I quote the Schwimmer letter in question almost in its entirety, as it contains the steps necessary to create auxiliary associations.

> The method of organization is, first and foremost, to gather enough members among those interested; if we could find members from the vicinity of Segesvár who in their neighborhood are not in enough numbers to establish a separate organization, then they could be accepted, so that on this basis they

could number 25 or 30. Naturally men can [also] be accepted, and indeed must be accepted. And if this number is reached, then the members would be convened for an inaugural meeting.

The branch association could be called "Segesvári Feministák Egyesülete" [Association of Feminists of Segesvár]. Or "Küküllő megyei Feministák Egyesülete" [Association of Feminists of Küküllő County] (if they are happy to involve feminists from across the county). Or if they think that they will include the whole of Transylvania, then it could be called "Erdélyi Feministák Egyesülete" [Association of Feminists of Transylvania]. For this, of course, the branch association would have to begin not with 25 or 30 members but with about 80 or 100. Vilma Glücklich, the director of our association, could go down for the inaugural meeting, and detail the program of work to be done. This program could be made up, of course tailored to local conditions, of holding social and educational meetings and parents' evenings. We in Budapest, for example, hold at least one such meeting a month, at which laypeople or teachers introduce a reform idea relating to education as a subject for debate. After this, it would be possible to hold a series of lectures relating the theory of feminism, at which the legal, economic and social situation of women would be introduced and debated. We could find a small feminist lending library to share the most important feminist journals among members. Our member Mrs. Oszkár Szirmai of Nagysáros, chair of our committee for the protection of children and mothers, would be happy to start organizing the voluntary work in child protection in the area. We could open a practical advice center, in which once or twice a week an official consultation session would be held for expert members to give advice on career choice and legal and other matters to those posing questions to them. We could continue a movement, as needed, in the interests of a gardening or other specialist school perhaps being established in the city, or in the interests of girls being accepted to boys' high schools. As for urging political rights, we could work shoulder to shoulder with the center and with the other branch associations—etc., etc. There is an enormous amount of work that could be done; the work, that is, is just waiting for someone to do it. We would be most delighted if you and your honorable colleagues would stand at the head of this movement, as this would guarantee real success that is permanent, not just transitory. Our other provincial branch associations, which work excellently, would also surely be happy to assist the young association with advice.[187]

The Segesvár branch was ultimately founded under the name Hungarian Women's Council, and it "[managed] to enlist the wife of the lord lieutenant as president, and as vice-presidents the wife of the educational inspector and the widow of the former lord lieutenant, with my good self [Mrs. Norbert Simon] as secretary, a young female teacher as clerk, and industrial inspector Mrs. Antal as treasurer." Mrs. Simon wasted no time destroying the enthusiasm of those in Budapest, however, as she warned them, "Here everything has to be started again at the beginning, and I am afraid that even in two years' time it will be too early to talk of a branch of the feminist association—unless enormous changes take place, as the ground is still so fresh and there is need for so much preparation work to be done."[188] In terms of these efforts as a whole, it is significant that in the provinces, too, FE encouraged the recruitment of men as members. Meanwhile, the sources reveal the approximate numbers that were needed to establish a group limited to a small town or a larger provincial group and show how they copied the objectives and programs of those in the capital.[189]

Why were auxiliary associations founded in these settlements in particular? The explanation for the establishment of the group in Upper Hungary is clear: in addition to the women who worked in the larger cities in this region, many women from bourgeois (and aristocratic) backgrounds who were open to feminist ideas would spend their summers at the spa towns there. The parent association made the best of this, as it regularly organized lectures and gatherings in the resorts of Tátrafüred and Pöstyén.[190] To attract wider attention, it also invited foreign guests, despite the costs this incurred: in the summer of 1912, for example, Cicely Corbett (born 1885 in Danehill and died 1959 in Danehill), a leading figure of the British women's movement, visited the Tatra Mountains at the invitation of FE.[191]

The "organizational route" outlined by Judit Acsády and Zsolt Mészáros may also have contributed to the geographical distribution of the subsidiary groups: the logical organizational route would suggest that NOE should primarily settle in those towns in which the Magántisztviselők Országos Szövetsége, which "financially and morally assisted" NOE's work, had successfully managed to establish its operations.[192] In addition to these considerations, the personal suitability of the leaders of provincial activism may have been an important factor: alongside Glücklich, Berta Engel, FE board member who embodied perfectly the ideal of the female entrepreneur of the period, played a key role in the creation of the branches in Upper Hungary. Similar individual initiatives appeared in the Nagyvárad and Kaposvár groups, whose organization was led by FE board members Mrs. Péter Ágoston and Franciska Schwimmer. The expanding train service was also crucial. Yet we also see signs of randomness and spontaneity in FE's provincial endeavors: members of the association did not reject a single invitation to the provinces, traveling to the farthest ends of the country to hold lectures and readings. In 1911, Glücklich even accepted an invitation to a charity evening in the northern Hungarian town of Balassagyarmat, where her hosts failed not only to pay her a fee but even to cover her travel expenses.[193]

In another sign of spontaneity, Balmazújvárosi Szabad Nőszervezet joined FE, as is first mentioned in the minutes for June 1908. From that moment onward, FE would suddenly and loudly praise the agrarian women from Balmazújváros, defending them against the atrocities visited on them by the local administrator.[194] In Schwimmer's official public interpretation, the behavior of the provincial women "highlights the great intelligence of the people, and their knowledge of laws and regulations." On the other side, it was already clear for Schwimmer in 1908 that FE's" lack of funds [was] the obstacle to . . . organizing them in the villages."[195] In the end, the organization, together with the Pápai Leányegyesület (Girls' Association of Pápa, which is a small town in central Hungary) and the Galilei Szabadkőműves Páholy (Galilei Freemason Lodge) in Budapest, was among the first officially to join FE.[196] Afterward, a cordial exchange of letters, imbued on the Balmazújváros side by childish awe, took place between those in Budapest and the leader of the branch, Mrs. István Bordás, née Sára Rokon Tóth (born 1880 in Balmazújváros and died 1957 in Balmazújváros). By 1918, their membership had risen to an impressive five hundred or so. Beginning in 1916, the peasant women also helped with selling the FE's new journal in their neighborhood. They were the first to ask for specimen copies of the new *Nők Lapja* (Women's Journal), the previously mentioned popular journal of the FE: in March they were given 50 copies to sell, and during the months that followed, they received a further 150. They did not excel at actually selling these: in August, Mrs. István Bordás reported that, because of summer agricultural work, there remained 56 copies that they had failed to sell, and so henceforth they required later 25 copies. In other words, the cost of an issue, at four fillérs, which was very low, was too much of a burden for the majority of the provincial agrarian population.[197]

According to a report in *A Nő és a Társadalom*, "the Free Women's Organization of the Balmazújváros was represented" at the 1908 IWSA congress of Amsterdam.[198] This must not be interpreted as meaning personal involvement. The letter written by Mrs. István Bordás, full of grammatical and stylistic errors, clearly indicates that they were not present in Amsterdam. She gives thanks for the postcards sent by FE members from Amsterdam and expresses her delight that, together with her fellow members, she can read the movement's official periodical: "Again, we do not know what we feel in our hearts so full of joy that we have read the journal A Nő and to read just how enthusiastic you all are about us."[199] Furthermore, as mentioned previously, Schwimmer had the whole group sent up to the IWSA congress in Budapest in 1913, as something of a spectacle for others to behold: apart from being photographed with prominent international delegates, the women of Balmazújváros were not given any other role there.

In light of the previous factors, I do not believe that this auxiliary association, despite its size and its level of activity, played a significant role. For Schwimmer and her colleagues, these women served as an ideal tool, not to mention a brilliant public relations move during the 1913 IWSA congress, but they do not seem to have been anything more. They offered a chance for FE to absolve itself of the charge brought against it in the daily press, which claimed, "The feminist movement fights only for the rights of bourgeois women."[200] Meanwhile, the letters from the women of Balmazújváros, written with much pathos but little real content, were often simply neglected by the FE leadership: in 1909, they waited

Figure 5.13. Women from the northeast Hungarian town Balmazújváros surrounded by delegates of the IWSA congress in Budapest. Schwimmer-Lloyd Collection, The New York Public Library.

in vain for any response to three letters, something that could surely not be put down to difficulties with the mail service.[201] All this serves to prove an important point: FE did not express the same message in its journal as in the association and private correspondence. The women of Balmazújváros did not bring any financial advantage, unable as they were even to collect membership fees or periodical subscriptions: we know from their letter of 27 July 1910 that, even though the association had 231 members, "unfortunately until now [their] income [was] only 12 crowns, what with [their] annual membership only being 60 fillérs."[202]

Finally, we should note that the activism of female agricultural laborers in Balmazújváros was not unique within the history of FE. According to the report of Ludmilla Jancsusko, who headed a local initiative, something similar had happened in 1913 in the settlement of Abaújszina in the northern Hungarian Hernád valley. Schwimmer replied almost immediately to her letter, mentioning the women of Balmazújváros as an example.[203]

As well as publishing columns on associations, the local press also often provided information about local events. These organizations' annual program of events, like that of the parent association, was regulated by (summer, or autumn–winter) plans of work. Committee meetings were held in August or September, and the leaders from Budapest were also invited. Twice a week there were library hours, association visiting times, and advice and administrative consultation sessions, where, alongside a discussion of activities to be undertaken, the legal, labor, and family problems facing the membership and those in need could be addressed. Board members of auxiliary associations attempted (in principle) to make up for deficiencies in secondary specialist education by holding language and practical courses (typing, stenography, business correspondence, etc.)—following the model used in Budapest. These courses in particular gave office workers and those employed in commerce an opportunity to improve their knowledge. The activists in the capital expected members of the branch organizations actively to join the work of the movement: their tasks were to recruit members, collect donations, and distribute propaganda material. In return, these members could avail themselves of offers of time at holiday resorts and members' discounts at baths and on trains.[204]

The effectiveness of the auxiliary associations varied. The groups in Szombathely, Upper Hungary, Nagyvárad, and Temesvár performed most reliably, though when writing up their reports the presidents may well have exaggerated their achievements to improve their own track records.

The organizers in Budapest, meanwhile, often expressed their dissatisfaction alongside their words of support. In 1907, they rebuked the provincial members: "Our provincial members (with a few honorable exceptions) cause considerable headache for our treasurer, as our enthusiastic debt collector cannot in this instance come to the rescue. Yet since our journal was launched our provincial members participate, albeit indirectly, in all the work of our association; please assist us conscientiously with our not inconsiderable costs."[205] The reason for the missed payments comes up regularly in the minutes: women in the provinces were simply unable to cover a membership fee in line with that in the capital—even after receiving payment reminders.[206]

The Budapest association complained that the associations in Pécs and Szeged did not operate on a continuous basis, and the latter "remained isolated" before in 1914 breaking off just about all contact with its parent organization. The development of the movement in Arad was for a long time held back by a lack of any available association headquarters, and progress in Szombathely was blocked by the typhus epidemic of 1908. In addition to these problems, in these places the elements of society that the activist leaders relied on were more rigidly constrained.

On the other side of the coin, it was not unknown for the provincial groups to voice criticisms of their own. The Szombathely organizers once complained to Vilma Glücklich that they could hardly cover the costs of their hall rental out of their income: "The life of our association is not satisfactory in any respect; numerically, we are decreasing, and we could surely do with both moral and financial success, because we can very much sense the lack of the latter as our obligation to pay our rent draws closer, and we are fearful that sooner or later we will become homeless."[207]

The three levels of the women's movement—that is, the local, the national, and the international or transnational—would from time to time become intertwined. In the history of such points of connection, the suffrage congresses held every two years enjoyed the greatest publicity. The 1913 congress held in Budapest was of key importance for the branch associations, as some of them were involved in the job of organizing it.[208] In addition, leaders of the women's movement abroad, like Carrie Chapman Catt, Cicely Corbett, or the German sociologist Anna Lindemann (born 1892 in Bielefeld and died 1959 in Wrocław), one of the youngest exponents of the pre-1918 German women's movement, came to Hungary and gave lectures in the provinces, which Schwimmer or Glücklich translated into Hungarian for the local audience. Catt, whom *A Nő és a Társadalom* referred to as "our great leader," spent considerable time in Hungary in the course of 1908, holding lectures for large audiences, not just in Budapest but also in Érsekújvár, Nyitra, Nagyvárad, Temesvár, Pécs, Szombathely, and Pozsony.[209]

After the outbreak of war, the provincial associations continued to follow the example set by Budapest, but they had numerous one-off initiatives, such as the keeping of community gardens on plots put at their disposal by the local settlement. In this regard, I consider that the key objective of the national conference convened by FE on 25 September 1914 was not to debate the organizational questions of the preceding ten years but to elaborate the strategies for the wartime work carried out on the home front. This is borne out by the following excerpt of the reports of the feminist association of Nagyvárad and the minutes of the Budapest board meeting of FE on 9 September: "One of the main subjects of the conference was the submission of the Nagyvárad Branch Association, which makes proposals for ways to see closer cooperation between branch associations and the center."[210] The minutes suggest that the meeting did not necessarily bring a "move from hierarchical management towards a decentralized, more democratic form," as Judit Acsády and Zsolt Mészáros suggest; rather, it laid down the foundation for closer and more concentrated cooperation.[211] Every representative of the provincial organizations was present at the national assembly, which achieved its goal.[212] Albeit with a lag of one and a half to two months compared to those in Budapest, the provincial labor exchange offices were put into action. In the October issue of *A Nő*, there was already a news story about how the offices in the provinces were working to solve the problems facing women seeking employment.[213] Of the branches set up before the outbreak of war, only a few would remain effective after 1914; those in Nagyvárad and Szeged, for example, were outstandingly successful.[214]

Even during the war years, the branches in the provinces remained loyal to the parent association: when, in the summer of 1916, at (according to Vilma Glücklich) the decision of the minister of the interior, the authorities banned the national feminist congress in Budapest, which had been planned for many months, an invitation came from Szeged for a substitute event to be held there.[215] In addition to the suffrage bill associated with liberal-bourgeois democratic politician Vilmos Vázsonyi, meanwhile, pressure from the parent association and from already-operating subsidiary groups contributed to the beginning of activist work in other settlements.[216] Between 1917 and the summer of 1918, representatives of FE intensified their efforts in all sixty-three Hungarian counties. They held meetings in, among other places, Beszterce (today Bistriţa), northern Hungarian Eger, Érsekújvár, western Hungarian Győr, Pápa, southern Hungarian Sásd, Szatmárnémeti (today Satu Mare), central Hungarian Székesfehérvár, eastern Hungarian Szolnok, and Trencsén (today Trenčín), where, in addition to holding lectures, they distributed badges and put up posters.[217]

To understand the dynamics of the institutional lives of these organizations, I considered it vital to survey not only the relationship between the Budapest associations and the transnational level of the women's movement but also the ties between these associations and the FE and NOE bodies in Budapest. The two associations started their organizational efforts in other towns and cities in Hungary together, but the bodies they formed there later split or followed different dynamics. Their success depended on the leaders of the local associations and the extent to which they worked closely with the Budapest headquarters. The war naturally affected the functioning of the branch organizations as well, but most of them continued to pursue work successfully despite the initial difficulties.

Hungary's Strengthening Positions in the International Women's Movement

In the discussion below, I first consider the public relations efforts used by the associations in parts of Hungary outside Budapest and then put their workings in a larger context and consider their place against the backdrop of the international women's movement. I examine the network among the members of FE and the transnational organizations, and more precisely the IWSA, which played a crucial role in FE's operations through personal contacts among their leaders. NOE was less prominent and less connected in the international arena, so the emphasis in the following pages falls on FE, although one certainly cannot ignore NOE, given the overlap between the two associations.

In western European countries, the investigation of the transnational dimensions of the women's movement began in the late 1980s. As well as an increase in general interest in international subjects, this, as Birgitta Bader-Zaar interprets it, is thanks to the UN resolution that paved the way to the announcement of the Decade of Women from 1975 to 1985.[218] Nowadays, a significant amount of international literature is available on this subject: methodological studies,[219] source publications,[220] and other works on the establishment and expansion, structural politics, and challenges of ICW, IWSA, and WILPF,[221] not to mention case studies of individual activists.[222] As the pre-1918 history of the movement can be interpreted as a series of European and North American congresses, the framework making this organization possible has also been studied. Who was in a position to participate in these meetings, and how? What travel strategies can be observed in the work of these activists? What languages did delegates at these sessions use to understand one another, and what obstacles were there to direct and indirect communication? How was one particular bond of friendship or act of hospitality able to influence the directions and dynamic of this enterprise?[223] Many of these studies start with the shared interests and collective identity of the members of these organizations and the way these were formed during World War I; this would ultimately lead to the institutionalization of the international peace movement.[224] Hungarian aspects of this issue have been studied by Judith Szapor and Susan Zimmermann. In her writings, Szapor relates to the international relations of FE before and after World War I, while Zimmermann examines the international embeddedness of the newly established FE on the basis of the sources in New York.[225]

I have outlined the main aspects of FE's network of relationships on the bases of the leading members' correspondences, press products, and other documents related to the operation of the associations, and in what follows, I share the first results of this work. I argue that FE's considerable international embeddedness was thanks to Schwimmer. She began building these connections, using her journalistic activities, at the beginning of the 1900s. Later, at FE committee meetings, it was she who always reported on letters arriving from abroad and on news from the international arena of the movement. Presumably, she personally handled almost all of the association's ever more intricate foreign correspondence. This in turn helped to advance her journalist career, as before 1914 she often reported on developments in Hungary in the press of the international associations.

The Schwimmer collection allows us fully to reconstruct the main trends of these connections. From this, we can form a picture of her views on politics and on social problems, as well as of the strategies she used to achieve FE's current plans and projects. Detailed descriptions can be found of her Hungarian and foreign colleagues and friends active in the international arena and of those in it who became her enemies. There were an increasing number of the latter: her conflict with Aletta Jacobs deepened in 1915, and in Hungary she had no shortage of detractors in MNSz or among the Social

Democrats and Christian-Socials. Glücklich and Schwimmer once described the president of MNSz, Auguszta Rosenberg, as being "impertinent" and even "mendacious."[226]

At this point, we need to clarify that, apart from a few attempts in her youth, Schwimmer did not keep a diary in the classical sense, but a mountain of slips of notepaper with the date marked have survived amid her letters, revealing her everyday tasks and her appointments both official and unofficial. These provide an interesting addition to FE's foreign connections.[227]

While Hungary was connected to ICW via MNSz, FE, together with Austria, Canada, Denmark, Italy, Norway, and Russia, became a full member of IWSA at the 1906 Copenhagen congress. Table 5.3 presents these acts of membership and indicates that BöF joined ICW in 1903.[228]

The first signs of Schwimmer's strategies to build her international network are from May and June 1901: this was when she established contact with the organization Kaufmännischer Hilfsverein für weibliche Angestellte in Germany and with Marie Lang.[229] Her first text in German to be published outside Hungary was in the pages of *Dokumente der Frauen*, for which she earned ten forints.[230] She exchanged her first letter with Aletta Jacobs in August 1901. Jacobs was interested not only in the charitable associations that dominated the Hungarian women's movement but also in the female prison in Márianosztra; she even suggested she might pay a visit to Hungary.[231] It is a sign of Schwimmer's initial lack of knowledge of English that she and Jacobs corresponded in German, which Schwimmer spoke perfectly. At the same time, Jacobs's German skills were not exactly well honed; her text is rife with grammatical errors, mistakes with verb agreement, and stylistic problems.

Jacobs in turn faced the challenge of deciphering Schwimmer's handwritten German in Gothic letters: "Again you have written your article in these damned German characters. This is unreadable. If it were written in Latin letters, this evening I would have put all my other work to one side and tried to publish it in one of the better journals.... Why should someone have to search for one single syllable for half an hour, if there are letters that the whole world uses and knows: send it back to me just as soon as you can."[232]

It is partly thanks to this intense exchange of letters that, together with Glücklich, Schwimmer not only participated in the 1904 Berlin congress of ICW but also gave a lecture there. This was made possible by the support of Schwimmer's uncle Lipót Kácser, who also earned his living as a journalist.[233] This congress proved pivotal in the history of international women's movements, as IWSA was established on this occasion.

What better evidence could there be that Hungary had found its way onto the map of the international women's movement than that Alice Salomon immediately called on Schwimmer to give two lectures on the ICW congress.

168 | *Progressive Women's Movements*

Table 5.3. The expansion of ICW, IWSA, and WILPF from 1888 to 1919

ICW	IWSA	WILPF
US 1888		
Canada 1893		
Germany 1897		
Great Britain, Sweden 1898		
Australia, Denmark, Netherlands 1899		
Italy, New Zealand 1900		
Argentina, France 1901		
Austria, Switzerland 1903		
Hungary, Norway 1904	Australia, Great Britain, Germany, Sweden, US 1904	
Belgium 1906	**Austria, Denmark, Canada, Hungary, Norway, Italy, Russia 1906**	
Bulgaria, Greece 1908	Bulgaria, Finland, South Africa, Switzerland 1908	
	Belgium, Czech Lands, France 1909	
Finland, Serbia 1911	Iceland, Serbia 1911	
South Africa 1913	China, Galicia, Portugal, Romania 1913	
Portugal 1914		
		Austria, Belgium, Canada, Denmark, France, Germany, Great Britain, Hungary, Italy, Netherlands, Norway, Sweden, US 1915
		Australia, Belgium, Finland, Ireland, Poland, Switzerland 1919

I used Leila J. Rupp's data to produce this table (Rupp 1994, 16–18).

In the name of the organizational committee, I commission you, during the discussion on 15 July in Section 2 of the International Congress, to give a report on the situation facing female post office administrators in Hungary. Miss Gronemann will be giving a talk on this subject relating to Austria, but we would also like to hear during the discussion about the conditions in Hungary. I would also like to ask you to give a brief talk on 14 June on the women workers' movement in Austria and Hungary; this would be about 15 minutes. I know that perhaps you have already agreed to this, but we would be grateful if, despite this, we could receive your assignation. We ask you to inform us as soon as possible, so that we can provisionally place your name in the program of events.[234]

Table 5.4. ICW, IWSA, and WILPF congresses from 1888 to 1921

ICW	IWSA	WILPF
Washington 1888		
Chicago 1893		
London 1899		
	Washington 1902	
Berlin 1904	Berlin 1904	
	Copenhagen 1906	
	Amsterdam 1908	
Toronto 1909	London 1909	
	Stockholm 1911	
	Budapest 1913	
Rome 1914		
		The Hague 1915
		Zurich 1919
Oslo 1920	Geneva 1920	
		Vienna 1921

I used Leila J. Rupp's data as the basis for this table (Rupp 1997, 74).

Thus, in a section jointly held with Caroline Gronemann (born 1869 in Vienna and died 1911 in Vienna), an Austrian pioneer of women's vocational education who called for women's rights to specialist education, Schwimmer gave a lecture on the situation facing working women.

Until 1920, Schwimmer was among the FE delegates at every IWSA congress. She also participated in the organization's 1920 meeting in Geneva, to which, as an émigré in Vienna, she traveled with Mrs. Meller. In the report on the event, her name is listed among FE members as a "specially invited member." Paradoxically, she gave a lecture as part of a panel to which Finnish female politicians and US senators were invited, which was entitled "Work of Women Members of Parliament, by Women Members of Parliament."[235] Right before she immigrated to the US, she also participated in the 1921 Vienna congress of WILPF.[236]

In the initial period, the Austrian and German parts of foreign relations of Schwimmer and through her FE were dominant; this can be put down to Schwimmer's limited knowledge of English and her journalistic bent, as well as to the fact that IWSA was founded in Berlin. Between 1901 and 1904, she exchanged letters with only two Americans, Carrie Chapman Catt and dancer and choreographer Isadora Duncan (born 1877 in San Francisco and died 1927 in Nice). In letters written in German, Schwimmer tried to tempt Duncan to visit Budapest in 1904, but her attempts were unsuccesful.[237] In her mail from outside Hungary, we mostly find letters from Vienna, Berlin, and the bastion of the German bourgeois women's movement, Leipzig. From Vienna, it was initially Adele Gerber,

Auguste Fickert, Leopoldine Kulka, and Marie Lang with whom she established cordial relations; later, she would add Henriette Herzfelder and Marianne Hainisch from the circles of BöF to the list. In 1908, she had a disagreement with Fickert when Schwimmer could hardly recognize an article she had submitted to *Neues Frauenleben*; as was her habit, Fickert had failed to inform her of the edits that had been made. Their relationship became frosty as a result, even though, just two years previously, when AöF had broken away from BöF, Schwimmer had mediated between Fickert, Hainisch, and IWSA, as borne out by Catt's letter: "I note what you say about the Oesterreichischer Frauenverein and Miss Fickert. I will talk with her when I go there about her Society [AöF] and learn what its objects are. . . . Will it offend Mrs. Hainisch? . . . We do not wish to be the means of creating unpleasant feelings of course. What do you think?"[238]

Schwimmer maintained a correspondence with some leaders of the radical wing of the bourgeois women's movement in Germany, including Anita Augspurg, Anna Pappritz (born 1861 in Ośno Lubuskie and died 1939 in Berlin), Alice Salomon (born 1872 in Berlin and died 1948 in New York), Käthe Schirmacher, and Helene Stöcker (born 1869 in Elberfeld and died 1943 in New York), all of whom she would remain in close cooperation with for decades.[239] Adele Schreiber (born 1872 in Vienna and died 1957 in Herrliberg) and Marie Stritt wrote particularly warm words to her. Before the official foundation of FE, Schwimmer arranged for a Budapest lecture given by Schreiber, a devout Catholic from an artistic Austrian family who lived in Berlin with her husband beginning in 1897.[240] Later Stritt, too, would go on a lecture tour of Hungary.[241] FE also looked to these activists to contribute to its new journal, as shown by Glücklich's list of potential authors. Apart from those from Austria and Germany, the only names on the list were Jacobs; a well-respected American feminist author of the period, Charlotte Gilman Perkins (born 1860 in Hartford and died 1935 in Pasadena); the British philosopher sociologist Bertrand Russell (born 1872 in Trellech and died 1970 in Penrhyndeudraeth); and a "Finnish woman."[242] FE intended to use these faces of the international women's movement to drum up interest in *A Nő és a Társadalom*.

> We are heading towards perfection. We are already at a point where we invite people to join us as colleagues. Please remove and add names as you see fit to the list on the other side. . . . The list of ordinary people with a variety of different interests serves the goal of the broadest and most distant group taking an interest in the distribution of the journal. . . . Yes, please, my dear, come back as soon as you can, because, even if I don't want to put it on the subscription list, I do want to put their "I do's" in the daily papers as good advertising for us.[243]

As a result of this gradual network building, a growing number of Austrian and German journals published articles by Schwimmer. Marie Lang made her a regular contributor to *Dokumente der Frauen*, sending her complimentary copies of the publication; Schwimmer's articles were then published in the pages of

Figure 5.14. Delegates of the IWSA congress in Budapest in front of the Vigadó concert hall. Schwimmer-Lloyd Collection, The New York Public Library.

Neues Frauenleben, Frauen-Rundschau, Die Frau, Illustrierte Frauen-Zeitung, and *Die Zeit.*[244]

Schwimmer was on friendly terms with many members of the German Verband fortschrittlicher Frauenvereine and the Austrian BöF, AöF, and the Frauenstimmrechtskomitee until the early 1920s. Aside from publishing in different journals, Schwimmer's lengthy exchanges of letters with foreign activists and women's rights associations discussed the present challenges faced by the women's movement and, beginning in 1914, the tasks of the peace movement. Indeed, in the early 1900s, Schwimmer often asked foreign activists for guidance on practical questions relating to women's education and employment. The 1912–1913 letters focus almost exclusively on the Budapest congress and the preliminary conference in Vienna.[245] Delegates from twenty-six countries were expected to attend the event in the Hungarian capital. Within the Austrian contingent, the leaders of BöF who were to make an appearance were Marianne Hainisch and Henriette Herzfelder, as well as Daisy Minor and Gisela Urban. Their participation was the cause of considerable pride among the leaders of FE.[246]

This presentation of the international system of contacts established by FE and Schwimmer must add nuance to those statements in the literature that overemphasize the importance of relationships with the English-speaking world. Needless to say, FE's connectedness of this kind constantly grew with the improvement in Schwimmer's competence in English.[247] In the early 1910s, meanwhile, three main trends were being established in FE's international relationships: it retained its traditionally close rapport with the German and Austrian associations and a few Swiss ones, which on an individual basis were not necessarily in direct contact with the international movement. These were primarily organizations or rights groups that gathered together narrowly professional communities, like teachers, office workers, employees in commerce, actors and singers, journalists, or restaurant staff. The second main tendency in its professional relationships cannot be limited to the English-speaking countries, however. These were in the main connections formed through IWSA, in which, alongside the British and US aspects, the Dutch and other northern European elements were becoming pronounced by the early 1910s. We can also mention a minimal amount of correspondence with the women's organizations of the Russian Empire, the Ottoman Empire, China, Iceland, and perhaps Australia. The third and less significant direction taken by the FE network involved countries such as those in southern Europe, southern Africa, or South America, which were on the periphery of the women's movement and with which FE came into contact in the course of organizing the 1913 congress.[248] During this period, FE established contacts with women's associations in Transylvania, the territory of present-day Slovakia, the Czech and South Slavic regions, and Galicia. After 1914, we should also note the deepening relationships with the peace movement, though I argue that these are principally not associated with FE so much as with Schwimmer and then Glücklich.

In point of fact, there is nothing extraordinary in how FE's contact network progressed: simple geography determined that German and Austrian connections would dominate Anglo-American ones. Any trend to the contrary would have been all the more surprising given the nature and level of development of the English-speaking women's movement. If we think of the number of women who could be mobilized, this would be true of Germany, too, where the social base of the women's movement was much broader than in Austria or Hungary. The German associations did, however, present an example for the Austrians and indeed Schwimmer and her coworkers to follow.[249] This, for all Schwimmer's Anglophilic tendencies, is surely relevant.

There are three reasons to believe that FE's working methods were adopted from the methods used by the German organizations, filtered through the Austrian ones. The first clear piece of evidence is found in the correspondence and in the articles by German and Austrian authors published in *A Nő és a Társadalom* or *A Nő*. We should not forget that the articles in these journals almost always expressed admiration for the work of their fellow women in the territories of the German Empire and Austria. Second, the list of speakers Schwimmer invited to Hungary also prove the influence of Germany and Austria. Of the thirty-one foreign lecturers arriving in Hungary between 1904 and 1917, half were German or Austrian citizens. There were only two guests from the United Kingdom and one each from the United States and France.[250] The majority of speakers, no doubt for reasons of financial expediency, willingly linked up their journeys to Prague, Vienna, Budapest, and perhaps some provincial Hungarian towns; this is what Schreiber did in 1904, Aletta Jacobs in 1906, Carrie Chapman Catt in 1908, and Cicely Corbett in 1912. In the course of a prolonged exchange of letters, Schreiber attempted to keep her activities in Budapest and Vienna in step: "I will probably come to Vienna in November. It is possible that I could come to Budapest afterwards, if it were possible to arrange a lecture there.... Please give me an entirely honest answer as to whether there is an organization prepared at least to cover the costs.... I would like an answer about the lecture as soon as possible, as I need to finalize my schedule."[251]

Third, we need to touch on indirect relations with women's movements abroad (and the way their example was followed)—that is, how foreign press was monitored and which foreign-language volumes were accumulated. The journals that FE subscribed to (at a favorable rate) or that were sent without charge because of Schwimmer's journalistic work also support the primacy of the German example: of the forty-nine journals—in addition to *Ius Suffragii*—to be found in the FE material, we find a total of eight periodicals published in the United Kingdom or the United States.[252] We see similar tendencies emerge with the monographs purchased from abroad, which have survived in the FE library: the association's archive holds twenty-nine works in Hungarian, forty in English, eleven in French, one each in Swedish and Italian, and fifty-five in German.[253]

The international relations of FE and, through it, NOE were thus inseparable from Rosika Schwimmer. Over the years, she became one of the faces not only of the Hungarian association but also of the international organization, and she worked hard to put her prominence to good use during the war years. Vilma Glücklich, who was secretary-general of the WILPF from 1922 to 1925, also became a respected figure in the international arena. It reveals a great deal about the women's movement in Hungary and the obstacles it faced in the interwar period that, after 1925, none of the leading figures of any of these international associations was Hungarian.

The Associations' Controversial Approaches to World War I

The outbreak of World War I was a turning point in the development of the Hungarian and international women's movements. As I have discussed, before August

1914, the associations used public activism, demonstrations, gatherings, posters, and leaflets to draw society's attention to the fact that there could be no further delay in achieving equal rights for women. This changed entirely in the last days of July 1914. In the discussion that follows, I consider NOE's and FE's somewhat ambivalent attitude toward the war and their wartime work on the home front. On the one hand, the associations made enormous efforts to participate in the war work, while on the other hand, from the outset, they sharply criticized the political establishment and the government of István Tisza (born 1861 in Pest and died 1918 in Budapest; in office 1913–1917) for failing to avoid armed conflict. In addition to their public relations and press efforts, they took action in this field as well, as illustrated by Schwimmer's peace negotiations abroad and the role of FE in the establishment of WILPF.

The first change in this regard was brought by the announcement on 26 July 1914 by Prime Minister Tisza that "it proved necessary to apply the exceptional powers introduced by article LXIII of 1912."[254] At the same time, regulation 12.001/I of 1914 introduced wartime censorship, and on 24 July (5479/1914) and 1 August (5735/1914), the formation of new associations or new subsidiary branches was forbidden.[255] In September 1915, members of FE were already complaining that the police were not allowing their "home agitation," and in May 1916, the police even took Vilma Glücklich in for questioning.[256] The national "feminist congress" planned by FE for the following month in Budapest was also banned, so the association was forced to distribute the text of the planned lectures in printed form. They had to swear they would stop their peace propaganda, for fear of imprisonment, the confiscation of their property, or the disbanding of the association.[257] In the August 1916 issue of A Nő, Mrs. Sándor Teleki complained, "The Budapest police punished one of our universally well-respected fellow feminist women [Szidónia Willhelm] with three days' imprisonment and a 50-crown fine, because she wished to demonstrate for peace."[258] In the end, beginning in June 1917, they were again able to hold public meetings without the authorities inspecting them; moreover, it was not hard to pay for these meetings, as their overall wealth had grown to as much as 50,000 crowns.[259]

Even though FE and NOE had from the very start of mobilization urged an immediate peace settlement and considered the situation to be "without doubt the ruin of male diplomacy and male civilization,"[260] they made the most active possible contribution to the war effort on the home front. By the first days of August, FE and NOE had taken the battle for political rights for women off their agendas, and, unlike AöF, they were concentrating their energies on providing help on the home front, on acting as a labor exchange, and on providing advice. Yet as early as the summer of 1915, the slogans of the fight for suffrage were seeping back into the pages of A Nő: "Ladies! They are even taking your 18-year-old sons! Would this be possible if we were able to participate in the managing of the state's affairs?"[261]

The newfound objectives of these organizations can be reconstructed from the special issues of *A Nő* published right after the outbreak of war.[262] The key declared goal was the prevention of economic collapse on the home front and the "protection of the extended family of the nation."[263] They considered it their "fundamental obligation" to "protect the material and intellectual treasures" that the decades of the dualist system had created.[264] The foundation of this mission was the labor exchange operated within the framework of the Gyakorlati Tanácsadó (Practical Advice Bureau) it should not be in italics c. to Pályaválasztási Tanácsadó on 177 of FE. They strove to find jobs for women forced to join the workforce by necessity, including those who had lost their livelihoods because of the worsening economic circumstances: for example, immediately after the outbreak of war, a great many female office workers found themselves out on the street, and, as in western Europe, many workers in the textile and food industries found themselves out of work.[265]

Regarding the labor exchange, given the nature of NOE's profile, its attention was focused on finding employment for female office workers; all other lines of work were the business of FE.[266] The associations did not forget about the protection of the rights of women who had already found work.[267] They tried to coordinate their efforts with a number of organizations in Budapest, as emphasized at their general meeting on 25 September: "There is a lack of harmonious cooperation... between the associations in the capital, so many things are done in parallel... and many in need of help do not... receive support, while others... make use of it from multiple sources. In order to coordinate work on this, a precise survey should be compiled of the tasks that each association has undertaken."[268]

After mobilization, the associations decided on the temporary suspension of *A Nő*: Vilma Glücklich "recommend[ed] that [they] announce a great general invitation on the cover of *A Nő*, which [they would] send not only to [their] subscribers but also bring to wider attention by distributing it on the street, bringing it to the awareness of the public that people can only effectively be helped by work rather than with handouts."[269] The membership expressed its deepest remorse for the war, as it had hoped "to the last minute" that "peace [would be] upheld" and that the monarchy would not join the war on the side of the German Empire.[270] Then they started to emphasize at their public meetings that the most important pillars of their work were organizing the economy of the home front, operating their labor exchange, defending the rights of mothers, and promoting health, vocational education, and child education. They provided support to deal with the problems of everyday living faced by those "left at home" by soldiers fighting at the front and those killed; the associations took on tasks that wartime social policy could not pay (enough) attention to. Under the banner of "wartime assistance for mothers," FE members in both Budapest and the provinces helped mothers who were on their own and unable to work: they helped with childcare, holding "peace-loving" storytelling afternoons for the little ones. In principle, they were willing to assist with problems faced by domestic servants (accommodation, professional training, contracts), though in practice this was limited to articles published in the pages of *A Nő*.[271]

They also operated communal gardening plots, giving talks on how to preserve fruit and vegetables.[272] Regarding the wartime role of AöF, the Hungarians reported only on the association's 1915 submission in the defense of victims of sexual violence.[273] Despite restrictions on which journals could be brought in from abroad, FE did not give up its monitoring of the foreign press but continued to make serious efforts to acquire not just German but also Swiss, British, and French periodicals.

In the first days of the war, FE, which at the time had a total of 1,195 members, devoted all its attention to filling with women the positions made vacant (by men leaving for the front) in Budapest factories and in the agricultural sector. At harvest time, this was all a strategic question, as produce could not remain unharvested in the fields.[274] The situation was made more difficult by the fact that in August, during the school vacation, many mothers were simply unable to find childcare.[275] This lack of care is closely connected to another problem that was never resolved during the decades of the dualist system: the low number of kindergartens and crèche facilities.[276] One of the first tasks in hand, then, was to provide institutional childcare for working mothers, something FE made significant progress with in a short space of time.[277] In August, with the help of the Pesti Izraelita Nőegylet, a number of day-care facilities, which operated until the start of the school year, were established in Budapest.[278] For the sake of completeness, we should mention that agricultural issues confronted FE members with serious challenges: "Only in the field of agricultural labor were we unable to achieve lasting results, as the majority of workers, for whatever reason, came back home after only a brief period of time."[279] The reason for this was, surely, that—apart from what they learned from the women of Balmazújváros—they had, even indirectly, no experience with this sector of the economy.

Special priority was given to "wartime assistance for mothers," or financial support for pregnant women: both FE and NOE demanded the introduction of an eight-hour workday for mothers; an end to working on Sundays, something that was only partially introduced previously; and strict adherence to the stipulations of the so-called closing-hours law passed in 1911.[280] They also distributed food vouchers and invited the needy to lunch.[281] FE did not forget the importance of health and health education: it took every opportunity to draw people's attention to the various viral and bacterial infections, such as cholera and sexually transmitted diseases, that were on the rise. Of course, they were aware that the more serious hygiene-related problems arose in small villages, where there was often no tradition of cleaning and disinfection at all. They had dealt with this even before 1914. And while they could not reach the remotest of places, in their publicity they did made efforts to draw the public's attention to these issues. They published articles on the shortcomings of midwife training and on the series of lectures held by experienced female doctors on the subject of maintaining good health.[282] They also endlessly advertised all kinds of cleaning and disinfection products.[283] As winter set in, they distributed aid in the form of medicine, clothes, and firewood on the streets of the capital.[284]

After receiving encouragement from the reform clothing movement in the early 1910s, in August 1914, they considered bringing into Hungary the wartime fashion based on comfortable, cheap materials, following the Austrian and French example, only then to reject the idea: "In Vienna they are attempting to avoid Parisian and London fashion and to create a Viennese fashion of their own. The question arises as to whether the association should formulate such a movement, employing the first tailoring companies, as this is a movement that can be put to economic use. The association does not yet deal with this issue, though it would sympathize with a fashion trend using Hungarian motifs, as more urgent professions are already using it."[285]

The objectives of the association were complex; their activities covered many different areas. Of these, I shall concentrate on the wartime work of the Practical Advice Bureau, as it was through this body that the Budapest associations organized the majority of the aid projects from 1914 to 1918. The Pályaválasztási Tanácsadó (Careers Advice Bureau) was also active, as parents' evenings were regularly held within its framework. Following the prewar practice, they continued to retrain women who had lost their jobs.[286] The obligation to coordinate the ever-growing list of tasks fell primarily to Vilma Glücklich and Paula Pogány. The membership was particularly grateful to the latter for her selfless efforts and often said as much; indeed, from December 1914 Glücklich repeatedly suggested that Pogány's pay be increased: "It is our obligation to raise Paula Pogány's pay, all the more because she does not only spend half a day on the association, as we agreed at the time, but her whole life, from early morning to late at night, which precludes her having any other kind of income." Her wage was increased in July 1917 (paid retrospectively from January onward) to include a 33 percent allowance for high costs. All this cannot have represented an unbearable burden for the association, as in 1918 it employed two office workers with monthly salaries of 180 crowns and 320 crowns, respectively.[287]

Until early 1917, the association could expect to see Schwimmer in person only during her short visits home, but Vilma Glücklich, Adél Spády, and Paula Pogány exchanged ideas with her via lengthy letters and could almost always rely on her advice. The whereabouts and circumstances of Schwimmer were often subjects of discussion at meetings, for the membership followed her work for the peace movement with awe blended with respect. When for a prolonged period they received no letter from her, they turned to the international press in alarm, looking for information as to where she was holding talks at that particular moment: "Our greeting telegram sent to Rosika Schwimmer, in which we wished to express our pleasure at her arrival in Europe, was not accepted as a private cable. It seems that the entirety of Rosika Schwimmer's correspondence has become stuck somewhere; no news has arrived from her, with the exception of a single cable reporting her arrival. Stories are always appearing in the newspapers that are false and cannot be confirmed."

In 1917, Glücklich tried to have "two . . . very important pieces of news" passed on to Schwimmer via Mihály Károlyi, as "she was unable [to reach Schwimmer] on the Vienna phone number given."[288]

In the first days of the war, FE opened its "club rooms" to those in need: the unemployed could come from 9:00 a.m. to 7:00 p.m., as often as every day of the week.[289] They made a number of announcements, however, to the effect that their resources were not unlimited, indicating that they could only accept those from the capital, and so they pointed those from the provinces to their local organizations. Meanwhile, they encouraged their branch associations to establish their own organizational frameworks.

These efforts on the part of the Hungarians were well received in Austria: AöF reported on their achievements on a number of occasions, and, at the invitation of the Frauenstimmrechtskomitee, Glücklich gave a lecture as early as November 1914 in Vienna on the sacrifices being made by Hungarian women and on the activities of the Practical Advice Bureau.[290] FE's greatest achievement was that "it managed to than 14000 women by March 1915.[291] Initially it also tried to place men in jobs, but, at the request of the Budapest authorities, it soon brought these attempts to an end.[292] The jobs offered to women fell into two categories. The first was dominated by the professions that traditionally employed women before 1914, ones mostly not held in very high regard (e.g., canning factories, light industry, the production of construction material, and domestic service[293]). The second, smaller, category concerned new opportunities for women to do jobs that before 1914 had almost always been performed by men.[294] Thus began the feminization of careers such as newspaper delivery, photography, high school teaching, and indeed street sweeping and ticket inspection on public transport.[295]

In May 1915, *A Nő* shared the following statistics about those who found jobs with the help of FE: "In April the following positions were filled thanks to our labor exchange: 6 saleswomen, 112 female factory workers, 16 bonnes [governesses], 77 domestic servants, 5 agricultural day laborers, 12 waitresses, 2 shop managers, 180 seamstresses, 6 tram ticket inspectors, a total of 416 women."[296] Here they also registered those women who were not immediately able to find paid work. In September 1914, there were already 1,566 names on the list: "65 nurses, 6 fashion sales assistants, 64 saleswomen, 15 wood and ice carriers, 7 photographers, 272 female factory workers, 14 nannies, 12 married housekeeper couples, 321 domestic servants, 16 workers in the fields, 65 governesses, teachers, lady's companions, 92 household workers, 31 hotel or spa employees, 55 newspaper sellers, 25 street sweepers, 67 shop assistants, 348 seamstresses, 91 women willing to do any kind of work." Alongside these monthly figures, they also published annual summary tables of the results of the Practical Advice Bureau.[297] These indicate that the career prospects for female office workers were even gloomier than they had been before the war. This made it harder for NOE to coordinate its labor exchange, and the difficulty was only heightened by the constant worsening of the economic situation, as well as by women's traditionally limited professional training.[298]

According to FE's statistics, the demand for women's labor was, understandably, most intense in agriculture (day laborers, workers in the fields) and in industry (factory workers). But we should not lose sight of the fact that in this period many of the large numbers of domestic servants were involved in small-scale agricultural production.[299] And the numbers of seamstresses and weavers rose so high in the association statistics because, following the German and Austrian example, FE offered workshops where unemployed women could earn a modest income by making military underwear and warm winter clothing for men in the armed forces. The number of positions arranged for newspaper sellers was also high, in part because the associations employed those in need of work to sell their own journals.[300]

A look at table 5.5 raises a question: Why did FE only operate a labor exchange in low-prestige occupations? The answers are partly to be found in the laws of supply and demand, in the lack of professional training that affected so many women, and in the fact that other associations (e.g., the Mária Dorothea Egyesület for elementary school teachers) also acted as employment agencies.[301] Yet even after the outbreak of war, FE and NOE both regularly warned that an improvement in the institutional framework for women's (professional) education, and likewise the opening of all university faculties to women, could be put off no longer.[302]

The associations distanced themselves from the distribution of handouts, while they encouraged women with contracts of employment to join the "organization of their profession."[303]

In early 1906, FE, with its 319 members, was a smaller association than AöF, but by July 1919, this figure had grown to 6,472. As a result of Vilmos Vázsonyi's electoral reform plan, beginning in the summer of 1917, huge numbers joined, and the membership doubled: by 24 July 1918, it stood at 5,312. The minutes of the committee meeting held at this time report on the "failure to achieve female suffrage."[304] With this, the growth in membership numbers slowed: in November 1918, there were 5,939 members, and in September 1919, this number declined to 5,438.[305]

Table 5.5. The statistics of the Practical Advice Bureau on the women who found employment thanks to its intervention (August 1914–March 1915)

Occupation	Aug.	Sept.	Oct.	Nov.	Dec.	Jan.	Feb.	Mar.	Σ
Nurse	5	61	29	12	1	15	27	10	160
Saleswoman	27	23	15	2	—	—	—	—	67
Lapidarist	—	—	—	2	—	2	12	—	16
Construction worker	48	—	33	—	—	—	—	—	81
Agricultural worker	418	—	—	—	—	—	—	—	418
Factory worker	610	120	106	259	235	114	35	34	1,513
Nanny	—	—	30	17	—	—	—	—	47
Domestic servant	1,898	840	190	160	101	98	74	93	3,454
Embroiderer	—	7	—	—	1	—	—	—	8
Office assistant	—	—	4	—	—	—	—	—	4
Commercial employee	—	—	—	—	17	9	25	30	81
Pot cleaner	58	—	—	—	—	—	—	—	58
Kitchen maid garden worker	—	—	—	—	—	—	—	28	28
Driver	—	—	—	—	—	—	1	—	1
Decorator	—	—	—	1	—	—	—	—	1
Day laborer	626	411	—	—	2	—	—	13	1,052
Governess, teacher	43	27	51	20	27	35	21	18	242
Furrier	—	—	12	3	—	4	1	2	22
Newspaper seller	394	8	7	6	—	—	—	—	415
Agent	—	—	—	1	—	—	—	—	1
Seamstress, weaver, etc.	828	824	1,274	921	498	524	383	257	5,509
Mixed occupation	53	28	12	3	—	4	1	2	103
Tram ticket inspector	—	—	—	9	—	—	—	13	22
Sack seamstress	—	34	—	—	—	—	—	—	34
Total	5,008	2,383	1,763	1,416	882	805	580	500	13,337

I based these statistics on the issues of *A Nő* between August 1914 and March 1915.

Table 5.6. The statistics of the Practical Advice Bureau on the women who found employment thanks to its intervention (February 1916–April 1916)

Occupation	Total
Seamstress	75
Domestic servant	118
Factory worker	110
Shop employee	34
Child's companion	15
Nurse	2
Day laborer	9
Electrotechnical apprentice	2
Laboratory worker	1
Hat decorator	1
Mixed occupation	15
Total	382

N 1916, 5, 78. The number of women looking for work was highest in the first months of the war because of the mass mobilization of men at the time.

Wartime conditions made it even harder than before to ensure the untroubled operation of FE. To overcome its financial woes, it had to cooperate with other Budapest associations; this also led to a more logical division of labor. Together with the Pesti Izraelita Nőegylet and the Jogvédő Egyesület (Legal Rights Association), FE collected letters of support and negotiation with employers.[306] The constant increase in printing and mailing costs presented a burden to the publishing company. Adél Spády argues that the financial problems were rooted in the cancellation of lectures held by visiting foreign guests that generated income and in the reduced willingness of members to donate. Because of the association's peace activism, the state authorities even confiscated some of its income;[307] meanwhile, in 1915, the minister for trade supported the labor exchange with 3,000 crowns as a sign of his respect for its work.[308] To ease the association's budget deficit, from 1915 it resumed the organization of lectures by foreign guests, with Adele Schreiber and Lida Gustava Heymann arriving in Budapest.[309] They also planned to invite Rosa Mayreder, but she was unable to leave Vienna on account of her husband's worsening depression.[310]

The associations were thus active on two fronts during the war. In the hinterland, they strove to help women in need and their children. On the international arena, working through IWSA and WILPF, they attempted to bring an end to armed conflict as soon as possible. NOE and especially FE had the committed support of the government, Budapest, and the provincial authorities, which gave them a high profile and contributed to a strong rise in membership. The upheavals that came in the wake of the war and the shrinking of the association's support base caught both NOE and FE completely unprepared.

Dissolution of the Associations

The dissolution of both NOE and FE falls outside the period examined in this volume, but it is nonetheless interesting to consider why NOE could not continue its activism after 1919, while FE adapted to the changing political climate and continued its pursuit of almost the same objectives it had espoused since its founding. Indeed, FE made every effort to remain active as part of the emerging women's movement of state socialism even after World War II, until it was finally banned in 1949.

Despite a year of intense pressure from FE, a vote in the Hungarian parliament on 27 July 1918 rejected the legislative proposal of Vilmos Vázsonyi, minister of justice. Those in favor of female suffrage remained in the minority, while the center of power forming around Schwimmer and her team began to lose its influence, even after women received the right to vote. Finally, the first People's Act (Néptörvény) of Mihály Károlyi's government introduced female suffrage for women if they were twenty-four years old, had held Hungarian citizenship for six years, and were literate (men received the right to vote if they had reached the age of twenty-one and had been Hungarian citizens for at least six years). This would have meant nine million voters in the territory of Hungary before the peace Treaty of Trianon (1920) under an electoral system that ultimately was never implemented because of the dramatic political changes of 1919.

The Hungarian Soviet Republic, which lasted from 21 March 1919 to 1 August 1919, lowered the voting age to eighteen. Women above this age—with the exception of feminists who were classified as bourgeois, such as Rosika Schwimmer and her coworkers—were also given the right to vote. On the basis of this provision, council elections were held on 7 April 1919. After the collapse of the Soviet Republic, the government of István Friedrich (born 1883 in Malacka and died 1951 in Vác) issued a new electoral decree on 17 November 1919 (Government Decree 5985). During this period, several different governments ruled Hungary, and the country suffered tremendous political, economic, and social instability. Women were granted the right to vote under the same conditions as men (twenty-four years of age, six years of Hungarian citizenship, and six months of residence or ownership of a dwelling in the same municipality), but they still had to be literate. On the basis of this government decree, nearly one and a half million women (1,433,000) were allowed to vote in post-Trianon Hungary. The first elections were held on 25 and 26 January 1920.

On 2 March 1922, the government of István Bethlen (born 1874 in Gernyeszeg and died 1946 in Moscow; prime minister of Hungary between 1921 and 1931) finally ushered in an era of relative political stability and regulated the right to vote by decree (Decree 2200/1922), raising the age limit for women to thirty and requiring them to complete six years of elementary school. If a woman was married or had at least three children, four years of elementary school education were sufficient. Anyone under the age of thirty who was self-supporting or had completed university studies could vote. The decree resulted in five hundred thousand women losing their right to vote. Although women were given the right to vote, few were able to play a real role in political life. Apart from the conservative Margit Slachta (born 1884 in Kassa and died 1974 in Buffalo, New York), the first female member of parliament, and the Social Democrat Anna Kéthly (born 1889 in Budapest and died 1976 in Blankenberge), who sat in parliament throughout the period, there were few women in parliament. Most of these women were members of the ruling party or a conservative party, and their speeches focused on various aspects of women's equality.[311]

At the beginning of the 1920s, the dynamic increase in the membership of FE immediately slowed, then stopped, and finally, the numbers began to wane.[312] As Balázs Sipos sees it, the enactment of the suffrage bill, which took place more than a year later, "mobilized certain groups of women to support conservative, right-wing and church or religious parties. . . . The recognition of this and . . . of the way women had stood their ground during the war resulted in the counter-revolutionary Christian-Social, nationalist government declaring in fall 1919 that it would ensure women the right to vote."[313] This view echoes contentions often found in the earlier international historical scholarship, which tended to celebrate the introduction of female suffrage in several European countries at the end of World War I as a triumph for both national and international women's movements. Recent interpretations have added dramatic shades of nuance to this view, however, and have suggested that the right to vote should not be interpreted as a reward that was given to women for the sacrifices they had made during the war.[314]

The history of FE after the end of World War I clearly harmonizes with the latter view, as the association could hardly claim female suffrage as the fruit of its own efforts over the course of the decade that had passed. The less active majority of the FE's bloated membership soon became disillusioned with the association and the principles of the movement. This is revealed in a pile of letters addressed to Glücklich in the course of 1918–1919, such as one that reads, "Forgive me, but after reading yesterday's papers, I cannot stop myself speaking out, for God's sake! . . . I have supported your cause with moral loyalty. I took on as my own all of your requests, if they were not laughable. . . . I ask for my departure from the association to be published in the journal, as dying for the homeland is an honor, but it is a curse to surrender the homeland in the wretchedness of ignobility."[315]

We can provide a number of reasons for the wave of mass departures from the association. Some members were so disillusioned that, contradicting the basic principle of the association—namely, that they could not be associated with any political party—they joined the broader circle of other parties, such as the Independence and 1848/Károlyi Parties. The operations of the association became more difficult when the Károlyi government gave Schwimmer a diplomatic mission: between November 1918 and January 1919, she tried, as Hungary's envoy to Switzerland, to balance between Hungary and the entente, but her Bern diplomatic mission would be a dismal failure.[316] In the end, the conservative turn after the collapse of the Hungarian Soviet Republic completely transformed the Hungarian political climate, as well as the frames of the women's movement, compared to what it had been before the war. The "political system strove to bring the social demobilization of women," and so the left-wing feminist organizations disappeared or lost much of their strength, more or less retreating into illegality.[317] Meanwhile, the right-wing, conservative women's groups increasingly came into positions of power. The revisionist propaganda of the interwar period, an increased reverence for religious, national ideas and for the woman's place in the home, together with the demonization of feminists, led to the emergence of an entirely new women's movement. At the center of this was Magyar Asszonyok Nemzeti Szövetsége (National Alliance of Hungarian Women), founded in January 1919 by the writer Cécile Tormay (born 1875 in Budapest and died 1937 in Mátraháza). The group's membership, according to some calculations, approached half a million by the eve of World War II.[318]

The earlier academic literature suggested that NOE was disbanded in the summer of 1919; in fact, the association had ceased its activities in April of that year. Part of the more radical membership, and even some of the leadership, had joined the Kommunisták Magyarországi Pártja (Party of Communists of Hungary): among them were president Janka Gergely, vice president Jolán Fehér, and Szidónia Willhelm, who at the time was the general secretary. A number of them decided to join FE.

The last issue of *Nőtisztviselők Lapja*, of 15 February, indicates that NOE had a quite different opinion on the preparations for the upcoming election: "Our fellow members . . . are surprised to discover that the leadership of our association keeps itself entirely separate from the preparations, that the members of our association, who have fought for more than a decade for female suffrage to be written into law, now pass the preparations by entirely inactively, reject the leadership tasks offered them from all sides, that our association publishes no election manifesto, in short, that we do now make the best of the rights we have acquired."[319]

In early 1919, there were even attempts to reorganize NOE: these concerned the possibility of the female office workers joining their male colleagues. Ultimately, the leadership rejected this idea, "for during the negotiations [they] became all the more strongly convinced that [they could] only conduct useful work as an association for fully independent female office workers."[320] Press sources suggest that NOE's last event was held on 6 March, when Elek Soltész, doctor at the Franz Joseph Commercial Hospital, gave a lecture entitled "Protection against the Various Infection Diseases" at the association's rooms at 3 Vigadó Square.[321] Of the contemporary papers, only *Pesti Napló* reported briefly on NOE's disbandment little more than a month later.[322]

In November, a journalist at *Az Újság*—who was writing an article on how female office workers were taken advantage of—could only find the association's former location on Vigadó Square. She described the dissolution of NOE with laconic succinctness: "We went up to the Nőtisztviselők Országos Egyesülete, which has long been operating as a labor exchange. We found its doors locked. The association has been disbanded. It seems there is no longer any need for employment agencies, as there are no job vacancies to be filled."[323]

In December 1918, the name of FE was changed to Feministák Pártközi Bizottsága (Interparty Committee of Feminists).[324] After 1918, the association had to confront problems similar to the ones AöF faced in Vienna. In and of itself, it must have been a terrible loss of face for Schwimmer and her colleagues that they could not claim the extension of suffrage to women as their own achievement. Compared to the membership numbers in 1918, the data for 1936 presents a drastic collapse: the membership of the main association in Budapest fell to just 280. Quite apart from the loss of influence this represented, it also meant an enormous loss in income. Nevertheless, we need to address two key factors relating to the workings of the association in the interwar period. As before, the FE association rooms were in downtown Budapest (at 16 Veres Pálné Street), close to the Egyetemet és Főiskolát Végzett Magyar Nők Egyesülete (Association for Hungarian Female University and College Graduates, the Hungarian auxiliary association of the International Federation of University Women), which was based at house number 25 on the same street. Both in its profile and in its membership, this group displayed an overlap with FE; in this period, it also had around three hundred members.[325] While we cannot infer broad tendencies from two items of data, I still think it impossible that the membership of organizations with liberal, feminist roots could have been much higher than this during the interwar period.

Although FE did continue to operate, it faced considerable challenges. From 1922 to 1925, Glücklich was general secretary of WILPF at its headquarters in Zurich; in 1927, she died. Schwimmer left Hungary in January 1920. The association was thus left without its two emblematic leaders and thereby lost much of its previously strong international embeddedness. In the wake of the restrictions imposed after 1918, the publication of *A Nő* became hectic by the second half of the 1920s, and in 1928, it was discontinued, and so the association, as run from 1927 by Mrs. Oszkár Szirmay, could not even rely on its own permanent

Figure 5.15. Members of FE in the interwar period, before 1927. Schwimmer-Lloyd Collection, The New York Public Library. *Seated left to right:* Melanie Vámbéry, Mrs. Mihály Havas, Mrs. Oszkár Szirmay, Unknown, Vilma Glücklich, Mrs. Eugénia Meller, née Miskolczy, Unknown. *Standing left to right:* Nóra Kunfi, Unknown, Gizella Fekete, Klára Kozma-Glücklich, Unknown, Laura Polányi, Unknown.

publication. As it happens, Glücklich, in letters addressed to Schwimmer, complained on repeated occasions from January 1926 onward that she did not even have time "to write a decent article" for the journal, and once she mentioned, "But you [Schwimmer] would laugh at me if you could see me struggling with it [the editing of the journal, a job she did together with Mrs. Szirmay from 1925 onward], and how poor it is!"[326] The questions, then, are just how large a role Glücklich's death played in the slow demise of the periodical and why Mrs. Szirmay did not think it important to keep it alive. Finally, we should touch on two things: there was no mention (in the sources studied thus far) of activism in the provinces in the interwar years; meanwhile, the association was also weakened by generational issues.

I will make only brief mention of the history of FE after World War I. Glücklich entrusted Mrs. Szirmay with the task of running the association when, shortly before her death, she left for Vienna for medical treatment. Mrs. Szirmay, in turn, would remain in the presidential chair until the association was disbanded, though for a period she shared it with Mrs. Eugénia Meller, née Miskolczy.[327]

Alongside her signature, that of Lilla Wágner (born 1903 in Budapest and died 1978 in London), who belonged to the younger generation, was also on the letter addressed to the minister of the interior, László Rajk, in November 1946, in which the executive committee of FE requested that the association be reorganized.

> We enclose the statutes of our reestablished association. These statutes are essentially entirely identical to the former ones. . . . The objective now is further to broaden and protect equal rights for women. To maintain women's social self-awareness to validate their rights in everyday life and for the benefit of the community. To protect the interests of women's labor. To serve the notion of reconciliation in every respect, with the intention that women's work serve the interests of humanity at every level.

They set membership fees to at least six forints a year, payable in advance in six-monthly installments. In addition, "anyone [could] become a supporting member who [paid] at least 25 forints a year or [made] a lifetime payment of at least 100 forints."[328]

The letter also refers to Mrs. Meller, who was the director when FE was banned in 1942: "One of the meetings prior to the disbandment, at which [members] dared to criticize the newly-passed legislation that contradicted any sense of justice and truth, was broken up by the police. As a continuation of this, the association was itself disbanded . . . the president was imprisoned and ultimately faced a martyr's fate."[329]

Mrs. Meller was a founding member of FE, and in 1907, thanks to Schwimmer's ever-longer foreign lecture tours, she joined the leadership of the Political Committee.[330] Melanie Vámbéry (born ca. 1880 and died 1944 in Auschwitz), who was secretary of FE from 1919 to 1938, also "faced a martyr's fate." She joined the association in 1906, but soon after this her name disappeared from the association's documents—probably on account of her marriage, then her divorce, and her relocation to the provinces. In October 1914, we again find her among the members, and from 1916, she served on the committee. The literature on her only mentions that she fell victim to the Holocaust.[331] The FE archive, meanwhile, holds relatively few specifics of her work.

> Mrs. Melanie Vámbéry, when quite a young girl, was contributor of a Journal, after her marriage organised and founded one of the Hungarian branches of the Feministák Egyesülete in a country-town. When she came to live in Budapest she worked for the Society here with zeal and devotion, took lively part in the struggle for woman suffrage and later on in the house-to-house peace propaganda. She is member of the Board and since 1919 Secretary of the Feministák Egyesülete and was delegate of the Society in the Peace Congress of Vienna in 1921 and the Hague 1921.[332]

Melanie Vámbéry's brother was the lawyer and bourgeois radical journalist Rusztem Vámbéry (born 1872 in Budapest and died 1948 in New York), the son of orientalist Ármin Vámbéry (born 1832 in Szentgyörgy and died 1913 in Budapest), and Melanie was the first wife of Zsigmond Kunfi (born 1879 in Nagykanizsa and died 1929 in Vienna); in 1944, Melanie and her daughter Nóra, likewise a member of FE, were deported and murdered.[333]

FE was eventually formed anew on 8 November 1946 at a ceremonious occasion at the offices of the Országos Iparegyesület (National Industry Association) on Zichy Jenő Street, not far from the association's headquarters newly furnished at 2 Perczel Mór Street. The FE's central office was again to be located in central Budapest.

Világ provided its readers with the following report on the ceremony and on the association's objectives: "At its general meeting . . . to reestablish itself . . . Feministák Egyesülete paid tribute to the association's former members who had died a martyr's death. . . . Dr. Lilla Wágner . . . gave a very impressive memorial lecture. In her introduction, Mrs. Oszkár Szirmay announced that the association would, true to its traditions of forty years' standing, continue its work for the broadest extension of human rights and for the cause of international peace and reconciliation."[334]

Previously, we thought that the members of the FE committee disbanded the association in the first days of 1949, in complete secrecy. Newly uncovered press sources suggest the opposite, however: according to announcements and reports in the daily press, the association continued to give home to a number of events, including lectures and debate evenings. These mostly sought the points of connection between people's democracy and the women's movement. The 17 December 1949 issue of *Magyar Közlöny* (Hungarian Gazette) reported on the closure of FE after nearly four and a half decades of operation: here, however, it merely states, laconically, that the minister of the interior had ordered the association to be disbanded.[335]

The decree to dissolve the association was obviously not unexpected by the members, and apart from the earlier change in the political climate, there were other signs that it might soon be disbanded. The first and most important of these signs was the death of Rosika Schwimmer on 3 August 1948 after a long hospital stay. Her charismatic personality and commitment had been a powerful motivation for the reorganization of FE, and with her death, this source of encouragement was lost. Members of the board who had been active from the outset and had survived the war, such as Mrs. Szirmay, Sarolta Steinberger, and Janka Dirnfeld, were also aging, and younger members, such as Lilla Wágner, did not feel the same ownership of the cause as the older members, who had been active from the very beginning.

6

Similarities and Differences among the Three Associations

FINALLY, it is worth considering the similarities and differences among Allgemeiner österreichischer Frauenverein (AöF), Nőtisztviselők Országos Egyesülete (NOE), and Feministák Egyesülete (FE). In general, while NOE and FE at first followed the examples set by AöF in many respects, they later followed different paths of development.

Regarding the establishment of the associations, three different tendencies can be observed. The creation of AöF can be connected to a single legislative proposal, while the primary motivation of NOE's establishment was provided by the workplace exploitation suffered by a growing number of women office workers in the first half of the 1890s. FE does not fit into this comparison, as its organization was motivated by completely different factors, and the key driver of its creation was the initiative of the International Woman Suffrage Alliance (IWSA). The idea was first thought up in 1902 by Aletta Jacobs, who started to correspond with Rosika Schwimmer at that time. At this stage of the organization, she was still thinking in terms of a joint Austro-Hungarian umbrella organization.[1] If one had formed, FE would have joined Bund österreichischer Frauenvereine (BöF), which brought together German-speaking bourgeois women's associations in Austria under the leadership of Marianne Hainisch. However, as the Czech women's associations had done, the Hungarians rejected this scenario. On the other hand, according to the membership lists of BöF, it formed a basis for rather fluid transitions of women's associations, as in the case of Jewish charitable associations and women's professional groups that also joined the BöF.[2]

The German Marxist politician August Bebel played a significant symbolic role in the founding of AöF as Auguste Fickert asked for his advice several times, and he was also a key symbolic figure for the leaders of the Hungarian associations as well.[3] In the light of this, it becomes clear that all three associations shared affinities with the Social Democratic branch of the women's movement. Fickert taught for several years at the Arbeiterinnen-Bildungsverein in Vienna, and Schwimmer helped organize the Social Democratic women's movement in Hungary in 1903. At the same time, they rejected the principles of the Christian-Social tendency of the movement, which they mocked at public events and in their press organs. In addition, they had constant conflicts with the more conservative groups of the bourgeois women's movement—namely, BöF and Magyarországi Nőegyesületek Szövetsége (MNSz) in Hungary. All this gradually changed for FE in the interwar period, as the political palette shifted, and FE moved closer to MNSz.

We do not have collections of statutes for AöF like the ones we have for NOE and FE, but other types of sources shed some light on the establishment of the association and its aims. The three associations were far ahead of their time in at least one respect: they sought to promote the status and rights of women in all walks of life. Of the three associations, NOE had the most specific objectives, including providing political, economic, and social support for female office workers. Although the profiles and goals of AöF, NOE, and FE were very similar, there could hardly be a greater difference in terms of their methods of leadership and management.[4] As in the cases of NOE and FE, the vice president and then president of AöF, Auguste Fickert, stayed in her posts for many long years, until her death. Yet if we dig a little deeper into the sources, it is clear that, unlike the Budapest groups, AöF filled (or left empty) the positions of president and vice president with little or no logic. Thus, NOE and FE were much more practical in their election of their leaders than AöF was. Indeed, they did not even see the preservation of the continuity of their leadership as necessary, nor did they leave positions unfilled after presidents or committee members resigned or passed away.[5] In addition, it is certain that neither Rosika Schwimmer nor Janka Gergely and Vilma Glücklich attempted to build an image or cult around themselves as leaders of the Hungarian associations in the same way that Fickert had done.

The manner in which the statutes were decided at the first general assembly says a lot about the differences between the working methods of AöF and FE. While members of AöF voted on the statutes en bloc, the same could never have happened in Budapest. At FE meetings, heated discussions always broke out among the committee members on just about all topics. None of the associations, however, openly committed to any political party. Rather, they were all happy to accept the support of different political groups.

The following examples illustrate exactly how the associations' boards and membership treated their leaders. In AöF's 1910 accounts, the cost of Auguste

Fickert's funeral and memorial events represent a separate item, which according to my calculations totaled 250 crowns—not overall such a conspicuous amount.[6] After this, *Neues Frauenleben* dedicated both a leading article and a separate article to Fickert's memory on the first anniversary of her death.[7] It is worth comparing this level of respect and commemoration with that afforded to Vilma Glücklich after her death that surprised the whole membership of FE in 1927, for the latter appears rather less contrived. At her death, she was remembered by her former Hungarian and international coworkers (including leading members of the International Council of Women, IWSA, and the Women's International League for Peace and Freedom) in *A Nő*, while at her funeral a speech was given by Anna Kéthly (born 1889 in Budapest and died 1976 in Blankenberge, Belgium), a leading Social Democratic woman politician of the era and the second female member of the National Assembly of Hungary (1922–1948).[8]

The factors outlined above probably affected the effectiveness of AöF and contributed to the failure within the association's limited membership to establish the same collegiate and even friendly relationships as seen in NOE or FE circles. That AöF members did not experience the same relaxed atmosphere as in the case of the Hungarian associations can largely be put down to Fickert's autocratic ways. Fickert's attitudes toward leadership could hardly have been more different from those embodied by Vilma Glücklich and Rosika Schwimmer.[9] And although the latter was developing a distinctly dominant character, her behavior did not come close to Fickert's autocratic attitude. As the correspondence among the three women reveals, their relationship was more than collegial. They became close friends over the years. AöF organized hardly any community activities of the kind that NOE and FE did on an almost continuous basis for their (board) members: the sources make no mention of AöF boat trips, meetings, or dinners on summer evenings or of the creation of vacation facilities. But what can explain this divergence? First, Schwimmer, Gergely, and Glücklich—all from Jewish families—joined their associations at a much younger age and with less hardened personalities than did Fickert, who was almost forty when AöF was founded.

At a number of points in this book, it has been necessary to cite the specifics of the development of the associations' journals, which represented the essential mode for these organizations to "express themselves." Where it is important, I try to draw the reader's attention to the connections between press history and women's history (e.g., legislation governing journal publication, censorship measures taken after 1914, the difficulties women journalists faced in earning a living). Taking only a brief detour to discuss the associations' press activities, I point out that the years 1902 and 1907—when, respectively, *Neues Frauenleben* and *A Nő és a Társadalom* began publication—can be interpreted as important turning points in the history of the press of the women's movement in Austria and in Hungary. Although the AöF's only official journal and the first journals published by FE and NOE began life rather later than their Western counterparts, by 1918 they played an absolutely crucial role in spreading the ideas of these progressive women's associations. We cannot avoid mentioning that the investigation of the surviving sources from these periodicals and the companies that published them has generated a number of new results. Perhaps the most important of these is that all three organizations attempted to mobilize capital well beyond their means and to cross-subsidize within their overall budgets to keep alive their journals, which from the outset were loss making but, as the associations emphasized at every possible opportunity, "morally prosperous."

There are also differences between the associations in the work around their official organs, at least before the death of Auguste Fickert. Enjoying the support of the Viennese Social Democratic political circles, AöF found itself in the fortunate position of acquiring a publication outlet immediately after its establishment. By contrast, NOE had to wait ten years for this, and FE, five. While Schwimmer shared editorial tasks with several coworkers, Fickert, because of her autocratic character and her attitude toward leadership, kept the editing of the journal in one hand. And although the editing of *Neues Frauenleben* followed a more clearly defined concept than that of *Dokumente der Frauen*,[10] she only delegated tasks to a much closer-knit group than Schwimmer did. This changed after her death in 1910, when Leopoldine Kulka, Christine Touaillon, Adele Gerber, and Emil Fickert worked on the publication of the journal.

None of the three groups had as many followers as, for example, the Social Democratic women's organizations. And in all three, the vast majority of the membership came from the (upper-)middle-class female and male population. In addition to being members from aristocratic backgrounds, many of them were university students. According to several sources, Fickert made certain efforts to exclude members of Jewish heritage from the AöF leadership and the editorial staff of *Neues Frauenleben*, but within the committee of NOE and even more so that of FE, women (and men) from Jewish families, albeit usually nonobservant ones, were in the majority. In terms of numbers, AöF had the smallest membership, followed by the FE, and the NOE had the largest. However, there are no exact data on the latter's membership figures from the years of World War I. Of the three associations, the FE had the lowest fluctuation in membership. For NOE, increases in membership were sometimes restrained and sometimes more dynamic, as in the case of FE. In contrast to the practice in Hungary, men paid the same subscription fee as women in AöF.

We can see from their membership lists that FE and NOE were able to reach and mobilize a far broader range of social groups than AöF was. Unlike AöF, from 1907 to 1918 the Hungarian organizations succeeded in forming more than ten provincial branches. These, after adapting the operating model of NOE and FE to their own purposes, began their own independent endeavors; during the years of World War I, these endeavors attained considerable significance. We need to think only of the Balmazújvárosi Szabad Nőszervezet (Free Women's Association of Balmazújváros), which formally became part of FE in 1908 and which provided an excellent basis on which Schwimmer and her associates could argue that the movement was fighting for the rights of women in every social class. Yet I also argue that the role of initiatives such as that in Balmazújváros must not be exaggerated and overinterpreted, as they only really functioned as a kind of shop window for the leadership, who otherwise knew little of these people and their problems firsthand.

For the associations in Budapest and Vienna, the year began in September and ended in May. Between June and the end of August, the associations put their work on hold for the summer. They generally held their annual meetings in April. Compared to the bourgeois women's associations in Germany, this was unique, as most of the German associations preferred to hold their annual meetings in the autumn months. The meetings held in Budapest and Vienna were quite different from those held in Germany. Annual meetings of Allgemeiner deutscher Frauenverein (AdF) were held in October and lasted several days, with much ceremony and many receptions and excursions. The AdF membership met, for example, in Gießen on 6–8 October 1913, where to end the series of events they visited a theater and held an excursion to Wetzlar. The three Austrian and Hungarian organizations examined in this book never did anything similar, even though a good proportion of its members would have been able to afford it.[11] Similarly to the youth section of AöF, a committee for young feminists was active within the framework of FE.[12]

Regarding the administrative workings of the three associations and the events organized by them, we can draw on the documents produced by their official organs, in addition to the archival sources. Furthermore, we can consider the announcements related to lectures, courses, and debate evenings as entirely authentic sources of information, as these disclosures served in Vienna and Budapest alike as invitations for members and those expressing an interest. Additionally, AöF, NOE, and FE marked the smallest items of income and expenditure in their reports, and so the rows of data can be compared meaningfully.

For both AöF and FE, donations were an important source of income. It is largely due to this and to external support that AöF managed to set up the long-planned centralized household (Heimhof) in Vienna. FE had plans for the creation of a similar residential building in Budapest, but these plans were never implemented because of the outbreak of World War I. No information is available on the donations received by NOE. In terms of expenditures, the largest cost for all three organizations was the rental of club rooms. In addition, their postage costs were initially very high because members were notified of the various programs and events by mail. It is not surprising, therefore, that the associations stopped this practice after the creation of their official organs and informed their members of their programs only through the association columns published in the journals.

Like AöF, FE and NOE also organized lectures on a monthly basis. Compared to FE, however, AöF spent disproportionately small amounts on organizing lectures and gatherings (e.g., 167.84 crowns in 1910), and there was no mention at all of joint travel or outings in the association. For comparison, FE's lectures in 1906 generated a profit of 1,038 crowns, and by 1910, the association had become so successful that it could spend 4,000 crowns a year on hosting lecturers from Austria and abroad.[13] Given the lack of resources at AöF, fewer foreign speakers came to Vienna than to Budapest, and AöF was accordingly also more modest in its entertainment allowance. There could be no question of the sort of luxurious receptions that FE organized, such as the one held at the Fishermen's Bastion in Budapest on 16 June 1913, where two thousand IWSA delegates were entertained. The bill for that event, amounting to 10,300 crowns, was footed by Mrs. Sándor Teleki. It has to be highlighted that this occasion was a particularly important one, but FE members were regular guests at the highly elegant Ritz hotel in Budapest; for example, upon the arrival of Anna Lindemann in 1914 or 1916, a "6 o'clock tea" was held in Schwimmer's honor.[14]

The Hungarian associations always paid honoraria to the (foreign) speakers, which AöF certainly could not afford to do. The sources contain no mention of any instance when a foreign speaker was not paid an honorarium by the Hungarian associations, even in wartime. Schwimmer, whom in 1917 it "proved possible ... to persuade to hold lectures entitled 'America during the war' in a number of provincial cities, was voted a 500 crown honorarium by the association for her efforts."[15] AöF could not allow itself to invite women's movement leaders from northern or western European countries, like Aletta Jacobs, Maikki Friberg, or Marie Stritt, to Vienna without paying them a fee. After 1904, for speakers arriving in Vienna, the next port of call was usually Prague or Budapest; in the latter, they would be hosted by the newly established MNSz or jointly by NOE and FE. In their correspondence with Schwimmer from before 1907, Aletta Jacobs and Marie Stritt made the dates of their Budapest and provincial visits contingent on their lectures in Vienna.[16]

The courses organized by the three associations were an important part of their annual programs. AöF's courses displayed less variety than those organized by FE and NOE: this could in part have been the result of the cultural, social, and economic differences between the two countries. In Vienna, there was clearly little demand for the teaching of correspondence and conversation in German, unlike in Hungary, where a number of otherwise Hungarian-speaking female officials were employed by companies that did business at least in part in German. Of course, AöF could have organized courses in French or English, but there was no precedent for this.

AöF's international relations proved overall much narrower than those of the Hungarian associations, especially FE. One reason for this is certainly Fickert's personality. Unlike Schwimmer, she avoided large-scale congresses, usually sending one of her coworkers to such events. This was the case with the 1904 abolitionist congress in London, which was attended by Leopoldine Kulka. It was here that Kulka first met Schwimmer, with whom she remained in relatively close contact until Kulka's death in 1920.[17] Schwimmer had been building up her contacts with members of the Austrian women's associations for years, and she even remained in contact with some of them (e.g., with some board members of BöF and Frauenstimmrechtskomitee) after her immigration to the US. In the case of FE, however, as with AöF, international connections were initially associated with a particular individual, such as Schwimmer before her emigration.

While, thanks to Schwimmer's efforts, FE developed increasingly strong international connections, AöF's worldwide network began to wither after it left BöF in 1906, and in particular after Fickert's death, in a process that lasted until 1914–1915. Not even with the active role it played in the international peace movement during World War I could AöF fully make up for this lag, which exerted its effect not just on AöF's diminished dynamism but also on its press publications. The best example of the international prominence and effectiveness of FE is the IWSA congress in June 1913, when for the better part of a week women's organizations all over the world focused their attention on Budapest. But the IWSA gave FE the right to organize the event in part because it was confident that Hungarian women would be granted the right to vote by 1913. In their view, the progressive suffrage bill introduced in 1912 provided a realistic chance of this happening. However, parliament rejected the bill in early 1913, and this cast a dark shadow over the event.

The effectiveness of FE and NOE is also the result of the supportive community that the leaders of the city of Budapest created in the István Bárczy era, between 1906 and 1918. This in part explains the differences compared to Vienna, which under the Christian-Social Karl Lueger hardly provided idyllic conditions for an organization fighting for the radical emancipation of women. In the Hungarian case, meanwhile, we should also make mention of the bourgeois radical movements in both culture and politics, and within this of the Társadalomtudományi Társaság (Social Science Society), which had a relatively close relationship with FE in the latter's early years. Aims of the Társadalomtudományi Társaság were sympathetic to FE and NOE, as they fought for the bourgeois radical transcendence of feudal positions, and they included not only bourgeois-liberal and bourgeois radical thinkers but also socialist thinkers. From press sources and the Schwimmer correspondence, however, we can conclude that the leadership of FE overestimated the value of this connection, to which Oszkár Jászi (born 1875, in Nagykároly and died 1957, in Oberlin), who was one of the key figures of Társadalomtudományi Társaság, and the other bourgeois radicals did not attribute such significance.

Fickert, Schwimmer, and to some extent Glücklich were obviously the faces of the Austrian and Hungarian bourgeois-liberal feminist movements. Though each had a distinctive personality, they had several important things in common. All three were convinced pacifists and devoted almost all their time to the movement. As teachers, Fickert and Glücklich both worked during school breaks and the summer holidays. The dynamics of Fickert's and Schwimmer's friendships are also similar in many respects. Consider Fickert's friendship with Maikki Friberg and that of Schwimmer with Aletta Jacobs; the correspondence between them clearly suggests a mentor-mentee relationship, which is true even though Fickert was a few years older than Friberg. Compared to the correspondence between Schwimmer and Jacobs, Fickert's communication with Friberg was not very practical in nature.

In many ways, the outbreak of World War I changed the scope and nature of the associations' operations. While AöF was passive, FE (and in part NOE) managed from the first moment of mobilization successfully to reconcile the role it played in the international peace movement with the aid work it undertook on the home front.[18] The attitude of AöF differed strongly from the approaches of BöF as well, as the Zentralkomitee actively participated in war work. The differences in attitudes between the Austrian and Hungarian associations were noticeable from the moment the war broke out. While *Neues Frauenleben* published an excerpt from *Die Waffen nieder* by Bertha von Suttner, the front page of *A Nő* announced, "Two bullets have made history at Sarajevo market. For reasons of politics, three children have been orphaned."[19] This reveals the disillusionment of AöF, foreshadowing its passivity toward war work and the proactive attitude that the Hungarian associations adopted. By contrast, inside AöF a highly intense and innovative pacifist movement emerged, one that obviated all activities intended to prevent economic and social collapse on the home front.

How could AöF's attitude toward the war differ so greatly from that of FE and NOE? How did the Hungarians reconcile their antimilitarist values with behavior that was tantamount to support for the war, and why did AöF not strive to do likewise? Let us not forget that in 1914 the leaders of FE and NOE were in their late thirties and early forties, while Auguste Fickert had been dead for four years, and Kulka's health continued to decline; this probably greatly determined their attitudes.[20] On the other hand, Kulka's opinion chimes perfectly with the way that Schwimmer and her colleagues saw MNSz.

The sources reveal that NOE and FE were more geared toward problem-solving than AöF was. Aside from accumulating expressions of encouragement, NOE's and FE's communications were much more pragmatic than those of AöF. For the Hungarians, it would have been unimaginable for the association pages to include reports of the achievements of domestic, let alone foreign, associations that they had no formal attachment to. They covered only their own activities, programs, and objectives. Yet, just like the Viennese, they regularly shared statistics on women's level of education or position in the labor market or reported on their members' participation in women's movement meetings, both at home and abroad. On the other hand, AöF intensively dealt with female suffrage during the war years, while similar tendencies can be seen in Hungary beginning in February 1917.

While NOE proved incapable of adapting its goals to the new challenges brought by the interim period after the end of the war, AöF managed to achieve this, at least in part, as the latest research shows that it remained in operation until around 1920 or 1922. It was FE that proved the most adaptable, as even though it never recovered its pre-1914 positions in the women's movement redefined by the interwar period, it did, with the exception of the years it was suppressed during and after the war, remain active for almost a further three decades.

Conclusion

IN AN INTERVIEW ON THE RECENT GENDER DEBATE IN HUNGARY, Andrea Pető sarcastically referred to Hungary as home to "ten million gender researchers."[1] Pető was referring to the way that this subject had become central to public debate in Hungary in the last few years. Politicians, journalists, and even the "influencer generation" on social media are now often found in bruising battles of words about whether the study of gender can be understood as an academic field.

By September 2012, one hundred thousand signatures had been collected on a petition to make domestic violence a criminal offense in Hungary. The government's stance was met with several spontaneous and preorganized demonstrations, which, however, died down within a short time. Subsequently, in May 2018, the European Parliament's Committee on Women's Rights and Gender Equality expressed its concern about the situation of Hungarian women. It did so because of the government's refusal to ratify the Istanbul Convention. Instead, leading politicians began saying that Hungarian women had an ethical duty to the nation to have more children, and the government in general kindled a panicked fear of the alleged threats of "gender ideology." According to women's rights activists, this could have triggered a third wave of feminism after the second wave, which never really gained any traction in Hungary in the first place because of the regime's control of most aspects of social life.[2] Judith Szapor recently made the frustratingly accurate contention that "Hungarian women seem to have removed themselves from—or possibly, allowed themselves to be pushed out of—the public sphere. Observers, whether domestic or foreign, have been at a loss to explain the post-communist period's dismal statistics on women's representation in

Parliament, the lowest in the European Union, political parties, and public life in general."[3] Apart from a few individual initiatives, which without exception take the Feministák Egyesülete (FE) and its membership as an example, there has not really been anything, from the perspective of feminist organization and association building, matching the fervor seen during the period of regime change at the beginning of the 1990s.[4] In Austria, the situation is similar, in that Allgemeiner österreichischer Frauenverein (AöF) and Auguste Fickert served as role models for the new women's movement that started in the 1970s.

In my discussion, I have focused on a distinct moment in the history of women's civil society in the Austro-Hungarian monarchy, when women joining the newly established modern women's associations began to advocate for women's interests. I offer a comparative look at the work of the three most powerful bourgeois-liberal feminist associations of the monarchy before 1918 and the distinctive features of their activism in the public sphere, where they made constant efforts to represent the interests of women. I argued that the most powerful Hungarian feminist associations, Nőtisztviselők Országos Egyesülete (NOE) and FE, took AöF, the leading Viennese bourgeois-liberal association, and a few progressive German associations filtered through AöF as a model for their activism at the turn of the century. I compared the everyday lives of the associations and described the different kinds of activities in which they engaged in the fight for women's rights, which included, for instance, providing legal advice and employment for women and organizing lecture tours on women's issues by leading activists. I showed that, in the end, NOE and FE became more successful than AöF, on the national and local levels and in the international arena.

Closely related to their achievements is the fact that not only was the work of the three associations based on the campaign for women's right to vote, which was sometimes intense, but they also worked to realize a number of other objectives. These included the protection of the rights of working women (including industrial workers, agricultural employees, and domestic servants, alongside those in professional careers), the campaign for the extension of women's institutional education, and the battle against prostitution and the trafficking of girls. The profile of the associations thus covered the most diverse aspects of the protection of women's rights, which they were to elaborate both at an organizational level and in their association journals.

I presented the pre-1918 history of the Hungarian feminist movement in detail, showing it not in isolation but rather in a broader comparative context alongside the development of the Austrian bourgeois-liberal women's movement. As the sources clearly reveal, AöF helped stimulate the newly founded NOE and FE, and FE became even more strident than AöF in its activism by the eve of World War I. The study of the relatively close-knit system of connections between these associations is in essence the first step in a systematic examination of the place of the

Hungarian women's movement in the larger international context before 1918. For this reason, I not only plead for the inclusion of the history of the feminist movement in the Hungarian historiography but also refuse the previously naturalizing perspective of this issue. It contributes not only to the history of women's movements in Hungary and Austria but also to gender and women's history in Central Europe. Thus, the women's movement should be understood as a broadly international trend with distinctive variations on different national stages. It would thus be crucial, I contend, to include the history of the feminist movement in the study of the history of Hungary. Furthermore, we should dispense with the "naturalizing perspective" in the study of the women's movement in Hungary. The women's associations in Hungary and in Austria should be studied not in the narrow, national context but rather as parts of the international women's movement. By placing them against this backdrop, as historians, we make a much more substantial contribution to the literature on and understanding of gender and women's history in Central Europe.

I have offered in my discussion an innovative comparative approach to the study of AöF in Vienna and NOE and FE in Hungary, none of which have actually been studied in the secondary literature in Austria or in Hungary. The six chapters of this book discuss their foundation, leadership, objectives, and publications, as well as their local, national, and international embeddedness, the role they played in World War I, and their eventual disbandment. Obviously, this is not intended as a comprehensive analysis of the women's movements in the multiethnic, multilingual Habsburg monarchy. Rather, it is a substantial step toward a nuanced grasp of the complex and intertwined histories of women's associations and activism in the region.

In the examination of the historical women's movement, with its strong transnational features, the "need to go beyond the national paradigm" has appeared in a serious fashion. As early as 1999, Susan Zimmermann stressed that the Hungarian women's movement cannot be presented exclusively at the national level. She justified this argument by pointing out that, from the last third of the nineteenth century, Hungarian women's associations became ever more intensively connected to the transnational dimensions of the movement. This is particularly true of FE, which, at Schwimmer's initiative, strove to become a part of the work of the international organization(s) even before it formally joined the International Woman Suffrage Alliance. Also, parts of this same process were Rosika Schwimmer's foreign lecture tours, the lectures given in Budapest and Hungary's provincial centers by leaders of international organizations, and the publication activity of a few activists, mostly in German, English, and French—to name but the most significant. A transnational examination is important because the activity of the women's movement at the international level is connected to its presence at the national one and to the patterns of conflict emerging in this regard.

Meanwhile, a study purely within the framework of the nation is less than effective because socioeconomic development affected women in most European countries in similar ways: we need to only think of the economic crisis of 1873 or the outbreak of World War I. Political, economic, and social changes of this kind serve as a perfect starting point for a comparative study of the women's organizations of individual countries.

The three organizations discussed at length above, which represented the radical left wing of women's organizations, had basically the same aims and profiles, and their members for the most part had the same social background as women of the middle and upper classes. They adopted almost identical approaches to the challenges women faced, and the strategies they developed to support working women were also similar. The associations also used similar communication and discursive strategies to encourage women's emancipation in every field of life. And importantly, contrary to the accusations of the Social Democratic and Christian-Social women's associations in both countries, the three associations encouraged the emancipation of more than upper- and middle-class women. They also strove to defend the interests of women who belonged to the lower classes.

As organizations founded on modern ideals, AöF, NOE, and FE rejected the principles of the traditional women's organizations of the early nineteenth century. Instead of charity work, they used practical tools to support women. They undertook a rich variety of political efforts related to women's work and carried out a wide range of activities related to job placement and the protection of working women's interests, which has been an understudied dimension of these organizations in scholarship on both countries. The journals published by these organizations also shared many affinities in their profiles, their structures, and the contents of their articles, as well as the strategies of their respective editorial offices. There were, of course, some significant differences in the strategies used by these organizations, however, and I naturally also took care to touch on them in the discussion above.

Regarding knowledge transfer among AöF, FE, and NOE, the personal contacts and relationships among the leaders of the two associations and members of the Vienna and Budapest editorial offices of *Neues Frauenleben, A Nő és a Társadalom*, and *A Nő. Feminista Folyóirat* were, of course, very significant. Indeed, the importance of these connections between the Austrian and the Hungarian bourgeois-liberal feminist women's movements strongly calls into question the usefulness of the nationalist perspective in the Hungarian scholarship on the movement and the methodological nationalism in the Austrian scholarship, which has resulted in an overemphasis on the German-speaking organizations of the monarchy.

In addition to offering a thorough look at Austrian, Hungarian, and more generally Central European women's activism before 1918, the discussion above also provides detailed information on the political agency of the charismatic protagonists of the women's movement, such as Rosika Schwimmer, Vilma Glücklich, and Auguste Fickert. Considering Schwimmer's extensive international network of contacts, the book makes a substantial contribution not only to the literature on Austrian and Hungarian history but also to the research on transnational women's movements.

The analysis above captures the moment when a self-aware but not yet politically empowered group of (upper-)middle-class Austrian and Hungarian women stepped out of obscurity and began leaving their mark on public life, in part through their activism and their press. *Neues Frauenleben*, *A Nő és a Társadalom*, and *A Nő. Feminista Folyóirat* are distinctive because they were the first modern feminist journals in the Austro-Hungarian monarchy that gave women a forum in which to make their voices heard on women's issues, which had hardly ever been discussed before in public. Thus, the leaders of the associations and editorial offices of the papers created an entirely new discursive space in which women's activism played a central role. The three associations and their journals were in close collaboration; thus, publishing and communicating with their respective supporters and the general public through the periodicals were important dimensions of their activism. All three organizations and periodicals, however, had a relatively restricted group of supporters (compared to the number of supporters of Social Democratic women's organizations in both countries, for instance). In terms of their social background, they were composed of (upper-)middle-class women and men living in Vienna and Budapest and, primarily in the case of Hungary, a few economically and socially more developed cities in the more rural parts of the country.

In the course of the reconstruction of the history of the Viennese organization operating from 1893 to 1922, it immediately becomes clear that the golden age of AöF was in the first decade of the new century, under the leadership of Auguste Fickert. Fickert was AöF's vice president from 1893 to 1897 and its president from 1897 to her death in 1910. The association and *Neues Frauenleben*, which existed for more than a decade and a half, were always in a close symbiosis, one that justified closer investigation.

AöF, which, in comparison to the groups in Hungary, operated with a modest membership throughout its span, was connected in myriad ways to Vienna and its middle class, which in turn limited the extent of its influence. Unlike in Hungary, Fickert and her colleagues never managed to establish bridgeheads in the provinces, even though the founding of branch organizations was on their agenda until 1910. Yet it would be a mistake to assume that AöF's influence was limited to a few districts in Vienna: even before 1910, Fickert had a relatively close working relationship with the progressive women's movement in Germany, with the activists in northern Europe, and with her counterparts in the Hungarian half of the monarchy.

The work of NOE and FE was inseparable from 1904 to early 1915. The women's movement in Hungary and in Budapest, developing rather later than that in Vienna, began to blossom, and to rise to a prominence similar to that of comparable organizations in the West, around the time of Fickert's death. Yet the two groups, with strong overlap in both their leadership and their membership, largely followed the path set by their colleagues in Vienna. This is entirely visible from the correspondence of Rosika Schwimmer, who from the early 1900s had a working relationship with Fickert, Marie Lang, Rosa Mayreder, and Adele Gerber. The discussion of these connections is a real innovation compared to the earlier literature, which largely examined the Budapest women's movement in isolation or else exaggerated the dominance of relations with the English-speaking world.

Although AöF, born into the intellectual ferment of the fin de siècle, began its work in a more progressive milieu, by the eve of World War I the Hungarian feminist movement had become more pervasive and in most regards had successfully reached the level set by similar organizations in western Europe. Thus, these Hungarian associations, often dominated by the personal initiatives of Rosika Schwimmer, Vilma Glücklich, and their handful of associates, in some senses outshone their fellow activists in the imperial capital. At several points, I highlighted the attitudes of Austrian and Hungarian men in general, and of leading politicians in particular, toward the associations' work. I reflected on the supportive community that the leaders of the city of Budapest created for the feminists in the István Bárczy era. This community in part explains the differences between Budapest and Vienna, which under the leadership of Christian-Social Karl Lueger hardly provided idyllic conditions for an organization fighting for the radical emancipation of women.

The editorial offices of AöF and FE were also closely connected. Schwimmer's first publications outside Hungary were published in the *Dokumente der Frauen* and later in *Neues Frauenleben*, to which she began contributing regularly, publishing articles on the situation and the perspectives of working women in Hungary. All three associations considered it crucial to secure their press, and they made significant financial sacrifices to keep their journals alive. The personal meetings of activists deepened the intensity of cooperation between the associations and the editorial offices.

The most important contribution I have sought to make with my discussion is to connect the histories of the Austrian and Hungarian bourgeois-liberal, feminist associations. My approach not only challenges the perspectives of the existing Austrian and Hungarian scholarship but also contradicts and offers an alternative to the widespread methodological nationalism in both countries. I hope that my work will serve as a model for similar studies connecting national histories of women's movements of different types inside and outside the Austro-Hungarian monarchy.

I have also sought to provide an analysis of the available membership data for the three associations and to give fresh insights into their financial circumstances. I give an in-depth study of the organizations' press activity, from both economic and institutional perspectives. My discussion of the activities of the official organs sheds light on the discursive strategies employed by the respective editorial offices, where there was a significant overlap with respect to personnel. As I have also shown, there were important similarities and differences in the ways in which AöF, NOE, and FE communicated with their followers and addressed the wider public. The primary aim of the editors and publicists was neither to castigate politicians nor to criticize men. Rather, both Austrians and Hungarians sought to promote women's emancipation and women's activism and to offer solutions to women's problems that had not yet been resolved by social policies. The (upper-)middle-class members of the association sought to safeguard the interests not only of women in the same social groups but also of those from the lower classes. However, they worked with limited means. The associations failed to achieve a breakthrough when promoting the organization of working women; their failure is probably closely connected to the low number of women joining trade unions in both Austria and Hungary on the eve of World War I.

Despite this, the activist efforts of the three organizations were still successful overall, especially if we consider that while the Social Democratic and Christian-Social women's organizations enjoyed the institutional support of political parties dominated by men, the bourgeois-liberal feminist groups pursued their work alone, formally independently of political parties. An important element of their activism was intensive communication with their followers, especially with (working) women from the (upper) middle classes. Their work in the field of education complemented this communication. As the years passed, NOE's and FE's communication strategies became more direct than those of their Austrian counterparts, largely because FE's activism was framed by the special institutions, such as the Career and Practical Advice Bureau. AöF's legal aid service could not carry out such a wide range of activities, but the association did try to fill some of this gap through the events it organized and through its official organ.

Notes

Introduction

1. Except for the NOE, whose members came from the middle classes and lower middle classes.
2. In an interview, I asked Judith Szapor about the origins of these in Hungary. Czeferner 2018.
3. Zimmermann 1999a, 49–66; Bader-Zaar 1995, 233–268.
4. Szapor 2004, 189–206.
5. Translation by Dóra Fedeles-Czeferner. Wischermann and Gerhard 1988, 268–284. Cf. Czeferner 2021.
6. From 1903 to 1908, an organization made up of state office employees (Beamtinnen-Sektion) operated within the framework of AöF. Its official publication, *Die Staatsbeamtin—Organ der Beamtinnen-Sektion*, appeared as a supplement of *Neues Frauenleben* from 1904 to 1907.
7. I owe a debt of thanks to Barbara Kunze at the Louise Otto-Peters Archiv in Leipzig for her assistance with this part of my research.
8. Hacker 1996, 97–106.
9. Bock 2014b, 204–240.
10. In 1906, a reporter with the *Daily Mail* coined the term *suffragette*, derived from *suffragist* (any person advocating for voting rights), for the members of WSPU, to belittle the women advocating women's suffrage. On the comparison of suffrage movements in different countries with different profiles and on terminology related to different types of suffrage, see Bock 2014b, 204–240.
11. On the different tendencies within the women's suffrage movement in the UK, its distinctive features, and the profiles of the main organizations, see Christensen-Nelson 2004; Bolt 1993.
12. Szapor 2011, 245–267.
13. E.g., at the ICW, founded in Washington, DC, in 1888, or at the IWSA.
14. AöF repeatedly published its call for the creation of a Fickert collection within the pages of *Neues Frauenleben*: "We repeat our request, however, that we wish for the other letters to be passed on to the Allg.[emeiner] österr.[eichischer] Frauenverein, or perhaps, for biographical reasons, to Herr Emil Fickert [Auguste Fickert's younger brother] ... or to Frau [Christine] Touaillon [a member of the AöF board] in Stainz bei Graz." Translation by Dóra Fedeles-Czeferner. *NFL* 1911, 6, 146. Tätigkeitsbericht 1910, 1–2.
15. On the latter, see Szapor 2004, 63–77; 2017, 1–19; 2018. Susan Zimmermann, Orsolya Kereszty, and Dagmar Wernitznig have also conducted research on the Schwimmer material. On this subject, also see Czeferner 2021; Zimmermann 1999b; Wernitznig 2017b, 262–279; Kereszty 2013, 92–107.

16. Cf. Vittorelli 2007, 15.
17. Czeferner 2021. New research has proven that leading members of the associations had contact with the ethnic women's associations.
18. For this see, e.g., Acsády and Mészáros 2018, 80–96; Árvai 2016; Kelbert 2013, 121–162.
19. Haan 2017, 501–536. Cf. Rupp 2010, 139–152.
20. Haan, Allen, et al. 2013, 2. Papers in this volume examine "how women in a variety of contexts and at different levels since the 1890s have challenged oppressive systems and worked for social justice." They also focus on women in movements and associations. Haan, Allen, et al. 2013.
21. Haan 2017, 501–536. As Haan, Margaret Allen, June Purvis, and Krassimira Daskalova highlight in the introduction to their edited volume "'women' are not a unitary category, and . . . their national and transnational activism has both challenged and reproduced existing power structures and institutions." Haan, Allen, et al. 2013, 2.
22. E.g., Rupp 1997.
23. Haan 2017, 501–536.
24. Rupp 2010, 139–152.
25. Haan 2017, 501–536.
26. Rupp 2010, 139–152.
27. Cf. Zimmermann 2003, 119–147; 2005, 87–117.
28. Carlier 2010, 503–522.
29. On the "serious political ambiguities and struggles" related to the construction of the inter- and transnational women's movements with examples from the multinational Habsburg monarchy, see Zimmermann 2003, 119–147; 2005, 87–117.
30. Zimmermann 2003, 119–147; 2005, 87–117.
31. Werner and Zimmermann 2006.
32. Haan 2017, 501–536.
33. Carlier 2010, 503–522.
34. On the challenges related to writing women's history by comparative perspectives and on Susan Pedersen's own experiences related to this practice, see Pedersen 2004, 85–102.
35. Cohen and O'Connor 2004, ix–xxiv. For greater details on the debates on comparative history and transfer history, see Kaelble 2003, 470–493.
36. On the category of the "everyday" and "ordinary" person, see Kotsonis 2011, 739–754.
37. Haan 2008, 65–78
38. Simonton 2006, 1–14.
39. Haan 2017, 501–536.

1. Scholarship on the Bourgeois-Liberal, Feminist Movement in Hungary and Austria

1. Szapor 2004, 189–206.
2. Szapor 2004, 189–206. Sylvia Paletschek and Bianca Pietrow-Ennker also emphasize that history was a key question for the women's emancipation movements

of the nineteenth century, as this was what gave them their legitimacy (Paletschek and Pietrow-Ennker 2004, 301–331). At the turn of the twentieth century, too, the women's associations documented their achievements in part to justify their existence. On this, see, e.g., Schwimmer 1907. Similar to the western European women's movements, Rosika Schwimmer traced the origins of the Hungarian women's movements back to the Enlightenment. In Austria, the biography of Mary Wollstonecraft as translated by Therese Schlesinger-Eckstein fit this tendency, as did Emma Adler's 1906 volume on the famous female figures of the French Revolution. Adler 1906; Godwin 1912.

3. "The state of women's and gender history in Hungary today: it demonstrates the infrastructural vacuum and institutional resistance against which a few committed practitioners of women's and gender history have been struggling to establish a foothold." Pető and Szapor 2007, 160–166.

4. Pető and Szapor 2007, 160–166.
5. Zimmermann 1999b.
6. E.g., Pető and Szapor 2004, 136–174.
7. Czeferner 2017a, 2017b.
8. Czeferner 2017a, 2017b.
9. Acsády 2007, 105–123; 2011, 309–331; Glant 2002, 35–51; Kovács 1996, 487–497; Papp 2004; Szapor 2004, 189–206; 2011, 245–265; 2017, 1–19; 2018; Schwartz 2008, 11; Loutfi 2009a, 371–391; 2009b, 81–101; McFadden 2006, 495–504; Zimmermann 1997a, 34–52; 1997c, 272–306; ; 1999b; 2002, 61–79; 2003, 119–147; 2005, 87–117. In particular: Zimmermann 2006a, 1359–1491. In the eighth part of this eleven-volume history of the Habsburg monarchy, she discusses the Hungarian women's movements of the period.

10. Gehmacher and Vittorelli 2009, 9–26.

11. The most important in this series of works is Martha Stephanie Braun, Ernestine Fürth, Marianne Hönig, Grete Laube, Bertha List-Ganser, and Clara Zaglits, eds., *Frauenbewegung, Frauenbildung und Frauenarbeit in Österreich* (Vienna, 1930). Edited by the Bund österreichischer Frauenvereine, especially Martha Stephanie Braun, Ernestine Fürth, Marianne Hönig, Grete Laube, Bertha List-Ganser, and Carla Zaglits (Vienna: Bund österreichischer Frauenvereine, 1930).

12. Fickert 1929; *60 Jahre BöF* 1965.
13. Braun-Prager 1936.
14. One of the high points of this was that the women's movement archive opened in Vienna in 1935 (Gehmacher and Vittorelli 2009, 9–23). In the same year, in New York, Rosika Schwimmer and Mary Ritter Beard embarked on establishing a similar collection (World Center for Women's Archives). Although the enterprise had collapsed by 1940, it set an example for the foundation of later collections with a similar profile. Relph 1979, 597–603.

15. Hauch 2003, 21–35.
16. Gehmacher and Mesner 2003, 7–17.
17. Hauch 2003, 21–35.
18. Jiří et al. 2013, 58.
19. With the participation of seventy-six researchers from twelve countries, the fifth Internationales Historikerinnen-treffen (International Historians' Meeting), held in

April 1984, acted as a catalyst for Austrian research into women's history. For more details, see Bechtel 1984.
20. Hauch 2003, 21–35; regarding Linz, also see Hauch 2013.
21. *Die Frau im Korsett: Wiener Frauenalltag zwischen Klischee und Wirklichkeit 1848–1920.* Tino 1984.
22. *Aufbruch in das Jahrhundert der Frau? Rosa Mayreder und der Feminismus in Wien um 1900.* Witzmann 1989.
23. *Aufmüpfig und angepaßt. Frauenleben in Österreich.* Vavra 1998.
24. "Sie meinen es politisch." *100 Jahre Frauenwahlrecht in Österreich.* For the volume to the exhibition, see Blaustrumpf ahoi! 2019.
25. Website based on Gehmacher and Vittorelli 2009. The background to the monograph was the workshop organized in 2007 titled Frauenbewegung vernetzt. Historiographie und Dokumentation. On this workshop, see Wöhrer 2007.
26. On a similar model, the online platform of the Digitales Deutsches Frauenarchiv was launched in September 2018 and is continuously extended (https://digitales-deutsches-frauenarchiv.de/, accessed 30 May 2023).
27. Much narrower in scope is the website Írónők a hálón [Women writers on the web], established as part of the project led by Anna Menyhért, but the webpage, unfortunately, does not exist anymore.
28. Gehmacher and Vittorelli 2009, 329–443.
29. *L'Homme* was the first journal in Austria to focus on women's history and gender research. Mazohl-Wallnig 1995, 9–27.
30. Translation by Dóra Fedeles-Czeferner. Bandhauer-Schöffmann 2009, 226–229.
31. Nagl-Docekal 1990, 7–18.
32. "Academic historians have in recent years learned (also) to include women in history." Translation by Dóra Fedeles-Czeferner. Mazohl-Wallnig 1995, 9–26.
33. "The trivialization of women's themes, which has done more harm than good to the original goal." Translation by Dóra Fedeles-Czeferner. Mazohl-Wallnig 1995, 9–26.
34. "In this short space of time much of the basic research into the history of women and gender has not yet taken place in systematic form." Translation by Dóra Fedeles-Czeferner. Mazohl-Wallnig 1995, 9–26.
35. Klingenstein 1997, 3–6.
36. Vittorelli 2009d, 103–133. The situation has changed little since 2009, alas. Cf. Carlier 2009, 233–237: In Marilyn Lake's view, "feminist scholarship is an international enterprise and feminism has a transnational history." Quoted in Carlier 2009, 233–237.
37. Zimmermann 2009, 63–80.
38. Bader-Zaar 1999, 365–383.
39. Geber 2013, 148–151; Flich 1990, 1–24; 2004, 43–55; Hacker 1996, 97–106; 1997; 1998; Prost 1986, 2–6; Unger 2009.
40. Bader-Zaar 2009, 297–328. Its subtitle in German was the same as for the English version, while its main title was changed to *Vision und Leidenschaft*. Anderson 1992. Of works in German translation, we might mention *A History of Their Own: Women in Europe from Prehistory to Present* by Bonnie S. Anderson and Judith

P. Zinsser, which was published in German as *Eine eigene Geschichte: Frauen in Europa* in 1992.

41. Chapters were written by Renate Flich, Gabriella Hauch, Birgitta Bader-Zaar, and Susan Zimmermann: Wandruszka and Rumpler 2006; Flich 2006, 940–964; Hauch 2006a, 965–1003; Bader-Zaar 2006a, 1005–1029; Zimmermann 2006a, 1359–1491.

42. E.g., Kehle 1952.

43. E.g., Beck 1964; Burmetler 1992; Kehle 1952; Mixa 1969; Krainer 1993; Truger 1986.

44. Auernig 1994.

45. "It would also be important to be able to gain access to unpublished material like associations' documents or correspondence. In this regard there is not always all that much at our disposal; searching is laborious and access . . . has to be fought for." Translation by Dóra Fedeles-Czeferner. Bader-Zaar 2009, 297–328.

46. E.g., Maderthaner 1986. The volume is a collection of studies from a symposium of Austrian and Hungarian historians. Other examples include Hauch 1986; Helmut 1984; Szapor et al. 2012; Viethen 1984.

47. E.g., Anderson 1992; Hacker 1996, 1997; Klingenstein 1997; Mazohl-Wallnig 1995.

48. E.g., Szapor et al. 2012; Winklbauer et al. 2016.

49. E.g., Raggam-Blesch 2005, 25–55; Malleier 2005, 79–101.

50. Raggam-Blesch 2005, 25–55.

51. Grandner and Saurer 2005; Saurer 1995.

52. On the aims of the project, see Frysak, Lanzinger, and Saurer 2004, 117–121. For the volume on the project's results, see Saurer 2006.

53. Similar projects appeared on the transnational arena from the 1990s onward, as evidenced by the international conferences held on the subject. Klösch-Melliwa 2001, 23–41.

54. Hämmerle 2012, 218–230; 2014; Hämmerle, Überegger, and Bader-Zaar 2014. Its second chapter covers Austro-Hungarian women. Also see Malleier 2004, 2005. Hämmerle's 2014 assessment of the situation still holds true in part for Austria and in full for Hungary: "An area of the new historical studies that has been thoroughly elaborated from a theoretical and methodological perspective often, precisely because of local military history, encounters apathy, or in luckier instances is marginalized, and just becomes a superficially appearing theme under the title of 'Woman.'" Translation by Dóra Fedeles-Czeferner. Hämmerle 2014, 10. On this, also see the 2018 issue of *L'Homme* on World War I.

55. E.g., the exhibition *1914—Frauen in dem ersten Weltkrieg* in Klagenfurt. For the catalog, see Pichler 2014.

56. Hämmerle counts eighty subsidiary groups of BöF in 1914, while Irene Schöffmann talks of seventy-four. Hämmerle 2014, 85; Bandhauer-Schöffmann 1986, 1.

57. Anderson 1994, 185.

58. Cf. Bader-Zaar 2009, 297–328.

59. Schmölzer 2002; Anderson 1985; Mayreder and Anderson 1988; Klaus and Wischermann 2013, 109–116.

60. Leisch-Prost 2006, 319–323.

61. Oesch's work also investigates the international connections of the Austrian women's movement and the peace movement following World War I. Oesch 2014. Also see Oesch 2008, 118–144; 2012, 509–514. On Schirmacher, see Gehmacher et al. 2018.

62. E.g., Lebensaft 2002, 757–759; Weiser 2004, 118–121; Arias 2000, 55–78; Andraschko 1993, 221–231; Keintzel 1993, 104–108; Raggam-Blesch 2012, 93–128; Geber 2013, 142–148; Hauch 2012, 71–91; Tichy 1989, 133–184.
63. Auernig 1994; Braun-Prager n.d.-a, n.d.-b; Flich 1990, 1–24; 2004, 43–55; Hacker 1996, 97–106; 1997, 101–109; Leon 1955, 51–63, 183–196; Geber 2013, 148–151.
64. E.g., Glant 2002, 32–51; Szapor 2017, 1–19; Zimmermann and Major 2006, 484–491.
65. E.g., Zimmermann 2006c, 162–166.
66. Haan et al. 2006.
67. Lóránd et al. 2024.

2. Austria-Hungary in the Fin de Siècle

1. Hanák 1971, 47.
2. Hanák 1971, 43.
3. For a critique of the hurried urban development of Budapest at the turn of the century, see Gyáni 2008, 65–68.
4. Frank 1990, 252–266.
5. Rumpler 1997.
6. Judson 2017, 332–338.
7. For the quotas divided between the two countries, which were used to finance the common issues, see Rumpler 1997, 413–414.
8. Judson 2017, 332–338.
9. Frank 1990, 252–266.
10. Frank 1990, 252–266.
11. Frank 1990, 252–266.
12. Rumpler 1997, 408–411.
13. On Lueger, see Boyer 2010.
14. Jeszenszky 1997, 267–294.
15. Bader-Zaar 2019, 37–60.
16. Hanák 1971, 53.
17. Jeszenszky 1997, 267–294.
18. Jeszenszky 1997, 267–294.
19. Rumpler 1997, 568–570.
20. For greater detail, see Hämmerle, Überegger, and Bader-Zaar 2014.
21. Jeszenszky 1997, 267–294.
22. On the supply situation, agricultural production, and the war economy, see the statistics in Rumpler and Schmied Kowarzik 2010.
23. Jeszenszky 1997, 267–294.
24. Judson 2017, 503–521.
25. Jeszenszky 1997, 267–294.
26. Katus 2007, 753–763.
27. Rumpler 1997, 426–445.
28. Dobszay and Fónagy 2005, 307–459. On the ethnic structures of the monarchy on the basis of the census of 1910, see Rumpler and Schmied Kowarzik 2010.

29. Frank 1990, 252–266; Judson 2017, 396–400.
30. Rumpler and Schmied Kowarzik 2010, 59–69.
31. Katus 2007, 753–763.
32. Jeszenszky 1997, 267–294.
33. Dobszay and Fónagy 2005, 307–459.
34. Jeszenszky 1997, 267–294.
35. Rumpler 1997, 456–486; Katus 2007, 678–695.
36. On the length of the railroad network, see Rumpler and Schmied Kowarzik 2010, 247–255.
37. Jeszenszky 1997, 267–294.
38. Rumpler 2010 and Schmied Kowarzik, 247–255.
39. Rumpler 1997, 468.
40. Frank 1990, 252–266.
41. Katus 2007, 678–695.
42. Katus 2007, 678–695; Rumpler 1997, 463–466.
43. Frank 1990, 252–266.
44. Katus 2007, 678–695.
45. Jeszenszky 1997, 267–294.
46. Frank 1990, 252–266; Katus 2007, 678–695.
47. Jeszenszky 1997, 267–294.
48. On the particularities of the population pyramid of the dualist era and the female surplus appearing in the older generations, see Gyáni and Kövér 2006, 19; Anderson 1992, 6.
49. Czeferner 2021.
50. Rumpler 1997, 488–495.
51. Frank 1990, 252–266.
52. Jeszenszky 1997, 267–294.
53. Ehmer 1996, 73–92.
54. Hanák 1998, 3–43.
55. Within this growth, on the numbers and proportions of the women's population of Budapest from 1880 to 1910, see Illyefalvi 1930, 7; Hanák 1998, 3–43.
56. The most important models in its development were Berlin and Vienna. Hanák 1998, 3–43; Melinz and Zimmermann 1996b, 15–34.
57. Zimmermann 1996b, 67–92. On care for the poor in Budapest and Vienna, see Zimmermann 2011.
58. Gyáni 2008.
59. Halmos 2006, 161–194; Hanák 1998, 118–120. On the many-layered meanings of the terminology of bourgeois development, see Kövér 2003, 35–45.
60. On the nineteenth-century history of Budapest's haute bourgeoisie, economic elite, and entrepreneurs, see Klement 2012, 78–106.
61. Jeszenszky 1997, 267–294.
62. Hanák 1971, 48.
63. Hanák 1971, 48. On the forms of entertainment available to women, see Géra and Szécsi 2018, 259–294; Kéri 2008, 159–198.
64. Wandruszka and Rumpler 2006.

65. Bader-Zaar 1995, 233–268; Hauch 2006a, 965–1003.
66. "If a nonpolitical association wishes to extend its activities to include political affairs, it has to submit itself to the applicable laws governing the founding of political associations. Whether an association can be considered political is determined by the national authority, or, in instances as listed in § 11, or on appeal, by the interior ministry." Translation by Dóra Fedeles-Czeferner. Gesetz vom 15. November 1867 (134/1867).
67. Judson 1992, 337–345.
68. Gyáni 2010, 285–295.
69. Reichsvolksschulgesetz 62/1869.
70. Hanák 1998, 63–97.
71. Act XXXVIII 1868.
72. For a comparison of the particularities of the development of the three cities in the period from 1867 to 1914, see Melinz and Zimmermann 1996b, 15–34.
73. Melinz and Zimmermann 1996a, 140–176.
74. Hanák 1998, 63–97.
75. Hanák 1998, 63–97.

3. The Austro-Hungarian Women's Movement until the Fin de Siècle and the Different Branches of the Women's Movement

1. Burucs 1993, 15–19.
2. On this, see Anderson 1992, 35–38; Bader-Zaar 2006a, 1005–1029.
3. Cited in Schwartz 2008, 11.
4. E.g., Szegvári 1969.
5. Schwartz 2008, 3.
6. Schwartz 2008, 6.
7. Witzmann 1989, 10–18.
8. Zimmermann 1997b, 171–204.
9. As Gabriella Hauch argues, in terms of research practice in Austria, four possible ideological tendencies can be differentiated: Social Democratic, Christian-Social/Catholic, national, and bourgeois-liberal women's associations. Another tendency can be found in federal national movements of the crown lands and in the extremely heterogeneous network of German-national patriotic and "völkische Hilfsvereine." Hauch 2009, 23–60.
10. Bund österreichischer Frauenvereine 1955, 9.
11. Cf. Szapor 2018, 11. The same can be observed in literary life.
12. Cf. Bader-Zaar 2009, 297–328.
13. Translation by Dóra Fedeles-Czeferner. ÖNB M F34, 361–364.
14. The author of these lines might be Käthe Braun-Prager, who in 1936 published a monograph on the key figures of the Austrian women's movement; she also wrote an article about Auguste Fickert when her memorial was unveiled (Braun-Prager 1936; Braun-Prager n.d.-a. ÖNB Han). It is also possible that the author was Rosa Mayreder, who participated in the work of the committee that decided on the erection of the Fickert memorial (Anderson 1994, 194). Another member of this committee was Marianne Hainisch (Burmetler 1992, 22). The plans for the memorial can be found in

the Fickert Collection. Situation für die Erbau eines Denkmales für Auguste Fickert in Türkenschanzpark, WR NF H.I.N. 71175/1-6.
15. Niederkofler 2011, 17-36.
16. I am using the term *civic school* as a translation of the Hungarian term *polgári iskola*. These schools were introduced in the Hungarian half of the Austro-Hungarian monarchy in 1868. In general, these schools emphasized practical subjects, such as accounting, geometry, the rudiments of exchange law, geography, history, and reading and writing in Hungarian and other languages. The Hungarian term *polgári* refers essentially to the urban burgher lifestyle, and these schools were intended to provide the education necessary for this lifestyle to flourish.
17. Zimmermann 2003, 119-147.
18. Hacker 1997, 75; Unger 2012, 18-30.
19. Hauch 2006c, 424-426.
20. Freismuth 1989, 27-36.
21. Statut 1848.
22. Hauch 2009, 23-60.
23. Translation by Dóra Fedeles-Czeferner. Weiland 1983, 187. Cf. Schmölzer 2002, 84-87.
24. Statut 1865, 1.
25. Translation by Dóra Fedeles-Czeferner. Schraut 2013, 110-137.
26. For an excellent survey of the various types of women's associations operating in the "center and periphery" of the Habsburg monarchy from the mid-nineteenth century, see Friedrich 1995, 125-175.
27. Weiland 1983, 187; Anderson 1992, 26-35.
28. Hauch 2009, 23-60.
29. Flich 2006, 946-947.
30. Hauch 2009, 23-60.
31. For a detailed analysis of this and of AöF's role in these campaigns, see Bandhauer-Schöffmann 1993, 49-78.
32. Bader-Zaar 2006b, 173-177; Hacker 1997, 75.
33. Clark 2008, 174, 168; Szegvári 1981, 127-128; Weiland 1983, 188.
34. Clark 2008, 174, 168; Szegvári 1981, 127-128.
35. Bandhauer-Schöffmann 1993, 49-78. From 1878, women were permitted to attend certain university lectures "in special circumstances." Clark 2008, 174.
36. Bandhauer-Schöffmann 1993, 49-78; Bader-Zaar 2006b, 173-177; Hacker 1997, 75.
37. When the first meeting of the Akademische Frauenverein (Academic Women's Association), which Auguste Fickert attended, took place in May 1908, around five hundred women were studying at the University of Vienna. Bandhauer-Schöffmann 1993, 49-78.
38. Anderson 1990, 189-201; Bader-Zaar 1999, 365-383. Christine Touaillon states the same in 1918 regarding the *Neues Frauenleben*. NFL 1918, 4-5, 76-81.
39. Bader-Zaar 1997, 547-561; "Wer wählt, gewinnt" 1989, 5. For more detail, see Anderson 1992, 39-40.
40. Bader-Zaar 1995, 233-268.
41. Auguste Fickert's name is also mentioned in the article; provincial teachers must have turned to her for guidance on organizational matters. *Lehrerinnen-Wart* 1889, 12, 24.

42. Bader-Zaar 1997, 547–561.
43. Cf. Anderson 1992, 10.
44. DF 1901, 145.
45. *NT* 1910, 144–146. Cf. Schwartz 2008, 13.
46. Burucs 1993, 15–19; Tóth 2005.
47. Szapor 2007, 129–144.
48. Schwartz 2008, 16.
49. Cf. Gyáni 2010, 485–495.
50. Szegvári 1981, 127–129.
51. Among other things, it maintained a residence for older unmarried female teachers unable to work (Burucs 1993, 15–19; Zimmermann 1997b, 171–204; 1999b, 22–25). It is significant, however, that in Hungary, as a result of the December 1895 Wlassics decree, the faculties of medicine (pharmacy) and humanities opened their doors to women a year before this happened in Austria.
52. Loutfi 2009a, 379–391.
53. Zimmermann 1999a, 49–66; Bader-Zaar 1995, 233–268.
54. Szapor 2004, 189–206.
55. Szapor 2004, 189–206. Cf. the approach of Karen Offen, who in her 2001 work discusses the different characteristics unique to the women's movement and the feminist movement. Offen 2001, 210–235.
56. Schwartz 2008, 8–9. Cf. Anderson 1990, 189–201; Gehmacher 2019, 3-44. Gisela Bock states that the term was used in England and the US since the 1910s, but not as a leading or title term, and it became well established in the interwar period. Bock 2014a, 100–152.
57. Gehmacher 2019, 4.
58. Gehmacher 2019, 5.
59. Gehmacher examines Käthe Schirmacher's role in this transfer. In one of her works written in French, Schirmacher used the word *féminisme*, which had been translated to *Frauenbewegung* in German. According to Schirmacher, "'Feminismus' was built on unhealthy eroticism and liberation only of carnal desires." Gehmacher 2019, 3–44. On this, most recently, see Gehmacher 2024.
60. Bock 2014a, 100–152.
61. Offen 2000.
62. Schwartz 2008, 12–13.
63. Schwartz 2008, 12–13.
64. Witzmann 1989, 10–18.
65. Anderson 1989, 6–12.
66. Witzmann 1989, 10–18.
67. Hauch 2009, 23–60.
68. For more detail on the structural framework of these and the connections between them, see Auernig 1994, 19–25.
69. This was published from 1 January 1891 as a supplement to the Arbeiter-Zeitung; until 1934, Adelheid Popp remained editor. Auernig 1994, 21.
70. Czeferner 2021, 9–14, 13, 15, 17, 65.

71. Witzmann 1989, 10–18.
72. I.e., the Social Democratic women's movement was a segment of the socialist movement as a whole. Witzmann 1989, 10–18.
73. Freismuth 1989, 27–36.
74. Bader-Zaar 2019, 37–60.
75. Hauch 2009, 23–60. For further information on Social Democratic women's movements, see Niggemann 1981; Prost 1989.
76. Witzmann 1989, 10–18.
77. Auernig 1994, 24.
78. Niederkofler 2011, 17–36.
79. Adler spoke in favor of female suffrage as early as 1907. Freismuth 1989, 27–36.
80. Hauch 2011, 221–243.
81. Mucsi 1980, 333–342.
82. Burucs 1993, 15–19.
83. Czeferner 2021.
84. Hauch 2009, 23–60.
85. Steinkellner 1985, 55–67.
86. Bader-Zaar 2009, 297–328.
87. Steinkellner 1985, 55–67.
88. Auernig 1994, 28.
89. Hauch 2009, 23–60. For further information on women's associations in Austria, see Klucsarits and Kürbisch 1975; Schernthaner 1985; Guschlbauer 1974.
90. In the space of a couple of years, they established sixteen girls' groups and twenty women's defense societies. Kéri 2008, 83.
91. Burucs 1993, 15–19.
92. Loutfi 2009a, 371–391.
93. Kéri 2008, 84.
94. Loutfi 2009a, 379–391.
95. Gehmacher and Vittorelli 2009, 297–444.
96. On the literature published on the Slovak women's movements before 2009, see Dudeková 2009, 329–350. For further literature, see Cviková 2006, 187–207.
97. Associations in the provinces were primarily devoted to philanthropy, and they were often connected with educational, patriotic, and religious aims. They facilitated women's participation in social life, however. Dudeková 2009, 329–350. Brno has been the center of the Social Democratic women's movement. Malečková 2004, 167–188.
98. Malečková 2004, 167–188.
99. Malečková also discusses the case of the first Czech female representatives in the Moravian diet (Malečková 2004, 167–188). This was a widely discussed issue in the Austrian and Hungarian women's press as well. Cf. Czeferner 2021.
100. Vittorelli 2009c, 393–410.
101. For further literature on the Czech women's movements, see Vosahlíková 2006, 209–218.
102. Rupp 1994, 16–18.

103. Malečková 2004, 167–188.
104. Vittorelli 2009c, 411–428. For further literature on the Polish and Galician women's movements, see Stegmann 2006, 241–255; Zhurzhenko 2006, 257–269; Lorence-Kot and Winiarz 2004, 206–220.
105. Stegmann 2000, 1, 22.
106. Stegmann 2000, 1–2.
107. Gogîltan 2009, 351–370.
108. Rupp 1994, 16–18.
109. Vittorelli 2007, 17, 128, 130.
110. Vittorelli 2009b, 429–443. A key milestone in the dialogue between women's historians in the Central and southeastern European regions is the 2006 German-language volume edited by Vesela Tutavac and Ilse Korotin, which holds the relationships and interdependences of women's associations in the Austro-Hungarian monarchy and the South Slav region under the microscope. Tutavac and Korotin 2016. For further literature on the women's movements of the South Slav region, see Morawetz 2006, 219–239; Vodopivec 1996, 141–164.

4. The Austrian Association

1. For a comparison of the circumstances of female teachers at Austrian civic schools with those in Germany, see Weiland 1983, 188–189. Cf., e.g., *NFL* 1910, 3, 89–91; 1911, 5, 124–125.
2. Anderson 1992, 41.
3. On this, see, e.g., *NFL* 1911, 3, 59–60. Cf. Weiland 1983, 211–213.
4. On the differences in the rights of women (teachers) in Vienna and Lower Austria, see Anderson 1992, 39–40. Cf., e.g., the assembly decree on forms of address for teachers at elementary and civic schools in Lower Austria: *NFL* 1905, 11, 21.
5. Anderson 1992, 39.
6. "As such the women's movement in Austria never became a single-issue movement as in England or the United States of America." Translation by Dóra Fedeles-Czeferner. Bader-Zaar 1997, 547–561.
7. Translation by Dóra Fedeles-Czeferner. Tätigkeitsbericht 1893, 1.
8. In her 2008 work, Gabriella Hauch suggests the statutes were sent back three times. Hauch 2008, 98–117. In her book, published one year later, she no longer mentions a number in this context: "After repeated unsuccessful attempts . . . the office for the police authorized the statutes [of AöF]." Translation by Dóra Fedeles-Czeferner. Hauch 2009, 23. In her collection on the AöF statutes, Fickert makes only passing mention of this public to-ing and fro-ing: "Our statutes were at first rejected by the Ministry of the Interior, and this is the reason why the association was not established last fall as had been planned in the 'circular letter.'" Translation by Dóra Fedeles-Czeferner. Protokoll 1893, 8–11.
9. "All citizens are equal before the law." Translation by Dóra Fedeles-Czeferner. Gesetz vom 15.
10. Protokoll 1893, 8–11.
11. Unger 2012, 18–31.
12. Cf. Festschrift 1913, 16.

13. "What are we missing, as women and in general? What prevents us from making progress? There are still too few of us in action, we hardly have any sense of solidarity, and we are completely undisciplined." Translation by Dóra Fedeles-Czeferner. Konvolut von Auguste Fickerts Reden und Schriften; WR NF, A-78003. Cf. Flich 1990, 1–24.

14. *Neuzeit* 1892, 4, 88. The organizational challenges of the meeting were described on two occasions in the official organ of AdF. *Neue Bahnen* (hereafter *NB*) 1892, 11, 86; *NB* 1892, 26, issue 14, 109–110.

15. Translation by Dóra Fedeles-Czeferner. Bertha von Suttner to Auguste Fickert, 14 April 1892, ÖNB M F.34.365.

16. Unger 2012, 17–30; Emilie Mataja to Auguste Fickert, 25 February 1892, ÖNB M F.34.365.

17. Together with her life partner, Ida Baumann, she held lectures until 1909 within the framework of the Arbeiterinnen-Bildungsverein. Klösch-Melliwa 2001, 127.

18. Auernig 1994.

19. Translation by Dóra Fedeles-Czeferner. Emilie Mataja to Augusre Fickert, 25 February 1892.

20. August Bebel to Auguste Fickert, 22 April 1899, WR NF H.I.N. 69831. Cf. Weiland 1983, 213. In Germany, the women's associations were genuinely afraid that the authorities would disband them were political agitation to occur.

21. Translation by Dóra Fedeles-Czeferner. August Bebel to Auguste Fickert, n.d., ÖNB M F.34.365.

22. "These questions are dealt with from a rather bourgeois perspective." Translation by Dóra Fedeles-Czeferner. *Arbeiterinnen-Zeitung* (hereafter *AZ*), 3 June 1892, cited in Hauch 2009, 24.

23. Anderson 1992, 40–41; Hauch 2009, 24; Tätigkeitsbericht 1893, 12; 1895, 19; 1897, 19; Hofmann-Weinberger 2016c.

24. Hauch 2006a, 965–1003.

25. Protokoll 1893, 8–11. Cf. Anderson 1992, 41.

26. Marianne Hainisch's memoirs incorrectly list the date of inauguration as 18 January. Hainisch 1930, 13–24. The news of the foundation was reported in *Neue Bahnen* with a slight delay, in March. *NB* 1893, 27, issue 5, 38.

27. Protokoll 1893.

28. Translation by Dóra Fedeles-Czeferner. The author of this article also explains that Fickert never spoke of her feelings and that her life was mostly loveless. *NFL* 1911, 6, 144–146.

29. Klaus and Wischermann 2013, 109–116.

30. Klaus and Wischermann 2013, 109–116.

31. Karoline Fellner to Auguste Fickert, 2 August 1870, WR NF H.I.N. 148.839. She remained in contact with her two teachers until the early 1900s. Mater Cassiana to Auguste Fickert, WR NF H.I.N.-69961–H.I.N.-69968; Mater Gisela to Auguste Fickert, WR NF H.I.N. 70.440/1–10.

32. Instituts-Zeugnis, 28 July 1870, WR NF H.I.N. 71178/4.

33. She passed her exams "with distinction." WR NF H.I.N. 711, 79/1.

34. Translation by Dóra Fedeles-Czeferner. Auguste Fickert, Tagebuch, 7 September 1874, WR NF H.I.N. 704.94.

35. Auguste Fickert, Tagebuch.

36. Schmölzer 2009, 109.
37. Lehmann 1859–1922.
38. Schmölzer 2009, 104.
39. Hacker 2006, 131–133. For the disciplinary proceedings that brought wage reductions and relocations, see the letters to Fickert from the school board in 1900. WR NF H.I.N. 71182/2–6. Cf. Flich 1990, 1–24.
40. In her letters, she regularly referred to her as "My dearest Fickert." E.g., Ida Baumann to Auguste Fickert n.d., WR H.I.N. 679.89.
41. Auguste Fickert, Tagebuch, 21 August 1872, WR NF H.I.N. 70494.
42. Her cousin responded, "That with your American idea! Who puts this madness into your head?" Translation by Dóra Fedeles-Czeferner. Karoline Fellner to Auguste Fickert, 24 May 1876, WR NF H.I.N. 148872.
43. Auguste Fickert, Tagebuch, WR NF H.I.N. 70494.
44. *NFL* 1911, 11, 1–7.
45. Schmölzer 2009, 112–113.
46. The literature makes no mention of this organizational question, with the exception of Hanna Hacker, who investigates the history of the Austrian women's movement through the conflicts between its leaders—yet even she offers no logical explanation for this problem. Hacker 1998, 103.
47. *NFL* 1911, 1, 15.
48. The names of the vice presidents are mentioned in the reports. See, e.g., *NFL* 1914, 7, 212–213.
49. *NFL* 1910, 7, 205–208.
50. Louise Fickert to Auguste Fickert, letters, 1891–1893, WR NF H.I.N.-153397–H.I.N.-153400.
51. At the time of the foundation of AöF, in Vienna and Lower Austria female teachers were not allowed to marry. Flich 2006, 941–964.
52. Tätigkeitsbericht 1898, 12; 1899, 13; 1900, 13.
53. Klösch-Melliwa 2001, 127–130. Around 1900, Baumann was in correspondence with Adele Gerber, later editor in chief of *Neues Frauenleben*, who on one occasion complained that Fickert did not take her seriously on account of her young age. Adele Gerber to Ida Baumann, 21 July 1902, WR NF H.I.N.-71161.
54. Auernig 1994, 52–53.
55. *NFL* 1902, 1, 1.
56. Tätigkeitsbericht 1901; *NFL* 1902, 1, 1, 19.
57. Hofmann-Weinberger 2016b.
58. Klingenstein 1999, 117–128.
59. Klingenstein 1999, 117–128.
60. Klingenstein 1999, 117–128.
61. From 1902 to 1910, these words adorned the first page of every issue of the journal: "Published in the middle of each month in Vienna, edited by Auguste Fickert." In 1911, they were changed to the following: "Founded by Auguste Fickert." Translation by Dóra Fedeles-Czeferner.
62. *NFL* 1902, 1, 1.
63. Hacker 1996, 97–106; sanatorium invoices made out to Emil Fickert, 3 July 1910, WR NF H.I.N. 71138/4.

64. Hacker 1996, 97–106.
65. On this, see, e.g., Auguste Fickert to Rosa Mayreder, WR NF H.I.N. 70862–H.I.N. 70875. See also WR NF H.I.N. 152.808–815; ÖNB M F.34.365.
66. L. WR NF H.I.N. 70478/2–70478/23. Cf. Hacker 1998, 89.
67. Klingenstein 1997, 313–314.
68. Leopoldine Kulka to Auguste Fickert, 1902–1910, WR NF H.I.N. 152.870–152.891; Christine Touaillon to Auguste Fickert, 22 March 1908, WR NF H.I.N. 152.900; Adele Gerber to Auguste Fickert, 19 April 1903, WR NF H.I.N. 70558/13. For more detail on Fickert's frosty responses to Mayreder's tenderer letters, see Schmölzer 2002, 92.
69. There are many suggestions of this in her letters: "I would be blessed if you came, you whom I love, who understands me, whom I understand. There are only half people everywhere here." Translation by Dóra Fedeles-Czeferner. Marie Lang to Auguste Fickert, 19 August 1897, WR NF H.I.N. 152899.
70. Marie Lang to Auguste Fickert, 15 March 1907, WR NF H.I.N. 123.710. Cf. Sparholz 1986, 44. Sparholz believes that the two women's breakup was a lasting one.
71. Malleier 2001, 50. Cf. Malleier 2005, 79–99.
72. Leopoldine Kulka, Dokumentation, WR NF AC10956995. See also Malleier 2001, 48–59.
73. Malleier 2001, 48–59.
74. Translation by Dóra Fedeles-Czeferner. Cited in Hacker 1996, 97–106. According to Hanna Hacker, Fickert's relationship with antisemitism was highly contradictory. In her own circles, she was at times called an antisemite, and she vehemently protested against this label. Hacker 1996, 97–106. Cf. the arguments of Elisabeth Malleier, according to which the question of Jewish origin played a role in succession discussions after Fickert's death. Malleier also contends that, "despite numerous Jewish friends, co-workers and patrons, Fickert had decreed in the years following her passing (1910) that the journal of the AöF, *Neues Frauenleben*, should not fall into Jewish hands." Malleier 2005, 79–101.
75. "It seems to me that you have not been quite yourself in the events of late." Translation by Dóra Fedeles-Czeferner. Cited in Sparholz 1986, 119.
76. Maikki Friberg to Auguste Fickert, 5 August [no year], WR NF H.I.N. 152.986.
77. Hacker 1996, 97–106.
78. *NFL* 1909, 5, 117–119; 1911, 11, 293–296.
79. Klaus and Wischermann 2013, 109–116; Hacker 1996, 97–106.
80. Protokoll 1893, 1.
81. Tätigkeitsbericht 1893, 1895–1900.
82. Tätigkeitsbericht 1910, 1–2.
83. Translation by Dóra Fedeles-Czeferner. E.g., *NFL* 1913, 1, 1.
84. *NFL* 1908, 8, 202–203; 1909, 9, 228–229.
85. Cf. the fact that in 1896 the report of the entire AöF was a mere two pages, while that of the *Rechtschutz-Sektion* was six. Tätigkeitsbericht 1896, 3–9.
86. Translation by Dóra Fedeles-Czeferner. Tätigkeitsbericht 1895, 1.
87. Tätigkeitsbericht 1896, 1–2.
88. For this, see the membership lists published with the reports. Tätigkeitsbericht 1893–1897.
89. Tätigkeitsbericht 1897, 3; *NFL* 1902, 1, 19.

90. Tätigkeitsbericht 1900, 4.
91. NFL 1904, 3, 19; 1907, 2, 23; 1903, 1, 1.
92. In the 1890s, her pay was 1,200 gulden a month. Wiener Bezirksschulfonde, 15 January 1892, WR NF H.I.N. 71180/a. By 1897, her pay had increased to 1,350 gulden. Bekenntnis zur Personaleinkommensteuer, 1897, WR NF H.I.N. 71179/1.
93. Translation by Dóra Fedeles-Czeferner. Louis Frank to Auguste Fickert, 15 January 1893, WR NF H.I.N. 70403/1; Auguste Schmidt to Auguste Fickert, 21 December 1892, WR NF H.I.N. 71000; Ferdinand Kronawetter to Auguste Fickert, 27 January 1893, H.I.N. 152.840; Protokoll 1893; Lemberger Frauenverein to AöF, 28 December 1892, WR NF H.I.N. 70824.
94. Protokoll 1893, 1–8.
95. Auguste Fickert to the National Educational Committee, 29 January 1875, WR NF H.I.N. 71176/1. Cf. Jammernegg 2016a; Auguste Bebel to Auguste Fickert, 22 April 1899, WR NF H.I.N. 69831.
96. Protokoll 1893, 15.
97. Hacker 1998, 107–112.
98. Protokoll 1893, 7.
99. Protokoll 1893, 15.
100. Translation by Dóra Fedeles-Czeferner. Protokoll 1893, 8–11.
101. Translation by Dóra Fedeles-Czeferner. Protokoll 1893, 7.
102. Protokoll 1893, 11.
103. Protokoll 1893, 12.
104. Translation by Dóra Fedeles-Czeferner. Protokoll 1893, 13.
105. NFL 1911, 6, 148–150.
106. NFL 1918, 4–5, 57–60.
107. Translation by Dóra Fedeles-Czeferner. In the 1898 report, Fickert again draws attention to the goals of the association: "This is also mentioned in the modest work of the AöF, the objective of which at its inception was to work on the transformation of women's thought and perspective." Translation by Dóra Fedeles-Czeferner. Tätigkeitsbericht 1898, 1.
108. Protokoll 1893, 14.
109. Cf. Anderson 1990, 189–201.
110. Tätigkeitsbericht 1910, 1–2; 1895, 18; 1893, 9.
111. E.g., on the basis of petitions published in the journal. Cf. Frysak 2002, 215–223.
112. Protokoll 1893, 1–7.
113. Konvolut von Artikeln über die Frauenfrage, WR NF H.I.N. 77991B.
114. The debate between Fickert and Lang and the reasons for it were described in the 1899 report: "Mrs. Lang . . . from the outset followed her intention to keep Auguste Fickert at arm's length from the editorial staff of the journal if possible." Translation by Dóra Fedeles-Czeferner. Tätigkeitsbericht 1899, 2.
115. In 1897, for example, they described this deficit as follows: "Despite cutting costs and 'limiting the household budget' every year at the association has closed with a deficit." Translation by Dóra Fedeles-Czeferner. Tätigkeitsbericht 1897, 1.
116. Hacker 1998, 78.
117. Tätigkeitsbericht 1899, 2.

118. Translation by Dóra Fedeles-Czeferner. Bertha von Suttner to Auguste Fickert, 21 October 1891, ÖNB M F.23.365.
119. Translation by Dóra Fedeles-Czeferner. Auguste Fickert to Ottilie Turnau, 21 October 1891, ÖNB M F.23.365.
120. Bader-Zaar 1999, 365–383; Frysak 2002, 215–223.
121. For the annual statistics, see Bader-Zaar 1999, 365–383. In 1909, they had 1,242 legal cases. Tätigkeitsbericht 1910, 3.
122. *NFL* 1908, 7, 182–183; 1908, 12, 302; 1911, 69; 1914, 4, 111–113.
123. Hofmann-Weinberger 2016b.
124. For greater detail on their conflicts, see Hacker 1998, 107–108.
125. Maikki Friberg to Auguste Fickert, 2 October 1906, WR NF H.I.N. 152.962.
126. Translation by Dóra Fedeles-Czeferner. Maikki Friberg to Auguste Fickert, n.d., WR NF H.I.N. 152.967.
127. Translation by Dóra Fedeles-Czeferner. Maikki Friberg to Auguste Fickert, 5 August [no year], WR NF H.I.N. 152.986.
128. *NFL* 1909, 8, issue 5, 118–119.
129. Wiener Bezirksschulfonde, 15 January 1892, WR NF H.I.N. 71180/a.
130. More precisely, the amount was "for membership cards not supplied because of missing address details." Translation by Dóra Fedeles-Czeferner. Tätigkeitsbericht 1895, 14.
131. Tätigkeitsbericht 1895, 14.
132. Tätigkeitsbericht 1897, 13; 1898, 12.
133. Tätigkeitsbericht 1910, 1.
134. The silver-based Austro-Hungarian gulden (in Hungary, forint) introduced in 1867 was replaced in 1892 by the gold-based crown. Gulden/forint banknotes nevertheless remained legal tender until the early 1900s.
135. *NFL* 1909, 5, 118–119; 1909, 10, 373; 1911, 11, 293–296; 1915, 6, 136.
136. Tätigkeitsbericht 1910, 1.
137. They visited the museum twice in 1895. Tätigkeitsbericht 1895, 18.
138. In the estate, there are a great many postcards that bear witness to these occasions. On the basis of these, Hacker has established the groups of hiking members each summer. Hacker 1998, 89.
139. Tätigkeitsbericht 1910, 1.
140. Klaus and Wischermann 2013, 109–116.
141. Klösch-Melliwa 2001, 127–130. Fickert had a high opinion of Lang's public-speaking abilities: "I would like to ask you give a welcome speech . . . at the meeting to be held in January . . . as it is my conviction that your encouraging way of speaking will be a much bigger success." Translation by Dóra Fedeles-Czeferner. Auguste Fickert to Marie Lang, 26 December 1896, WR NF H.I.N. 152904.
142. *NFL* 1909, 5, 118–119; 1909, 10, 373; 1911, 11, 293–296; 1915, 6, 136; Aufruf—Bau- und Wohngenossenschaft "Heimhof," 1909, WR NF AC11118278.
143. Tätigkeitsbericht 1895, 11.
144. Hofmann-Weinberger 2016a. In the initial period, *Neue Bahnen* also regularly reported on these courses. NB 1894, 27, issue 2, 12; 1894, 27, issue 4, 30; 1895, 28, issue 4, 30.
145. Tätigkeitsbericht 1895, 11.

146. Translation by Dóra Fedeles-Czeferner. *NFL* 1906, 5, 22–26.
147. *NFL* 1908, 7, 171–176; 1908, 12, 299; 1909, 7, 169–173; 1918, 3, 45–46.
148. Protokoll 1893, 20. At the general meeting of 1907, sixty-three full members voted on the nomination. *NFL* 1907, 6, 22–23.
149. Minutes of the FE committee meeting of 27 January 1917, MNL OL P999, box 2, item 3.
150. The Heimhof was constructed at 30 Peter Jordanstraße, not far from the headquarters of AöF. *NFL* 1911, 11, 293–296.
151. Ferdinand Kronawetter to Auguste Fickert, 27 January 1893, WR NF H.I.N. 152.840; Protokoll 1893, 1–7.
152. Translation by Dóra Fedeles-Czeferner. Tätigkeitsbericht 1897, 1.
153. Tätigkeitsbericht 1897, 3. On the journal, see also Wolff 2017, 128–137.
154. Jank 2018.
155. E.g., Minna Cauer, letter to the editors of *Neues Frauenleben*, 19 September 1910, WR NF H.I.N. 63316.
156. This seems rather a high number, if we consider that in 1897 the association had 320 members. Tätigkeitsbericht 1897.
157. The report reveals that one person voted against the motion, while everyone else supported it. Tätigkeitsbericht 1897, 3.
158. On this, see Konvolut von Artikeln über die Frauenfrage, WR NF H.I.N. 77991B.
159. Translation by Dóra Fedeles-Czeferner. Tätigkeitsbericht 1898, 2.
160. Translation by Dóra Fedeles-Czeferner. Minna Cauer to Auguste Fickert, 14 December 1898, WR NF H.I.N. 69970.
161. Schmölzer 2002. Cf. Klingenstein 1997, 300. Lang's letters prove that the paper was very important to her: "The newspaper is my youngest child." Marie Lang to Auguste Fickert, 20 December 1898, WR NF H.I.N. 152908.
162. Aufruf—Dokumente der Frauen, 1897, WR NF AC11118278. On one occasion Fickert offered up the honorarium of 110 gulden she received from *Neue Freie Presse* and *Volksstimme*. Tätigkeitsbericht 1898, 8.
163. Tätigkeitsbericht 1899, 10.
164. Tätigkeitsbericht 1900.
165. Translation by Dóra Fedeles-Czeferner. *DF* 1899, 1, issue 1, 1–4 (my italics).
166. For greater detail on this, see Czeferner 2021.
167. E.g., Anderson 1992, 45–50; Hacker 1998, 83–89; 2006, 131–134.
168. Translation by Dóra Fedeles-Czeferner. *DF* 1900, 2, issue 1, 1.
169. Tätigkeitsbericht 1900, 13.
170. Sparholz 1986, 68.
171. Klingenstein 1997, 313–314.
172. Tätigkeitsbericht 1900, 6–8.
173. Schmölzer 2002, 86. Cf. Anderson 1992, 42. Tätigkeitsbericht 1893. Cf. Hauch 2006a, 965–1003.
174. Malleier 2001, 24–29.
175. Protokoll 1893, 20; Tätigkeitsbericht 1893.
176. Hacker 1996, 97–106; Jammernegg 2016a.

177. Tätigkeitsbericht 1898.
178. Anderson 1990, 189–201.
179. Translation by Dóra Fedeles-Czeferner. Tätigkeitsbericht 1895, 6. Kulka also cited this at the twenty-fifth jubilee of AöF. NFL 1918, 4–5, 57–60.
180. Translation by Dóra Fedeles-Czeferner. Tätigkeitsbericht 1895, 6.
181. NFL 1918, 4–5, 57–60.
182. NFL 1904, 6, 16.
183. NFL 1902, 4, 18–20; Hacker 1996, 97–106; Hofmann-Weinberger 2016d.
184. We know little about the life of Misař, who worked as an author and a journalist; we have little information about her beyond her role in the administration of these associations. Jammernegg 2016c.
185. Jammernegg 2016a.
186. *Der Bund* 1906, 6, 10–11.
187. Tätigkeitsbericht 1900, 4.
188. Klösch-Melliwa 2001, 127.
189. Klösch-Melliwa 2001, 129.
190. NFL 1903, 1, 1; NFL 1904, 1, 1.
191. NFL 1902, 5, 16–18. Cf. Schwartz 2008, 14.
192. Anderson 1992, 71.
193. Hauch 2006b, 479–483; 2012, 71–91.
194. Hauch 2012, 71–91; Schmölzer 2002, 93–95.
195. Anderson 1992, 52–56.
196. Hauch 2012, 71–91; Schmölzer 2002, 93–95; Auguste Fickert, Tagebuch, WR NF H.I.N. 70494.
197. Anderson 1992, 102.
198. Hauch 2012, 71–91; Schmölzer 2002, 93–95.
199. Tätigkeitsberichte 1893–1900.
200. Protokoll 1893, 1.
201. Anderson 1991, 259–291; Leisch-Prost 2006, 319–323.
202. Schmölzer 2002, 130. Cf. Anderson's idea that "Mayreder's position in the association was altogether ambiguous and her feelings ambivalent." Anderson 1992, 263.
203. Mayreder portrays Fickert as a "moral genius" and a "leading moral force." Translation by Dóra Fedeles-Czeferner. Anderson 1994, 194.
204. Malleier 2001, 48–59.
205. For more detail on these, see Hacker 1996, 97–106.
206. Jammernegg 2016a.
207. Jammernegg 2016c.
208. Szapor 2004, 189–205.
209. Tätigkeitsbericht 1896.
210. NFL 1908, 7, 171.
211. Tätigkeitsbericht 1910.
212. Translation by Dóra Fedeles-Czeferner. Tätigkeitsbericht 1910.
213. E.g., NFL 1904, 4, 19–21; 1908, 8, 202–203.
214. Translation by Dóra Fedeles-Czeferner. NFL 1909, 1, 1.

215. Beginning in 1893, she corresponded with Raschke about the Viennese women's legal rights organization. WR NF H.I.N. 70943/1.
216. Augspurg rejected Fickert's request to write an article, claiming that she did not have the time. Anita Augspurg to Auguste Fickert, 9 June 1902, WR NF H.I.N. 69775.
217. The biographical data is from the Digitales Deutsches Frauenarchiv n.d.
218. Bjørnstjerne Bjørnson to Auguste Fickert, 29 January 1899, 15 February 1902, WR NF H.I.N. 69877–69878.
219. In elementary school and at the school of the English Sisters, Fickert learned French, but at teacher training college, she was always given the grades "very good" or "good" in English. WR NF H.I.N. 71178/2–10.
220. Fickert's archive is rife with documents relating to the time she took off for medical treatment and to do association business; it seems the district school board ignored her absences from school. WR NF H.I.N. 71183/6–7; H.I.N. 71184/2–3.
221. Marie Lang to Auguste Fickert, n.d., WR NF H.I.N. 152.902.
222. This is where she met Rosika Schwimmer for the first time. *NFL* 1904, 6, 1–5; Leopoldine Kulka to Auguste Fickert, 10 July 1904, WR NF H.I.N. 152883.
223. *NFL* 1910, 3, 77–78; 1913, 5, 128–129.
224. Translation by Dóra Fedeles-Czeferner. Martina Kramers to Rosika Schwimmer, 23 April 1906, NYPL RSP I, box 9; Martina Kramers to Rosika Schwimmer, 11 September 1906, NYPL RSP I, box 10.
225. Martina Kramers to Rosika Schwimmer, 6 October 1906. NYPL RSP I, box 10.
226. Translation by Dóra Fedeles-Czeferner. Martina Kramers to Rosika Schwimmer, 6 October 1906. NYPL RSP I, box 10.
227. Bader-Zaar 1997, 547–526; Hauch 2011, 221–243. The conflicts between the different branches of the movement concern these same analogies and models. Hacker 1996, 97–106.
228. Anderson 1994, 185.
229. See *NFL* 1918, 1–2, 1–7.
230. Translation by Dóra Fedeles-Czeferner. Cited in Hämmerle 2014, 84.
231. Translation by Dóra Fedeles-Czeferner. *NFL* 1914, 8–9, 237–238; 1914, 10, 257–260.
232. *NFL* 1914, 8–9, 237–238. Cf. Anderson 1994, 185.
233. Translation by Dóra Fedeles-Czeferner. *NFL* 1914, 8–9, 237–238.
234. *NFL* 1914, 8–9, 238–242. The model was not without controversy: for example, Lily Braun, one of its best-known journalists, was regularly critical of it.
235. In and of itself, this was not unusual. On how similar opinions emerged in other countries at war, see Hämmerle, Überegger, and Bader-Zaar 2014; Leisch-Prost 2006, 319–323.
236. One of the occasions for this was the death of Suttner on 21 June 1914. *NFL* 1914, 7, 197–200.
237. Translation by Dóra Fedeles-Czeferner. *NFL* 1911, 6, 156–158. For more on this, see *NFL* 1914, 6, 177–179. This last report on the BöF meeting was written by Kulka.
238. Cf. Leisch-Prost 2006, 319–323. On Rosa Mayreder's antiwar writings, see Tanzer 2013, 46–61.
239. Translation by Dóra Fedeles-Czeferner. Cited in Anderson 1992, 192.

240. Schmölzer 2002, 195.
241. *NFL* 1914, 7, 212–213.
242. On the Zionist activists in the Austrian bourgeois women's movement, see Malleier 2001; 2005, 79–102.
243. As Kulka's deputy, she worked as vice president. *NFL* 1918, 4–5, 92. Cf. Hacker 1998, 82.
244. She was born Mathilde Lucca; in the journal, she usually wrote articles under the nom de plume Erich Holm. *NFL* 1910, 1, 1–5; 1913, 2, 33–37; 1916, 4, 74–77.
245. She became best known for her efforts in founding and supporting philanthropic organizations during World War I. Raggam-Blesch 2005, 25–55.
246. Jammernegg 2016b.
247. E.g., *NFL* 1916, 3, 63. The Hungarians followed a similar practice. E.g., *N* 1915, 3, 43.
248. *NFL* 1915, 6, 136.
249. On its foundation see *NFL* 1917, 8–9, 176–182; 1917, 10, 195–199.
250. Oesch 2014, 100–148; Urban 1930, 25–64.
251. Translation by Dóra Fedeles-Czeferner. "Women's Influence on Culture and the Future," *AZ*, 28 November 1915, 11; *Neues Wiener Tagblatt* (hereafter *NWT*), 30 May 1916, 43; *Neue Freie Presse* (hereafter *NFP*), 2 December 1917, 10.
252. *NFP*, 14 December 1915, 8; *Reichspost*, 14 December 1915, 7; *NWT*, 12 December 1915, 17.
253. Translation by Dóra Fedeles-Czeferner. Cf. *NFL* 1915, 12, 270–273.
254. Urban 1930, 25–64.
255. *NFP*, 14 December 1915, 8. The dates for the foundation and dissolution of the associations, as well as their official addresses, are all from the Ariadne database.
256. In the journal, see, e.g., *NFL* 1915, 6, 128–133, 133–136. Cf. Hauch 2011, 221–243.
257. Bader-Zaar 2006a, 1025.
258. Translation by Dóra Fedeles-Czeferner. *NFL* 1915, 1, 16–17.
259. *NFL* 1917, 1, 1.
260. Anderson 1992, 192.
261. After 1914, their letters focused exclusively on the peace movement. Leopoldine Kulka to Rosika Schwimmer, MNL OL P999, box 18, 15, no. 160–162. In late October 1918, Schwimmer had talks in Vienna with Kulka and Rudolf Goldscheid regarding the peace treaty. Rosika Schwimmer, diary note, 30 October 1918, NYPL RSP I, box 101. As well as being a supporter of AöF and a regular contributor to *Neues Frauenleben*, Goldscheid also submitted articles to the official organs of the Hungarian associations. *NT* 1909, 10, 163–166.
262. *NFL* 1915, 4, 85–87. Despite her worsening illness, Kulka took part in the organization's second congress in Zurich on 12–19 May 1919 (Malleier 2016). In her article on Marianne Hainisch, Birgitta Bader-Zaar writes that, as a representative of BöF, she, too, traveled to the congress, but the literature and press sources contradict this. Bader-Zaar 2006b, 173–177. Cf. Anderson 1994, 192.
263. *NFL* 1914, 10, 260; 1914, 11, 268; 1915, 3, 63–65; 1915, 6, 137.
264. The winter of 1916–1917 is considered the "winter of hunger." Hauch 2011, 221–243. Cf. *NFL* 1918, 1–2, 1–7.
265. Jammernegg 2016a.

266. "Many women from the radical wing of the bourgeois women's movement, who prior to World War I pursued their activities within the framework of AöF, at the time of the First Republic transferred their political activities to the international level, finding a home in the Women's International League for Peace and Freedom." Translation by Dóra Fedeles-Czeferner. Jammernegg 2016a.
267. Hauch 2009, 142.
268. Gehmacher 2001, 159–175; Hauch 2009, 129–151; 2011, 221–243; Unger 2012, 18–30.
269. *NFL* 1918, 4–5.
270. *NFL* 1918, 92.
271. Hacker 1996, 97–106.
272. Bader-Zaar 1997, 547–562.
273. The decision to establish the temporary inclusion of female deputies in the Austrian national assembly was made on 10 October 1918, the inaugural session was held on 21 October, and it exercised its legislative power until 26 February of the following year. 65 Christian-Social, 37 Social Democratic, and 106 German national or liberal deputies took up their places in the assembly room; of these, 10 were women. Anderson 1994, 178.
274. Bader-Zaar 2019, 37–60.
275. Cf. Anderson 1994, 184; Bader-Zaar 1997, 547–562.
276. Bader-Zaar 2019, 37–60. For more details on female suffrage in Austria, see Bader-Zaar 2018, 101–112.
277. Bader-Zaar 2019, 37–60.
278. Translation by Dóra Fedeles-Czeferner. Bader-Zaar 1997, 547–562.
279. Anderson 1994, 181; Hofmann-Weinberger 2016b.
280. Translation by Dóra Fedeles-Czeferner. *AZ*, 4 January 1920, 7.
281. In this case, I did not use the 1992 English edition but the German version, which includes a more detailed introductory study.
282. Anderson 1994, 180.
283. *Allgemeiner Tiroler Zeitung*, 1 September 1922.
284. Bundesverfassungsgesetz 1920.
285. B, (1918): 6, 11–12. The *Zeitschrift für Frauenstimmrecht* also ran a short news item about this. (*Zeitschrift für Frauenstimmrecht*, [1918]: 5, 5.) Aside from having an important role in the Frauenstimmrechtskomitee, Urban acted as chair of the BöF press committee and as a member of the IWSA press committee, as well as editing *Wiener Mode*. Festschrift 1913, 6.
286. *Der Bund*, 1918, 8–7; *AZ*, 9 February 1919.
287. *AZ*, 30 September 1920; Tätigkeitsbericht 1897, 4. Cf. Bader-Zaar 1999, 365–383.
288. *Der Bund*, 1918, 10, 15.
289. Report 1920, 16.
290. Report 1920, 16. On the Hungarian aspects of the congress, see Szapor 2011, 245–267.
291. Gabriella Hauch openly refers to the members of AöF as "old ladies" (*alte Damen*). Hauch 2009, 142.

292. Urban 1930, 25–64.
293. Cf. Hauch 2009, 129–149.

5. The Hungarian Associations

1. The sources vary as to the date of its foundation: Burucs and Szapor insist on the year 1896, as mentioned in the memoirs of Janka Gergely, the "chronicler of the feminist movement," which have survived from the 1940s in manuscript form (Janka Gergely: A feminizmus története [A history of feminism], MNL OL P999, box 17). Katalin Kéri and Claudia Papp, partly citing Susan Zimmermann and partly the 1913 work of lawyer and FE board member Andor Máday, accept the 1897 date. Zimmermann also cites a newspaper article of 8 August 1897 reporting on the beginnings of NOE's activity, but she mentions no precise details (Zimmermann 1999b, 38). As we saw for AöF, however, the foundation of the association and the acceptance of its statutes did not necessarily coincide with the time of the first, celebratory general assembly, which the article Zimmermann cites reports on. I myself, in line with Janka Gergely's description, prefer the 1896 date.

2. Máday 1913, 177.

3. A letter to her childhood friend Irma Kubicsek, who stayed in Temesvár (today Timişoara, Romania), paints a revealing picture of the difficulties Schwimmer faced as a female official: "Be glad, my dear, that you have become free after such a short space of time, as I know that you would not have been brave enough to give him your resignation anytime soon. But . . . it would be smarter if you again took up a position as a governess . . . rather than as an official, as in that case you have to find board and lodging—unless you stay with your aunt—and I don't think they pay so well, either." Irma Kubicsek to Rosika Schwimmer, 28 January 1896, NYPL RSP I, box 1.

4. Miksa Iritz to Rosika Schwimmer, 1900, NYPL RSP I, box 2.

5. NYPL RSP I, box 1–2.

6. MNL OL P987. The spelling of Mrs. Szirmay's name is not consistent in the sources; it is sometimes written with an *i* at the end and sometimes with a *y*. As this was originally an old Hungarian aristocratic family, I use the latter, Szirmay.

7. Női Tisztviselők Országos Egyesülete [National Association of Female Office Workers] to Rosika Schwimmer, 7 May 1900, NYPL RSP I, box 2.

8. For the letters exchanged with women office workers placed in jobs or with commercial employees, see NYPL RSP I, box 1–5.

9. The source cites Schwimmer's customary annual lecture tour in the fall. On this, see, e.g., the letters she exchanged with Adele Schreiber in 1906–1907: NYPL RSP I, box 10–11; *NT* 1907, 5, 92.

10. *NT* 1908, 5, 87.

11. *NT* 1908, 5, 88; 1909, 5, 78; *N*, 1914, 9, 193.

12. *NT* 1908, 5, 88.

13. An exception is Zimmermann 1997a, 175–204.

14. Kaba 2008, 8–18.

15. Zimmermann 1997a, 175–204.

16. Auguszta Rosenberg to Rosika Schwimmer, 4 December 1904, NYPL RSP I, box 6.

17. Vilma Glücklich to Rosika Schwimmer, later than 26 December 1904, NYPL RSP I, box 6; Mrs. Ignácz Glücklich, widow, to Rosika Schwimmer, 1 January 1905, NYPL RSP I, box 6.
18. Remembering Vilma Glücklich, MNL OL P999, box 1, 2/a.
19. Minutes of the committee meeting held on 20 February 1908, NYPL RSP I, box 6.
20. Minutes of the committee meeting held on 20 April 1910, NYPL RSP I, box 6.
21. This will be important with regard to the social class of the membership and the committee. Minutes of the committee meeting held on 24 April 1911, NYPL RSP I, box 6.
22. Vilma Glücklich to Mrs. Oszkár Szirmay, MNL OL P999, box 5, item 6, no. 245.
23. Carrie Chapman Catt to Rosika Schwimmer, 22 April 1905, NYPL RPS, box 7. Cf. Zimmermann 2006b, 119–169.
24. Translation by Dóra Fedeles-Czeferner. Aletta Jacobs to Rosika Schwimmer, 16 February 1906, NYPL RSP I, box 6.
25. Vilma Glücklich to Rosika Schwimmer, 1901, NYPL RSP I, box 2.
26. Cf. Zimmermann 1996a, 57–92. Schwimmer and Mrs. Szirmay continued their correspondence until 1948 with rather tender letters like this one: "My dear friend Irma, we always talk of how one morning you will get on a place to N.Y. and [unreadable word] arrive at our place. . . . I just want to talk and talk. But we would both enjoy that. So please come, come, my dear! Until then, please hug and kiss our friend in our place. . . . Your [unreadable word] worried and loving Rózsika." Rosika Schwimmer to Mrs. Oszkár Szirmay, 1947, MNL OL P987, box 1, item 3. (Courtesy of Judith Szapor.) Mrs. Szirmay did not have a chance to visit Schwimmer in New York.
27. The planned grave inscription follows: "Here lies Rozika Schwimmer, who lost so much in life, that for this reason she lost her life." NYPL RSP I, box 1.
28. On one occasion, Kubicsek wrote: "And I hope that your health is fully returned to normal, else, if you keep up your drinking, you will turn into a real flighty alcoholic. Which would be a real shame." Irma Kubicsek to Rosika Schwimmer, 9 March 1894, NYPL RSP, box 1. On one occasion, Aletta Jacobs reflected on Schwimmer's morphine addiction. Aletta Jacobs to Rosika Schwimmer, 16 February 1905, NYPL RSP I, box 7.
29. Janka Gergely and Vilma Glücklich to Rosika Schwimmer, May 1906, NYPL RSP I, box 9.
30. Szapor 2018, 19.
31. NYPL RSP I, box 86–97. In her letters written in English and German, Schwimmer addressed her fellow activists as "Dear Family," bidding farewell to them with a kiss. Rosika Schwimmer to FE from Osnabrück, 21–22 July 1917, NYPL RSP I, box 90. In 1917, Mrs. Meller began her detailed report "Dearest Schwimmer," explained why she was writing in English, and expressed her hope that Schwimmer would return home in the course of the following few weeks: "I write you English, that this letter shall not have to pass two censors and I do hope you will get it in time. . . . It would be splendid, if you would be back in time. All your questions I have answered before. . . . The meeting on the 13th was very successful, the great hall and the galleries packed. . . . Our president was ground. . . . I have just finished the Nők Lapja." Mrs.

Eugénia Meller née Miskolczy to Rosika Schwimmer, 20 July 1917, NYPL RSP I, box 90 (emphasis in the original).

32. In the Hungarian-language literature, her name appears as Róza Schwimmer or Rózsa/Róza Bédy-Schwimmer, while in other languages it is written as Rosika Schwimmer. I myself insist on the form Rosika Schwimmer (in the original Hungarian name order: Schwimmer Rózsa), as she herself usually preferred this. Cf. the postcard sent to Aletta Jacobs, her mentor and friend, who in 1904 had asked her, "Why are you called Bédy-Schwimmer all of a sudden?" Translation by Dóra Fedeles-Czeferner. Aletta Jacobs to Rosika Schwimmer, 26 April 1904, NYPL RSP I, box 5.

33. Aletta Jacobs to Rosika Schwimmer, 16 February 1905, NYPL RSP I, box 7.

34. Aletta Jacobs to Rosika Schwimmer, 20 April 1905, NYPL RSP I, box 7.

35. NYPL RSP I, box 6–9.

36. Aletta Jacobs to Rosika Schwimmer, 8 November 1906, NYPL RSP I, box 10.

37. This is true not just of the bourgeois-feminist branch but also of the Christian-Social and Social Democratic schools, as these publications provided ideal forums for spreading the ideas of the movement. The advance of women's journalism was nowhere near as significant in the Austro-Hungarian context. On this, see Klaus and Wischermann 2013, 66.

38. A list, not exhaustive, of Austrian and German journals in which she published before 1907: *Die Zeit* (The Time), *Wiener Mode, Arbeiterinnen-Zeitung, Neues Frauenleben, Illustrierte Frauen-Rundschau* (Illustrated Women's Review), *Etische Kultur* (Ethic Culture), and *Dokumente des Fortschritts* (Documents of Progress). For the series of letters exchanged with the editors of these papers, see NYPL RSP I.A., box 1–11. For the articles, see NYPL RSP II.A., box 466, folder 10; box 467, folder 1–3.

39. We know this from those pamphlets whose income and expenditure she recorded. NYPL RSP I.A.

40. The letters she exchanged with Aletta Jacobs also tell of this. E.g., Aletta Jacobs to Rosika Schwimmer, 1 August 1902, NYPL RSP I, box 2. She first published in the journal in September 1901. Editors of *Frauenleben* to Rosika Schwimmer, 7 September 1901, NYPL RSP I, box 2.

41. *NT* 1907, 64–66.

42. Draft contract, 9 September 1906, NYPL RSP IX, box 555, folder 3.

43. Minutes of the FE committee meeting on 21 December 1906, MNL OL P999, box 2, item 3.

44. Minutes of the FE committee meetings on 22 October, 25 November, and 20 December 1907 and on 20 February, 15 March, and 23 April 1908, MNL OL P999, box 2, item 3.

45. Minutes of the FE committee meeting on 9 December 1909, MNL OL P999, box 2, item 3.

46. Minutes of the FE committee meeting on 28 February 1914, MNL OL P999, box 2, item 3.

47. Minutes of the FE committee meeting on 23 March 1914, MNL OL P999, box 2, item 3. Given the wealth of her aristocratic family, however, it is unlikely that Mrs. Teleki would have accepted the wage.

48. Rupp 1997, 16–18, 28.

49. Minutes of the FE committee meeting on 29 January 1917, MNL OL P999, box 2, item 3.
50. Wernitznig 2017b.
51. Rosika Schwimmer to Mrs. Eugénia Meller, née Miskolczy, 27 January 1939, MNL OL P999, box 2, item 3, no. 130.
52. Rosika Schwimmer to Mrs. Eugénia Meller, née Miskolczy, 27 January 1939, MNL OL P999, box 2, item 3, no. 130.
53. Rosika Schwimmer to Mrs. Eugénia Meller, née Miskolczy, 24 February 1939, 11 April 1939, MNL OL P999, box 2, item 3, no. 142, 161. The material sent included the correspondence in German and Italian relating to the preparations for the 1913 congress. Today, it can be found in boxes 499–500 of the New York Public Library. NYPL RSP I, box 499–500.
54. Rosika Schwimmer to Mrs. Eugénia Meller, née Miskolczy, 6 June 1939, MNL OL P999, box 2, item 3, no. 178.
55. For Schwimmer's fake passport and the official documents relating to her emigration, see NYPL RSP X, box 554, 555.
56. Schwimmer's journey can be reconstructed using the letters she wrote to FE members and her diary notes: she traveled in a first class cabin on the boat, in "fairytale" conditions, eating "a lot, and well," reading, and attending concerts. During processing at Ellis Island, one immigration officer asked her, "Are you the celebrated Mme. Sch.[wimmer]?" Rosika Schwimmer to her family, from the boat across the Atlantic, 25 August 1921, NYPL RSP I, box 130; Rosika Schwimmer to her family, from Rotterdam and from New York, 6 August 1921, 26 August 1921, NYPL RSP I, box 130.
57. NYPL RSP X, box 554, 555.
58. NYPL RSP Index.
59. Solinger 2019, 87.
60. The majority of their letters were not included in the published Károlyi letters, presumably because Edith Wynner (née Weiner, born 1915 in Budapest and died 2003 in New York), who was for many decades in charge of the estate, did not give them to the editor, György Litván. Wynner's work to organize the material, as well as her notes, makes it much easier to navigate. Part of this was done while Schwimmer was still alive. Litván 1978.
61. Report 1920, 16.
62. Vilma Glücklich to Rosika Schwimmer, 15 January 1926, 14 May 1926, NYPL RSP.
63. On this, see, e.g., Medical records, January, May, December 1926, NYPL RSP I, box 159–161.
64. Rosika Schwimmer, diary note, 21 June 1948, NYPL RSP X, box 586.
65. NOE 1909.
66. Amendment of the FE statutes in 1905, MNL OL P999, box 1, item 1/a.
67. NOE 1909, §2–10.
68. *N* 1915, 4, 58–67.
69. Aletta Jacobs to Rosika Schwimmer, 5 November 1902, NYPL RSP I, box 2.
70. March 1904, NYPL RSP I, box 5.
71. *Feministák Egyesülete* 1905, 3–4.
72. *NT* 1907, 4, 88–93 (my emphasis).

73. On this at NOE, see *NT* 1907, 6, 88–93. On the case of FE, see *NT* 1907, 4, 64–66.
74. *NT* 1911, 9, 143.
75. FE, annual report of 1907, MNL OL P999, box 1, item 2/a; *NT* 1909, 4, 63.
76. *NT* 1907, 2, 30.
77. *N* 1914, 1, 1.
78. *NT* 1908, 2, 32.
79. FE constitutional amendments of 1905 and 1911, MNL OL P999, box 1, item 1/a.
80. Minutes of the FE committee meeting on 25 October 1915 and the general assembly of 22 December 1918, MNL OL P999, box 2, item 3; 1917 amendment to the FE statutes, MNL OL P999, box 2, item 3.
81. Minutes of the annual meeting of FE on 24 April 1913 and its national conference on 25 September 1914, MNL OL P999, box 1, item 2/a, No. 3; MNL OL P999, box 1, item 2/b.
82. *NT* 1912, 7, 13.
83. Minutes of the annual meeting of FE on 15 April 1909, MNL OL P999, box 2, item 3.
84. Typing was considered a special case among the courses offered; attendees could practice this in the NOE association offices. *NT* 1907, 9, 158.
85. In 1906, the courses jointly held by the associations "were attended by 192 students. Book-keeping: 12, stenography: 57, typing: 58, German grammar: 38, English: 5, Esperanto: 22" (*NT* 1907, 5, 89).
86. *NT* 1912, 9, 169.
87. E.g., *N* 1914, 17, 3.
88. E.g., *NT* 1907, 7. In its financial reports, FE accounted for the last few crowns spent on such excursions. Minutes of the committee meeting of FE on 17 May 1907, MNL OL P999, box 2, item 3.
89. *N* 1914, 5, 96.
90. *NT* 1907, 9, 158; 1908, 4, 66.
91. *NT* 1911, 7, 120 (emphasis in the original).
92. On the visits to museums, see, e.g., *NT* 1907, 10, 176; 1909, 11.
93. *NT* 1907, 5, 88–93; 1908, 5, 88–94.
94. Minutes of the FE committee meeting on 1 April 1910, MNL OL P999, box 2, item 3.
95. *NT* 1907, 4, 62.
96. *NT* 1907, 5, 88–93.
97. Minutes of the ordinary general meetings of FE on 17 March 1907 and 24 April 1913 and of the committee meeting of 23 March 1914, MNL OL P999, box 1, item 2/a; MNL OL P999, box 2, item 3; *NT* 1907, 5, 88–93; 1911, 11, 191; Postal addresses of the Budapest members of FE, MNL OL P999, box 23, item 32/a; Mrs. Sándor Teleki to the members of FE, November 1912, NYPL RSP I, box 497; *NT* 1912, 10, 190; 1912, 11, 207.
98. E.g., *NT* 1907, 1, 30.
99. After Steinberger's lecture in January 1908, the leadership of NOE was satisfied with the audience of around one hundred. *NT* 1908, 2, 33.
100. The minutes indicate that she usually offered part of this fee to the Political Committee. MNL OL P999, box 2, item 3.

101. Minutes of the committee meeting of FE on 6 April 1906, MNL OL P999, box 2, item 3.
102. *NT* 1908, 1, 13.
103. *NT* 1913, 11, 196.
104. *NT* 1913, 3, 50.
105. The data is from the minutes of the FE committee meetings from 1907 to 1914, MNL OL P999, box 2, item 3.
106. Minutes of the FE committee meeting of 23 June 1911, MNL OL P999, box 2, item 3.
107. For more detail on this, see the minutes of the committee meetings of FE and its annual general meetings. General assembly minutes and secretarial reports, MNL OL P999, box 1, item 2/a; Minutes of the committee meetings, MNL OL P999, box 2, item 3; *NT* 1907, 4, 61; 1910, 4, 64. Cf. the debates on the closing-time law in the journals. *NT*, 1907, 8, 138; 1911, 4, 59–60; 1913, 6, 115–117, 131.
108. *NT*, 1908, 7, 123; 1910, 8, 141.
109. *NT* 1912, 9, 170.
110. Cf. the FE data, according to which three thousand guests, who "represented 8 million women," arrived in Budapest. *NT* 1913, 7–8, 129–130.
111. Minutes of the FE committee meeting on 10 March 1906, MNL OL P999, box 2, item 3.
112. *FÉ* 1906, 12, 4; NYPL RSP II.A., box 482, folder 12.
113. Gergely Janka to Rosika Schwimmer, 1907, NYPL RSP I, box 9; Subscription list, NYPL RSP I, box 9.
114. *NT* 1913, 6, 109.
115. Vilma Glücklich to Rosika Schwimmer, December 1906, NYPL RSP I, box 10.
116. Marianne Hainisch to Rosika Schwimmer, n.d., NYPL RSP I, box 11.
117. At Christmastime, the proofs, which Glücklich was "burning to see," were still with Schwimmer; the work for the journal must have become more intense. Vilma Glücklich to Rosika Schwimmer, 25 December 1906, NYPL RSP I, box 11.
118. Minutes of the FE committee meeting of 27 November 1913, MNL OL P999, box 2, item 3.
119. In the first issue, the editors expressed their hope that the journal would in due course be published weekly. *N* 1914, 1, 1.
120. Zimmermann 1999b, 49–66; Acsády and Mészáros 2016, 486–502.
121. Papp 2004, 101; Zimmermann 1997b, 171–204.
122. NOE 1909.
123. *N* 1914, 12, 251–252.
124. NOE 1909.
125. *NT* 1907, 5, 87–89.
126. Zimmermann 1997b, 171–204; 1999b.
127. Szapor 2004, 189–205.
128. Glücklich and Dirnfeld 1910, 2–4.
129. *NT* 1912, 3, 49.
130. Minutes of the FE committee meeting on 20 September 1910, MNL OL P999, box 2, item 3.

131. Minutes of the FE committee meeting on 22 March 1915, MNL OL P999, box 2, item 3.
132. Cf. Zimmermann 1996a, 57–92.
133. These were kept by board members and sometimes by Vilma Glücklich. Minutes of the FE committee from 1906 to 1914, MNL OL P999, box 2, item 3.
134. Minutes of FE committee meetings from 1914 to 1918, MNL OL P999, box 2, item 3.
135. Szapor 2006, 54–277. Cf. Szapor 2004, 189–205, which states, "Another source mentions 30,000 members in 1918, which seems too high."
136. On this, also see Szapor 2018, 27.
137. Szapor 2018, 27; Minutes of FE committee meetings from 1914 to 1918, MNL OL P999, box 2, item 3.
138. List of FE members resident in Budapest and logbooks of members, 1912–1922, n.d., MNL OL P999, box 23, item 32/a–c. Reasons given for the departure of members include "got married," "is married," "travelled away," "died," "disappeared," "said she is not a member," "is unknown," "is not in Budapest," "[emigrated] to America."
139. NOE 1909.
140. NT 1907, 6, 88–95. The sum put aside for this purpose was 2,400 crowns in 1907; in 1914, it was increased to 4,000.
141. *Pesti Napló*, 19 January 1893, 11, cited in Bódy 2003, 81–82.
142. Bódy 2003, 94–95.
143. Bódy 2003, 98–99.
144. Bódy 2003.
145. The information here is from the minutes of FE's (extraordinary) committee meetings and annual general meetings and from NOE's reports. Minutes of FE committee meetings, MNL OL P999, box 2, item 3; Issues of *A Nő és a Társadalom* 1907–1913 and *A Nő* from 1914.
146. Szapor 2017, 52.
147. On this, see, e.g., NT 1907, 4, 64–65.
148. The constitutional amendment accepted at the 1905 annual general meeting of FE, MNL OL P999, box 1, item 1/a.
149. FE financial report from 1906, MNL OL P999, box 2, item 3.
150. Treasurer's balance statement from 1906, MNL OL P999, box 2, item 3; NT 1907, 4, 64–69.
151. Amendments to the FE statutes in 1915 and 1918, MNL OL P999, box 1, item 1/a; Minutes of the annual general meeting of FE on 24 April 1913, MNL OL P999, box 2, item 3.
152. NT 1911, 11, 191.
153. On this, see, e.g., N 1914, 7, 146.
154. NT 1911, 7, 119.
155. Susan Zimmermann, considering the men joining FE to be "of the second rank," did not list them among the influential public figures of Budapest. Zimmermann 1999a.
156. In this regard, the following inspiring slogans were regularly repeated in *A Nő és a Társadalom* and *A Nő*: "Let us gather subscribers and members for the association

and the peace committee!" (*N* 1915, 12, 105). Board members of FE and editorial office of *A Nő* attempted to attract an audience for Adele Schreiber's 1915 lecture with this call to arms: "Let us all be there and act in line with the proposal of our fellow member Countess Sándor Teleki: everyone should bring with them at least one antifeminist acquaintance!" (*N* 1915, 11, 191).

157. In the case of many association members, it is only these photographs that survive. Feminist Gallery, NYPL Digital Collection.

158. List of FE members in Budapest and logbooks of members, 1912–1922, MNL OL P999, box 23, item 32/a.

159. List of FE members living in Budapest and logbooks of members, 1912–1922, n.d., MNL OL P999, box 23, item 32/a. Several works and poetry translations by Dezső Kosztolányi—including translations of the poem *The Scream*, by Polish writer and actress Eleonora Kalkowska (born 1883 in Warsaw and died 1937 in Bern), which *Neues Frauenleben* also published—appear in the pages of *A Nő*. 1915, 8, 122; 1915, 12, 187; 1917, 2, 19.

160. Members' enthusiasm for these tasks generally depended on their health and on their holidays. The letters of Szidónia Willhelm and Janka Gergely provide pictures that go into almost every detail. Mrs. Sándor Teleki generally retreated from her FE tasks during her stays in the mountain resort of Ótátrafüred.

161. Zimmermann 1996a, 57–92.

162. Glücklich and Dirnfeld 1910, 1–2.

163. NOE 1909; *NT* 1907, 10, 165–166.

164. *NT* 1907, 10, 165–166. Lecturers from Budapest regularly paid for their own journeys. The leadership of FE repeatedly applied to the minister for commercial affairs to ask for "free train tickets" for their members, but such requests were generally rejected. Ministerial councillor to Rosika Schwimmer, 31 January 1907, NYPL RSP I, box 11. In 1914, the association's "members from aristocratic backgrounds" wished to acquire free or discounted train tickets, thanks to an intervention from Mrs. Sándor Teleki. Hungarian Royal Ministry for Commercial Affairs to Mrs. Sándor Teleki, 3 February 1914, MNL OL P999, box 3, item 5, no. 346.

165. *NT* 1907, 10, 172.

166. FE to József Halász, 21 February 1913, NYPL RSP I, box 497. Glücklich informed Schwimmer of her results: "The committee gave an enthusiastic welcome to my proposal, and mandates me both in the Kaposvár and the Fiume case, if Babare's [Adél Babare, member of the FE board] response is favorable." Vilma Glücklich to Rosika Schwimmer, 4 November 1905, NYPL RSP I, box 8. Cf. Acsády and Mészáros 2016, 486–502. Acsády and Mészáros estimate that the real work took place in late 1906, at the time of Glücklich's lecture in Nagyvárad.

167. Vilma Glücklich to Rosika Schwimmer, 4 November 1905, NYPL RSP I, box 8.

168. FE treasurer's report for 1906, MNL OL P999, box 1, item 2/a, 1906–1914.

169. *NT* 1907, 5, 88–93.

170. *NT* 1907, 10, 176; 1911, 6, 98; 1907, 10, 176.

171. Acsády and Mészáros 2016, 486–502.

172. These cities supported extending suffrage to women (Szegvári 1981, 135). On this and the role played by the association in the suffrage blocs, see also the

correspondence among FE, Schwimmer, and Mihály Károlyi between the fall of 1917 and the summer of 1918 (Litván 1978, 189–193, 216). In October 1917, the Pécs branch of FE and its group in Kassa reflected on Károlyi's attempts to introduce female suffrage (Litván 1978, 197, 200–201). Minutes of the FE committee meeting of 30 July 1917, MNL OL P999, box 2, item 3.

173. *NT* 1909, 6, 103–110.
174. The FE statutes and their amendments, 1911, MNL OL P999, box 1, item 1/a.
175. Bittermann-Wille and Hofmann-Weinberger 2001, 355–384.
176. It is not clear which provincial group this refers to. Minutes of the FE committee meeting on 7 January 1918, MNL OL P999, box 2, item 3.
177. Minutes of the FE committee meeting of 23 June 1911, MNL OL P999, box 2, item 3.
178. Minutes of the FE committee meeting of 25 October 1907, MNL OL P999, box 2, item 3.
179. Janka Gergely and Szidónia Willhelm discussed the subject in *A Nő és a Társadalom* (e.g., *NT* 1907, 11, 185–186).
180. János Benedek to FE, 3 August 1910, MNL OL P999, box 5, item 64.
181. *NT* 1907, 11, 88–94.
182. *NT* 1907, 11, 88–94.
183. *N* 1907, 11, 179; *NT* 1908, 1, 6.
184. *N* 1914, 2, 53.
185. I.e., groups of a feminist nature. *NT* 1907, 11, 189.
186. Mrs. Norbert Simon to Rosika Schwimmer, 17 February 1913, NYPL RSP I, box 497. Mrs. Simon was on the list of members with a Budapest address (8 Andrássy Boulevard). The list of FE members living in Budapest and the logbooks of members, 1912–1922, n.d., MNL OL P999, box 23, item 32/a.
187. Rosika Schwimmer to Mrs. Norbert Simon, 26 February 1913, NYPL RSP I, box 497.
188. Rosika Schwimmer to Mrs. Norbert Simon, 19 March 1913, NYPL RSP I, box 497.
189. Rosika Schwimmer to Mrs. Norbert Simon, 26 February 1913, NYPL RSP I, box 497.
190. *NT* 1908, 5, 89. Similar attempts in spa towns by Lake Balaton proved unsuccessful.
191. Lengthy correspondence relating to her lectures can be found in the Schwimmer archive. NYPL RSP I.A., box 499.
192. Acsády and Mészáros 2016, 486–502.
193. Charity for the Free Distribution of Coal and Wood (*Emberszeretet ingyen szén- és faosztás*) to Vilma Glücklich, 11 December 1911, MNL OL P999, box 3, item 5, no. 227.
194. On this, see Acsády and Mészáros 2018, 80–96; Zimmermann and Nagy 2018, 121–133. Cf. Mrs. István Bordás to FE, 3 June 1906, MNL OL P999, box 3, item 5, no. 42.
195. Minutes of the committee meeting of FE on 5 June 1908, MNL OL P999, box 2, item 3. Cf. the interpretation of FE, which, as a rhetorical device, calls on "aristocratic ladies who consider themselves ignorant about politics" to "go among Hungarian peasant women, to go and learn from them." *NT* 1908, 6, 93.
196. Minutes of the FE committee meeting of 26 January 1911, MNL OL P999, box 2, item 3. Cf. Acsády and Mészáros 2018, 80–96.

197. Mrs. István Bordás to FE, MNL OL P999, box 3, item 5, no. 36–96; MNL OL P999, box 2, item 3. Cf. Acsády and Mészáros 2018, 80–96, esp. 89.
198. NT 1907, 7, 113–114.
199. Mrs. István Bordás to FE, 14 July 1908, MNL OL P999, box 3, item 5, no. 43.
200. NT 1907, 5, 76.
201. Mrs. István Bordás to FE, 30 January 1909, MNL OL P999, box 3, item 5, no. 45; Mrs. István Bordás to FE, n.d., MNL OL P999, box 3, item 5, no. 50.
202. Mrs. István Bordás to FE, 27 July 1910, MNL OL P999, box 3, item 5, no. 51.
203. Rosika Schwimmer to Ludmilla Jancsusko, 17 February 1913, NYPL RSP I, box 497. The association was most likely never actually founded.
204. NT 1908, 106.
205. NT 1907, 7, 125.
206. Minutes of the FE committee meetings of 20 September 1910, January 1914, 27 December 1915, MNL OL P999, box 2, item 3. In 1917, FE gave up on its increase in the subscription charge for *A Nő* on account of provincial members' inability to pay. It stated, "It would be a decisive blow to our propaganda were the subscription fee for our journal to be increased." Minutes of the FE meeting of 29 January 1917, MNL OL P999, box 2, item 3.
207. Erzsébet Trombitás to Vilma Glücklich, 23 November 1910, NYPL RSP I, box 497.
208. NT 1911, 11, 191.
209. NT 1909, 3, 33. Anna Lindemann held a lecture, entitled *Ehe und Wahlrecht*, within the association. Annual report of the feminist association of Nagyvárad, MNL OL P999, box 1, item 2/a, no. 4.
210. Reports of the feminist association of Nagyvárad, 1914–1917, MNL OL P999, box 4, item 5.
211. Acsády and Mészáros 2016, 486–502. Cf. Reports of the feminist association of Nagyvárad, 1914–1917, MNL OL P999, box 4, item 5. Minutes of the committee meeting of FE on 9 September 1914, MNL OL P999, box 2, item 3.
212. Minutes of the extraordinary committee meeting of FE on 14 September 1914, MNL OL P999, box 2, item 3.
213. N 1914, 18, 206.
214. N 1917, 1, 13–14.
215. Minutes of the FE extraordinary committee meeting on 11 June 1916, MNL OL P999, box 2, item 3.
216. For more on the legislative proposal, see Szegvári 1981, 137–141.
217. Minutes of the FE committee meeting on 19 September 1917, MNL OL P999, box 2, item 3; Szegvári 1981, 142.
218. Bader-Zaar 2008, 107–128.
219. Bader-Zaar 2008, 107–128; Gehmacher 2011, 58–64; Weckert and Wischermann 2006; Zinsser and Anderson 2005.
220. Bosch and Kloosterman 1990.
221. Here I list the works relevant from a Hungarian perspective, while emphasizing that Leila J. Rupp dedicated a whole volume to the subject. Haan and Allen 2013; Rupp 1994, 1571–1660; 1997; 2010, 139–152; Zimmermann 2002, 61–79; 2003, 119–147; 2005, 87–117; 2006b, 119–167; 2009, 226–227.

222. E.g., Gehmacher, Heinrich, and Oesch 2018; Oesch 2008, 118–144; 2012, 509–514; 2014; Wernitznig 2015, 102–108; 2017a, 91–114; 2017b, 262–279.
223. Cf. Gehmacher 2011, 58–64.
224. Bader-Zaar 2008, 107–128; Rupp 1994, 1571–1660; 2010, 139–152.
225. E.g., Szapor 2018; Zimmermann 1999b; 2002, 61–79; 2003, 119–147.
226. Vilma Glücklich to Rosika Schwimmer, 30 October 1906, NYPL RSP I, box 10.
227. The documents were written in French, Italian, and Dutch, in addition to Hungarian, English, and German.
228. Rupp 1994, 16–18.
229. In 1906, Lang gave a lecture on the work of housewives. *FÉ* 1906, 3, 5.
230. Journal of the Kaufmännischer Hilfsverein für weibliche Angestellte, n.d.; Marie Lang to Rosika Schwimmer, 17 July 1901, NYPL RSP I, box 2. Schwimmer published a twelve-line piece on the vocational schools in commerce open to women (*DF* 1901, 3, issue 9, 287).
231. "I cannot yet establish when we will come to Hungary; I only know that we cannot come before 13 or 14 September. . . . More than anything in Hungary and first of all I would like to see the women's prison in Márianosztra; is it far? I cannot find it on the map": "Ich kann jetzt noch nicht feststellen, wenn wir in Ungarn kommen, nur weiss ich dass wir nicht eher 13 oder 14 sept. [*sic*] kommen können. . . . Am liebsten und erste möchte ich in Ungarn das Gefaengnis für Frauen in Maria Nostra sehen, ist das weit? Ich kann es nicht auf die Karte finden." Aletta Jacobs to Rosika Schwimmer, 2 August 1901, NYPL RSP I, box 2.
232. "Da hast du wirklich wieder in die Verdammte Deutsche Buchstaben dein Artikel geschrieben. Das ist nicht zu lesen. Wenn es in lateinische Buchstaben geschrieben war, hatte ich heute all meine Arbeit liegen lassen um es zu übersetzen und zu probieren es in eine bessere Zeitschrift publiziert zu bekommen. . . . Warum soll man eine halbe Stunde suchen nach eine Syllable [*sic*], wenn es Buchstaben gibt welche durch die ganze Welt gebraucht und bekannt sind: Sende es mir so bald wie möglich zurück." Aletta Jacobs to Rosika Schwimmer, 5 March 1904, NYPL RSP I, box 5.
233. To participate, Schwimmer needed to have a press pass; in this, too, her uncle assisted. Marie Stritt to Rosika Schwimmer, 18 May 1904, NYPL RSP I, box 5. Adelheid von Welczek and Anita Augspurg, presidents of the ICW organizational committee, sent invitations to the inaugural session of IWSA. Augspurg was already aware of Schwimmer's name, thanks to an article published in the Viennese *Die Zeit*. Adelheid von Welczek to Rosika Schwimmer, June 1904, NYPL RSP I, box 5; Anita Augspurg to Rosika Schwimmer, 14 April 1904, NYPL RSP I, box 5.
234. Translation by Dóra Fedeles-Czeferner. Alice Salomon to Rosika Schwimmer, 27 April 1904, NYPL RSP I, box 5.
235. Report 1920, 6.
236. In the FE report of 1922, she commented on her participation: "Our much-respected fellow member, Rózsa Bédy-Schwimmer, who lives abroad, was the invited guest of our congress. It is with satisfaction and great pleasure that we have observed the great respect and acknowledgment that women rallied from all over the world fighting for peace have afforded the most ardent fighter for our cause." So Wernitznig's claim about Schwimmer's isolation does not hold for this period either.

Minutes of the FE annual general meeting held on 5 April 1922, MNL OL P999, box 1, item 2/a. Cf. Wernitznig 2015, 102–108; 2017a, 91–114; 2017b, 262–279.
237. Isadora Duncan to Rosika Schwimmer, 1904, NYPL RSP I, box 5.
238. Carrie Chapman Catt to Rosika Schwimmer, [September or October] 1906. [Along with Edith Wynner's handwritten note], NYPL RSP I, box 10. The letter in which Catt asks Schwimmer to mediate between her and the Austrians suggests BöF's relative passivity: "I will be very glad if you would also write to your friends in Vienna and urge them to send delegates to Copenhagen; we want them to be with us very much." Carrie Chapman Catt to Rosika Schwimmer, 24 April 1906, NYPL RSP I, box 9.
239. NYPL RSP I, box 2–6.
240. Her mother, Clara Schreiber (born 1848 in Vienna and died 1905 in Meran), was the author of poems and essays, and the family operated a popular salon in its home in Bad Aussee, where it hosted liberal politicians, artists, and journalists devoted to the cause of women's rights. Korotin 2016b, 2249.
241. At Stritt's invitation, Schwimmer made her lecture tour of Germany in 1906. Marie Stritt to Rosika Schwimmer, 10 November 1906, NYPL RSP I, box 10.
242. Schwimmer met her through Jacobs and corresponded with her from February 1905 onward. NYPL RSP I, box 5–6.
243. Vilma Glücklich to Rosika Schwimmer, 1906, NYPL RSP I, box 8.
244. Apart from telegrams detailing the payment Schwimmer would receive, there were also rejections, for example, from the editors of *Wiener Mode*. Editors of *Wiener Mode* to Rosika Schwimmer, 14 February 1908, NYPL RSP I, box 16.
245. NYPL RSP, box 497, folder 9–box 498, folder 8; Festschrift 1913. Rather paradoxically, the celebratory publication that accompanied this event, as well as describing the life of Marianne Hainisch, shares the most information about the work of Auguste Fickert, who died three years earlier (Festschrift 1913, 19). The brochure also introduced the Hungarian organizers of the congress (24–27).
246. *NT* 1913, 3, 57; NYPL RSP I, box 499.
247. Even before FE was founded, Schwimmer attended English classes, but for years she made excuses to Catt for her limited English skills (Vilma Glücklich to Rosika Schwimmer, October 1904, NYPL RSP I, box 5). Catt was quick to reassure her: "You need not apologize for your English. You will not need to work so very hard to quite master it. I have been studying German since I came home from Berlin, but a busy woman, such as I am, has so many interruptions, that study of any kind is difficult. If I could only write German as well as you write English, I should be very much encouraged. Nevertheless, I am persevering, and hope to be able to read at least understandingly. When I do, I shall come over to Budapest and pay the Hungarian society a visit perhaps." This was the first time she broached the subject of her potential visit to Hungary. Carrie Chapman Catt to Rosika Schwimmer, 22 April 1905, NYPL RSP I, box 7.
248. These countries joined the international women's movement in the course of 1913–1914. Rupp 1997, 16–18, 74.
249. Cf. Weiland 1983.
250. The list of names can be reconstructed from the minutes of the committee meetings, from the FE journals, and from the Schwimmer correspondence: Aletta Jacobs,

Carrie Chapman Catt, Henriette Fürth, Anna Lindemann, Gertrud Woker, Marie Lang, Wilhelm Rein, Marie Lischnewska, Dora Montefiore, Adele Schreiber, Alexandra Gripenberg, Nelly Roussel, Hans Dorn, Cicely Corbett, Hermann Bahr, Hedwig Buschmann, Lida Gustava Heymann, Hellmut von Gerlach, Käthe Schirmacher, Otto Fick, Helene Stöcker, Marie Stritt, Gina Krog, Bertha von Suttner, Minna Cauer, "leader of the Serbian women's movement," Robert Michels, Florence W. Keys, I. A. Davodssohn, and "Mrs. Dina van Schaid." Catt, Jacobs, and Corbett visited Hungary on a number of occasions.

251. Translation by Dóra Fedeles-Czeferner. Adele Schreiber to Schwimmer, 28 September 1902, NYPL RSP I, box 5. On the negotiations concerning the itinerary in Hungary of Catt and Jacobs and then of Corbett, see NYPL RSP I, box 9–10, 28–32. On the financial backing for lecture tours of this kind, see Gehmacher 2011, 58–64.

252. Apart from these, there is one journal published in the Netherlands. MNL OL P999, box 50–68.

253. MNL OL P999, box 43–50.

254. Törvény a kivételes hatalomról 1912.

255. Kókay, Buzinkay, and Murányi 2001. The regulations on the founding of associations were eased by the regulation of 26 April 1916 (1442/1916). Censors removed an increasing number of articles from the issues of *A Nő* after October 1915. The missing empty pages are most obvious in December 1916, when all of the pacifist articles were redacted. For the uncensored copies, see NYPL RSP I, box 482.

256. Minutes of the FE committee meetings of 15 September 1915 and 8 May 1916, MNL OL P999, box 2, item 3.

257. Minutes of the FE committee meeting on 28 December 1916, MNL OL P999, box 2, item 3.

258. *N* 1916, 8, 117.

259. *N* 1917, 12, 195–202; 1916, 2, 33. In November 1915, Glücklich "announce[d], as a welcome piece of news, that . . . the minister of commerce gave 3000 crowns for [the] labor exchange. While [they] received this sum as a lifetime contribution, [they] hope[d] that it [was] not final in nature" (Minutes from the FE committee meeting on 17 November 1915, MNL OL P999, box 2, item 3). In the summer of 1917, the ministerial councillor Zoltán Bosnyák had 4,500 crowns transferred to FE. Minutes of the FE committee meeting on 9 July 1917, MNL OL P999, box 2, item 3.

260. *N* 1916, 5.

261. *N* 1915, 7, 108.

262. These issues were just a few pages in length. Before August 1914 and after January 1915, the publication was typically twenty to twenty-five pages long.

263. E.g., *N* 1914, 15, 1.

264. *N* 1914, 15, 1.

265. *N* 1914, 18, 211; Branca 2013, 12–72.

266. Minutes of the committee meeting of FE on 19 October 1914, MNL OL P999, box 2, item 3.

267. *N* 1914, 18, 7.

268. Minutes of the national conference of FE on 25 September 1914, MNL OL P999, box 1, item 2/b.

269. Minutes of the FE committee meeting on 31 July 1914, MNL OL P999, box 2, item 3.
270. *N* 1914, 15, 1.
271. *N* 1914, 19, 216.
272. *N* 1917, 6, 97–98.
273. *N* 1915, 8, 122–123.
274. *N* 1914, 15, 2.
275. On this, see FE to Budapest Metropolitan Council, 16 September 1914, MNL OL P999, box 3, item 5, no. 135.
276. *N* 1914, 17, 2. There were 3,187 kindergartens in Hungary in 1908; most struggled with being overcrowded. The first crèche was opened only in 1907, late even by Central European standards. Koncz 1982, 57.
277. On this, see the correspondence between FE and Budapest Metropolitan Council between July and September 1914, MNL OL P999, box 3, item 5, no. 141–148.
278. *N* 1914, 17, 2.
279. Minutes of the FE committee meeting on 31 July 1914, MNL OL P999, box 2, item 3.
280. *N* 1917, 3, 39; 1917, 6, 97.
281. *N* 1914, 17, 3. On how FE members, during the winter of 1914–1915, provided milk and bread for children in need, see *N* 1915, 1, 12.
282. *NT* 1908, 5, 80–81. The issues of the "midwife question" in Hungary were even discussed in *Neues Frauenleben*. *NFL* 1911, 2, 264–270.
283. They published advertisements for specialist hand disinfectants and toothpastes. *N* 1915, 10, 155; 1915, 1, 10.
284. *N* 1914, 18, 207.
285. Minutes of the FE committee meeting on 9 September 1914, MNL OL P999, box 2, item 3.
286. On the reports of the associations' career meetings, see, e.g., *N* 1915, 7, 114–116. Cf. the minutes of the FE committee meetings, where they also turn to the problems of the labor exchange. In February 1916, Paula Pogány studied, within a Berlin association, the state of the labor exchange and the work of the career adviser, "as at home [they were] at a loss as [they were] faced by the ever-worsening situation for labor exchange" (Minutes of the FE committee meeting on 9 February 1916, MNL OL P999, box 2, item 3). On the courses held for female office workers in Budapest and in the provinces, as well as for entirely uneducated or illiterate women, see, e.g., *N* 1915, 3, 43; 1916, 8, 127.
287. Minutes of the FE committee meeting on 12 December 1914, MNL OL P999, box 2, item 3; Minutes of the FE committee meeting held 9 July 1917, MNL OL P999, box 2, item 3; Minutes of the FE committee meeting on 26 April 1918, MNL OL P999, box 2, item 3.
288. Minutes of the extraordinary FE committee meeting on 27 December 1915, MNL OL P999, box 2, item 3.
289. E.g., *N* 1914, 15. The association's telephone lines also smoothed communications with state authorities and the State Labor Exchange. *N* 1914, 9, 178.

290. *N* 1914, 19, 214. The title of the lecture was "Die Ungarischen Frauen und der Krieg." Minutes of the FE committee meeting on 16 November 1914, MNL OL P999, box 2, item 3.
291. Even in the first special issue of the journal, there are a number of job advertisements (*N* 1914, 15, 1–2). We encounter nothing like this in the pages of *Neues Frauenleben*.
292. This task was taken over by the State Labor Exchange Authority. *N* 1914, 16, 2.
293. The numbers of domestic servants began to fall in western Europe and in the United States in the first years of the century. Given Hungary's different economic and social path, many, especially girls who were not yet married, were still working in these roles, even in the interwar period. Gyáni 1983.
294. There has not yet been a comprehensive work on the feminization of certain careers in Hungary. With regard to Vienna, see Appelt 1985, 212–216.
295. FE played an important role in the latter. *N* 1914, 15, 1–2; 1914, 17, 2.
296. *N* 1915, 5, 81.
297. *N* 1914, 17, 2; 1914, 18, 206.
298. Their limited knowledge of German continued to cause problems. We find numerous examples of this among the letters in the Schwimmer Collection (e.g., *NT* 1908, 7, 125–127; 1909, 4, 57–58). This was precisely the reason that women office worker Mária Farkas, for example, refused the job offered her. Mária Farkas to Rosika Schwimmer, 20 May 1900, NYPL RSP I, box 2.
299. Gyáni 1983, Kéri 2008, 130–133.
300. *N* 1914, 3, 55. FE hoped that it could also raise income from this enterprise.
301. Burucs 1993, 15–19.
302. On this, see, e.g., *N* 1916, 2, 22–25.
303. As they emphasized, they did not wish to be "dependent on men on a gender basis." *N* 1916, 1, 4.
304. FE logbooks of its members, MNL OL P999, box 23, item 32/b; Minutes of the FE committee meeting on 27 July 1918, MNL OL P999, item 2, box 3. Cf. Szapor 2018, 33.
305. FE logbooks of its members, MNL OL P999, box 23, item 32/b.
306. We do not know quite why FE worked together with these groups in particular. The Jewish heritage of many FE members can perhaps explain the choice of the Pesti Izraelita Nőegylet. This association, founded in 1866, assisted women who were "poor, ill, unable to work, who had recently given birth, or were widowed," as well as orphaned girls, but it also provided childcare and operated a soup kitchen (Burucs 1993, 15–19). As its members mostly did charity work, its profile was not really compatible with that of FE.
307. Minutes of the FE committee meeting on 29 January 1917, MNL OL P999, box 2, item 3.
308. Minutes of the FE committee meeting on 17 November 1915, MNL OL P999, box 2, item 3.
309. Paula Pogány's opinion of the budget and the lectures follows: "I would very much like it if the Viennese also invited them, as this would made the costs for us even lower." Minutes of the FE committee meeting on 12 December 1914, MNL OL P999, box 2, item 3.

310. Minutes of the FE committee meeting on 6 March 1916, MNL OL P999, box 2, item 3.
311. Szapor 2018.
312. FE logbooks of its members, MNL OL P999, box 23, item 32/b; Szegvári 1981, 143–147.
313. Sipos 2018, 192–202.
314. On this, see Gottlieb et al. 2017, 29–75.
315. Mrs. Mihály Greiger [?] to Vilma Glücklich, 18 October 1918, MNL OL P999, box 5, item 6, no. 339.
316. On Schwimmer's diplomatic service in Bern, see Glant 2002, 34–51; Pastor 1975, 282–292.
317. Sipos 2018, 192–202.
318. Dobrovits 1936, 120.
319. *Nőtisztviselők Lapja* 1919, 1–2, 3.
320. *Nőtisztviselők Lapja* 1919, 4–5 (emphasis in the original).
321. *Világ*, 6 March 1919, 6.
322. *Pesti Napló*, 23 April 1919, 7.
323. *Az Újság*, 6 November 1919, 2.
324. Minutes of the FE committee meeting on 22 December 1918, MNL OL P999, box 2, item 3.
325. Dobrovits 1936, 165.
326. Vilma Glücklich to Rosika Schwimmer, 25 January 1926 and 14 May 1926, NYPL RSP.
327. From 1907 to 1918, we constantly find Mrs. Szirmay among the members of the FE committee. MNL OL P999, box 1, item 1/b; box 2, item 3.
328. FE to minister of the interior László Rajk, 22 November 1946, MNL OL P999, box 1, item 2/a.
329. FE to Minister of the Interior László Rajk, 22 November 1946, MNL OL P999, box 1, item 2/a.
330. The Budapest archive of FE is home to Mrs. Meller's correspondence with various international organizations for women's and human rights and to her papers, which include her autobiography, family photographs, and family tree. MNL OL P999, box 42, item 79; FE annual report for 1922, MNL OL P999, box 1, item 2/a.
331. Minutes of the committee meetings of FE on 23 June 1906 and 19 October 1914, MNL OL P999, box 1, item 1/b; box 2, item 3. Cf. Papp and Zimmermann 2006, 331–335; FE annual report for 1922, MNL OL P999, box 1, item 2/a.
332. Biographies of the leading members of FE, n.d., MNL OL P999, box 23, item 32/a.
333. The courtesy of Benedek Várkonyi and Judith Szapor.
334. *Világ*, 10 November 1946, 5.
335. *Magyar Közlöny*, 17 December 1949, 261–262.

6. Similarities and Differences among the Three Associations

1. "But could the Hungarian associations not join Marianne Hainisch in Vienna and form an Austro-Hungarian alliance? Marianne Hainisch has already brought together 13 large associations." Aletta Jacobs to Rosika Schwimmer, 1 August 1902,

NYPL RSP I. Box 3. Cf. Zimmermann's work on the possibility of establishing a joint Austro-Hungarian umbrella organization: Zimmermann 2003, 119–147.
2. Bader-Zaar 2009, 297–328.
3. On this, see, e.g., *N* 1914, 1, 5.
4. Cf. Schwartz 2008, 11–16.
5. Glücklich did not remain the "honorary" leader of FE after 1927 either. The places on the committee left by the deaths of male members Dezső Márkus (born 1862 in Paks and died 1912 in Budapest) and Gusztáv Dirner (born 1855 in Gölnicbánya and died 1912 in Budapest) were immediately filled, if only because of the impending IWSA congress. A memorial celebration was organized in their honor, and memorial foundations, akin to the Auguste Fickert Stiftung, were set up (Minutes of the committee meeting on 20 December 1912, where the first item on the agenda was the deaths of Dezső Márkus and Gusztáv Dirner, MNL OL P999, box 1, item 2/a). During the war years, FE, despite its views on the flawed logic of "giving out handouts," assisted Márkus's widow, something Glücklich had had enough of in 1916: "We would truly be acting against Márkus's spirit were we to allow his family, which is completely alien to him in its way of thinking, to see us as an object constantly to be tapped for money." Vilma Glücklich to Mrs. Oszkár Szirmay, 21 May 1915, MNL OL P999, box 5, item 6, no. 238.
6. Tätigkeitsbericht 1910, 7.
7. *NFL* 1911, 6, 143–148.
8. *N* 1928, 1. Another memorial to an FE member has remained. Mrs. Rudolf Balló, remembrances of Vilma Glücklich, n.d., MNL OL P999, box 1, item 2/b, no. 170.
9. Braun-Prager n.d.-a, n.d.-b; Remembrance of Vilma Glücklich, MNL OL P999, box 1, item 2/a.
10. Klingenstein 1997, 313–314; Schmölzer 2002, 93–95.
11. On the meeting in Gießen, see *NB* 1913, 17, 129–130; 1913, 18, 138. A report on the event can be read in the issue of *Neue Bahnen* from late October 1913: *NB* 1913, 20, 153–158. The schedule of the calendar for associations in Germany was not altered by the outbreak of war. On this situation in 1915, see, e.g., *NB* 1915, 17, 129–130; 1915, 18, 137–138; 1915, 20, 161–166.
12. *NFL* 1906, 5, 24.
13. Minutes of the second and fifth annual general meetings of FE, MNL OL P999, box 1, item 2/a—1906–1914.
14. Receipt from the Gerbeaud café, 6 June 1913, NYPL RSP I, box 500; Minutes of the electoral session of 24 April 1914, MNL OL P999, box 1, item 2/a—1906–1914; Minutes of the electoral session of 25 September 1916, MNL OL P999, box 1, item 2/a—1916.
15. Minutes of the FE committee meeting of 27 January 1917, MNL OL P999, box 2, item 3.
16. NYPL RSP I, box 2–10. We do not have any information as to whether these activists visited other provincial capitals.
17. *NFL* 1904, 6, 1–5; Leopoldine Kulka to Auguste Fickert, 10 July 1904, WR NF H.I.N. 152883.
18. *A Nő* regularly reported on this. E.g., *N* 1914, 18, 206; 1915, 3, 40.
19. *N*, 1914, 13, 257.

20. After their meeting on 30 October 1918, Schwimmer noted that Kulka "look[ed] terrible." Rosika Schwimmer, journal entry on 30 October 1918, NYPL RSP I, box 101.

Conclusion

1. Szilvay 2018.
2. Antoni 2015.
3. Szapor 2018, 148.
4. Antoni 2015.

Bibliography

Archive Sources

Braun-Prager n.d.-a	Braun-Prager, Käthe. n.d.-a. "Auguste Fickert." Musiksammlung. Nachlass Emil Fickert. F.34. Fickert. Österreichische Nationalbibliothek.
Braun-Prager n.d.-b	Braun-Prager, Käthe. n.d.-b. "Auguste Fickert." Cod. Ser. n. 27844. Österreichische Nationalbibliothek Sammlung von Handschriften und alten Drucken.
Festschrift 1913	Österreichische Frauenstimmrechtskomitee, ed. 1913. "Das Frauenstimmrecht. Festschrift. Anlässlich der Internationalen Frauenstimmrechtskonferenz in Wien 11. und 12. Juni 1913." St. Stefan, Vienna.
Kulka	Kulka, Leopoldine. Dokumentation. AC10956995. Wienbibliothek im Rathaus.
MNL OL P987	Szirmay Oszkárné irathagyatéka [Papers of Mrs. Oszkár Szirmay]. P987. Magyar Nemzeti Levéltár Országos Levéltára [National Archives of Hungary].
MNL OL P999	Feministák Egyesülete. P999. Magyar Nemzeti Levéltár Országos Levéltára [National Archives of Hungary].
Nachlass Schirmacher	Nachlass Käthe Schirmacher. Dr. Käthe Schirmacher. Schenkung an der Universitätsbibliothek Rostock. Historische Quellen der Frauenbewegung und Geschlechtspolitik. Fischer, Erlangen, 2000. Mikrofiche-Ed.
NYPL RSP	Rosika Schwimmer Papers. MssCol 6398. Manuscript and Archives Division. New York Public Library.
NYPL RSP Digital Collection	Rosika Schwimmer Papers. New York Public Library Digital Collections. Accessed 31 May 2023. https://digitalcollections.nypl.org/search/index?utf8=%E2%9C%93&keywords=rosika+schwimmer#.
NYPL RSP Index	Rosika Schwimmer Papers. Comprehensive Alphabetical Index of Individual Correspondents Represented in the Rosika Schwimmer Collection. Manuscript and Archives Division. New York Public Library.
ÖNB M F34	Nachlass Emil Fickert. F34.Fickert. Österreichische Nationalbibliothek. Musiksammlung.

Protokoll 1893	Stenographisches Protokoll über die Constituierende Versammlung des Allgemeinen österreichischen Frauenvereines. Allgemeiner österreichischer Frauenverein, Vienna, 1893.
Report 1920	IWSA Report of Eighth Congress. Geneva, Switzerland, June 6–12, 1920. Manchester: Hotspu Press.
Statut 1848	Statut der Ersten Wiener demokratischer Frauenverein. Vienna, 28 August 1848.
Statut 1865	Statuten des Allgemeinen deutschen Frauenvereines. Leipzig, 17 Oktober 1865. Louise Otto-Peters Archiv, Leipzig.
Tätigkeitsbericht	Tätigkeitsberichte des Allgemeinen österreichischen Frauenvereines. Allgemeiner österreichischer Frauenverein. Holzwarth & Berger, Vienna, 1893, 1894, 1895, 1896, 1897, 1898, 1899, 1900, 1901, 1902, 1903, 1904, 1905, 1906, 1907, 1908, 1909, 1910.
Teleky	Teleky, Dora. Dokumentation. Wienbibliothek im Rathaus. TP-005972.
Touaillon	Touaillon, Christine. Dokumentation. TP-052549. Wienbibliothek im Rathaus.
WR NF	Nachlass Auguste Fickert. LQH0003431. Wienbibliothek im Rathaus.

Legislation

Act XXXVIII 1868	Act XXXVIII [Act XXXVIII]. 1868. Törvénycikk a népiskolai közoktatás tárgyában [Act on the subject of public education in public schools]. https://net.jogtar.hu/ezer-ev-torveny?docid=86800038.TV.
Gesetz vom 15. November	Gesetz vom 15. November 1867 (134/1867). ALEX. Historische Rechts- und Gesetztexte Online. http://alex.onb.ac.at/cgi-content/alex?aid=rgb&datum=18670004&seite=00000377.
Kaiserliche Verordnung 1917/122	Kaiserliche Verordnung, betreffend die Regelung von Lohn- und Arbeitsverhältnissen in den militärischen Zwecken dienenden Betrieben. 1917. http://alex.onb.ac.at/cgi-content/alex?aid=rgb&datum=19170004&seite=00000289.
Reichsvolksschulgesetz 62/1869	Gesetz, durch welches die Grundsätze des Unterrichtswesens bezüglich der Volksschulen festgestellt werden. 1869. https://www.ris.bka.gv.at/Dokument.wxe?Abfrage=BgblAlt&Dokumentnummer=rgb1869_0062_00277.

Törvény a kivételes hatalomról 1912 — Törvény a háború esetére szóló kivételes intézkedésekről [Law on special measures in the event of war]. 1912. Article LXIII. In *Az első világháború sajtójogi forrásai. Sajtójog a kivételes hatalom árnyékában* [Sources for press rights in World War I. Press rights in the shadow of exceptional authority], edited by Roland Kelemen, 66–69. Budapest: Médiatudományi Intézet [Institute for Media Studies], 2017.

Periodicals

Allgemeiner Tiroler Zeitung (Innsbruck), 1919–1922.
A Nő és a Társadalom (NT) [Women and Society] (Budapest), 1907–1913.
A Nő. Feminista Folyóirat (N) [The Woman. Feminist Journal] (Budapest), 1914–1928.
Arbeiter-Zeitung (Vienna), 1911–1919.
Az Újság [The News] (Budapest), 1903–1944.
Der Bund. Zentralblatt des Bundes österreichischen Frauenvereine (Vienna), 1905–1919.
Dokumente der Frauen (DF) [Women's Documents] (Vienna), 1899–1902.
Feminista Értesítő (FÉ) [Feminist Bulletin] (Budapest), 1906.
Lehrerinnen-Wart, Monatsblatt für die Interessen des Lehrerinnenthumes (Vienna), 1889/1890–1901.
Magyar Közlöny [Hungarian Gazette] (Budapest), 1945–.
Neue Freie Presse (NFP) (Vienna), 1864–1939.
Neues Frauenleben (NFL) (Vienna), 1902–1918.
Neues Wiener Journal (Vienna), 1893–1939.
Neues Wiener Tagblatt (NWT) (Vienna), 1867–1945.
Neuzeit (Vienna), 1861–1903.
Nőtisztviselők Lapja [Journal of Women Office Workers] (Budapest), 1915–1919.
Österreichische Volks-Zeitung (Vienna), 1888–1918.
Pesti Napló [Pest Journal] (Budapest), 1850–1939.
Reichspost (Vienna), 1894–1938.
Világ [World] (Budapest), 1945–1949.
Wiener Zeitung (Vienna), 1902–.
Zeitschrift für Frauenstimmrecht (Berlin), 1907–1918.

Printed Sources

Adler, Emma. 1906. *Die berühmtesten Frauen der französischen Revolution 1789–1795*. Vienna: C. W. Stern.
Braun-Prager, Käthe. 1936. *Große Frauen der Heimat*. Vienna: Steyrermühl.
Cviková, Jana. 2006. "'Sinnlose' oder 'sinnvolle' Emanzipation. Über die Entstehung des feministischen Bewusstseins in der Slowakei." In *Frauenbilder, feministische Praxis und nationales Bewußtsein in Österreich-Ungarn 1867–1918*, edited by Waltraud Heindl, Edit Király, and Alexandra Millner, 187–207. Basel: Francke.
Feministák Egyesülete: Tájékoztatás a Feministák Egyesületének céljairól és munkatervéről [Report on the objectives and plan of work of Feminists' Association]. 1905. Budapest: Márkus Samu könyvnyomdája.

Fickert, Auguste. 1929. *Zur Enthüllung ihres Denkmals am 22. Juni 1929*. Vienna: Holzwarth und Berger.
Glücklich, Vilma, and Janka Dirnfeld, eds. 1910. *A Feministák Egyesületének alapszabályai* [The statutes of feminists' association]. Budapest. https://mtda.hu/books/a_feminista _egyesuletek_alapszabalyai.pdf.
Godwin, William. 1912. *Erinnerungen an Mary Wollstonecraft*. Translated by Therese Schlesinger-Eckstein. Halle.
Hainisch, Marianne. 1930. "Zur Geschichte der österreichischen Frauenbewegung: aus meinen Erinnerungen." In *Frauenbewegung, Frauenbildung und Frauenarbeit in Österreich*, edited by Bund österreichischer Frauenvereine, 13–24. Vienna: BöF.
Illyefalvi, I. Lajos. 1930. *A kenyérkereső nő Budapesten* [Working Woman in Budapest]. Budapest: Budapest Főváros Statisztikai Hivatala.
Leon, Dora. 1955. "Auguste Fickert: 1855–1910." In *Frauenbilder aus Österreich: eine Sammlung von zwölf Essays*, edited by Bund österreichischer Frauenvereine, 51–63. Vienna: Obelisk.
Máday, Andor. 1913. *A magyar nő jogai a múltban és jelenben* [The rights of Hungarian women past and present]. Budapest: Athenaeum.
MTDA. n.d. *Az MTDA feminista archívuma a XIX–XX. századi nemzetközi és magyar nőmozgalma prominens képviselőinek arcképcsarnoka* [The MTDA feminist archive. Gallery of the prominent representatives of the international and Hungarian women's movement in the nineteenth and twentieth centuries]. Accessed 31 May 2023. http:// mtda.hu/Fema.html.
A Nőtisztviselők Országos Egyesületének (NOE) Alapszabályai [The statues of the National Association of Female Clerks]. 1909. Budapest: Markovits és Garai Könyvnyomdája.
Österreichische Frauenstimmrechtskomitee, ed. 1913. *Das Frauenstimmrecht. Festschrift anlässlich der Internationalen Frauenstimmrechtskonferenz in Wien 11. und 12. Juni 1913*. St. Stefan, Vienna.
Schwimmer, Rózsa. 1907. *A magyar nőmozgalom régi dokumentumai* [Old documents of the Hungarian women's movement]. Budapest. http://mtdaportal.extra.hu/books/Bedy_s _r_a_magyar_nomozgalom.pdf.
60 Jahre Bund österreichischer Frauenvereine. 1965. Design by Wilma Franck. Vienna: Ludwig Schölers Buchdruckerei.
Tormay, Cécile. 1925. *Bujdosó könyv* [An outlaw's diary]. Vol. 1. Budapest: Singer és Wolfner.
Urban, Gisela. 1930. "Die Entwicklung der Österreichischen Frauenbewegung im Spiegel der wichtigsten Vereinsgründungen." In *Frauenbewegung, Frauenbildung und Frauenarbeit in Österreich*, edited by Bund österreichischer Frauenvereine, 25–64. Vienna: BöF.

Books and Articles

Ablonczy, Balázs. 2016. *Keletre, magyar! A magyar turanizmus története* [Go east! History of the Hungarian Turanism]. Budapest: Jaffa.
Acsády, Judit. 2007. "In a Different Voice: Responses of Hungarian Feminism to the First World War." In *The Women's Movement in Wartime: International Perspectives, 1914–1919*, edited by S. Alison Fell and Ingrid Sharp, 105–123. Basingstoke: Palgrave Macmillan.
———. 2011. "Diverse Constructions: Feminist and Conservative Women's Movements and Their Contribution to the (Re-)construction of Gender Relations in Hungary after the

First World War." In *Aftermaths of War: Women's Movements and Female Activists, 1918–1923*, edited by Ingrid Sharp and Matthew Stibbe, 309–332. Leiden: Brill.

Acsády, Judit, and Zsolt Mészáros. 2016. "Feminizmus a fővárosban és vidéken a múlt századelőn" [Feminism in the capital and in the provinces at the turn of the last century]. In *Vidéki élet és vidéki társadalom Magyarországon: a Hajnal István Kör Társadalomtörténeti Egyesület 2014. évi, egri konferenciájának kötete* [Provincial life and provincial society in Hungary: The annals of the 2014 Eger Conference of the István Hajnal Circle Social History Association], edited by József Pap and Árpád Tóth, 486–502. Budapest: Hajnal István Kör Társadalomtörténeti Egyesület.

———. 2018. "A Balmazújvárosi Szabad Nőszervezet és a Feministák Egyesülete közötti kapcsolat (1908–1929): A női szolidaritás megnyilvánulásai a hazai feminista mozgalomban" [Relations between the Balmazújvárosi Szabad Nőszervezet and the Feminists' Association (1908–1929): Expressions of female solidarity in the Hungarian feminist movement]. *TNTeF* 2:80–96.

Aloni, Micaela. 2016. "Nadja Brodsky (Stein, Orstein)." Hohenems Genealogy. Jewish Family Research in Vorarlberg and Tyrol. Accessed 31 October 2020. http://www.hohenemsgenealogie.at/en/genealogy/getperson.php?personID=I12462&tree=Hohenems.

Anderson, Harriet. 1985. "Beyond a Critique of Femininity: The Thought of Rosa Mayreder." PhD diss., University of London.

———. 1989. "Zwischen Modernismus und Sozialreform: Rosa Mayreder und die Kultur der Wiener Jahrhundertwende." *Mitteilungen des Instituts für Wissenschaft und Kunst, Wien* 44:6–12.

———. 1990. "'Mir wird es immer unmöglicher', 'die Männer' als die Feinde der Frauensache zu betrachten.' Zur Beteiligung von Männern an den Bestrebungen der österreichischen Frauenbewegung um 1900." In *"Das Weib existiert nicht für sich": Geschlechterbeziehungen in der bürgerlichen Gesellschaft*, edited by Helene Dienst and Edith Saurer, 189–201. Vienna: Verein Kritische Sozialwissenschaft und Politische Bildung.

———. 1992. *Utopian Feminism: Women's Movements in Fin-de-Siècle Vienna*. New Haven, CT: Yale University Press.

———. 1994. *Vision und Leidenschaft. Die Frauenbewegung im Fin de Siècle Wiens*. Vienna: Deuticke.

Andraschko, Elisabeth. 1993. "Elise Richter—eine Skizze ihres Lebens." In *"Durch Erkenntnis zu Freiheit und Glück . . ." Frauen an der Universität Wien (ab 1897)*, edited by Waltraud Heindl and Marina Tichy, 221–231. Vienna: Universitätsverlag.

Antoni, Rita. 2015. "A magyarországi feminista megmozdulások története" [The history of feminist movements in Hungary]. Nőkért.hu. Accessed 19 June 2023. https://nokert.hu/sun-20151129-1022/1371/6/magyarorszagi-feminista-megmozdulasok-tortenete#4.

Appelt, Erna. 1985. *Von Ladenmädchen, Schreibfräulein und Gouvernanten 1900–1934. Angestellten Wiens zwischen 1900 und 1934*. Vienna: Verlag für Gesellschaftskritik.

Arias, Ingrid. 2000. "Die ersten Ärztinnen in Wien: ärztliche Karrieren von Frauen zwischen 1900 und 1938." In *Töchter des Hippokrates. 100 Jahre akademische Ärztinnen in Österreich*, edited by Birgit Bolognese-Leuchtenmüller, 55–78. Vienna: Verlag der Österreichischen Arztkammer.

Árvai, Tünde. 2016. *Városanyák. Mozaikok a pécsi nők 19-20. századi történetéből* ["City mothers." Mosaics from the history of women in Pécs in the 19th–20th centuries]. Pécs: Kronosz.

Auernig, Karola. 1994. "'Sehr geehrtes Fräulein' Die Briefe der Stefanie Kummer (1868–1942) an Auguste Fickert (1855–1910) von ca. 1891–1907." Master's thesis, Universität Wien.

Bibliography

Bader-Zaar, Birgitta. 1995. "'Weise Mäßigung' und 'Ungetrübter Blick' die Streben nach politischer Gleichberechtigung." In *Bürgerliche Frauenkultur im 19. Jahrhundert*, edited by Brigitte Mazohl-Wallnig, 233–268. Vienna: Böhlau.

——. 1997. "Bürgerrechte und Geschlecht. Zur Frage der politischen Gleichberechtigung von Frauen in Österreich, 1848–1918." In *Frauen in der Geschichte des Rechts von der frühen Neuzeit bis zur Gegenwart*, edited by Ute Gerhard, 547–562. Munich: C. H. Beck.

——. 1999. "Die Wiener Frauenbewegung und der Rechtsschutz für Frauen, 1895–1914." In *Geschichte und Recht: Festschrift für Gerald Stourzh zum 70. Geburtstag*, edited by Thomas Angerer and Gerald Stourzh, 365–383. Vienna: Böhlau.

——. 2006a. "Frauenbewegungen und Frauenwahlrecht." In *Die Habsburgermonarchie 1848–1918. Politische Öffentlichkeit und Zivilgesellschaft, Teilband 1. Vereine, Parteien und Interessenverbände als Träger der politischen Partizipation*, edited by Helmut Rumpler and Peter Urbanitsch, 1005–1027. Vienna: Österreichische Akademie der Wissenschaften.

——. 2006b. "Marianne Hainisch (1839–1936)." In *A Biographical Dictionary of Women's Movements and Feminism: Central, Eastern, and South Eastern Europe, 19th and 20th Centuries*, edited by Francisca de Haan et al., 173–177. Budapest: CEU Press.

——. 2008. "Zur Geschichte der internationalen Frauenbewegungen. Von transatlantischen Kontakten über institutionalisierte Organisationen zu globalen Netzwerken." In *Internationalismen: Transformation weltweiter Ungleichheit im 19. und 20. Jahrhundert*, edited by Karin Fischer and Susan Zimmermann, 107–128. Vienna: Historische Sozialkunde, Internationale Entwicklung, Promedia.

——. 2009. "Die deutschsprachigen österreichischen Frauenbewegungen bis 1918. Bibliographie und Kommentar." In *Wie Frauenbewegung geschrieben wird. Historiographie, Dokumentation, Stellungnahmen, Bibliographien*, edited by Johanna Gehmacher and Natascha Vittorelli, 297–328. Vienna: Löcker.

——. 2018. "Die Demokratisierung des Wahlrechts." In *Die junge Republik. Österreich 1918/1919*, edited by Robert Kreichbaumer, Michaela Maier, and Maria Mesner, 101–112. Vienna: Böhlau.

——. 2019. "Die Forderung des Frauenwahlrechts. Akreur_innen, Strategien, Diskurse in der österreichischen Reichshälfte der Habsburgermonarchie (1848–1918)." In *"Sie meinen es politisch!" 100 Jahre Frauenwahlrecht in Österreich. Geschlechterdemokratie als gesellschaftspolitische Herausforderung*, edited by Blaustrumpf ahoi!, 37–60. Vienna: Löcker.

Bandhauer-Schöffmann, Irene. 1986. "Die bürgerliche Frauenbewegung im Austrofaschismus: eine Studie zur Krise des Geschlechterverhältnisses am Beispiel des Bundes Österreichischer Frauenvereine und der Katholischen Frauenorganisation für die Erzdiözese Wien." PhD diss., Universität Wien.

——. 1993. "Frauenbewegung und Studentinnen. Zum Engagement der österreichischen Frauenvereine für das Frauenstudium." In *"Durch Erkenntnis zu Freiheit und Glück..." Frauen an der Universität Wien (ab 1897)*, edited by Waltraud Heindl and Marina Tichy. Vienna: Universitätsverlag.

——. 2009. "Historische Grabungsarbeiten zur Frauenbewegung in Wien der 1980-er Jahren." In *Wie Frauenbewegung geschrieben wird*, edited by Johanna Gehmacher and Natascha Vittorelli, 226–229. Vienna: Historiographie, Dokumentation, Stellungnahmen, Bibliographien, Löcker.

Bechtel, Beatrix, Hg. 1984. *Die ungeschriebene Geschichte: historische Frauenforschung; Dokumentation des 5. Historikerinnentreffens in Wien, 16. bis 19. April 1984.* Vienna: Wiener Frauenverlag.

Beck, Elfride. 1964. "'Die Wienerin und ihre Zeit': Frauen- und Familienzeitschriften der 2. Hälfte des 19. Jahrhunderts als Zeitdokumente." Diss., Universität Wien.

Bittermann-Wille, Christina, and Helga Hofmann-Weinberger. 2001. "Von der Zeitschrift Dokumente der Frauen zur Dokumentation von Frauenzeitschriften." Accessed 31 May 2023. https://www.demokratiezentrum.org/wp-content/uploads/2022/10/bittermann_frauenzeitschriften.pdf.

———. 2009. "Frauen in Bewegung (1848–1918). Aus der Praxis eines themenzentrierten Dokumentationsprojekts zur österreichischen historischen Frauenbewegung." In *Wie Frauenbewegung geschrieben wird. Historiographie, Dokumentation, Stellungnahmen, Bibliographien*, edited by Johanna Gehmacher and Natascha Vittorelli, 183–196. Vienna: Löcker.

Blaustrumpf ahoi!, Hg. 2019. *"Sie meinen es politisch!" 100 Jahre Frauenwahlrecht in Österreich. Geschlechterdemokratie als gesellschaftspolitische Herausforderung.* Vienna: Löcker.

Bock, Gisela. 2014a. "Begriffsgeschichten: 'Frauenemanzipation' im Kontext der Emanzipationsbewegungen des 19. Jahrhunderts." In *Geschlechtergeschichten der Neuzeit. Ideen, Politik, Praxis*, edited by Gisela Bock, 100–154. Göttingen: V&R.

———. 2014b. "Wege zur demokratischen Bürgerschaft: transnationale Perspektiven." In *Geschlechtergeschichten der Neuzeit. Ideen, Politik, Praxis*, edited by Gisela Bock, 204–242. Göttingen: V&R.

Bódy, Zsombor. 2003. *Egy társadalmi osztály születése. A magántisztviselők társadalomtörténete 1890–1938* [Birth of a social class: The social history of private office workers, 1890–1938]. Budapest: L'Harmattan.

Bolt, Christine. 1993. *The Women's Movements in the United States and Britain from the 1790s to the 1920s.* Hertfordshire: Harvester Wheatshelf.

Bosch, Mineke, and Annamarie Kloosterman, eds. 1990. *Politics and Friendship: Letters from the International Women Suffrage Alliance, 1902–1942.* Columbus: Ohio State University.

Boyer, John W. 2010. *Karl Lueger (1844–1910). Christlichsoziale Politik als Beruf.* Vienna: Böhlau.

Branca, Patricia. 2013. *Women in Europe since 1750.* Oxford: Routledge.

Bundesverfassungsgesetz. 1920. "Gesetz vom 1." Oktober. Accessed 15 January 2025. http://alex.onb.ac.at/cgi-content/alex?aid=sgb&datum=1920&page=1873&size=45.

Bund österreichischer Frauenvereine. 1955. *Frauenbilder aus Österreich: eine Sammlung von zwölf Essays.* Vienna: Obelisk.

Burmetler, Maria. 1992. "Frauenarbeit in Österreich mit einem kurzen Einblick in die ersten politischen Frauenorganisationen." Master's thesis, Vienna.

Burucs, Kornélia. 1993. "Nők az egyesületekben" [Women in the associations]. *História* 2:15–19.

Carlier, Julie. 2009. "How the Women's Movements Can (or Should) Be Written from a Transnational Perspective?" In *Wie Frauenbewegung geschrieben wird. Historiographie, Dokumentation, Stellungnahmen, Bibliographien*, edited by Johanna Gehmacher and Natascha Vittorelli, 233–237. Vienna: Löcker.

———. 2010. "Forgotten Transnational Connections and National Contexts: An 'Entangled History' of the Political Transfers That Shaped Belgian Feminism, 1890–1914." *Women's History Review* 4:503–522.

Christensen-Nelson, Carolyn. 2004. *Literature of the Women's Suffrage Campaign in England*. Peterborough: Broadview.
Clark, L. Linda. 2008. *Women and Achievement in Nineteenth-Century Europe*. Cambridge: Cambridge University Press.
Cohen, Deborah, and Maura O'Connor. 2004. "Comparative History, Cross-National History—Definitions." In *Comparison and History: Europe in Cross-National Perspective*, edited by Deborah Cohen and Maura O'Connor, ix–xxiv. New York: Routledge.
Czeferner, Dóra. 2017a. "A jelen és a jövő sokkal jobban érdekel, mint a múlt—Interjú Pető Andreával" [The present and the future interest me much more than the past—interview with Andrea Pető]. *Újkor.hu—A velünk élő történelem* [History we live with]. Accessed 31 May 2023. http://ujkor.hu/content/a-jelen-es-a-jovo-sokkal-jobban-erdekel-mint-a-mult-interju-peto-andreaval.
———. 2017b. "Nő és neveléstörténet felsőfokon—Interjú Kéri Katalinnal" [Women's and educational history at an advanced level—interview with Katalin Kéri]. *Újkor.hu—A velünk élő történelem* [History we live with]. Accessed 31 May 2023. http://ujkor.hu/content/no-es-nevelestortenet-felsofokon-interju-keri-katalinnal.
———. 2018. "'Egy korszakról sem kaphatunk átfogó képet, ha a nőket kihagyjuk a vizsgálatból'—Interjú Szapor Judittal" ["There is no period we can get a full picture of if we leave women out of our investigation"—interview with Judith Szapor]. *Újkor.hu—A velünk élő történelem* [History we live with]. Accessed 30 October 2020. http://ujkor.hu/content/interju-szapor-judittal.
———. 2021. *Kultúrmisszió vagy propaganda? Feminista lapok és olvasóik Bécsben és Budapesten* [Cultural mission or Propaganda? Feminist journals and their readers in Vienna and Budapest]. Budapest: ELKH–BTK.
Dobrovits, Sándor. 1936. *Statisztikai Közlemények. Budapest egyesületei* [Statistical bulletins: Budapest's associations]. Edited by Illyefalvi I. Lajos. Budapest: Székesfőváros Statisztikai Hivatala.
Dobszay, Tamás, and Zoltán Fónagy. 2005. "Magyarország társadalma a 19. század második felében" [Hungarian society in the second half of the 19th century]. In *Magyarország története a 19. században* [History of Hungary in the 19th century], edited by András Gergely, 397–459. Budapest: Osiris.
Digitales Deutsches Frauenarchiv. n.d. Accessed 15 January 2025. https://www.digitales-deutsches-frauenarchiv.de/.
Dudeková, Gabriela. 2009. "Frauenbewegung in der Slowakei bis 1918. Bibliographie und Kommentar." In *Wie Frauenbewegung geschrieben wird. Historiographie, Dokumentation, Stellungnahmen, Bibliographien*, edited by Johanna Gehmacher and Natascha Vittorelli, 329–350. Vienna: Löcker.
Ehmer, Josef. 1996. "Zur sozialen Schichtung der Wiener Bevölkerung. 1857 bis 1910." In *Wien–Prag–Budapest. Urbanisierung, Kommunalpolitik, gesellschaftliche Konflikte (1867–1918)*, edited by Gerhard Melinz and Susan Zimmermann, 73–83. Vienna: Promedia.
Flich, Renate. 1990. "Der Fall Auguste Fickert—eine Lehrerin macht Schlagzeilen." *Wiener Geschichtsblätter* 45 (1): 1–24.
———. 2004. "Auguste Fickert: 'rote' Lehrerin und radikal bürgerliche Feministin?" In *Die Revolutionierung des Alltags: zur intellektuellen Kultur von Frauen im Wien der Zwischenkriegszeit*, edited by Doris Ingrisch, 43–55. Frankfurt am Main: Lang.
———. 2006. "Bildungsbestrebungen und Frauenbewegungen." In *Die Habsburgermonarchie 1848–1918*, vol. 8, *Politische Öffentlichkeit und Zivilgesellschaft, Teilband 1.: Vereine,*

Parteien und Interessenverbände als Träger der politischen Partizipation, edited by Adam Wandruszka and Helmut Rumpler, 941–964. Vienna: Verlag der Österreichischer Akademie der Wissenschaften.

Frank, Tibor. 1990. "Hungary and the Dual Monarchy 1867–1890." In *A History of Hungary*, edited by Sugar F. Peter, Péter Hanák, and Tibor Frank, 252–266. Bloomington: Indiana University Press.

———. 1997. "Hungary and the Dual Monarchy." In *A History of Hungary*, edited by Peter F. Sugar, Péter Hanák, and Tibor Frank, 252–266. Bloomington: Indiana University Press.

Freismuth, Elisabeth. 1989. "Der Weg zum Frauenstimmrecht." In *Aufbruch in das Jahrhundert der Frau? Rosa Mayreder und der Feminismus in Wien um 1900. Sonderausstellung des Historischen Museums der Stadt Wien*, edited by Reingard Witzmann, 27–36. Vienna: Museum der Stadt Wien.

Friedrich, Margaret. 1995. "Vereinigung der Kräfte, Sammlung des kleinen Gutes zu einem gemeinschaftlichen Vermögen, kurz die Assoziation ist hier die einzige Rettung. Zur Tätigkeit und Bedeutung der Frauenvereine im 19. Jahrhundert in Metropote und Provinz." In *Bürgerliche Frauenkultur im 19. Jahrhundert*, edited by Brigitte Mazohl-Wallnig, Vienna: Böhlau.

Frysak, Elisabeth. 2002. "Legale Kämpfe. Petitieren als Konsequenz von Unrechtserfahrung(en) österreichischer bürgerlicher Frauenvereinen." In *Erfahrung: Alles nur Diskurs? Zur Verwendung des Erfahrungsbegriffs in der Geschlechtergeschichte. Beiträge der 11. Schweizerischen Historikerinnentagung*, edited by Marguérite Bos, Bettina Vincenz, and Tanja Wirz, 215–223. Zurich: Chronos.

Frysak, Elisabeth, Margareth Lanzinger, and Edith Saurer. 2004. "Frauenbewegung(en), Feminismen und Genderkonzepte in Zentral-, Ost- und Südosteuropa." *L'Homme* 1:117–121.

Geber, Eva. 2013. *Der Typus der kämpfenden Frau: Frauen schreiben über Frauen in der Arbeiterzeitung von 1900–1933*. Vienna: Mandelbaum.

Gehmacher, Johanna. 2001. "Nachfolgeansprüche. Deutschnationale und nationalsozialistische Politik und die bürgerliche Frauenbewegung. Österreich 1918–1938." In *Feminismus und Demokratie*, edited by Ute Gerhard, 159–175. Königstein: Taunus.

———. 2011. "Reisende in Sachen Frauenbewegung. Käthe Schirmacher zwischen Internationalismus und nationaler Identifikation." *Ariadne* 60:58–64.

———. 2019. "In/visible Transfers: Translation as a Crucial Practice in Transnational Women's Movements around 1900." *German Historical Institute London Bulletin* 41 (2): 3–44.

———. 2024. *Feminist Activism, Travel and Translation around 1900: Transnational Practices of Mediation and the Case of Käthe Schirmacher*. London: Palgrave Macmillan.

Gehmacher, Johanna, Elisa Heinrich, and Corinna Oesch. 2018. *Käthe Schirmacher: Agitation und autobiographische Praxis zwischen radikaler Frauenbewegung und völkischer Politik*. Vienna: Böhlau.

Gehmacher, Johanna, and Maria Mesner, eds. 2003. *Frauen- und Geschlechtergeschichte. Positionen, Perspektiven*. Innsbruck: Studien.

Gehmacher, Johanna and Natascha Vittorelli, eds. 2009. *Wie Frauenbewegung geschrieben wird*. Historiographie, Dokumentation, Stellungnahmen, Bibliographien, Vienna: Löcker.

Géra, Eleonóra and Szécsi Noémi. 2018. *A budapesti úrinő magánélete (1860–1914)* [Private Life of the Budapest Lady (1860–1914)]. Budapest: Európa.

Glant, Tibor. 2002. "Against All Odds: Vira B. Whitehouse and Rosika Schwimmer in Switzerland, 1918." *American Studies International* 40 (1): 34–51.

Gogîltan, Anca. 2009. "Women's Emancipation Movements in Transylvania, Banat, Crişana, and Maramureş (Nineteenth Century until 1918): Bibliography and Commentary." In *Wie Frauenbewegung geschrieben wird, Historiographie, Dokumentation, Stellungnahmen, Bibliographien*, edited by Johanna Gehmacher and Natascha Vittorelli, 351–370. Vienna: Löcker.

Gottlieb, Julie, Judith Szapor, Tiina Lintunen, and Dagmar Wernitznig. 2017. "Suffrage and Nationalism in Comparative Perspective: Britain, Hungary, Finland, and the Transnational Experience of Rosika Schwimmer." In *Women Activists between War and Peace: Europe, 1918–1923*, edited by Ingrid Sharp and Matthew Stibbe, 29–75. London: Bloomsbury Academic.

Grandner, Margarete and Edith Saurer, eds. 2005. *Geschlecht, Region und Engagement. Die jüdischen Frauenbewegungen in deutschsprachigen Raum 19. und frühes 20. Jahrhundert*. Vienna: Böhlau.

Guschlbauer, Elisabeth. 1974. "Der Beginn der politischen Emanzipation der Frau in Österreich (1848–1919)." PhD diss., Universität Salzburg.

Gyáni, Gábor. 1983. *Család, háztartás és városi cselédség* [Family, household, and the urban servantry]. Budapest: Magvető.

———. 2008. *Budapest—túl jón és rosszon. A nagyvárosi múlt mint tapasztalat* [Budapest—beyond good and bad: The metropolitan past as experience]. Budapest: Napvilág.

———. 2010. "Individualizálódás és civil társadalom. Történeti érvek, elméleti megfontolások" [Individualisation and civil society. Historical arguments, theoretical considerations]. *Történelmi Szemle* [Historical Review] 52 (4): 485–495.

———. 2011. "A nők, avagy a nemek története: fogalmak és helyzetkép" [A history of women, or of the genders: Concepts and the state of affairs]. In *A vászoncselédtől a vállalkozó nőig. A nő a Jászkunság társadalmában . . .* [From the linen maid to the female entrepreneur: Women in the society of the Jászkunság . . .], edited by Bathó Edit and Tóth Péter, 8–15. Jászberény: Jász Múzeumért Alapítvány.

Gyáni, Gábor, and György Kövér. 2006. *Magyarország társadalomtörténete a reformkortól a második világháborúig* [The Social History of Hungary from the Reform Era until World War II]. Budapest: Osiris.

Haan, Francisca de. 2008. "On Retrieving Women's Cultural Heritage—Especially the History of Women's Movements in Central, Eastern, and South Eastern Europe." In *Traveling Heritages. New Perspectives on Collecting, Preserving and Sharing Women's History*, edited by Saskia Wieringa, 65–78. Amsterdam: Aksant.

———. 2017. "Writing Inter/Transnational History: The Case of Women's Movements and Feminisms." In *Internationale Geschichte in Theorie und Praxis/International History in Theory and Practice*, edited by Barbara Haider-Wilson, William D. Godsey, and Wolfgang Mueller, 501–536. Vienna: Verlag der Österreichischen Akademie der Wissenschaften.

Haan, Francisca de, Krassimira Daskalova, and Anna Loutfi. 2006. *A Biographical Dictionary of Women's Movements and Feminism: Central, Eastern, and South Eastern Europe, 19th and 20th Centuries*. Budapest: CEU Press.

Haan, Francisca de, Margaret Allen, June Purvis, and Krassimira Daskalova. 2013. *Women's Activism: Global Perspectives from the 1890s to the Present*. London: Routledge.

Hacker, Hanna. 1996. "Wer gewinnt? Wer verliert? Wer tritt aus dem Schatten? Machtkämpfe und Beziehungsstrukturen nach dem Tod der 'großen Feministin' Auguste Fickert (1910)." *L'Homme. Tausendeinen Geschichten aus Österreich* 7:97–106.

———. 1997. "Zeremonien der Verdrängung: Konfliktsmuster in der bürgerlichen Frauenbewegung um 1900." In *Die Frauen der Wiener Moderne*, edited by Lisa Fischer, 101–109. Munich: Verlag für Geschichte und Politik.

———. 1998. *Gewalt ist keine Frau: der Akteurin oder eine Geschichte der Transgression*. Königstein: Helmer.

———. 2006. "Auguste Fickert (1855–1910)." In *A Biographical Dictionary of Women's Movements and Feminism: Central, Eastern, and South Eastern Europe, 19th and 20th Centuries*, edited by Francisca de Haan el al., 131–133. Budapest: CEU Press.

Halmos, Károly. 2006. "Besitzbürgertum Magyarországon. A virilizmus" [Besitzbürgertum in Hungary: Virilism]. In *Zsombékok. Középosztályok és iskoláztatás Magyarországon a 19. század elejétől a 20. század közepéig. Társadalomtörténeti tanulmányok* ["Zsombéks": Middle classes and education in Hungary from the early 19th century to the mid-20th century; Studies in social history], edited by Kövér György, 161–194. Budapest: Századvég.

Hamann, Brigitte. 1989. "Österreichische Frauen in der Friedensbewegung." In *Aufbruch in das Jahrhundert der Frau? Rosa Mayreder und der Feminismus in Wien um 1900. Sonder ausstellung des Historischen Museums der Stadt Wien*, edited by Reingard Witzmann, 134–143. Vienna: Museum der Stadt Wien.

Hämmerle, Christa. 2012. "Der Erste Weltkrieg aus frauen- und geschlechtergeschichtlicher Perspektive. Forschungsthemen und -desiderate in Österreich." *Österreich in Geschichte und Literatur (ÖGL) mit Geographie* 56 (3): 218–230.

———. 2014. *Heimat/Front: Geschlechtergeschichte/n des Ersten Weltkriegs in Österreich-Ungarn*. Vienna: Böhlau.

Hämmerle, Chrsita, Oswald Überegger, and Birgitta Bader-Zaar, eds. 2014. *Gender and the First World War*. London: Palgrave Macmillan.

Hanák, Péter. 1971. *A dualizmus korának történeti problémái* [The historical problems of the period of dualism]. Budapest: Tankönyvkiadó.

———. 1998. *The Garden and the Workshop. Essays on the Cultural History of Vienna and Budapest*. Princeton, NJ: Princeton University Press.

Hauch, Gabriella, ed. 1986. *Arbeitsmigration und Arbeiterbewegung als Historisches Problem. International Conference of Historians of the Labour Movement, Linzer Konferenz, 22, 1986, Linz*. Vienna: Europaverlag.

———. 2003. "'Wir, die viele Geschichten haben . . .' Zur Genese der historischen Frauenforschung in gesellschaftlichen und wissenschaftlichen Kontext." In *Frauen- und Geschlechtergeschichte. Positionen, Perspektiven*, edited by Johanna Gehmacher and Maria Mesner, 21–35. Innsbruck: Studien.

———. 2006a. "'Arbeit, Recht und Sittlichkeit'—Themen der Frauenbewegungen in der Habsburgermonarchie." In *Die Habsburgermonarchie 1848–1918*, vol. 8, *Politische Öffentlichkeit und Zivilgesellschaft, Teilband 1.: Vereine, Parteien und Interessenverbände als Träger der politischen Partizipation*, edited by Adam Wandruszka and Helmut Rumpler, 965–1003. Vienna: Verlag der Österreichischer Akademie der Wissenschaften.

———. 2006b. "Therese Schlesinger (1863–1940)." In *A Biographical Dictionary of Women's Movements and Feminism: Central, Eastern, and South Eastern Europe, 19th and 20th Centuries*, edited by Francisca de Haan et al., 479–483. Budapest: CEU Press.

———. 2006c. "Perin-Gradenstein, Karoline Freifrau von." In *Biographical Dictionary of Women's Movements and Feminisms in Central, Eastern, and South Eastern Europe:*

19th and 20th Centuries, edited by Francisca de Haan et al., 424–426. Budapest: CEU Press.

——. 2008. "Schreiben über eine Fremde. Therese Schlesinger (1863 Wien–1940 Blois bei Paris)." *Österreichische Zeitschrift für Geschichtswissenschaften* 2:98–117.

——. 2009. *Frauen bewegen Politik Österreich 1848–1938*. Innsbruck: Studien.

——. 2011. "Sisters and Comrades: Women's Movements and the 'Austrian Revolution'; Gender in Insurrection, the Räte Movement, Parties, and Parliament." In *Aftermaths of War: Women's Movements and Female Activists, 1918–1923*, edited by Ingrid Sharp and Matthew Stibbe, 221–243. Leiden: Brill.

——. 2012. "'Against the Mock Battle of Words'—Therese Schlesinger, née Eckstein (1863–1940), a Radical Seeker." In *Austrian Lives*, edited by Günter Bischof et al., 71–91. New Orleans: University of New Orleans Press.

——. 2013. *Frauen. Leben. Linz. Eine Frauen- und Geschlechtergeschichte im 19. und 20. Jahrhundert. Historisches Jahrbuch der Stadt Linz 2013*. Linz.

Helmut, Konrad, ed. 1984. *Neuere Studien zur Arbeitergeschichte: zum fünfundzwanzigjährigen Bestehen des Vereins für Geschichte der Arbeiterbewegung*. Vol. 1, *Beiträge zur Wirtschafts- und Sozialgeschichte*. Vienna: Europaverlag.

Hofmann-Weinberger, Helga. 2016a. "Else Beer-Angerer." *Ariadne*. Accessed 31 May 2023. http://www.fraueninbewegung.onb.ac.at/Pages/PersonDetail.aspx?p_iPersonenID=8675106.

——. 2016b. "Frauenstimmrechtskomitee (Bund österreichischer Frauenvereine)." *Ariadne*. Accessed 31 May 2023. http://www.fraueninbewegung.onb.ac.at/Pages/OrganisationenDetail.aspx?p_iOrganisationID=12235615.

——. 2016c. "Verein der Lehrerinnen und Erzieherinnen." *Ariadne*. Accessed 31 October 2023. http://www.fraueninbewegung.onb.ac.at/Pages/OrganisationenDetail.aspx?p_iOrganisationID=8675205.

——. 2016d. "Zentralverein der Postbeamtinnen." *Ariadne*. Accessed 31 May 2023. http://www.fraueninbewegung.onb.ac.at/Pages/OrganisationenDetail.aspx?p_iOrganisationID=12550639.

Horváth, J. András. 2010. *A megigényelt világváros. Budapest hatósága és lakossága a városegyesítés éveiben* [World city in demand: The authorities and the population of Budapest during the years of the city's unification]. Budapest: Budapest Főváros Levéltára [Budapest City Archives].

Jammernegg, Lydia. 2016a. "Allgemeiner österreichischer Frauenverein. Historischer Überblick." *Ariadne*. Accessed 31 May 2023. http://www.fraueninbewegung.onb.ac.at/Pages/OrganisationenDetail.aspx?p_iOrganisationID=8675071.

——. 2016b. "Gisela Urban." *Ariadne*. Accessed 31 May 2023. http://www.fraueninbewegung.onb.ac.at/Pages/PersonDetail.aspx?p_iPersonenID=8675482.

——. 2016c. "Olga Misař." *Ariadne*. Accessed 31 May 2023. http://www.fraueninbewegung.onb.ac.at/Pages/PersonDetail.aspx?p_iPersonenID=8674839.

Jank, Dagmar. 2018. "Minna Cauer." Digitales Deutsches Frauenarchiv. Accessed 31 May 2023. https://www.digitales-deutsches-frauenarchiv.de/akteurinnen/minna-cauer.

Jeszenszky, Géza. 1997. "Hungary through World War I and the End of the Dual Monarchy." In *A History of Hungary*, edited by Peter F. Sugar, Péter Hanák, and Tibor Frank, 267–194. Bloomington: Indiana University Press.

Jiří, Pešek, Oliver Rathkolb, et al. 2013. *Zeitgeschichte in Bewegung. Die österreichische Erforschung des 20. Jahrhunderts*. Prague: Karolinum.

Judson, Pieter. 1992. "Die unpolitische Bürgerin im politisierenden Verein. Zu einigen Paradoxa des bürgerlichen Weltbildes im 19. Jahrhundert." In *Durch Arbeit, Besitz, Wissen und Gerechtigkeit. Bürgertum in der Habsburgermonarchie*, edited by Ernst Bruckmüller, Hans Heiss, Hannes Stekl, and Hannes Urbanitsch, 337–345. Vienna: Böhlau.
———. 2017. *Habsburg. Geschichte eines Imperiums 1740–1918*. Munich: C.H. Beck.
Kaba, Eszter. 2008. "'... nagyjából és általánosan harcoltunk mindenért.' Munkásnőegylet a századforduló Magyarországán" ["... We fought together and in general for everything." Working Women's Association in fin-de-siècle Hungary]. *Múltunk* 2:8–18.
Kaelble, Hartmut. 2003. "Die interdisziplinären Debatten über Vergleich und Transfer." In *Komparatistik in den Sozial-, Geschichts- und Kulturwissenschaften*, edited by Hartmut Kaelble and Jürgen Schriewer, 469–493. Frankfurt: Campus.
Katus, László. 2007. "Magyarország a Habsburg birodalomban" [Hungary in the Habsburg Empire]. In *Magyarország története* [History of Hungary], edited by Ignác Romsics, 488–772. Budapest: Osiris.
Kehle, Hertha. 1952. "Hertha Kehle: Die Frauenzeitschrift. Ihre Anfänge und ihre Entwicklung in Österreich." PhD diss., Universität Wien.
Keintzel, Brigitta. 1993. "Elise Richter." In *Wir sind die ersten, die es wagen: Biographien deutschsprachiger Wissenschaftlerinnen, Forscherinnen, intellektueller Frauen*, edited by Ilse Korotin, 104–108. Vienna: Bundesministerium für Unterricht und Kunst.
Kelbert, Krisztina. 2013. "A feministák pionírjai vidéken. A Szombathelyi Nőtisztviselők Országos Egyesültének tevékenysége és szerepe a XX. század első felének magyarországi nőmozgalmában" [Feminist pioneers in the provinces: The activities and role of Nőtisztviselők Országos Egyesülete of Szombathely in the Hungarian women's movement of the first half of the 20th century]. *Századvég* 2:121–162.
Kereszty, Orsolya. 2013. "A Great Endeavour: The Creation of the Hungarian Feminist Journal *A Nő és a Társadalom* (Woman and Society) and Its Role in the Women's Movement, 1907–1913." *Aspasia* 7:92–107.
Kéri, Katalin. 2008. *Hölgyek napernyővel. Nők a dualizmus kori Magyarországon 1867–1914* [Ladies with parasols: Women in Hungary in the era of dualism, 1867–1914]. Pécs: Pro Pannonia.
Klaus, Elisabeth, and Ulla Wischermann. 2013. *Journalistinnen. Eine Geschichte in Biographien und Texten 1848–1990*. Vienna: LIT.
Klement, Judit. 2012. *Hazai vállalkozók a hőskorban. A budapesti gőzmalomipar vállalkozói a 19. század második felében* [Hungarian entrepreneurs in a heroic era: Entrepreneurs in the Budapest steam mill industry in the second half of the 19th century]. Budapest: ELTE Eötvös Kiadó.
Klingenstein, Eva. 1997. *Die Frau mit Eigenschaften. Literatur und Geschlecht in der Wiener Frauenpresse*. Vienna: Böhlau.
———. 1999. "'Die Frauen müssen ganz andere Worte hören.' Die Anfänge der engagierten Frauenpresse in Österreich und Deutschland." In *Frauen—Literatur—Geschichte. Schreibende Frauen vom Mittelalter bis zu der Gegenwart*, edited by Hiltrud Gnüg and Renate Möhrmann, 117–128. Stuttgart: J. B. Metzler.
Klösch-Melliwa, Helga. 2001. "Forschungsüberblick zur frauenrelevanten/feministischen Informationsarbeit mit Schwerpunkt Österreich." In *Kolloquia. Frauenbezonege/feministische Dokumentation und Informationsarbeit in Österreich Lehr- und Forschungsmaterialen*, edited by Frida—Verein zur Förderung und Vernetzung frauenspezifischer

Informations- und Dokumentationseinrichtungen in Österreich, 23–41. Vienna: Bundesministerium für Bildung, Wissenschaft und Kultur.

Klucsarits, Richard, and Friedrich G. Kürbisch. 1975. *Arbeiterinnen kämpfen um ihr Recht. Autobiographische Texte zum Kampf rechtloser und entrechteter "Frauenpersonen" in Deutschland, Österreich und die Schweiz des 19. und 20. Jahrhunderts*. Wuppertal: Peter Hammer Verlag.

Kókay, György, Géza Buzinkay, and Gábor Murányi. 2001. *A magyar sajtó története* [The history of the press in Hungary]. Budapest: Sajtóház.

Koncz, Katalin. 1982. *Nők a munka világában* [Women in the world of work]. Budapest: Kossuth.

Korotin, Ilse, ed. 2016. *biografiA. Lexikon österreichischer Frauen*. Band 1. Vienna: Böhlau.

———. 2016. *biografiA. Lexikon österreichischer Frauen*. Band 2. Vienna: Böhlau.

Kotsonis, Yanni. 2011. "Ordinary People in Russian and Soviet History." *Kritika, Explorations in Russian and Eurasian History* 3:739–754.

Kovács, Mária M. 1996. "Ambiguities of Emancipation: Women and the Ethnic Question in Hungary." *Women's History Review* 4:487–497.

Kövér, György. 2003. "Kulturális rétegződés és társadalmi értékrend a magyar középosztály történetében" [Cultural stratification and the social value system in the history of the Hungarian middle class]. In *Társadalom és kultúra Magyarországon a 19–20. században* [Society and culture in Hungary in the 19th–20th century], edited by József Vonyó, 35–45. Pécs: Pro Pannonia.

Krainer, Larissa. 1993. "Österreichische Frauenzeitschriften. Im Spannungsfeld zwischen kapitalorientierten Marktkräften und frauenbewegter Bewusstseinsbildung, zwischen Kommerz- und Alternativmedien." PhD diss., Universität Klagenfurt.

Lebensaft, Elisabeth. 2002. "Christine Touaillon." In *Wissenschaftlerinnen in und aus Österreich. Leben—Werk—Wirkung. Zur Geschlechtersymetrie in der österreichischen Wissenschaftsgeschichte*, edited by Ilse Korotin, 757–759. Vienna: Österreichische Nationalbibliothek.

Lehmann, Adolph. 1859–1922. *Adolph Lehmann's allgemeiner Wohnungs-Anzeiger nebst Handels- u. Gewerbe-Adressbuch für d. k.k. Reichshaupt- u. Residenzstadt Wien u. Umgebung*. Vienna: Druck und Verlag von Friedrich Förster.

Leisch-Prost, Edith. 2006. "Rosa Mayreder." In *A Biographical Dictionary of Women's Movements and Feminism: Central, Eastern, and South Eastern Europe, 19th and 20th Centuries*, edited by Francisca de Haan et al, 319–323. Budapest: CEU Press.

Litván, György. 1978. *Károlyi Mihály levelezése* [The correspondence of Mihály Károlyi]. Vol. 1, *1905–1920*. Budapest: Akadémiai.

Lóránd, Zsófia, Adele Hîncu, Jovana Mihajlović Trbovc, and Katarzyna Stańczak-Wiślicz, eds. 2024. *Texts and Contexts from the History of Feminism and Women's Rights. East Central Europe, Second Half of the Twentieth Century*. Budapest: CEU Press.

Lorence-Kot, Bogna, and Adam Winiarz. 2004. "The Polish Women's Movement to 1914." In *Women's Emancipation Movements in the Nineteenth Century: A European Perspective*, edited by Sylvia Paletschek and Bianca Pietrow-Ennker, 167–188. Stanford, CA: Stanford University Press, 206–220.

Loutfi, Anna. 2009a. "First-Wave Hungarian Women's Movement (Late Nineteenth/Early Twentieth Centuries). Bibliography and Commentary." In *Wie Frauenbewegung geschrieben wird. Historiographie, Dokumentation, Stellungnahmen, Bibliographien*, edited by Johanna Gehmacher and Natascha Vittorelli, 371–391. Vienna: Löcker.

———. 2009b. "Politics and Hegemony in the Historiography of Women's Movements (Nineteenth and Twentieth Century): A Call for New Debates." In *Wie Frauenbewegung geschrieben wird. Historiographie, Dokumentation, Stellungnahmen, Bibliographien*, edited by Johanna Gehmacher and Natascha Vittorelli, 81–101. Vienna: Löcker.

Maderthaner, Wolfgang, ed. 1986. *Arbeiterbewegung in Österreich und Ungarn bis 1914. Referats des österreich-ungarischen Historikersymposiums in Graz vom 5–9. September 1986.* Vienna: Europaverlag.

Malečková, Jitka. 2004. "The Emancipation of Women for the Benefit of the Nation: The Czech Women's Movement." In *Women's Emancipation Movements in the Nineteenth Century: A European Perspective*, edited by Sylvia Paletschek and Bianca Pietrow-Ennker, 167–188. Stanford, CA: Stanford University Press.

Malleier, Elisabeth. 2001. *Jüdische Frauen in der Wiener bürgerlichen Frauenbewegung 1890–1938*. Vienna: Manuskript–Forschungsbericht.

———. 2004. *Jüdische Frauen in Wien. 1816–1938: Wohlfahrt—Mädchenbildung—Frauenarbeit.* Vienna: Mandelbaum.

———. 2005. "Jüdische Feministinnen in der Wiener bürgerlichen Frauenbewegung von 1938." In *Geschlecht, Region und Engagement. Die jüdischen Frauenbewegungen in deutschsprachigen Raum 19. und frühes 20. Jahrhundert*, edited by Margarete Grandner and Edith Saurer, 79–102. Vienna: Böhlau.

———. 2009. "'Jeder Sieg der Frauen muss ein Sieg der Freiheit sein, oder ist es kleiner.' Jüdische Feministinnen in der Wiener bürgerlichen Frauenbewegung und internationalen Frauenbewegungsorganisationen." In *Wien und die jüdische Erfahrung. 1900–1938. Akkulturation—Antisemitismus—Zionismus*, edited by Frank Stern and Barbara Eichinger, 277–295. Vienna: Böhlau.

———. 2016. "Ernestine Fürth." *Ariadne.* Accessed 31 May 2023. http://www.fraueninbewegung.onb.ac.at/Pages/PersonDetail.aspx?p_iPersonenID=8675290.

Mayreder, Rosa, and Harriet Anderson, eds. 1988. *Tagebücher 1873–1937*. Frankfurt am Main: Insel.

Mazohl-Wallnig, Brigitte, ed. 1995. *Bürgerliche Frauenkultur im 19. Jahrhundert*. Vienna: Böhlau.

McFadden, Margaret. 2006. "A Radical Exchange: Rosika Schwimmer, Emma Goldman, Hella Wuolijoki and Red-White Struggles for Women." In *Women's Movements: Networks and Debates in Post-Communist Countries in the 19th and 20th Centuries*, edited by Edith Saurer, 494–504. Cologne: Böhlau.

Melinz, Gerhard, and Susan Zimmermann. 1996a. "Die aktive Stadt. Kommunale Politik zur Gestaltung städtischer Lebensbedingungen in Budapest, Prag und Wien (1867–1914)." In *Wien–Prag–Budapest. Urbanisierung, Kommunalpolitik, gesellschaftliche Konflikte (1867–1918)*, edited by Gerhard Melinz and Susan Zimmermann, 140–176. Vienna: Promedia.

———. 1996b. "Großstadtgeschichte und Modernisierung in der Habsburgermonarchie." In *Wien–Prag–Budapest. Urbanisierung, Kommunalpolitik, gesellschaftliche Konflikte (1867–1918)*, edited by Gerhard Melinz and Susan Zimmermann, 15–34. Vienna: Promedia.

Mixa, Franz. 1969. "Die ersten Wiener Frauenzeitschriften des 18. Jahrhunderts als Zeitdokumente." PhD diss., Universität Wien.

Morawetz, Martina. 2006. "Der Beginn der Frauenpresse in Slowenien zur Zeit der Habsburger Monarchie." In *Frauenbilder, feministische Praxis und nationales*

Bewußtsein in Österreich-Ungarn 1867–1918, edited by Waltraud Heindl, Edit Király, and Alexandra Millner, 219–239. Basel: Francke.

Mucsi, Ferenc. 1980. "Weibliche Industriearbeit und sozialistische Frauen-Arbeiterbewegung in Ungarn vor dem Ersten Weltkrieg." In *Die Frau in der Arbeiterbewegung 1900–1939*, edited by Gerhard Botz, 333–342. Vienna: Europaverlag.

Nagl-Docekal, Herta. 1990. "Feministische Geschichtswissenschaft—ein unverzichtbares Projekt." *L'Homme* 1:7–18.

Niederkofler, Heidi. 2011. "Es war einmal... Gründungsgeschichten des (Internationalen) Frauentags." In *Frauentag! Erfindung und Karriere einer Tradition. Begleitbuch zur Ausstellung "Feste.Kämpfe. 100 Jahre Frauentag," veranstaltet vom Kreisky-Archiv, vom Johanna-Dohnal-Archiv und vom Österreichischen Museum für Volkskunde vom 4. März bis 30. Juni 2011 im Österreichischen Museum für Volkskunde, Wien*, edited by Heidi Niederkofler, 17–36. Vienna: Löcker.

Niggemann, Heinz. 1981. *Emanzipation zwischen Sozialismus und Feminismus. Die sozialdemokratische Frauenbewegung im Kaiserreich*. Wuppertal: Peter Hammer.

Oesch, Corinna. 2008. "Yella Hertzka (1873–1948): Eine Auto/Biographie von Beziehungen." *Österreichische Zeitschrift für Geschichtswissenschaften* 2:118–144.

———. 2012. "Yella Hertzka (1873–1948): Transnationale Handlungsräume und Vernetzungen." In *Update! Perspektiven der Zeitgeschichte: Zeitgeschichtetage 2010*, edited by Linda Erker et al., 509–514. Vienna: Studien.

———. 2014. *Yella Hertzka (1873–1948): Vernetzungen und Handlungsräume in der österreichischen und internationalen Frauenbewegung*. Innsbruck: Studien.

Offen, Karen. 2000. *European Feminisms: A History, 1700–1950*. Stanford, CA: Stanford University Press.

———. 2001. "Umstände, Unwägbarkeiten: Feministinnen der zwanziger Jahre zwischen Krieg, Revolution und neuem Wissensstreit." In *Feminismus und Demokratie: europäische Frauenbewegungen der 1920er Jahre*, edited by Ute Gerhad, 210–235. Königstein: Helmer.

Paletschek, Sylvia, and Bianca Pietrow-Ennker. 2004. "Women's Emancipation Movements in Europe in the Long Nineteenth Century: Conclusions." In *Women's Emancipation Movements in the Nineteenth Century: A European Perspective*, edited by Sylvia Paletschek and Bianca Pietrow-Ennker, 301–331. Stanford, CA: Stanford University Press.

Papp, Claudia. 2004. *Die Kraft der weiblichen Seele: Feminismus in Ungarn, 1918–1941*. Münster: LIT.

Papp, Claudia, and Susan Zimmermann. 2006. "Meller, Mrs Artur, Eugénia Miskolczy." In *A Biographical Dictionary of Women's Movements and Feminism: Central, Eastern, and South Eastern Europe, 19th and 20th Centuries*, edited by Francisca de Haan et al., 331–335. Budapest: CEU Press.

Pastor, Peter. 1975. "The Diplomatic Fiasco of the Modern World's First Woman Ambassador, Rosa Bedy-Schwimmer." *East European Quarterly* 3:273–282.

Pedersen, Susan. 2004. "Comparative History and Women's History: Explaining Convergence and Divergence." In *Comparison and History: Europe in Cross-National Perspective*, edited by Deborah Cohen and Maura O'Connor, 85–102. New York: Routledge.

Pető, Andrea, and Judit Szapor. 2004. "A női esélyegyenlőségre vonatkozó női felfogás hatása a magyar választójogi gondolkodásra 1848–1990. Az 'állam érdekében adományozott jog' feminista megközelítésben" [The effect of women's concept of equal rights for women on Hungarian electoral thought, 1848–1990: A feminist perspective on "rights given in the interests of the state"]. In *Recepció és kreativitás. Nyitott magyar kultúra. Befogadás és eredetiség a jogban és jogtudományban* [Reception and creativity: Open Hungarian culture; Acceptance and originality in law and jurisprudence], *Recepció és kreativitás*, series edited by Gábor Palló, 136–174. Budapest: Áron.

———. 2007. "The State of Women's and Gender History in Eastern Europe: The Case of Hungary." *Journal of Women's History* 19 (1): 160–166.

Pichler, Heinz Stefan. 1914. *Frauen im Ersten Weltkrieg. Ausstellungskatalog*. Klagenfurt: Kammer für Arbeiter und Angestellte in Kärnten.

Prost, Edith. 1986. "Weiblichkeit und Bürgertum." *Mitteilungen des Instituts für Wissenschaft und Kunst* 46 (1): 2–6.

———, ed. 1989. *"Die Partei hat mich nie enttäuscht..." Österreichische Sozialdemokratinnen.* Unter Mitarbeit von Brigitta Wiesinger. Vienna: Verlag für Gesellschaftskritik.

Raggam-Blesch, Michaela. 2005. "Frauen zwischen den Fronten. Jüdinnen in feministischen und philanthropischen Bewegungen in Wien an der Wende des 19. zum 20. Jahrhundert." In *Geschlecht, Region und Engagement. Die jüdischen Frauenbewegungen in deutschsprachigen Raum 19. und frühes 20. Jahrhundert*, edited by Margarete Grandner and Edith Saurer, 25–55. Vienna: Böhlau.

———. 2012. "A Pioneer in Academia: Elise Richter." In *Jewish Intellectual Women in Central Europe, 1860–2000: Twelve Biographical Essays*, edited by Judith Szapor et al., 93–128. New York: Edwin Mellen.

Relph, Anne Kimbell. 1979. "The World Center for Women's Archives, 1935–1940." *Signs* 4:597–603.

Rumpler, Helmut. 1997. *Österreichische Geschichte 1904–1914. Eine Chance für Mitteleuropa. Bürgerliche Emanzipation und Staatsvervall in der Habsburgermonarchie*. Vienna: Ueberreuter.

Rumpler, Helmut, and Anatol Schmied Kowarzik. 2010. *Die Habsburgermonarchie 1848–1918.* Vol. 11, 2. Teilband. *Weltkriegsstatistik, Österreich-Ungarn 1914–1918*. Vienna: Verlag der Österreichischen Akademie der Wissenschaften.

Rumpler, Helmut, and Martin Seger. 2010. *Die Habsburgermonarchie 1848–1918*. Vol. 9, 2. Teilband. *Die Gesellschaft der Habsburgermonarchie*. Vienna: Verlag der Österreichischen Akademie der Wissenschaften.

Rupp, Leila J. 1994. "Constructing Internationalism: The Case of Transnational Women's Organizations, 1888–1945." *American Historical Review* 99 (5): 1571–1600.

———. 2010. "Constructing Internationalism: The Case of Transnational Women's Organizations, 1888–1945." In *Globalizing Feminisms, 1789–1945*, edited by Karen Offen, 139–152. London: Routledge.

Rupp, Leila J. 1997. *Worlds of Women: The Making of an International Women's Movement*. Princeton, NJ: Princeton University Press.

Sághy, Marianne. 1994. "A nők városa" [City of women]. *Café Bábel* 4 (11–12): 109–118.

Saurer, Edith. 1995. *Die Religion der Geschlechter. Historische Aspekte religiöser Mentalitäten*. L'Homme Schriften 1. Vienna: Böhlau.

———. 2006. *Women's Movements: Networks and Debates in Post-Communist Countries in the 19th and 20th Centuries*. Vienna: Böhlau.

Schernthaner, Maria. 1985. "Die katholische Frauenbewegung in Wien 1848–1914." PhD diss., Universität Wien.

Schmölzer, Hilde. 2002. *Rosa Mayreder: ein Leben zwischen Utopie und Wirklichkeit*. Vienna: Promedia.

———. 2009. *Frauenliebe: Berühmte weibliche Liebespaare der Geschichte*. Vienna: Promedia.
Schwartz, Agatha. 2008. *Shifting Voices: Feminist Thought and Women's Writing in Finde-Siècle Austria and Hungary*. Ottawa: University of Ottawa Press.
———. 1992. "Women's History." In *New Perspectives on Historical Writing*, 2nd ed., edited by Peter Burke, 42–66. Oxford: Polity.
Schraut, Sylvia. 2013. *Bürgerinnen im Kaiserreich: Biografie eines Lebensstils*. Stuttgart: Kohlhammer.
Simonton, Deborah. 2006. *The Routledge History of Women in Europe*. New York: Routledge.
Sipos, Balázs. 2018. "Összegabalyodott nőtörténet. Nemzeti és transznacionális nőtípusok találkozása az első világháború utáni Magyarországon" [The tangled web of women's history: A meeting of national and transnational types of women in Hungary after World War I]. In *Homoklapátolás Nemesércért. A 70 éves Standeisky Éva tiszteletére* [Shoveling sand for rare ore: In honor of Éva Standeisky at 70], edited by Eszter Balázs, Gábor Koltai, and Takács Róbert, 192–202. Budapest: Napvilág.
Solinger, Rickie. 2019. *Pregnancy and Power: A History of Reproductive Politics in the United States*. New York: New York University Press.
Sparholz, Irmgard. 1986. "Marie Lang und ihre Bedeutung für Sozialreformen in Österreich im Ausgehenden Neunzehnten Jahrhundert." Master's thesis, Vienna.
Stegmann, Natali. 2000. *Die Töchter der geschlagenen Helden "Frauenfrage," Feminismus und Frauenbewegung in Polen 1863–1919*. Wiesbaden: Harrassowitz.
———. 2006. "Der Platz polnischer Feministinnen im galizischen Machtgefüge der 1890-er Jahre bis 1914." In *Frauenbilder, feministische Praxis und nationales Bewußtsein in Österreich-Ungarn 1867–1918*, edited by Waltraud Heindl, Edit Király, and Alexandra Millner, 241–255. Basel: Francke.
Steinkellner, Friedrich. 1985. "Emanzipatorische Tendenzen im christlichen Wiener Frauenbund und in der Katholischen Reichsfrauenorganisation Österreichs." In *Unterdrückung und Emanzipation: Festschrift für Erika Weinzierl; zum 60. Geburtstag*, edited by Rudolf G. Ardelt, 55–68. Vienna: Geyer-Ed.
Szapor, Judith. 2004. "Sisters of Foes: The Shifting Front Lines of the Hungarian Women's Movement." In *Women's Emancipation Movements in the Nineteenth Century: A European Perspective*, edited by Sylvia Paletschek and Bianca Pietrow-Ennker, 189–205. Stanford, CA: Stanford University Press.
———. 2005. *The Hungarian Pocahontas: The Life and Times of Laura Polanyi Stricker, 1882–1957*. Boulder, CO: East European Monographs.
———. 2006. "Feministák és 'radikális asszonyok': Női politikusok az 1918-as demokratikus forradalomban" [Feminists and "radical women": Female politicians in the democratic revolution of 1918]. In *Nők a modernizálódó magyar társadalomban* [Women in modernizing Hungarian society], edited by Gábor Gyáni and Beáta Nagy, 254–277. Debrecen: Csokonai.
———. 2007. "A magánszférából a politikai közéletbe: a női politizálás története Magyarországon a kezdetektől 1945-ig" [From the Private to the Public Sphere: Women in the History of Women's Politics in Hungary from the Beginning to 1945]. In *A nő és a politikum. A nők politikai szerepvállalása Magyarországon* [Women and Politics. Women in Politics in Hungary], 129–144. Budapest: Napvilág.
———. 2011. "Who Represents Hungarian Women? The Demise of the Liberal Bourgeois Women's Rights Movement and the Rise of the Rightwing Women's Movement in the

Aftermath of World War I." In *Aftermaths of War: Women's Movements and Female Activists, 1918–1923*, edited by Ingrid Sharp and Matthew Stibbe, 245–267. Leiden: Brill.

———. 2017. "'Good Hungarian Women' vs. 'Radicals, Feminists, and Jewish Intellectuals': Rosika Schwimmer and the Hungarian Women's Debating Club in 1918–1919." In "Agency, Activism and Organization," special issue, *Women's History Review* 6:1–19.

———. 2018. *Hungarian Women's Activism in the Wake of the First World War: From Rights to Revanche*. London: Bloomsbury Academic.

Szapor, Judith, Andrea Pető, Maura Hametz, and Marina Calloni. 2012. *Jewish Intellectual Women in Central Europe, 1860–2000: Twelve Biographical Essays*. New York: Edwin Mellen.

Szegvári, Katalin N. 1969. *A nők művelődési jogaiért folytatott harc hazánkban, 1777–1918* [The battle in Hungary for women's educational rights, 1777–1918]. Budapest: Közgazdasági és Jogi Könyvkiadó.

———. 1981. *Út a női egyenjogúsághoz* [The road to equal rights for women]. Budapest: Magyar Nők Országos Tanácsa/Kossuth.

———. 2001. *A női választójog külföldön és hazánkban* [Female suffrage in Hungary and abroad]. Budapest: HVG-ORAC.

Szilvay, Gergely. 2018. "A tízmillió gendertudós országában élünk—Pető Andrea a gendervitákról" [We live in a country of ten million gender experts—Andrea Pető on the gender debates]. Mandiner, 10 September 2018. https://mandiner.hu/cikk/20180910_peto_andrea_interju.

Tanzer, Ulrike. 2013. "Feminism and Pacifism: Rosa Mayreder's Writing against War." In *Culture at War: Austria-Hungary, 1914–1918*, edited by Florian Krobb, 46–61. Cambridge: Modern Humanities Research Association.

Tichy, Marina. 1989. "'Ich hatte immer Angst, unwissend zu sterben'—Therese Schlesinger, Bürgerin und Sozialistin." In *"Die Partei hat mich nie enttäuscht . . .": österreichische Sozialdemokratinnen*, edited by Edith Leisch-Prost, 133–184. Vienna: Verlag für Gesellschaftskritik.

Tino, Erben, ed. 1984. *Die Frau im Korsett: Wiener Frauenalltag zwischen Klischee und Wirklichkeit 1848–1920. Sonderausstellung des Historischen Museums der Stadt Wien*. Vienna: Museum der Stadt Wien.

Tóth, Árpád. 2005. *Önszervező polgárok. A pesti egyesületek társadalomtörténete a reformkorban* [Citizens organizing themselves: The social history of Budapest associations during the reform era]. Budapest: L'Harmattan.

Truger, Marion. 1986. "Das Frauenbild um 1900 in den Frauenzeitschriften." Master's thesis, Universität Wien.

Tutavac, Vesela, and Ilse Korotin, eds. 2016. *"Wir wollen der Gerechtigkeit und Menschenliebe dienen . . .": Frauenbildung und Emanzipation in der Habsburgermonarchie—der südslawische Raum und seine Wechselwirkung mit Wien, Prag und Budapest*. Wien: Praesens.

Unger, Petra. 2009. *Mut zur Freiheit: faszinierende Frauen—bewegte Leben*. Vienna: Metroverlag.

———. 2012. "'Sie wollen das Leben . . . !': Skizze zur Ersten Frauenbewegung in Österreich." In *Frauen-Fragen. 100 Jahre Bewegung. Reflexion, Vision*, edited by Birge Krondorfer and Hilde Grammel, 18–30. Vienna: Promedia.

Vavra, Elisabeth. 1998. *Aufmüpfig und angepasst. Frauenleben in Österreich; Niederösterreichische Landesausstellung '98*. Vienna: Böhlau.

Viethen, Eva. 1984. "Wiener Arbeiterinnen: Leben zwischen Familie, Lohnarbeit und politischem Engagement." Vols. 1–5. PhD diss., Universität Wien.

Vittorelli, Natascha. 2007. *Frauenbewegung um 1900: über Triest nach Zagreb*. Vienna: Löcker.

———. 2009a. "Kommentierte Bibliographie zu Frauenbewegungen in der habsburgischen Verwaltungseinheit Galizien." In *Wie Frauenbewegung geschrieben wird. Historiographie, Dokumentation, Stellungnahmen, Bibliographien*, edited by Johanna Gehmacher and Natascha Vittorelli, 411–428. Vienna: Löcker.

———. 2009b. "Kommentierte Bibliographie zu südslawischen Frauenbewegungen." In *Wie Frauenbewegung geschrieben wird. Historiographie, Dokumentation, Stellungnahmen, Bibliographien*, edited by Johanna Gehmacher and Natascha Vittorelli, 429–443. Vienna: Löcker.

———. 2009c. "Kommentierte Bibliographie zu vornehmlich tschechisch definierten Frauenbewegungen in Böhmen und Mähren." In *Wie Frauenbewegung geschrieben wird. Historiographie, Dokumentation, Stellungnahmen, Bibliographien*, edited by Johanna Gehmacher and Natascha Vittorelli, 393–410. Vienna: Löcker.

———. 2009d. "Wie Frauenbewegung geschrieben wird." In *Wie Frauenbewegung geschrieben wird. Historiographie, Dokumentation, Stellungnahmen, Bibliographien*, edited by Johanna Gehmacher and Natascha Vittorelli, 103–133. Vienna: Löcker.

Vodopivec, Peter. 1996. "Wie die Frauen im slowenischen Raum im 19. Jahrhundert am öffentlichen Leben teilnahmen." In *Von Bürgern und Ihre Frauen*, edited by Margaret Friedrich and Peter Urbanitsch, 141–164. Wien–Köln–Weimar: Böhlau.

Vosahlíková, Pavla. 2006. "Die Beziehung der tschechischen Feministinnen zur Nationalbewegung unter Kaiser Franz Joseph I." In *Frauenbilder, feministische Praxis und nationales Bewußtsein in Österreich-Ungarn 1867–1918*, edited by Waltraud Heindl, Edit Király, and Alexandra Millner, 209–218. Basel: Francke.

Wandruszka, Adam, and Helmut Rumpler, eds. 2006. *Die Habsburgermonarchie 1848–1918*. Vol. 8, *Politische Öffentlichkeit und Zivilgesellschaft, Teilband 1.: Vereine, Parteien und Interessenverbände als Träger der politischen Partizipation*. Vienna: Verlag der Österreichischer Akademie der Wissenschaften.

Weckert, Anja, and Ulla Wischermann. 2006. *Das Jahrhundert Feminismus. Streifzüge durch nationale und internationale Bewegungen und Theorien*. Frankfurt am Main: Ulrike Helmer.

Weiland, Daniela. 1983. *Geschichte der Frauenemanzipation in Deutschland und Österreich: Biographien, Programme, Organisationen*. Düsseldorf: Econ.

Weiser, Ilse. 2004. "Christine Touaillon—Pionierin in der Literaturwissenschaft." In *Women! Würdigung der Grazer FrauenStadtGeschichte; Dokumentation und Lesebuch*, edited by Bettina Behr and Ilse Weisner, 118–121. Innsbruck: Studien.

Werner, Michael-Zimmermann. 2006. "Beyond Comparison: Histoire Croisée and the Challenge of Reflexivity." *History and Theory* 45 (1): 30–50.

Wernitznig, Dagmar. 2015. *"It Is a Strange Thing Not to Belong to Any Country, as Is My Case Now": Fascism, Refugees, Statelessness, and Rosika Schwimmer (1877–1948)*. Venice: Rivista DEP: Deportate, Esuli, Profughe.

———. 2017a. "Between Front Lines: The Militant Pacifist Rosika Schwimmer (1877–1948) and Her Total Peace Effort." In *Reconsidering Peace and Patriotism during the First World War*, edited by Justin Quinn Olmstead, 91–114. New York: Palgrave Macmillan.

———. 2017b. "Out of Her Time? Rosika Schwimmer's Transnational Activism after the First World War." *Women's History Review* 2:262–279.

"Wer wählt, gewinnt." 1989. In *Ausstellung fand vom 16. Februar 1989 bis 16. März 1989 im WuK*, edited by Monika Bernold. Vienna: Initiative 70 Jahre Frauenwahlrecht.

Winklbauer, Andrea, and Sabine Fellner. 2016. *Die bessere Hälfte: jüdische Künstlerinnen bis 1938.* Vienna: Ausstellungskatalog, Jüdisches Museum.

Wischermann, Ulla, and Ute Gerhard. 1988. "Liberalismus—Sozialismus—Feminismus. Zeitschriften der Frauenbewegung um die Jahrhundertwende." In *Deutsche Literatur von Frauen,* edited by Gisela Brinkler-Gabler, 268–284. Munich: Beck.

Witzmann, Reingard. 1989. "Frauenbewegung und Gesellschaft in Wien um die Jahrhundertwende." In *Aufbruch in das Jahrhundert der Frau? Rosa Mayreder und der Feminismus in Wien um 1900. Sonderausstellung des Historischen Museums der Stadt Wien,* edited by Reingard Witzmann, 10–19. Vienna: Museum der Stadt Wien.

Wöhrer, Veronika. 2007. "Bericht: Frauenbewegung vernetzt." Historiographie und Dokumentation. Salon 21, 20 April 2007. http://www.univie.ac.at/Geschichte/salon21/?p=160.

Wolff, Kerstin. 2017. "Eine eigene Geschichte schreiben—Frauenbewegungszeitschrifte als vergessene Orte einer frühen Frauengeschichte." *Feministische Studien* 1:128–137.

Zhurzhenko, Tatiana. 2006. "Ukrainian Women in Galicia: Origins of the Feminist Tradition and the Challenges of Nationalism." In *Frauenbilder, feministische Praxis und nationales Bewußtsein in Österreich-Ungarn 1867–1918,* edited by Waltraud Heindl, Edit Király, and Alexandra Millner, 257–269. Basel: Francke.

Zimmermann, Susan. 1996a. "Hogyan lettek feministák? Gárdos Mariska és Schwimmer Rózsika a századfordulto Magyarországán" [How did they become feminists? Mariska Gárdos and Rosika Schwimmer in fin-de-siècle Hungary]. *Eszmélet* 8 (32): 57–92.

———. 1996b. "Making a Living from Disgrace: The Politics of Prostitution, Female Poverty and Urban Gender Codes in Budapest and Vienna, 1860–1920." In *CEU History Department Yearbook, 1994/95,* edited by Andrea Pető, 67–92. Budapest: Central European University.

———. 1997a. "Frauenarbeit, soziale Politiken und Umgestaltung von Geschlechterverhältnissen im Wien der Habsburgermonarchie." In *Die Frauen der Wiener Moderne,* edited by Lisa Fischer and Emil Brix, 34–52. Munich: Verlag für Geschichte und Politik.

———. 1997b. "Frauenbestrebungen und Frauenbewegungen in Ungarn." In *Szerep és alkotás. Női szerepek a társadalomban és az alkotóművészetben* [Role and Creativity. Female Roles in Society and Art], edited by Nagy Beáta and S. Sárdi Margit, 171–204. Debrecen: Csokonai.

———. 1997c. "Wie sie Feministinnen wurden. Wege in die Frauenbewegung in Zentraleuropa der Jahrhundertwende." *L'Homme* 2:272–306.

———. 1999a. "A magyar nőmozgalom és a 'szexuális kérdés' a XX. század elején" [The Hungarian women's movement and the "sexual question" in the early 20th century]. *Eszmélet* 11 (42): 49–66.

———. 1999b. *Die bessere Hälfte? Frauenbewegungen und Frauenbestrebungen im Ungarn der Habsburgermonarchie 1848 bis 1918.* Vienna: Promedia.

———. 2002. "Women's and Gender Studies in Global-Local Perspective: Developing the Frame." In *Societies in Transition—Challenges to Women's and Gender Studies,* edited by Heike Fleßner and Lydia Potts, 61–79. Opladen: Leske + Budrich.

———. 2003. "Jenseits von Ost und West. Entwicklungswege zentral-osteuropäischer Frauenbewegungen in transnationalen Kontext." In *Brüche, Geschlecht, Gesellschaft. Gender Studies zwischen Ost und West,* edited by Alice Pechriggl and Marlen Bidwell-Steiner, 119–147. Vienna: Bundesministerium für Bildung, Wissenschaft und Kultur.

———. 2005. "The Challenge of Multinational Empire for the International Women's Movement: The Habsburg Monarchy and the Development of Feminist Inter/National Politics." *Journal of Women's History* 2:87–117.

---. 2006a. "Frauenbewegungen und Frauenbestrebungen im Königreich Ungarn." In *Die Habsburgermonarchie 1848–1918*, vol. 8, *Politische Öffentlichkeit und Zivilgesellschaft*, Teilband 1.: *Vereine, Parteien und Interessenverbände als Träger der politischen Partizipation*, edited by Adam Wandruszka and Helmut Rumpler, 1359–1491. Vienna: Verlag der Österreichischen Akademie der Wissenschaften.

---. 2006b. "Reich, Nation und Internationalismus. Kooperation und Konflikte der Frauenbewegungen der Habsburger Monarchie im Spannungsfeld internationaler Organisation und Politik." In Frauenbilder, feministische Praxis und nationales Bewußtsein in Österreich-Ungarn 1867–1918, edited by Waltraud Heindl, Edit Király, and Alexan dra Millner, 119–167. Basel: Francke.

---. 2006c. "Vilma Glücklich." In *A Biographical Dictionary of Women's Movements and Feminism: Central, Eastern, and South Eastern Europe, 19th and 20th Centuries*, edited by Francisca de Haan et al., 162–166. Budapest: CEU Press.

---. 2009. "Auf dem Weg zu einer Geschichte der vielen Geschichten der Frauen—Aktivismus weltweit." In *Wie Frauenbewegung geschrieben wird: Historiographie, Dokumentation, Stellungnahmen, Bibliographien*, edited by Johanna Gehmacher and Natascha Vittorelli, 226–229. Vienna: Löcker.

---. 2011. *Divide, Provide, and Rule: An Integrative History of Poverty Policy, Social Reform, and Social Policy in Hungary under the Habsburg Monarchy*. Budapest: Central European University Press.

Zimmermann, Susan, and Borbála Major. 2006. "Róza Schwimmer." In *A Biographical Dictionary of Women's Movements and Feminism: Central, Eastern, and South Eastern Europe, 19th and 20th Centuries*, edited by Francisca de Haan et al., 484–491. Budapest: CEU Press.

Zimmermann, Susan, and Piroska Nagy. 2018. "Female Agrarian Workers in Early Twentieth-Century Hungary." *Aspasia* 1:121–133.

Zinsser, Judith P., and Bonnie S. Anderson. 2005. "Women in Early and Modern Europe: A Transnational Approach." In *Women's History in Global Perspective*, edited by Bonnie G. Smith, vol. 3, 111–145. Urbana: University of Illinois Press.

Index

A Nő és a Társadalom, ix, xi, 6, 11, 52, 56, 113, 118–120, 127, 136, 146, 151, 153–154, 161, 164, 170, 172, 191, 201–202, 233n156, 235n179
A Nő. Feminista Folyóirat, ix, xii, 7, 107, 120–121, 123, 127, 129, 136–137, 140, 151–152–153, 161, 164, 173–176, 178, 180, 185, 191, 196, 201, 202, 233n156, 236n206, 239n255, 243n18
Acsády, Judit, 18–19, 114, 138, 156, 160, 164, 234n166
activism, xii, 2–5, 12–13, 15–18, 23, 25, 44–46, 51–52, 58, 61–63, 88, 90, 94, 97–98, 107, 115, 155–158, 160, 162, 174, 181–182, 186, 199–204, 206n21,
Adler, Emma, 207n2
Adler, Viktor, 35, 51, 53, 64, 215n79
Ady, Endre, 123
Ágoston, Mrs. Peter, 160
Allgemeiner deutscher Frauenverein, ix, 7, 43, 76, 104–105, 193, 217n13,
Allgemeiner österreichischer Frauenverein, ix, xi–xii, 3, 5–14, 16, 19, 23, 24–26, 37, 40–41, 43, 45–46, 49, 50–53, 55, 61–66, 68–111, 120, 123, 128–131, 136, 138, 140, 142, 151–152, 154, 170–171, 174, 176, 178–179, 185, 189–197, 199–204, 205n6, 205n14, 216n8, 218n51, 219n74, 219n85, 202n107, 222n150, 223n179, 225n261, 226n266, 226n291, 227n1
Alsergrund, 79, 92
Anderson, Bonnie S., 208n40
Anderson, Harriet, 11, 25, 40, 43, 45, 49, 62, 64, 89, 94, 102,
Andrássy, Gyula, 29–30
Andrássy, Ilona (Mrs Batthyány, Lajos), 126
antisemitism, 94, 219n74
Arbeiterinnen-Bildungsverein, 50–51, 84, 92, 190, 217n17
Arbeiterinnen-Zeitung, 51, 229n38
Ariadne, Frauen in Bewegung, 1848–1938 21, 107

Auernig, Karola, 24, 26
Augspurg, Anita, 99, 105, 170, 224n216, 237n233
Auguste Fickert Stiftung, 104, 243n5
Auschwitz, 116, 187
Austrian Women's Day, 42, 55, 63– 65, 78
Austro-Hungarian Compromise, xi, 28–32, 34, 36, 38, 40–41, 46–47, 59, 71,
auxiliary/branch associations/organizations, 13–14, 37, 54, 61, 58, 90, 98, 104, 115, 127, 155–165, 185,

Babare, Adél, 234
Bader-Zaar, Birgitta, 23–24, 45, 62, 108, 165, 225n262
Bahr, Hermann, 239n250
Balmazújváros, 9, 158, 160–162, 176, 193
Balmazújvárosi Szabad Nőszervezet, 9, 154, 160, 193
Banat, 22, 59
Bandhauer-Schöffmann, Irene, 22, 44
Bárczy, István, xi, 1, 50, 130–131, 195, 203
Baumann, Ida, 7, 66–69, 71–73, 84, 95, 217n17
Bäumer, Gertrud, 100
Beamtinnen-Sektion, 82, 90, 205n6,
Bebel, August, 64, 190
Bédy, Béla, 120
Beer-Angerer, Elsa, 103–104, 106
Békássy, Flóra, 140
Békássy, Mrs. Elemér, 141
Berlin, xi, 1, 6–7, 30, 43, 48, 63, 86–87, 99–100, 167, 169, 211n56, 238n247, 240n286
Bern, 105, 122, 184, 242n316
Besenyő, Béla, 151
Biró, Gizella (née Kaiser), 112
Bjørnson, Bjørnsterne, 69, 100
Black Friday (stock exchange panic of 1873), 34
Blumgrund, Janka, 151
Bock, Gisela, 48, 214n55

267

Bódy, Zsombor, 150
Bordás, Sára (née Rokon Tóth), 161
Bosnyák, Zoltán, 239n259
bourgeois-liberal, 1–5, 10, 17, 19, 24–26, 29, 36–37, 40, 45, 48, 51, 53, 55–56, 63, 65, 69, 85, 94, 195–196, 199, 201, 203–204
Braun, Lily, 73, 224n234
Braun-Prager, Käthe, 26, 212n14
British Women's Social and Political Union (WSPU), 8, 205n10
Brno, 39, 49–50, 58, 215n97
Broch, Hermann, 27
Brodsky, Nadja, 103
Brüll, Alfréd, 133
Budapest, xi, 1–6, 8, 12, 18, 23, 26–27, 29, 34, 36, 38–42, 44, 46–48, 50, 52–53, 55, 58–59, 77, 98, 101, 111–112, 114–118, 120, 126, 129–134, 136, 138, *139*, 140–142, 146, 148–149, 151, 153–155, 157, 159, 161, *162*, 163–165, *169*, 170, *171*, 173–178, 181, 183–185, 187–188, 190–191, 193–195, 200–203, 210n2, 211n55, 211n57, 232n110, 234n164, 238n247, 240n286
Bukovina, 2
Bund deutscher Frauenvereine, x, 100, 116
Bund österreichischer Frauenvereine, ix, xi, 2, 13, 19, 25, 44–45, 49, 55, 70, 77, 81–82, 91, 94, 98–99, 101, 103–106, 109, 126, 167, 170–171, 189–190, 195–196, 209n56, 224n237, 225n262, 226n285
Buschmann, Hedwig, 238n250

Carlier, Julie, 14–15
Cauer, Minna, 86–87, 99–100
census, 32, 35, 150, 210n28; property census, 30; education census, 30; tax census, 51
Central Allies, 106
Central European University (CEU), 18, 23, 26
centralized household, 97, 135–136, 193
changes of regime / regime change, 2, 4, 17, 199
Chaplin, Charlie, 123
Chapman Catt, Carrie, 115, 123, 157, 164, 169, 173, 238n238, 238n247, 238n250, 239n251
Charles IV/I, 28, 31
Chicago, 41, 122, 169

Christian Social women's movement, 4, 12, 36, 41–42, 49, 53–56, 70, 94, 98, 102, 104–105, 116, 190, 201, 204, 212n9, 226n273, 229n37
Churchill, Winston, 123
Clark, Linda L., 44
comparative and transfer studies, 5, 15, 199–201
comparative history, 15
connected or shared history, 15
Corbett, Cicely, 160, 164, 173, 238n250, 239n251
Cowman, Krista, 22
Crişana, 59
Croatia, 2, 31, 60, 108, 155
cross national history, 15
Czech Lands, 19, 22, 76, 98, *168*, 172
Czech Republic, 2, 58
Czech women's movements, 57–58
Czechoslovak, 58

Das Recht der Frau, 86
Deák, Ferenc, 29
Dénes, Zsófia, 153
Der Bund, 91, 105, 109
Deutscher Verband für Frauenstimmrecht, 99
Die Frau, 80, 100, 171
Die Frau mit Eigenschaften, 23
Die Frauenbewegung, 80, 86
Die Habsburgermonarchie, 1848–1918, 24
Die Waffen nieder, 103, 196
Dirner, Gusztáv, 153–154, 243n5
Dirnfeld, Janka, 119, *121*, 122, 153–154, 188
Döbling, 93
Dresden, 64, 98, 100
Dulemba, Marie von, 97,
Duncan, Isadora, 169

Egyesület, Mária Dorothea, 179
Egyetemet és Főiskolát Végzett Nők Egyesülete, 185
Eine eigene Geschichte: Frauen in Europa, 209n40
Einküchenhaus, 73
Einstein, Albert, 39, 123

Engel, Berta, 160
enrollment fee, 75–77, 83, 129–131, 139–140
entangled history / histoire croisée / Verflechtungsgeschichte, 14–16
entente, 30, 184
envoy, xii, 11, 117, 122, 184
Enzersdorf, Maria, 7, 73
Eötvös, József, 38,
Eötvös, Loránd, 39
Erster Wiener demokratischer Frauenverein, ix, 43, 75
Erzsébetváros, 148
ethnic groups / minorities, 31, 38, 56–57
ethnic women's associations/organizations, 12, 206n17
European Parliament's Committee on Women's Rights and Gender Equality, 198
expansion of IWSA, 168

Favoriten, 92–93, 109
Fehér, Jolán, 184
Fellner, Karoline, 66
female/women office workers, 3, 55, 105, 112–113, 115, 126, 139–140, 150–151, 154–158, 163, 172, 175, 177, 179, 184–185, 189–190, 240n286,
female/women's labor/work, 25, 53, 154, 187, 201
female/women's suffrage, 8, 21, 25, 43, 51–52, 60, 105, 108, 127, 146, 157, 179, 182–185, 187, 189, 197, 205n10, 205n11, 215n79, 226n276, 234n172
feminism, 3–5, 13–14, 16, 21–23, 26, 48–49, 56, 94, 159, 198, 208n36
Feminismus, 48
feminist, 1–5, 7–9, 12–13, 15, 17–19, 21, 24–25, 48, 50–51, 53, 56–57, 60, 100, 110–111, 118, 125, 128, 137, 138, 156–161, 164–165, 170, 174, 184–185, 196, 199–204, 208n36, 214n55, 227n1, 229n37, 235n185
Feminista Értesítő, xi, 135
Feministák Egyesülete, xi, xi–xii, 1–16, 41–43, 47–51, 56–58, 111–116, 118–148, 151–158, 160–162, 164–167, 169–176, 178–179, 180–197, 199–201, 203–204, 228n31, 230n56, 231n79, 231n88, 232n107, 232n110, 233n154,
234n156, 234n160, 234n164, 234n166, 234n172, 235n195, 236n206, 237n236, 238n247, 238n250, 240n286, 241n295, 241n300, 241n306, 242n327, 242n330, 243n5, 243n8
Ferencváros, 1
Feszty, Árpád, 153
Fick, Otto, 238n250
Fickert, Auguste, xi, 7, 9–11, 19, 20, 25–26, 45–46, 49–51, 61–66, 67, 68–89, 93–95, 96, 97–101, 103–104, 106, 108–109, 117, 151, 154, 170, 190–192, 196, 199, 202–203, 205n14, 212n4, 213n37, 216n8, 217n28, 218n39, 218n40, 218n53, 219n74, 220n107, 220n114, 221n141, 223n203, 238n245
Fickert, Emil, 72, 83, 95, 97, 192, 205n14
Fickert, Marianne, 71
Fickert memorial, 212n14
Flich, Renate, 11, 23, 26
Ford, Henry, 120
Ford Peace Ship, 121
Frank, Tibor, 28–29, 34
Franz Ferdinand, 30
Franz Joseph I, 28, 31, 38–39
Frauenhilfsaktionen, 102
Frauenleben, 70, 80, 118,
Frauen-Rundschau, 7, 171, 229n38
Frauenstimmrechtskomitee, 2, 52, 81, 90–91, 105, 108, 171, 178, 195, 226n285
Freud, Sigmund, 27
Friberg, Maikki, 73, 82, 100, 194, 196
Frisch, Anna, 107
fröhliche Apokalypse, 27
Frysak, Elisabeth, 25, 209n52
Fuchs, Malvi, 46
Fürth, Ernestine, 81, 91, 207n11
Fürth, Henriette, 100, 238n250

Gabriela Dudeková, 57–58, 215n96
Galicia, 2, 22, 31, 43, 59, 72, 108, *168*, 172
Galilei Szabadkőműves Páholy, 161
Galló, Paula, 216
Gárdos, Mariska, 52–53, 118
Geber, Eva, 23
Gehmacher, Johanna, viii, 19, 21–22, 25, 48, 214n59

gender, 13, 18, 21, 24–25, 51, 57, 64, 66, 107, 140, 150, 198, 200, 207n3, 208n29, n34, 241n303
Gerber, Adele, 71–72, 79, 84, 97, 99, 103, 105, 154, 169, 192, 203, 218n53
Gerhalter, Li, 21
Gerhard, Ute, 6
Gerlach, Hellmut von, 239
Giesswein, Sándor, 153
Gilman Perkins, Charlotte, 170
Glant, Tibor, 19
Glücklich, Mrs. Ignác, 114
Glücklich, Vilma, xi–xii, 1–2, 8, 10, 26, 41, 106, 114–120, 122–123, *124*, 127, 129, 131, 133, 135–136, 142, 151, 154–155, 157, 159–160, 163–165, 167, 172–175, 177–178, 183, 185, *186*, 190–191, 196, 202–203, 232n117, 234n166, 243n5
Goldmann, Lisa M., 110, 123
Goldscheid, Marie, 95
Goldscheid, Rudolf, 95, 225n261
Grandner, Margarete, 24
Graz, 21, 26, 30, 52, 98, 205n14
Gripenberg, Alexandra, 100, 238n250
Gronemann, Caroline, 252
Grossmann (Gergely), Janka, 113, 115–116, 119, 127, 132, 140, 145, 151–153, 184, 190–191, 227n1, 234n159,
Guschlbauer, Elisabeth, 89
Gyakorlati Tanácsadó, 175
Gyáni, Gábor, 37

Haan, Francisca de, 13, 16, 22
Hacker, Hanna, 11, 23, 26, 80, 89, 218n46, 219n74, 221n138
Hague, The, xii, 100, 104, 106, *169*, 187
Hainisch, Marianne, 2, 41, 44, 49, 81, 91, 101–102, 108, 136, 170–171, 189, 212n14, 225n262, 238n245, 242n1
Haller, Mrs. György, 114, 152
Hämmerle, Christa, 25, 209n54, 209n56, 224n235
Hanzel-Hübner, Mathilde, 97
Hauch, Gabriella, 22, 65, 89, 107, 212n9, 216n8, 226n291
Heimhof, 73, 80, 82–85, 88, 97, 135, 193, 222n150
Helsinki, 73, 100

Hertzka, Yella, 21, 25, 104
Herzfelder, Henriette, 91, 101, 170–171
Heymann, Lida Gustava, 99, 104–106, 181, 238n150
Holm, Erich, 225n244
Holocaust, 153, 187
Hoover, Herbert, 123
Horticultural school in Vienna-Grinzing, 25
Hüchtker, Dietlind, 21
Hungarian National Council, xii, 146
Hungarian Soviet Republic, 122, 182, 184
Hungerwinter, 31,

ICW, IWSA, and WILPF congresses, *169*
industrial revolution / industrialization, 27, 33–35, 42, 46; international, 1, 3–4, 6, 8–16, 19, 21, 23, 25–26, 30, 42, 48, 58, 65, 76, 81–82, 97–102, 104–107, 109–111, 115, 117–118, 121, 126, 145, 153, 157, 161, 164–170, 172–173, 177, 181, 183, 185, 188, 191, 195–196, 199–200, 202, 208n36, 209n53, 209n61, 226n266, 238n248, 242n330; transnational 3, 9, 13–16, 23, 42, 48, 61, 145, 151, 164–165, 200, 202, 206n21, 206n29, 208n36, 209n52
International Council of Women, ix, xi, 3, 13–14, 101, 126, 166–167, *168–169*, 205n13, 237n233
International Woman Suffrage Alliance, ix, xi, xii, 1–3, 6, 8, 13–14, 42, 50, 58–59, 81–82, 99, 101, 110–111, 113, 115, 116–118, 120, *121*, 123, 125–126, 128–130, *131*, 132, 134–136, 145, 152–153, 156, 158, 161, *162*, 165–167, *168*, *169*, 170, *171*, 172, 181, 189, 191, 194–195, 226n285, 237n233, 243n5
Internationale Frauenliga für Frieden und Freiheit, österreichischer Zweig, 104
Internationales Historikerinnen-Treffen, 207n19
interwar period, 26, 57–58, 173, 185, *186*, 190, 214n56
Iritz, Miksa, 112
Ius Suffragii, 101, 118, 173
IWSA Congress, Budapest, 1913, xi, 1–2, 6, 42, 50, 59, 101, 111, 116, 120, *121*, 127–130, *131*, 132–136, 145–146, 152–153, 158, 161, *162*, 164–165, 167, 171, *171*, 172, 195, 230n53

Jacobs, Aletta, 100, 101, 115, 117, 120, 126, 136, 166–167, 170, 173, 189, 194, 196, 228, 28, 229n32, 238n250, 238n241, 23n251, 242n1
Jammernegg, Lydia, 89
Jászai, Mari, 133, 153
Jászi, Oszkár, 195
Jewish question, 27
Jewish/Jews, 3, 8, 11, 24, 59, 66–67, 72–73, 81, 99, 115, 117, 123, 138, 153, 189, 191–192, 219n73, 241n306
Joseph II, 46

Kaba, Eszter, 113
Kácser, Lipót, 151, 167, 237n233
Kaffka, Margit, 41
Kalkowska, Eleonora, 234n159
Kánya, Emília, 47
Károly, Katinka (née Andrássy), 123
Károlyi, Mihály, xii, 11, 117, 121–123, 178, 184, 230n60, 235n172
Kende, Júlia (married to Sándor Teleki), 41, 46, 120, 152, 174, 194, 229n47, 234n156, 234n160, 234n164
Kéri, Katalin, 18, 140, 227n1
Kéthly, Anna, 123, 154, 183, 191
Key, Ellen, 100
Keys, Florence W., 239n250
Klingenstein, Eva, 23–25, 70
knowledge transfer / exchange of knowledge, 7, 13, 201
Kőbánya, 148
Kodály, Zoltán, 123
Kommunisták Magyarországi Pártja, 184
Kosztolányi, Dezső, 154, 234n159
Kovács, Ilona, 122
Kovács, Mária M., 19
Kozma-Glücklich, Klára, *186*
Kramers, Martina G., 101
Krog, Gina, 238n250
Kronawetter, Ferdinand, 76, 85, 88
Kubicsek, Irma, 227n3, 228n28
Kulka, Leopoldine, 2, 68, 71–72, 74, 79–80, 83–84, 90, *96*, 97, 101, 103–104, 106–109, 123, 154, 170, 192, 195, 225n261, 244n20
Kunfi, Nóra, *186*, 188
Kunfi, Zsigmond, 188

Kunze, Barbara, 205n7
Kveder, Zofka, 60

labor exchange, 9, 48, 102, 113, 126, 130, 132, 140, 164, 174–175, 178–179, 181, 185, 239n259, 240n286, 240n289
labor movement, 35
Lagerlöf, Selma, 100
Lang, Marie, 72, 80, 82, 84, 87–88, 91, 95–96, 100, 106, 167, 170, 203, 220n114, 237n229, 238n250
Lanzinger, Margareth, 25
law on associations, 37–38, 52–53, 62, 77–78, 81, 107, 109; § 30, 37, 62, 72, 77–78
Lehár, Franz, 39
Lehrerinnen-Wart, 45, 70
Leichter, Käthe, 19
Leipzig, 39, 43, 76, 169, 205n7
Leon, Dora, 26
Leopoldstadt, 91
Lette-Verein, 43
L'Homme – Europäische Zeitschrift für feministische Geschichtswissenschaft 22, 208n29
Liebknecht, Karl, 123
Lindemann, Anna, 164
Linz, 21, 52, 208n21
Lipótváros, 148
Lischnewska, Marie, 238n250
Liszt, Franz, 39
Littmann, Helene, 70
Litván, György, 230n60
Ljubljana, 60
Lölich, Franz, 79
London xii, 8, 28, 91, 100, 120, *169*, 177, 187, 195
Lóránd, Zsófia, 26
Loutfi, Anna, 19, 55–56
Lovas, Renée, 123
Lower Austria, 21, 45–46, 62, 105, 216n4, 218n51
Lueger, Karl, xi, 29, 36, 54–55, 70, 84–85, 195, 203
Lux, Terka, 153

Mach, Ernst, 39
Máday, Andor, 227n1

Magántisztviselők Országos Szövetsége, 112, 135, 150–151, 160
Magyar Asszonyok Nemzeti Szövetsége, ix, 184
Magyar Közlöny, 188 188
Magyarization, 32, 59
Magyarországi Munkásnő Egyesület, ix, xi, 118
Magyarországi Nőegyesületek Szövetsége, ix, 114, 116, 126, 135, 166–167, 190, 194, 196,
male suffrage, 30, 33, 51–52, 64, 183
Malečková, Jitka, 58
Malleier, Elisabeth, 24, 73, 89, 219n74
Manchester, 8
Mann, Thomas, 123
Maramureș, 59
Mark, Toni, 103
Márkus Dezső, 153, 243n5
Marxist, 64, 190
Marxist historiography, 17
Marxist ideology, 4
Mataja, Emilie, 64
Máté, Olga (née Mautner), 153
Maverick Lloyd, Lola, 122
Mayreder, Karl, 84, 95
Mayreder, Rosa, 25, 41, 49, 68, 72–73, 80, 83, 87–88, 94–96, 103, 106, 108, 154, 181, 203
Mazohl-Wallnig, Brigitte, 22
McFadden, Margaret H., 19
Megyeri, Mrs. Izidor, 133
Meisel-Heß, Grete, 41
Meller, Eugénia (née Miskolczy), 116, 121–122, 134, 152–153, 169, 186, 187, 228n31
Mesner, Maria, 19
Mészáros, Zsolt, 138, 156, 160, 164
Michels, Robert, 134, 238n250
Mikes, Mrs. Ármin, 152
militant suffragette movement, 8
Minerva, 44
Minor, Daisy, 91, 171
Misař, Olga, 91, 97, 106, 223n184
Montefiore, Dora, 239
Moravia, 2, 58, 76
multiethnic, 12, 14, 27, 31, 56–57, 200
Musill, Marie, 96

Nagl-Docekal, Herta, 22
Nagyvárad, 41, 155–158, 160, 163–164, 234n166
National Council, xii, 146
national minorities, 12, 28, 30–32, 36, 42, 56, 59
national narrative, 12
national paradigm, 13, 30–31, 35, 58, 200
nationalism, 201, 203
nationalist perspective, 201
Neue Bahnen, 7, 217n26, 221n144, 243n11
Neuer Wiener Frauenclub, 55, 76, 81
Neurath, Anna Schapire, 95
Neurath, Otto, 95
Neuzeit, 70
new or second women's movement, 21
New York, 1, 12, 121–123, 125, 153, 166, 170, 183, 187, 207n14, 230n56
Nietzsche, Friedrich, 27
Nobel Peace Prize, xii, 103, 117
Nők Lapja, 7, 27, 107, 161, 228
Nőmunkás, 51, 53, 136
Norbert, Mrs. Simon, 159
Nőtisztviselők Lapja, 7, 107, 113, 184
Nőtisztviselők Országos Egyesülete, ix, xi–xii, 3, 5–10, 12–14, 16, 41–42, 47, 50–51, 111–113, 115–116, 118, 125–136, 138–142, 145, 148, 150–152, 154–158, 160, 165, 173–174, 176, 179, 181–182, 184–185, 189–197, 199–204, 205n1, 231n84, 231n99

Oesch, Corinna, 25, 209n61
Offen, Karen, 22, 49
Ofner, Julius, 68, 84, 88
old or first women's movement, 21
"ordinary" or "everyday" women, 15, 206n36
Országos Nőképző Egylet, 44
Oscar II, 121,
Österreichische Friedensgesellschaft, 80
Ottakring, 93
Otto-Peters, Louise, 43, 76, 99

pacifism, 101, 102–103
pacifist, 6, 9, 102m, 110, 120, 122, 196, 239n255
Paletschek, Sylvia, 206n2,
Pankhurst, Emmeline, 8, 101
Papp, Claudia, 19, 138, 227n1

Pappritz, Anna, 170
peace congress, xii, 187
peace movement, 9, 50, 80, 98–99, 102,
  105–107, 122, 124, 166, 171–172, 177, 195–196,
  209n61, 225n261
Pécs, 151, 155–158, 163–164, 235n172
Pejacsevich, Katinka, 152
Perczel, Flóra (née Kozma), 116, 151, 188
Perin, Karoline von, 43, 75
periodical press, 12, 22, 104
Pető, Andrea, 17–19, 198
Pietrow-Ennker, Bianca, 206n2
Pogány, Paula, 113, 116, 119–120, *121*, 127, 151,
  156, 177, 240n286
Pogány, Vilmos/Willy, 53
Polányi, Laura, 146, *186*
Political Committee, 1, 8, 115, 187
Pope Leo XIII, 55
Popp, Adelheid, 51–52, 108, 214n69
postcolonial and transnational
  approaches, 16
Prager Frauen-Erwerb-Verein, 43
Prager-Holm, Mathilde, 103
Prague, 19, 35, 39, 41, 43–44, 49, 58, 60, 63, 81,
  98, 103, 173, 194
Pressburg/Bratislava/Pozsony, 57, 157,
  164
progressive women's movement, 57, 84,
  111, 202
Prost, Edith, 23
Puskás, Tivadar, 39

radical feminism, 4–5
Raggam-Blesch, Michaela, 24
Rajk, László, 187
Raschke, Marie, 99, 224n215
Rechtschutz-Sektion, 23, 75, 219n85
Regen, Sophie 97
Reichsverein der Post- und
  Telegraphenmanipulantinnen und
  Posthilfsbeamtinnen, 82
Reichsverein der Postoffizienten, 105
Reinitz, Ernő, 151
Rerum Novarum, 55
Richter, Elise, 26, 45, 110
right to vote, xi, 2, 8, 30, 100, 105, 108,
  182–183, 199

Ritoók, Emma, 41
Ritter Beard, Mary, 122, 207n14
Rosenberg, Auguszta, 114, 116, 167
Rosenthal, Marie, 97
Roth, Joseph, 49
Roussel, Nelly, 136n250
Rupp, Leila J., 14, *168–169*, 236n221
Russell, Bertrand, 170

Saint-Germain-en-Laye peace treaty, 31
Salomon, Alice, 167, 170
Salzburg, 21, 41, 52, 98
Sammlung Frauennachlässe, 21
Sanger, Margaret, 123
Saurer, Edith, 24–25
Schirmacher, Käthe, 21, 26, 116, 170, 209n61,
  214n59, 238n250
Schlesinger-Eckstein, Therese, 26, 94–95,
  207n2
Schmidt, Auguste, 43, 76, 99
Schmölzer, Hilde, 43, 68, 88
Schnur, Nelly, 113, 151, 239n250
Schreiber, Adele, 116, 170, 173, 181, 227n8,
  239n250
Schreiber, Clara, 238n240
Schwartz, Agatha, 19, 48
Schwartz, Marie, 45–46, 63, 65, 91
Schwimmer, Béla, 117, 123
Schwimmer, Franciska, 117, 120, *121*, 122–123,
  132, 160
Schwimmer, Rosika, xi–xii, 1–2, 8–12, 26, 41,
  48, 50–51, 53, 97, 101, 106, 110–118, *119*, 120, *121*,
  122–127, 132, 134–136, 151–154, 156–158, 160–161,
  164, 166–167, 169–173, 177–178, 182, 184–186,
  188–196, 202–203, 205n15, 207n2, 207n14,
  224n222, 225n261, 227n3, 228n26, 228n27,
  228n28, 228n31, 229n32, 230n56, 230n60,
  232n117, 234n164, 234n166, 234n172, 237n230,
  237n233, 237n236, 28n238, 238n241, 238n242,
  238n244, 238n247, 238n250, 244n20
Segesvár, 100, 158–159
Seifert, Franz, 19
Sektion Friedenspartei, 104, 106
Sektion Jugend, 90, 141
Semmelweis, Ignác, 39
Serbia, xii, 2, 97, 102, 108, 154, 157–158,
  168

sexual education, 78, 125
Simmering, 92–93
Simonton, Deborah, 16
Sipos, Balázs, 183
Slavonia, 2
Slovak, 57–58, 215n96
Slovakia, 1, 58, 153, 157, 172
Social Democratic women's movement, 12, 24–25, 50–53, 56, 63–64, 94, 105–106, 136, 190, 192, 201–202, 204, 215n72, 215n97
Social Democratic Workers' Party in Hungary, 35
socialism, 4, 35, 56, 182
South Slavic, 31, 172
Sozialdemokratische Partei Österreichs, 64
soziale Frage, 9, 84
Spády, Adél, 120, 156, 177, 181
Sparholz, Irmgard, 88
Spitzer, Mrs. Róza, 151
Springer, Otto von, 76, 92, 130
state socialism, 4, 182
Stegmann, Natali, 59
Steinberger, Sarolta, 134, 151, 153, 188
Steiner, Riza, 134
Stöcker, Helene, 170, 238n250
Strauss, Johann, 39
Strauss, Richard, 39
Stritt, Marie, 100, 170, 194, 238n250
suffragist, 8, 105, 205n10
surplus of women, 35, 211n48
Suttner, Bertha von, 63, 103, 196, 238n250
Suttner-Gesellschaft, 80
Switzerland, xii, 11, 34, 72, 76, 117, 122, 168, 184
Szapor, Judith, 17–19, 140, 147, 166, 198, 205n2, 227n1
Szeged, 153, 157–158, 163–165
Szenczy, Gizella, 113
Szenczy, Margit, 151
Szirmay, Károly, 141
Szirmay, Mrs. Oszkár, 11, 112, 114, 123, 136, 141, 154, 159, 185–186, 186, 188, 227n6, 228n26
Szombathely, 151, 156–158, 163–164

Taubner, Margit, 151
Teleki, Blanka, 46

Teleky, Dora, 26, 84, 110
Temesvár, 115, 117, 156–158, 163–164
Terézváros, 148
Tisza, István, 174
Tormay, Cécile, 184
Touaillon, Christine, 26, 66, 71–72, 97, 103, 154, 192, 205n14, 213n38
trafficking of girls, 53, 125, 199
transfer, 15, 201, 206n35, 214n59
transnational, 3, 9, 13–16, 23, 42, 48, 61, 145, 151, 164–165, 200, 202, 206n21, 206n29, 208n36, 209n53,
transnational dimensions, 13, 145, 165, 200
transnational/international women's movement, 1, 3, 6, 19, 26, 48, 61, 82, 99, 104–105, 106, 109–110, 115, 117, 165, 167, 170, 173, 183, 121, 200, 202, 206n29, 238n247,
Transylvania, 22, 31–33, 59, 158–159, 172
Trianon peace treaty, 31, 182
Trieste, 34, 60
Troll-Borostyani, Irma von, 40, 76
Trombitás, Erzsébet, 151
Türkenschanzpark, 19
türkische influenza, 73
Turnau, Ottilie, 81, 96
Tutavac, Vesela, 216n110

Unger, Petra, 23
universal suffrage, xii, 46, 51–52, 109
university 26, 39, 45, 80–81, 110, 123, 148, 153, 179, 183, 192, 213n35
University of Budapest, 26
University of Prague, 39
University of Vienna, 21–23, 26, 39, 45, 213n37
Upper Hungary, 33, 157–158, 160, 163
Urban, Gisela, 105, 109, 171, 226n285
urbanization, 33–34, 37, 40
US citizenship, 122
Utopian Feminism: Women's Movements in Fin-de-Siècle Vienna (Anderson), 62, 65

Vágújhely, 1, 157
Vámbéry, Ármin, 187
Vámbéry, Melanie, 153, *186*, 187–188
Vámbéry, Rusztem, 187
Vázsonyi, Vilmos, 146, 165, 179, 182

Verband der akademischen Frauen
   Österreichs, 110
Verband fortschrittlicher Frauenvereine, ix,
   86, 171
Verband österreichischer Staatsbürgerinnen,
   108
Verein der Lehrerinnen und Erzieherinnen,
   ix, 37, 45–46, 62–63, 65–66, 71, 77, 81, 105
Verein für Frauenstimmrecht, 108
Vereinsgesetz xii, 37
Veres, Hermin (née Bekiczky), 47, 185
Vienna, xi–xii, 1–2, 5–7, 9, 12, 18–19,
   21–28, 34–46, 50–52, 54–55, 61–68,
   71–72, 75–77, 79–82, 84–85, 87–88,
   91–95, 97–106, 108–111, 113, 117, 122–123,
   135, 148, 154, *169*, 170–171, 173, 177–178,
   181, 185–188, 190, 193–195, 200–203,
   207n14, 211n56, 213n37, 216n4, 218n51,
   225n261, 237n238, 242n1
Vigadó (Budapest), 130, 132, 134, *171*
Vittorelli, Natascha, 19, 22–23, 58, 60
Volksstimme, 63, 83, 85–86
Vorkonferenz, 2
votes for women, 127

Wágner, Lilla, 187–188
Währing, 19, 92–93
Washington, DC, 3, 81, *169*, 205n13
Welczek, Adelheid von, 237, 233
Werner, Michael, 14
Wernitznig, Dagmar, 121, 205n15
Wie Frauenbewegung geschrieben wird, 22
Wiener Frauenerwerbverein, ix, 43,
   49, 104

Wiener Mode, 88, 100, 229n38, 238n244
Willhelm, Szidónia 115–116, 145, 151, 174, 184,
   234n160
Wischermann, Ulla, 6
Wittgenstein, Karl, 39
Wittgenstein, Ludwig, 39
Wlassics, Gyula, 44, 214n51
Woker, Gertrud, 238n250
Wollstonecraft, Mary, 207
Women's International League for Peace and
   Freedom, ix, xii, 13, 102, 104, 106–107, 117,
   125, 166, *168*, *169*, 173–174, 181, 185,
World Center for Women's Archives,
   207n14
World Peace Prize, xii, 117
World War I, xii, 1, 3, 6–7, 9–10, 17, 19, 25, 30,
   32, 35, 37–38, 41, 53, 61, 81, 90, 98, 101, 107,
   110, 117, 122–123, 135, 153, 166, 173, 183, 186,
   192–193, 195–196, 199–201, 203–204, 209,
   61, 225n244, 226n266
World War II, 13, 19, 26, 153, 182, 184
Wynner (née Weiner), Edith, 120, 230n60

Zagreb, 19, 60, 96
Zeitschrift für Frauenstimmrecht, 81, 109,
   226n285
Zetkin, Clara, 100
Zimmermann, Bénédicte, 14–15
Zimmermann, Susan, viii, 19, 23, 40, 114, 138,
   140, 166, 200, 227n1, 233n155
Zipernovszky, Mrs. Károly, 154
Zirzen Janka, 48
Živena, 57
Zycha, Marianne, 103

Dóra Fedeles-Czeferner is Research Fellow at the HUN REN Research Centre for the Humanities, Institute of History. She is the author of two monographs in Hungarian. This is her first book to be published in English.

For Indiana University Press

Sabrina Black, Editorial Assistant
Tony Brewer, Artist and Book Designer
Anna Garnai, Production Coordinator
Sophia Hebert, Assistant Acquisitions Editor
Samantha Heffner, Marketing and Publicity Manager
Katie Huggins, Production Manager
Gigi Lamm, Director of Sales and Marketing
Nancy Lightfoot, Project Manager/Editor
Annie L. Martin, Editorial Director
Bethany Mowry, Acquisitions Editor
Dan Pyle, Online Publishing Manager
Michael Regoli, Director of Publishing Operations
Pamela Rude, Senior Artist and Book Designer